THE LANDLORD'S LAW BOOK

VOL. 2 : EVICTIONS

by ATTORNEY DAVID BROWN

Edited by

STEVE ELIAS

MARY RANDOLPH

MARCIA STEWART

RALPH WARNER

Illustrated by Linda Allison

NOLO PRESS BERKELEY

**please
read
this**

Your Responsibility When Using A Self-Help Law Book

We've done our best to give you useful and accurate information in this book. But laws and procedures change frequently and are subject to differing interpretations. If you want legal advice backed by a guarantee, see a lawyer. If you use this book, it's your responsibility to make sure that the facts and general advice contained in it are applicable to your situation.

Keeping Up-To-Date

To keep its books up-to-date, Nolo Press issues new printings and new editions periodically. New printings reflect minor legal changes and technical corrections. New editions contain major legal changes, major text additions or major reorganizations. To find out if a later printing or edition of any Nolo book is available, call Nolo Press at (510) 549-1976 or check the catalog in the *Nolo News*, our quarterly newspaper.

To stay current, follow the "Update" service in the *Nolo News*. You can get the paper free by sending us the registration card in the back of the book. In another effort to help you use Nolo's latest materials, we offer a 25% discount off the purchase of any new Nolo book if you turn in any earlier printing or edition. (See the "Recycle Offer" in the back of the book.)

This book was last revised in: **August 1993.**

FOURTH EDITION	March 1993
Second Printing	August 1993
Production	Stephanie Harolde
Book Design	Toni Ihara
	Jackie Mancuso
Proofreading	Ely Newman
Index	Jane Meyerhofer
Printing	Delta Lithograph

ISSN 1042-6582
ISBN 0-87337-160-7

Library of Congress Card Catalog No.: 89-642318

printed on recycled paper

thank you

This book could not have been published without the generous assistance of many people. A special thank you to Mary Randolph, Steve Elias, Jake Warner and Marcia Stewart, who all tirelessly read the entire manuscript several times and made numerous helpful suggestions, nearly all of which were incorporated. If you find this book easy to follow and enjoyable to read (well, not like a novel), Mary, Steve, Jake and Marcia deserve most of the credit.

Thanks also to Amy Ihara, John O'Donnell, Barbara Hodovan, Kate Thill, Carol Pladsen, Stephanie Harolde, Julie Christianson, David Cole, Ann Heron, Jack Devaney, Susan Quinn, Alison Towle, and especially Toni Ihara and Jackie Mancuso, who were responsible for the layout of this book and the wonderful front cover design. Ira Serkes, past president of the Rental Housing Association of Contra Costa County, read the manuscript and made helpful suggestions.

Finally, I would like to express my special thanks to my wife, Nancy Brown, for her support, patience and encouragement in putting together this book.

contents

1

EVICTIONS IN CALIFORNIA: AN OVERVIEW

2

EVICTION FOR NONPAYMENT OF RENT

3

EVICTION AFTER TERMINATION OF MONTH-TO-MONTH TENANCY BY 30-DAY NOTICE

4

EVICTION FOR LEASE VIOLATIONS, PROPERTY DAMAGE OR NUISANCE

5

EVICTION WITHOUT A THREE-DAY OR 30-DAY NOTICE

6

FILING AND SERVING YOUR UNLAWFUL DETAINER COMPLAINT

7

TAKING A DEFAULT JUDGMENT

8

CONTESTED CASES

9

COLLECTING YOUR MONEY JUDGMENT

10

WHEN A TENANT FILES FOR BANKRUPTCY

APPENDIX

Rent Control Chart

Forms

In Re Smith

Evictions in California: An Overview

Sometimes even the most sincere and professional attempts at conscientious landlording fail, and you have to consider evicting a tenant. This is a do-it-yourself eviction manual for California landlords. It shows you, step-by-step, how to file and conduct an uncontested eviction lawsuit against a residential tenant. It does not cover how to evict a hotel guest or a tenant in a mobile home park.

A. The Landlord's Role in Evictions

Strictly speaking, the word "evict" refers to the process of a sheriff or marshal ordering a tenant to get out or be forcibly removed. It is illegal for you to try to physically evict a tenant yourself. The sheriff or marshal will only evict a tenant pursuant to a court order known as an "unlawful detainer judgment." To get such a judgment, you must bring an eviction lawsuit, called an "unlawful detainer action," against the tenant.

The linchpin of an unlawful detainer suit is proper termination of the tenancy; you can't get a judgment without it. This usually means giving your tenant adequate written notice, in a specified way. The law sets out very detailed requirements for landlords who want to end a tenancy. If you don't meet them exactly, you will lose your suit even if your tenant has bounced checks, including your rent check, from here to Mandalay.

This legal strictness is not accidental; it reflects the law's bias in favor of tenants. The law used to be heavily weighted on the landowner's side, but attitudes have changed, and today it puts more value on a tenant's right to shelter than a landlord's right to property. As one court put it, "Our courts were never intended to serve as rubber stamps for landlords seeking to evict their tenants, but rather to see that justice be done before a man is evicted from his home." (*Maldanado v. Superior Court* (1984) 162 Cal. App. 3d 1259, 1268-69.)

Because an eviction judgment means the tenant won't have a roof over his head (and his children's heads), judges are very demanding of the landlord. In addition, many California cities go beyond state law, which allows the termination of periodic tenancies at the will of the landlord, and require the landlord to show a "just cause" for eviction. In these cities, nonpayment of rent is still a straightforward ground for eviction, but there are few others.

Why do we emphasize the negatives of evicting a tenant? Because we want you to understand at the outset that even if you properly bring and conduct an unlawful detainer action, you are not assured of winning and having the tenant evicted if the tenant decides to file a defense. In other words, despite the merits of your position, you may face a judge who will hold you to every technicality and bend over backwards to sustain the tenant's position. A tenant can raise many substantive, as well as procedural, objections to an unlawful detainer suit. Essentially, any breach by you of any duty imposed on landlords by state or local law can be used by your tenant as a defense to your action. Simply put, unless you thoroughly know your legal rights and duties as a landlord before you go to court, and unless you dot every "i" and cross every "t," you may end up on the losing side. Our advice: especially if your action is contested, be meticulous in your preparation.

Before you proceed with an unlawful detainer lawsuit, consider that even paying the tenant a few hundred dollars to leave right away may be cheaper in the long run. For example, paying a tenant $500 to leave right away (with payment made only as the tenant leaves and hands you the keys) may be cheaper than spending $100 to file suit and going without rent for three to eight weeks while the tenant contests the lawsuit and stays. The alternative of a several-month-long eviction lawsuit—during which you can't accept rent that you may be unable to collect even after winning a judgment—may, in the long run, be more expensive and frustrating than paying the tenant to leave and starting over with a better tenant quickly.

Note of Sanity. Between 80% and 90% of all unlawful detainer actions are won by landlords because the tenant fails to show up. So the odds favor relatively smooth sailing in your unlawful detainer action.

B. Proceed With Caution When Evicting a Tenant

The moment relations between you and one of your tenants begin to sour, you will be wise to remember a cardinal truth. Any activity by you that might be construed by your tenant as illegal, threatening, humiliating, abusive or invasive of his privacy can potentially give rise to a lawsuit against you for big bucks. So, although the unlawful detainer procedure can be tedious, it's important to understand that it is the only game in town.

Shortcuts such as threats, intimidation, utility shutoffs or attempts to physically remove a tenant are illegal and dangerous, and if you resort to them you may well find yourself on the wrong end of a lawsuit for such personal injuries as trespass, assault, battery, slander and libel, intentional infliction of emotional distress and wrongful eviction. A San Francisco landlord was ordered to pay 23 tenants $1.48 million in 1988, after a jury found he had cut off tenants' water, invaded their privacy and threatened to physically throw them out. (The verdict was reduced on appeal, to half a million dollars.) (*Balmoral Hotel Tenants Association v. Lee* (1990) 226 Cal. App. 3d 686, 276 Cal. Rptr. 640.)

To avoid such liability, we recommend that you avoid all unnecessary one-on-one personal contact with the tenant during the eviction process unless it occurs in a structured setting (for example, during mediation, at a neighborhood dispute resolution center or in the presence of a neutral third party). Also keep your written communications to the point and as neutral as you can, even if you are boiling inside. Remember, any manifestations of anger on your part can come back to legally haunt you somewhere down the line. Finally, treat the tenant like she has a right to remain on the premises, even though it is your position that she doesn't. Until the day the sheriff or marshal shows up with a writ of possession, the tenant's home is legally her castle, and you may come to regret any actions on your part that don't recognize that fact.

C. A Reason for Which You Must Evict—Drug Dealing

In cases of drug dealing, it's not a question of whether or not it's permissible to evict a tenant—it's imperative to do so. In fact, a landlord who fails to evict a tenant who deals illegal drugs on the property can face lawsuits from other tenants, neighbors and local authorities. Many landlords have been held liable for tens of thousands of dollars in damages for failing to evict a drug-dealing tenant. A landlord can also face loss of the property.

When it's a month-to-month tenancy, terminate the tenancy with a 30-day notice as soon as you suspect illegal drug activity by the tenant or any members of the tenant's family. If the tenant has a fixed-term lease, you will have to follow the procedures in Chapter 4. Evictions for drug dealing may be a little more difficult in rent control cities with "just-cause eviction" provisions in their rent control ordinances; even so, a landlord faced with a drug-dealing tenant should do everything he or she can to evict, and should begin gathering evidence against the drug dealer—including getting tenants and neighbors to keep records of heavy traffic in and out of the suspected tenant's home at odd hours.

D. Evictions in Rent Control Cities

Cities With Rent Control

Some form of rent regulation now exists in 15 California cities:

Berkeley	Oakland
Beverly Hills	Palm Springs
Campbell (mediation only)	San Francisco
Cotati	San Jose
East Palo Alto	Santa Monica
Hayward	Thousand Oaks
Los Angeles	West Hollywood
Los Gatos	

If you think all local rent control laws do is control rents, you have a surprise coming. They also affect evictions in two important ways. First, many rent control ordinances and regulations impose important restrictions or additional procedural requirements on evictions. For example, the ordinances of some cities require a landlord to have a "just cause" (good reason) to evict a tenant. Local ordinances also commonly require tenancy termination notices and complaints to contain statements not required by state law.

Second, any violation of any provision of a rent control law may provide a tenant with a defense to your eviction lawsuit. Even failure to register your rental units with the local rent board, if that is required under the ordinance, may provide a tenant with a successful defense against an eviction suit. The Appendix in this book lists the requirements each rent control city imposes on eviction lawsuits—such as any applicable registration requirements or extra information required in three-day or 30-day notices or in the eviction complaint itself.

No two cities' rent control ordinances are exactly alike, and each one seems to change in some respect every year. We cannot give you an iron-clad guarantee as to the effects your particular ordinance may have on evictions carried out under it. You must always check a current copy of your city's rent control ordinance and regulations before you evict in a rent control city. The Appendix tells you what to look for when you read your rent control ordinance.

E. Evicting a Resident Manager

If you fire a resident manager, or if he quits, you will often want him to move out of your property, particularly if he occupies a special manager's unit or if the firing or quitting has generated (or resulted from) ill will. Eviction lawsuits against former managers can be extremely complicated. This is especially true if the management agreement requires good cause for termination of employment or a certain period of notice. Such lawsuits can also be complicated where a single combined management/rental agreement is used or if local rent control laws impose special requirements. While all rent control cities do allow

eviction of fired managers, some cities impose restrictions on it.

This section outlines some of the basic issues involved in evicting a resident manager. We do not, and can not, provide you complete advice on how to evict a resident manager. In many cases, you will need an experienced attorney who specializes in landlord-tenant law to evict a former manager, particularly if the ex-manager questions whether the firing was legally effective or proper.

1. Separate Management and Rental Agreements

To evict a tenant-manager with whom you signed separate management and rental agreements, that allowed you to terminate the employment at any time, you will have to give a normal 30-day written termination notice, subject to any just-cause eviction requirements in rent control cities. (See Chapter 3.) If the tenant has a separate fixed-term lease, you cannot terminate the tenancy until the lease expires.

2. Single Management/Rental Agreement

What happens to the tenancy when you fire a manager (or he quits) depends on the kind of agreement you and the manager had.

a. If the Manager Occupied a Special Manager's Unit

If your manager occupies a specially constructed manager's unit (such as one with a reception area or built-in desk) which must be used by the manager, or if she receives an apartment rent-free as part or all of her compensation, your ability to evict the ex-manager depends on:

- the terms of the management/rental agreement, and
- local rent control provisions.

If the agreement says nothing about the tenancy continuing if the manager quits or is fired, termination of the employment also terminates the tenancy. You can insist that the ex-manager leave right away, without serving any three-day or 30-day notice, and can file an eviction lawsuit the next day if the ex-manager refuses to leave. (See C.C.P. § 1161 (1).) (See the Checklist in Chapter 5, Section C.)

The just-cause eviction provisions of any applicable rent control law, however, may still require a separate notice, or otherwise restrict your ability to evict a fired manager.

b. If the Manager Didn't Occupy a Manager's Unit

If the manager was simply compensated by a rent reduction, and there is no separate employment agreement, there may be confusion as to whether the rent can be "increased" after the manager is fired.

If an ex-manager refuses to pay the full rent, you will have to serve a Three-Day Notice To Pay Rent or Quit, demanding the unpaid rent. If she still won't pay, you'll have to follow up with an eviction lawsuit. (See Chapter 2.)

F. Attorneys and Eviction Services

While you can do most evictions yourself, there are a few circumstances when you may want to consult an attorney who specializes in landlord-tenant law:

* The property you own is too far from where you live. Since you must file an eviction lawsuit where the property is located, the time and travel involved in representing yourself may be too great.

* Your tenant is already represented by a lawyer, even before you proceed with an eviction.

* Your property is subject to rent control and local ordinances governing evictions.

* The tenant you are evicting is an ex-manager who you have fired. (See Section E, above.)

* Your tenant contests the eviction in court. (See Chapter 8, Section B, for more details on hiring an attorney in contested cases.)

* Your tenant files for bankruptcy. (See Chapter 10.)

If you simply want someone to handle the paperwork and eviction details, you can use an "eviction service." (Check the Yellow Pages under this heading.) Because eviction services can not represent you in court, however, they are not helpful where the tenant contests the eviction in court.

G. How To Use This Book

This book is a companion volume to *Volume 1, The Landlord's Law Book: Rights and Responsibilities*, which discusses the legal rules of renting residential real property, with an eye toward avoiding legal problems and fostering good tenant relations. Although you can use this book as a self-contained do-it-yourself eviction manual, we strongly recommend that you use it along with *Volume 1*. It's not just that we want to sell more books—*Volume 1* provides crucial information on the substance of landlord-tenant law that you almost certainly will need to know to win an unlawful detainer lawsuit. For example, it discusses leases, co-tenants, subtenants, roommates, deposits, rent increases, rent control laws, privacy, discrimination, your duty to provide safe housing, and many more crucially important areas of landlord-tenant law. Even more important, *Volume 1* provides a good overview of your duties as a landlord so that you can minimize the need to evict tenants as much as possible or at least know in advance whether you're vulnerable to any of the commonly-used tenant defenses.

Some *Volume 1* material is necessarily repeated here and discussed in the eviction context. For example, information on three-day notices is important for both rent collection (discussed in *Volume 1*) and for eviction. For the most part, however, this volume makes extensive references to *Volume 1* for detailed discussions of substantive law instead of repeating them.

Now let's take a minute to get an overview of how this volume works. Chapters 2 through 5 explain the legal grounds for eviction. The entire list looks like this:

• The tenant has failed to leave or pay the rent due within three days of having received from you a written Three-Day Notice To Pay Rent or Quit (Chapter 2).

• A month-to-month tenant has failed to leave within 30 days of having received from you a written 30-day notice terminating the tenancy (Chapter 3).

• The tenant has failed to leave or comply with a provision of her lease or rental agreement within three days after having received your written three-day notice to correct the violation or quit (Chapter 4).

• The tenant has sublet the property contrary to the lease or rental agreement, has caused or allowed a nuisance or serious damage to the property, or has used the property for an illegal purpose, and has failed to leave within three days of having received from you an unconditional three-day notice to vacate (Chapter 4).

• A tenant whose fixed-term lease has expired and has not been renewed has failed to leave (Chapter 5).

• A month-to-month tenant has failed to leave within the stated time after having given you a written 30-day notice terminating the tenancy (Chapter 5).

After the tenancy is terminated (in almost all cases, by a three- or 30-day notice), most of the procedures in unlawful detainer lawsuits are the same no matter which reason your suit is based on. Thus, after you read either Chapter 2, 3, 4 or 5, depending on the way you're terminating the tenancy, go next to the chapters that explain the court procedures. These begin with Chapter 6 on filing a complaint to begin your unlawful detainer lawsuit.

If your tenant doesn't contest the lawsuit within five days after being served with a copy of your complaint, you will go next to Chapter 7 on getting an eviction judgment by default.

If the tenant does contest your unlawful detainer suit, you will proceed directly to Chapter 8, which tells you how to handle contested actions and when the services of a lawyer are advisable. Chapter 10 discusses your options when a tenant files for bankruptcy.

Chapter 9, on collecting your money judgment, will be your last stop after you win the lawsuit.

The whole eviction process typically takes from one to two months.

If you live in a city with a rent control ordinance, you will be referred to the Appendix from time to time for more detailed information on your locality's ordinance.

Here are two examples of common pathways through this book:

EXAMPLE

A tenant in your Los Angeles apartment building, Roy, doesn't pay the rent when it's due on the first of the month. A few days pass, and you decide he's probably never going to pay it. You turn to Chapter 2 on nonpayment of rent. Following the instructions, you serve Roy with a three-day notice to pay rent or quit (after checking the Appendix in this book and a copy of the current Los Angeles rent control ordinance to see if there are any special requirements you should know about).

Roy neither pays the rent nor moves in three days. You then turn to Chapter 6, which tells you how to begin an unlawful detainer suit by filing a complaint with the court and serving a copy of the complaint and a summons on the tenant. Roy does not respond to your complaint in five days, and Chapter 6 steers you to Chapter 7 on how to get a default judgment. You are entitled to a default judgment when the other side does not do the things necessary to contest a case. After you successfully use Chapter 7 to take default judgments both for possession of the premises and the money Roy owes you, your final step is to turn to Chapter 9 for advice on how to collect the money.

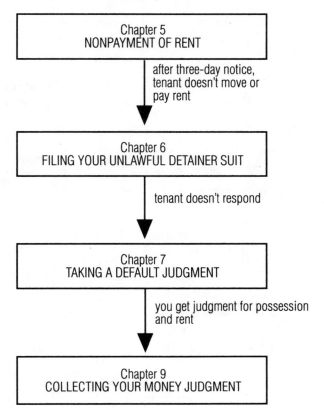

Eviction for Nonpayment of Rent

Chapter 5
NONPAYMENT OF RENT

after three-day notice,
tenant doesn't move or
pay rent

Chapter 6
FILING YOUR UNLAWFUL DETAINER SUIT

tenant doesn't respond

Chapter 7
TAKING A DEFAULT JUDGMENT

you get judgment for possession
and rent

Chapter 9
COLLECTING YOUR MONEY JUDGMENT

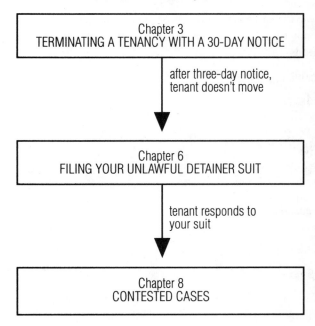

Eviction With 30-Day Notice

Chapter 3
TERMINATING A TENANCY WITH A 30-DAY NOTICE

after three-day notice,
tenant doesn't move

Chapter 6
FILING YOUR UNLAWFUL DETAINER SUIT

tenant responds to
your suit

Chapter 8
CONTESTED CASES

EXAMPLE

You decide that you want to move a new tenant into the house you rent out in Sacramento. The current tenant, Maria, occupies the house under a month-to-month rental agreement. She pays her rent on time, and you've never had any serious problems with her, but you would rather have your friend Jim live there. You turn to Chapter 3 and follow the instructions to prepare and serve a 30-day notice terminating Maria's tenancy. Maria doesn't leave after her 30 days are up, so you go to Chapter 6 for instructions on how to file your unlawful detainer suit. After you serve her with the summons and complaint, Maria files a written response with the court. You then go to Chapter 8 to read about contested lawsuits.

Valuable Resources
You should have ready access to current editions of the California Civil Code *and the* California Code of Civil Procedure. *Although we often refer to and explain the relevant code sections, there are times when you will want to look at the entire statute. These resources are available at most public and all law libraries. You can also order the paperback versions from Nolo Press. (See the order form in the back of this book.) Chapter 8 of* Volume 1 *shows you how to find and use statutes and other legal resources if you want to do more research on a particular subject.*

To go further, we recommend two excellent resources. The first is Legal Research: How To Find and Understand the Law, *by Stephen Elias and Susan Levinkind (Nolo Press), which gives easy-to-use, step-by-step instructions on how to find legal information. The other is* Legal Research Made Easy: A Roadmap Through the Law Library Maze, *by Robert C. Berring (Nolo Press), a videotape presentation on the subject. (See order information at the back of this book.)*

Abbreviations Used in This Book

We use these standard abbreviations throughout this book for important statutes and court cases covering evictions.

California Codes

Bus. & Prof.	Business & Professions
Civ.	Civil
C.C.P.	Civil Procedure
Evid.	Evidence
Gov't.	Government
Mil. & Vet.	Military & Veterans

Federal Laws

C.F.R.	Code of Federal Regulations
U.S.C.	United States Code

Cases

Cal. App.	California Court of Appeal
Cal.	California Supreme Court
F. Supp.	Federal District Court
U.S.	United States Supreme Court

Icons Used in This Book

 Caution. This icon alerts you to potential problems.

 See an Expert. This icon lets you know when you need the advice of an attorney or other expert.

 Fast Track. This icon lets you know when you can skip information that may not be relevant to your situation.

 Recommended Reading. This icon refers you to other books or resources.

 Rent Control. This icon indicates special considerations for rent control cities. ■

EVERYTHING YOU NEED TO BE A SUPER LANDLORD ... PLUS TRUTH, JUSTICE AND THE AMERICAN WAY.

Eviction for Nonpayment of Rent

Approximately nine out of ten unlawful detainer lawsuits are brought because of the tenant's failure to pay rent when due. Although you don't want to sue your tenants every time they're twenty minutes late with the rent, obviously it's unwise to let a tenant get very far behind. You have to use your own best judgment to decide how long to wait.

Once you've decided that your tenants either can't or won't pay the rent within a reasonable time (or move out), you will want to evict them as fast as possible. As we stressed in the previous chapter, the only legal way to do this is with an "unlawful detainer" lawsuit. This chapter shows you how to do this step by step.

A. Overview of the Process

Before you can file an unlawful detainer lawsuit against a tenant, the law requires that you terminate the tenancy. To properly terminate a tenancy for nonpayment of rent, you must give the tenant three days' written notice using a form called a "Notice To Pay Rent or Quit." This is normally referred to as a three-day notice.

If within three days after you properly serve the tenant with this notice (you don't count the first day) she offers you the entire rent demanded, the termination is ineffective and the tenant can legally stay. If, however, the tenant neither pays nor moves by the end of the third day (assuming the third day doesn't fall on a Saturday, Sunday or holiday), you can begin your lawsuit.

You do not have to accept payment offered after the end of the third day (unless it falls on a Saturday, Sunday or holiday, in which case the tenant has until the end of the next business day to pay up). If you do accept the rent, you no longer have the right to evict the tenant based on the three-day notice.

EXAMPLE

Tillie's lease requires her to pay $600 rent to her landlord, Lenny, on the first day of each month in advance. Tillie fails to pay November's rent on November 1. By November 9, it's evident to Lenny that Tillie has no intention of paying the rent, so he serves her with a Three-Day Notice To Pay Rent or Quit following the instructions set out below. The day the notice is given doesn't count, and Tillie has three days, starting on the 10th, to pay. Tillie doesn't pay the rent on the 10th, 11th or 12th. However, since the 12th is a Saturday, Tillie is not legally required to pay until the close of the next business day, which is November 15 (because November 13 is a Sunday and the 14th is a holiday—Veteran's Day.) In other words, Lenny cannot bring his lawsuit until November 16.

Lenny will be very lucky if he can get Tillie out by the end of the month, partly because he waited so long before giving her the three-day notice. If Lenny had given Tillie the notice on November 4, the third day after that would have been November 7. Lenny could have filed his suit on the 8th and gotten Tillie out a week sooner.

Checklist for Uncontested Three-Day Notice Eviction

Here are the steps involved in evicting on the grounds covered in this chapter, if the tenant defaults. We cover some of the subjects (for example, filing a complaint and default judgments) in later chapters. As you work your way through the book you may want to return to this chart to see where you are in the process.

CHECKLIST FOR UNCONTESTED THREE-DAY NOTICE EVICTION

Step	Earliest Time To Do It
☐ 1. Prepare and serve the three-day notice on the tenant.	Any day after the rent is due—for example, on or after the second of the month when the rent is due on the first. (If rent due date falls on Saturday, Sunday or holiday, it's due the next business day.)
☐ 2. Prepare the summons (or summonses, if there is more than one tenant) and complaint and make copies. (Chapter 6)	Late in the third day after service of the three-day notice.
☐ 3. File the complaint at the courthouse and have the summons(es) issued. (Chapter 6)	The fourth day after service of the three-day notice, or, if the third day after service falls on a Saturday, Sunday or holiday, the second business day after that third day.
☐ 4. Have the sheriff, marshal or a friend serve the summons and complaint. (Chapter 6)	As soon as possible after filing the complaint and having the summons(es) issued.
☐ 5. Prepare Request for Entry of Default, Judgment, Declaration and Writ of Possession. (Chapter 7)	While you're waiting for five-day (or 15-day, if complaint not personally served) response time to pass.
☐ 6. Call the court to find out whether or not tenant(s) have filed written response.	Just before closing on the fifth day after service of summons, or early on the sixth day. (If fifth day after service falls on weekend or holiday, count the first business day after that as the fifth day.)
☐ 7. Mail copy of Request for Entry of Default to tenant(s), file original at courthouse. Also file Declaration and Proof of Service, and have clerk issue Judgment and Writ for Possession for the property. (Chapter 7)	Sixth day after service of summons and complaint. (Again, count first business day after fifth day that falls on weekend or holiday.)
☐ 8. Prepare letter of instruction for, and give writ and copies to, sheriff or marshal. (Chapter 7)	As soon as possible after above step. Sheriff or marshal won't evict for at least five days after posting notice.
☐ 9. Change locks after tenant vacates.	As soon as possible.

for money judgment

Step	Earliest Time To Do It
☐ 10. Prepare Request for Entry of Default, Judgment and, if allowed by local rule, Declaration in Support of Default Judgment (or a Declaration in Lieu of Testimony). (Chapter 7)	As soon as possible after property is vacant.
☐ 11. Mail Request for Entry of Default copy to tenant, file request at courthouse. If Declaration in Lieu of Testimony allowed, file that too, and give clerk judgment and writ forms for money part of judgment. If testimony required, ask clerk for default hearing. (Chapter 7)	As soon as possible after above.
☐ 12. If testimony required, attend default hearing before judge, testify and turn in your judgment form for entry of money judgment. (Chapter 7)	When scheduled by court clerk.
☐ 13. Apply security deposit to cleaning and repair of property, and to any rent not accounted for in judgment, then apply balance to judgment amount. Notify tenant in writing of deductions, keeping a copy. Refund any balance remaining. If deposit does not cover entire judgment, collect balance of judgment. (Chapter 9)	As soon as possible after default hearing. Deposit must be accounted for within two weeks of when the tenants vacate.

B. Preparing the Three-Day Notice To Pay Rent or Quit

Pay very close attention to the formalities of preparing and giving the notice. Any mistake in the notice, however slight, may give your tenant (or her attorney) an excuse to contest the eviction lawsuit. At worst, a mistake in the three-day notice may render your unlawful detainer lawsuit "fatally defective"—which means you not only lose, but very likely will have to pay the tenant's court costs and attorney's fees if she is represented by a lawyer, and have to start all over again with a correct three-day notice.

1. Requirements of a Three-Day Notice

In addition to stating the correct amount of past due rent and the dates for which it is due (see subsection 2, below), your three-day notice must contain the following:

- Your tenant(s)'s name(s);

- A description of the property—street address and apartment or unit number, city, county and state;

- A demand that the tenant(s) pay the stated amount of rent due within three days or move. If you just demand the rent and do not set out the alternative of leaving, your notice is fatally defective;

- A statement that you will pursue legal action (or declare the lease/rental agreement "forfeited") if the tenant does not pay the entire rent due or move; and

- An indication—such as a signature by you, your manager, or other person you authorize to sign three-day notices—that the notice is from you. You don't need to date the notice, but it doesn't hurt.

Some rent control ordinances require three-day notices to pay rent or quit to contain special warnings. Check the Appendix and your ordinance if your property is subject to rent control.

2. How To Determine the Amount of Rent Due

It's essential that you ask for the correct amount of rent in your three-day notice. That may seem easy, but a demand for an improper amount is the most common defect in a three-day notice.

To calculate the correct amount, follow these rules:

Rule 1: Never demand anything in a Three-Day Notice To Pay Rent or Quit other than the amount of the past due rent. Do not include late charges, check-bounce or other fees of any kind, interest, utility charges or anything else, even if a written lease or rental agreement says you're entitled to them.

Does this mean that you cannot legally collect these charges? No. It simply means you can't legally include them in the Three-Day Notice To Pay Rent or Quit or recover them in an unlawful detainer lawsuit. You can deduct these amounts from the security deposit or sue for them later in small claims court. (See Chapter 20 of *Volume 1*.) You can evict a tenant for failure to pay legitimate utility or other non-rent charges, even though you can't recover or ask for those charges in an unlawful detainer lawsuit. (See Chapter 4, Section C.)

Rule 2: Assuming the rent is due once a month and the tenant simply does not pay the rent for the month, you are entitled to ask for the full month's rent in your notice. The amount of rent due is not based on the date the three-day notice is served, but on the whole rental period. Thus, if rent is due in advance the first of every month, and you serve a three-day notice on the 5th, you should ask for the whole month's rent—that's what's overdue.

Rule 3: If the tenancy is already scheduled to terminate because you have given a 30-day notice to that effect, you must pro-rate the rent due. We don't recommend this. If you serve a three-day ntice on top of a 30-day notice, you risk confusing the tenant, irritating a judge and losing an unlawful detainer action. (See Chapter 3.)

Rule 4: To arrive at a daily rental amount, always divide the monthly rent by 30 (do this even in 28-, 29- or 31-day months).

Rule 5: If the tenant has paid part of the rent due, your demand for rent must reflect the partial payment. For example, if the monthly rent is $500, and your tenant has paid $200 of that amount, your three-day notice must demand no more than the $300 balance owed.

Rule 6: You do not have to credit any part of a security deposit (even if you called it last month's rent) toward the amount of rent you ask for in the three-day notice. In other words, you have a right to wait until the tenant has moved, to see if you should apply the deposit to cover any necessary damages or cleaning. (See *Volume 1*, Chapter 5.) Even if you called the money "last month's rent," the tenant is entitled to have this credited only if and when he properly terminates the tenancy with a 30-day notice or actually moves out.

Here are a few examples of how rent should be calculated for purposes of a three-day notice:

EXAMPLE

Tom has been paying $500 rent to Loretta on the first of each month, as provided by a written rental agreement. On October 6, Tom still hasn't paid his rent, and Loretta serves him with a three-day notice to pay the $500 or leave. (Loretta has, in effect, given Tom a five-day grace period; she could have given him the notice on October 2.) Even though the rental agreement provides for a $10 late charge after the second day, Loretta should not list that amount in the three-day notice.

EXAMPLE

Teresa's rent of $450 is due the 15th of each month for the period of the 15th through the 14th of the next month. Teresa's check for the period from October 15 through November 14 bounces, but Linda, her landlord, doesn't discover this until November 15. Now Teresa not only refuses to make good on the check, but also refuses to pay the rent due for November 15 through December 14. It's now November 20. Teresa owes Linda $900 for the period October 15-December 14, and that's what the notice should demand. Linda should not add check-bouncing charges or late fees to the amount. And even though Teresa promises to leave "in a few days," rent for the entire period of November 15 through December 14 is already past due, and Linda has the right to demand it.

EXAMPLE

Terri and her landlord, Leo, agree that Terri will move out on July 20. Terri's rent is due the first of each month, in advance for the entire month. Terri will only owe rent for the first twenty days of July, due on the first day of that month. If Terri doesn't pay up on July 1, the three-day notice Leo should serve her shortly thereafter should demand this twenty days' rent, or 1/30th of the monthly rent ($350/30 = $11.66/day) for each of the twenty days, a total of $233.20.

EXAMPLE

Tony pays $500 rent on the first of each month under a one-year lease that expires July 31. On June 30, he confirms to his landlord, Lana, that he'll be leaving at the end of July and asks her to consider his $500 security deposit as the last month's rent for July. Lana has no obligation to let Tony do this, and can serve him a three-day notice demanding July's rent of $500 on July 2, the day after it's due. As a practical matter, however, Lana might be wiser to ask Tony for permission to inspect the property to see if it's in good enough condition to justify the eventual return of the security deposit. If so, there's little to be gained by giving Tony a three-day notice and suing for unpaid rent, since by the time the case gets before a judge, Lana will have to return the security deposit. (This must be done within 14 days after Tony leaves. See *Volume 1*, Chapter 20.)

3. Special Rules for Rent Control Cities

You can't evict a tenant for refusal to pay a rent increase that was illegal under a rent control ordinance, even if the tenant also refuses to pay the part of the rent that is legal under the ordinance.

EXAMPLE

Owsley rents out his Berkeley two-bedroom apartments for a reasonable $550 per month. After a year of renting to Tina on a month-to-month basis, Owsley gave Tina a 30-day notice raising the rent to $575. When Tina refused to pay the increase, Owsley served her with a three-day notice demanding that she pay the additional $25 or move. Unfortunately for Owsley, Berkeley's rent control board allowed only a 2% increase that year, so that the most Owsley can legally charge is $561. Since the three-day notice demanded more rent than was legally due (under the rent control ordinance), Tina will win any lawsuit based on the three-day notice.

EXAMPLE

Suppose Tina refused to pay any rent at all, in protest of the increase. Tina does owe Owsley the old and legal rent of $550. But since Owsley's three-day notice demanded $575, more rent than was legally due, the notice is defective. Owsley will lose any eviction lawsuit based on this defective notice, even though Tina refuses to pay even the legal portion of the rent, because the three-day notice must precisely demand the correct rent.

A three-day notice is also defective under a rent control ordinance if the landlord at any time collected rents in excess of those allowed under the ordinance and failed to credit the tenant with the overcharges, even though she now charges the correct rent and seeks to evict based only on nonpayment of the legal rent. Since the previously-collected excess rents must be credited against unpaid legal rent, any three-day notice that doesn't give the tenant credit for previous overcharges is legally ineffective because it demands too much rent.

EXAMPLE

Lois rented the apartments in her Los Angeles building for $500 a month. In April, she served Taylor with a 30-day notice increasing the rent to $600, effective May 1. Taylor paid the increase (without complaint) in May and June. In July, when Taylor was unable to pay any rent at all, Lois learned, after checking with the Rent Adjustment Commission, that the maximum legal rent was $523.45. She therefore served Taylor with a three-day notice demanding this amount as the rent for July.

After filing an unlawful detainer complaint based on the nonpayment of this amount, Lois lost the case and had to pay Taylor's court costs and attorney's fees. Why? First, since her rent increase notice had demanded an illegally high rent, it was void. The legal rent therefore was still $500. Second, in May and June, Lois collected a total of $200 more than that legal rent, which had to be credited against the $500 Taylor did owe. Taylor therefore owed only $300. Since Lois' three-day notice demanded more than this, it was ineffective.

Some rent control ordinances impose special requirements on rent increase notices. Under state law, all that's required is a 30-day notice that clearly states the address of the property and the new rent—see Chapter 14 of *Volume 1*. Quite a few require rent increase notices to list a justification or itemization of rent increases. A rent increase notice that fails to comply with all requirements imposed by both state and local law is of no effect. Therefore, any later Three-Day Notice To Pay Rent or Quit based on the tenant's failure to pay the increased amount is void because, by definition, it demands payment of more rent than is legally owed, either by asking for the increased rent or by failing to credit previous "excess" payments. In short, a landlord will lose any eviction lawsuit based on this sort of defective notice.

EXAMPLE

When Opal raised the rent on her Beverly Hills apartment unit from $500 to $540, an increase allowed under that city's rent control ordinance, she thought everything was okay. When she prepared her 30-day rent increase notice, however, she forgot about the part of the ordinance requiring a landlord to justify and itemize the rent increase and state in the notice that her records were open to inspection by the tenant. Opal collected the $540 rent for three months. The next month, when her tenant Renee failed to pay rent, Opal served her with a three-day notice demanding $540. When the case got to court, the judge told Opal her rent increase notice hadn't complied with city requirements and was ineffective, leaving the legal rent at $500. Since Renee had paid the extra $40 for three months, she was also entitled to a $120 credit against this amount, so that she owed $380. Since Opal's three-day notice demanded $540, it too was ineffective, and Renee won the eviction lawsuit.

These problems occur most often in cities with "strict" or even "moderate" rent control ordinances, which set fixed rents that a landlord cannot legally exceed without board permission. (See *Volume 1*, Chapter 4.) To remind you, strict and moderate rent control cities include Berkeley, Santa Monica, Cotati, Palm Springs, East Palo Alto, Thousand Oaks, Hayward, West Hollywood, Los Angeles, San Francisco and Beverly Hills. They are far less likely to occur in cities with "mild" rent control, including Oakland, San Jose, Los Gatos, and Campbell, where if the tenant fails to contest a rent increase the increase is usually considered legally valid. Even if the tenant does contest the increase in these "mild" cities, the proper legal rent will be quickly decided by a hearing officer, making it less likely the landlord will be caught by surprise later if she has to evict for nonpayment of rent.

The moral of all this is simple: pay close attention to any rent control ordinance in the city in which your property is located. Ask yourself the following questions:

- Have you owned the premises at all times when the tenant was living there?

- If not, did the previous owner fully comply with your rent control law?

- If so, have you fully complied with the notice requirements for rent increases and charged the correct rent?

If your answer is "no" to either of the last two questions, your tenant may be due a refund before you can evict for nonpayment of rent.

If your answer to these questions is "yes," have you fully complied with all other provisions of the rent control ordinance? If so, you are probably in a position to legally evict the tenant for nonpayment of rent.

Good Faith Mistakes
Cities that require registration of rents (Berkeley, Santa Monica, Cotati, East Palo Alto, Los Angeles, Palm Springs, Thousand Oaks and West Hollywood) must limit the sanctions against landlords who make good-faith mistakes in the calculation of rents. (Civ. Code § 1947.7.) The statute doesn't mention or seem to apply to unlawful detainer suits.

---

4. How To Fill Out a Three-Day Notice

A sample Three-Day Notice To Pay Rent or Quit and instructions for filling it out appear below. A blank tear-out form is included in the forms section in the back of this book. You may tear out the form or use a photocopy. We recommend using a photocopy, because you will probably use this form more than once.

Step 1: Fill in the Tenant's Name

The first blank is for the name(s) of the tenant(s) to whom the three-day notice is addressed. This normally should include the tenant(s) whose name(s) is (are) listed on a written lease or rental agreement, or with whom you orally entered into a rental agreement, plus the names, if known, of any other adult occupants of the property.

The California Supreme Court has ruled that in order to evict an adult who claims to be a tenant but is not on the lease or rental agreement, the landlord must provide the person with notice of the unlawful detainer action and an opportunity to be heard. This usually means naming the person as a defendant in the suit. For example, if a married couple occupies an apartment, but only the husband signed the lease, the landlord must still name both the husband and wife as defendants. Although this rule technically only applies to unlawful detainer complaints (see Chapter 6), not necessarily the three-day notice, it's still a good idea to follow it here as well and name all adult occupants in the notice. (*Arrieta v. Mahon* (1982) 31 Cal. 3d 381, 182 Cal. Rptr. 770.)

Step 2: Fill in the Address

The next spaces are for the address of the premises. Include the street address, city, and county, and the apartment number if your tenant lives in an apartment or condominium.

In the unlikely event the unit has no street address, use the legal description of the premises from your deed to the property, along with an ordinary understandable description of where the place is located (for example, "the small log cabin behind the first gas station going north on River Road from Pokeyville"). You can retype the notice to make room for the legal description or staple a separate property description as an attachment to the notice and type "the property described in the attachment to this notice" in place of the address.

Step 3: Fill in the Rent Due

The next space is for the amount of rent due and the dates for which it is due. You must state this figure accurately. (See subsection 2, above.)

Step 4: Sign and Date the Notice and Make Copies

The "ultimatum" language—that the tenant either pay the rent within three days or move out, or you'll bring legal action—and the "forfeiture" language are already included in our printed form. All you need to add are your signature and the date you signed it. The date is not legally required, but it helps to clarify when the rent was demanded. This date must not be the same day the rent was due, but at least one day later.

Be sure to make several photocopies for your records; the original goes to the tenant. If you serve a notice on more than one tenant (see Section C, below), you can give the others copies.

Step 5: Complete the Proof of Service Box on Your Copy

At the bottom of the Three-Day Notice To Pay Rent or Quit is a "Proof of Service," which indicates the name of the person served, the manner of service and the date(s) of service. You or whoever served the notice on the tenant should fill out the Proof of Service on your copy of the three-day notice and sign it. You do not fill out the Proof of Service on the original notice that is given to the tenant. If more than one person is served with the notice, there should be a separate Proof of Service (on a copy of the notice) for each person served. Save the filled-out Proof(s) of Service—you'll need this information when you fill out the Complaint and other eviction forms.

C. Serving the Three-Day Notice on the Tenant

The law is very strict about when and how the Three-Day Notice To Pay Rent or Quit must be given to ("served on") your tenant(s). Even a slight departure from the rules may cause the loss of your unlawful detainer lawsuit if it is contested.

THREE-DAY NOTICE TO PAY RENT OR QUIT

To: _____Tyrone Tenant_____ ,

(name)

Tenant(s) in possession of the premises at

_____123 Market Street, Apartment 4_____ ,

(street address)

City of _____San Diego_____ , County of _____San Diego____ , California.

Please take notice that the rent on these premises occupied by you, in the amount of $__400_, for the period from_____June 1, 19—_____ to _____June 30, 19—_____ , is now due and payable.

You Are Hereby Required to pay this amount within THREE (3) days from the date of service on you of this notice or to vacate and surrender possession of the premises. In the event you fail to do so, legal proceedings will be instituted against you to recover possession of the premises, declare the forfeiture of the rental agreement or lease under which you occupy the premises, and recover rents, damages and costs of suit.

Date:___June 5, 19—_____ _____*Lou Landlord*_____

Owner/Manager

....

PROOF OF SERVICE

I, the undersigned, being at least 18 years of age, served this notice, of which this is a true copy, on _____ , one of the occupants listed above as follows:

☐ On _____ , 19____ , I delivered the notice to the occupant personally.

☐ On _____ , 19____ , I delivered the notice to a person of suitable age and discretion at the occupant's residence/business after having attempted personal service at the occupant's residence, and business if known. On _____ , 19____ , I mailed a second copy to the occupant at his or her residence.

☐ On _____ , 19____ , I posted the notice in a conspicuous place on the property, after having attempted personal service at the occupant's residence, and business, if known, and after having been unable to find there a person of suitable age and discretion. On _____ , 19____ , I mailed a second copy to the occupant at the property.

I declare under penalty of perjury under the laws of the State of California that the foregoing is true and correct.

Dated: _____ , 19____ _____

Signature

1. When To Serve the Notice

The three-day notice can be given to your tenant any day after the rent is due, but not on the day it is due. For example, if the rent is due on the first day of each month, a notice given to the tenant on that day has no legal effect. If the due date falls on a Saturday, Sunday or holiday, rent is due on the next business day, and the three-day notice cannot be given until the day after that.

EXAMPLE

Tyson pays monthly rent, due in advance on the first of each month. If the first falls on a Monday holiday, Tyson's rent is not legally due until Tuesday. This means the three-day notice cannot be served until Wednesday.

This is one of the many technicalities of eviction law that can haunt an unlawful detainer action from the very beginning. Bizarre as it sounds, if you give the notice only a day prematurely, and the tenant still doesn't pay the rent during the two to three weeks he contests the lawsuit, you may still lose the case if the tenant spots your mistake.

EXAMPLE

When Tiffany didn't pay her $400 rent to Leslie on Friday, January 1, Leslie prepared a Three-Day Notice To Pay Rent or Quit, giving it to Tiffany the next day. Unfortunately for Leslie, the rent wasn't actually due until January 4, even though Tiffany's lease said it was due on the first, because January 1, New Year's Day, was a legal holiday, January 2 was a Saturday and January 3 was a Sunday. Oblivious to all this, Leslie waited the three days, and, as Tiffany still hadn't paid the rent, Leslie filed her unlawful detainer suit on January 6. Tiffany contested it, and the case finally went to court on February 5. Even though Tiffany clearly owed Leslie the rent for January and February, Leslie lost the lawsuit because she gave Tiffany the three-day notice before the rent was legally past due. Now Leslie will have to pay Tiffany's court costs as well as her own. Assuming Tiffany has still not paid the rent, Leslie can, of course, serve a new three-day notice and begin the eviction procedure again, poorer but wiser.

> **If You Routinely Accept Late Rent**
> *There is no law that gives tenants a five-day or any other grace period when it comes to paying the rent. If, however, you regularly allow your tenant to pay rent several days or even weeks late, you may have problems evicting the tenant. If your three-day notice demands the rent sooner than the tenant is accustomed to paying it, the tenant might be able to successfully defend an eviction based on that three-day notice.*

EXAMPLE

You routinely allowed the tenant to pay by the fifth of the month, even though the rental agreement states that the rent is due on the first. If you now serve a notice on the second or third day of the month, the tenant may be able to convince a judge that you served the notice too early.

This is called an "estoppel defense" in legalese. This means that one person (you) who consistently fails to insist on strict compliance with the terms of an agreement (in this case, prepayment of rent on time) may be prevented or stopped ("estopped") from insisting on strict compliance at a later time.

To avoid problems, wait until after any traditional grace period, (that is, one that you've given regularly in the past), has expired, before serving the three-day notice. Or, if the tenancy is one from month-to-month, and the rental agreement requires that rent be paid on the first of the month, you can reinstate the original payment terms with a 30-day written notice. Doing so allows you to insist that rent be paid on the first of the month, regardless of past custom. (See *Volume 1*, Chapter 3, Section F for a discussion on and Sample Notice of Reinstatement of Terms of Tenancy.)

2. Who Should Serve the Three-Day Notice

Anyone at least 18 years old (including you) can legally give the three-day notice to the tenant. It's often best to have it served by someone else. That way, if the tenant refuses to pay the rent and contests the resulting eviction suit by falsely claiming he didn't receive the notice (this is rare), at trial you can present the testimony of someone not a party to the lawsuit who is more likely to be believed by a judge. Of course, you must weigh this advantage against any time, trouble or expense it takes to get someone else to accomplish the service and, if necessary, appear in court.

3. Who Should Receive the Notice

Ideally, each person named on the three-day notice should be personally handed a copy of it. This isn't always possible, though, and under certain circumstances it isn't necessary. If you rented your property to just one tenant, whose name alone appears on any written rental agreement or lease, serve that person with the three-day notice. (However, as discussed below in Section C4, you can sometimes actually give the notice to a co-occupant of the property who isn't listed on the lease if you can't locate the tenant who is listed on the lease.)

If you rented to more than one tenant, it is legally sufficient to serve just one. (*University of Southern Califor-*

nia v. Weiss (1962) 208 Cal. App. 2d 759, 769, 25 Cal. Rptr. 475.) However, if possible, it's better to serve separate copies of the three-day notice on each. We recommend doing this to minimize the possibility that a nonserved tenant will try to defend against any subsequent eviction lawsuit on the ground that he didn't receive the notice.

You normally have no obligation to serve the three-day notice on occupants who are not named in the written rental agreement or lease and with whom you've had no dealings in renting the property. (*Chinese Hospital Foundation Fund v. Patterson* (1969) 1 Cal. App. 3d 627, 632, 8 Cal. Rptr. 795.) However, as discussed above (Section B4), it's best to serve all adult occupants of the premises.

4. How To Serve the Three-Day Notice on the Tenant

The law is very strict on how the three-day notice must be served on the tenant. It is not enough that you mail the notice or simply post it on the door. There are three legal methods of service for a three-day notice.

a. Personal Service

The best method of service of a three-day notice is to simply have someone over 18 hand your tenant the notice.

If the tenant refuses to accept the notice, it is sufficient to drop or lay it at his feet. It is unnecessary and possibly illegal to force it on the tenant's person. If the tenant slams the door in your face before you can leave it at her feet, or talks to you through the door while refusing to open it, it's okay to slide it under the door or shout, "I'm leaving a notice on your doormat" while doing so.

Handing the notice to any other person, such as someone who lives with your tenant but is not listed as a co-tenant on the written rental agreement, is not sufficient except as described just below under "Substituted Service on Another Person."

b.   Substituted Service on Another Person

If the tenant to whom you're attempting to give the three-day notice never seems to be home, and you know where she is employed, you should try to personally serve her there. If you are unable to locate the tenant at either place, the law allows you to use "substituted service" in lieu of personally giving the notice to the tenant. In order to serve the notice this way, you must:

1. Make at least one attempt to personally serve the tenant at her home, but not succeed; and

2. Make one attempt to serve her with the notice at work, but still not succeed; and

3. Leave a copy of the notice with an adult at the tenant's home or workplace; and

4. Mail another copy to the tenant at home by ordinary first-class mail. (C.C.P. § 1162(2).)

Ask for the name of the person with whom you leave the notice; you'll need to include it in the complaint you'll file to begin your lawsuit (Chapter 6). If you can't get a name, you can just put a description of the person.

Accomplishing Substituted Service. Substituted service of the notice is not completed, and the three-day period specified in the notice does not start running, until you have left the copy with the "substitute" person *and* mailed the second copy to the tenant at home. The first day of the notice's three-day period is the day after both these steps are accomplished.

EXAMPLE

Tad should have paid you his rent on the first of the month. By the fifth, you're ready to serve him with a Three-Day Notice To Pay Rent or Quit. When you try to personally serve it on him at home, a somewhat hostile buddy of Tad's answers the door, saying he's not home. Your next step is to try his workplace—the one listed on the rental application he filled out when he moved in. You go there only to find that Tad called in sick that day. You can give the notice to one of his co-workers or to his friend at home, with instructions to give it to Tad when they see him. After that, you must mail another copy of the notice to Tad at home by ordinary first-class mail. Substituted service is complete only after both steps have been accomplished.

Although the law is unclear, if you use any method of service that involves mailing we recommend that you give the tenant an extra five days to pay the rent or leave (under C.C.P. § 1013, which allows a party in a lawsuit five extra days to respond to mailed notices). This means that you need to wait until eight days after the mailing of the notice has elapsed (or longer if the 8th day falls on a Saturday, Sunday or holiday). For this reason, it's best to diligently attempt personal service before resorting to substituted service or the posting-and-mailing method described below.

c.   "Posting-and-Mailing" Service

If you can't find the tenant or anyone else at her home or work (or if you don't know where she is employed), you may serve the three-day notice through a procedure known as "posting and mailing" (often referred to as "nail-and-mail"). To serve the notice this way, you must do the following, in the order indicated:

1. Make at least one unsuccessful attempt to personally serve the tenant at home;

2. If you know where the tenant works, try unsuccessfully to serve her at work;

3. Post a copy of the notice on the tenant's front door; and

4. Mail another copy to the tenant at home by first-class mail. (C.C.P. § 1162(3).)

You may want to send the letter by certified mail and save the mailing receipt the Postal Service gives you. You can send it return receipt requested, so you know when the tenant received it; on the other hand, some people routinely refuse to sign for and accept certified mail.

Another way around this problem is to talk to the tenant—before you file an eviction lawsuit—and pin her down as to having received the notice. (Don't ask, "Did you get my three-day notice?" Ask, "When are you going to pay the rent I asked for in the three-day notice I left you?")

EXAMPLE

Tyler's rent is due on the 15th of each month, but he still hasn't paid Lyle, his landlord, by the 20th. Lyle can seldom find Tyler (or anyone else) at home, and doesn't know where (or if) Tyler works. Since that leaves no one to personally or substitute serve with the three-day notice, Lyle has only the "posting-and-mailing" alternative. Lyle can tape one copy to the door of the property and mail a second copy to Tyler at that address by first-class mail. Lyle should begin counting the three days the day after both of these tasks are accomplished. Because the notice was mailed, Lyle should wait five extra days (a total of eight or more if the 8th day falls on a Saturday, Sunday, or holiday) before he can file an unlawful detainer suit.

Proof of Service. Be sure the person who serves the three-day notice completes the Proof of Service at the bottom on an extra copy of the notice. (See Section B3, above.)

> ### When Posting-and-Mailing Is Effective
>
> *An appeals court in Santa Clara County has ruled that posting-and-mailing service isn't effective, and the notice's three-day period doesn't begin running, until the first day after the tenant actually receives the notice. Davidson v. Quinn (1982) 138 Cal. App. 3d Supp. 9, 188 Cal. Rptr. 421. A more recent case from Sacramento County, Walters v. Meyers (1990) 226 Cal. App. 3d Supp. 15, says just the opposite—that the three-day period begins to run the day after the second notice is mailed, and that there is no five-day extension under C.C.P. § 1013.*
>
> *Neither of these cases is binding precedent outside of the county where the case was decided. So, in Sacramento County, posting-and-mailing service should be no problem, while in Santa Clara County, the three-day period won't start to run until the tenant actually receives the notice.*
>
> *Judges in other counties can follow either case, but are more likely to follow Walters v. Meyers and rule that the three-day period begins to run the day after the mailing, rather than the day the tenant happened to receive the notice.*

D. After the Three-Day Notice Is Served

Your course of action after the three-day notice is served depends on whether or not the tenant pays the rent in full and whether the tenant stays or leaves.

1. The Tenant Stays

If the tenant offers the rent in full any time before the end of the three-day (or eight-day) period, you must accept it if it's offered in cash, certified check or money order. If you've routinely accepted rent payments by personal check, you must accept a personal check in response to a three-day notice unless you notified the tenant otherwise in the notice itself. If you refuse to accept the rent (or if you insist on more money than demanded in the notice, such as late charges) and file your lawsuit anyway, your tenant will be able to contest it and win. (The only way to evict a month-to-month tenant who never pays until threatened with a three-day notice is to terminate his tenancy with a 30-day notice—see Chapter 3.)

If a properly-notified tenant doesn't pay before the notice period passes, the tenancy is terminated. You then have a legal right to the property, which you can enforce by bringing an unlawful detainer action. (See Section E, below, and Chapter 6.)

You Do Not Have To Accept Rent After the End of the Notice Period. In fact, if you do accept rent (even part payments) you reinstate the tenancy and waive your right to evict based on the three-day notice. For example, if on the third day after service of a three-day notice demanding $300 rent, you accept $100, along with a promise to pay the remaining $200 "in a few days," you will have to start over again with a three-day notice demanding only the balance of $200, and base your lawsuit on that. If you proceed with the lawsuit based on the three-day notice demanding all the rent, the tenant may be able to successfully defend the lawsuit on the ground that you waived the three-day notice by accepting part of the rent. Of course, you may want the partial payment badly enough to be willing to serve a new notice. In that case, accept it with one hand and serve a three-day notice for the difference with the other.

2. The Tenant Moves Out

Once in a great while, a tenant will respond to a Three-Day Notice To Pay Rent or Quit by actually moving out within the three days. If the tenant doesn't pay the rent, but simply moves after receiving the three-day notice, he still owes you a full month's rent since rent is due in advance. The tenant's security deposit may cover all or most of the rent owed. If not, you may decide to sue the tenant in small claims court for the balance.

Nolo's book *Everyone's Guide to Small Claims Court (California Edition)*, by Ralph Warner, shows how to sue in small claims court.

What if the tenant simply sneaks out within the three-day period, but doesn't give you the keys or otherwise make it clear he's turning over possession of the property to you? In that case, you can't legally enter and take possession unless you either use a procedure called "abandonment" or file an eviction suit anyway. If you file suit, you must serve the summons and complaint by posting and mailing, as described in Chapter 6, Section H4, and obtain a judgment. For more information on the abandonment alternative, and to decide whether it may be suitable under your circumstances, see *Volume 1*, Chapter 19.

E. When To File Your Lawsuit

As we have stressed, you cannot begin your unlawful detainer lawsuit until the three-day notice period expires. The rules for counting the days are as follows:

- Service is complete when you personally serve the three-day notice or, if you serve the notice by "substituted service" or "posting-and-mailing" service, five days after you have mailed the notice and either given it to another adult or posted it (as described above).

Los Angeles County Note

The court in Highland Plastics Inc. v. Enders *(1980) 109 Cal. App. 3d Supp. 1, 167 Cal. Rptr. 353 ruled that service is complete after mailing and that you needn't wait five extra days. This ruling is binding only in Los Angeles County. We recommend that you not rely on it, even in Los Angeles, but instead allow an extra five days.*

- If you serve more than one tenant with notices, but not all on the same day, start counting only after the last tenant is served.
- Do not count the day of service as the first day. The first day to count is the day *after* service of the notice was completed.
- Do not file your lawsuit on the third day after service is complete. The tenant must have three (or eight)

full days after service to pay the rent or leave before you file suit.

- If the third day is a business day, you may file your lawsuit on the next business day after that.
- If the third day falls on a Saturday, Sunday or legal holiday, the tenant has until the end of the next business day to pay the rent. You cannot file your suit on that business day, but must wait until the day after that.

EXAMPLE

Toni failed to pay the rent due on Monday, November 1. On November 11, Les personally served Toni with the three-day notice at home. The first day after service is Friday the 12th, the second day is Saturday the 13th, and the third day is Sunday the 14th. Since the third day falls on a Sunday, Toni has until the end of the next business day—Monday the 15th—to pay the rent or leave. Only on the 16th can Les file suit. ■

Eviction After Termination of Month-to-Month Tenancy by 30-Day Notice

The second most common basis for unlawful detainer lawsuits (after failure to pay rent) is the tenant's failure to move after receiving a 30-day notice terminating the tenant's month-to-month tenancy.

A. Overview of the Process

Before you can file an unlawful detainer lawsuit against a tenant, you must legally terminate the tenancy. If the tenant has a month-to-month tenancy, you can use a 30-day notice to terminate the tenancy. In most circumstances, you don't have to state a reason for terminating the tenancy. This general rule, however, has some very important exceptions, discussed below.

If the tenant doesn't leave by the end of the 30 days, you can file your lawsuit to evict the tenant.

Checklist for 30-Day Notice Eviction

Below is an overview of steps involved in evicting on the grounds covered in this chapter, assuming that the tenant defaults. We cover some of the subjects (for example, filing a complaint and default judgment) in later chapters. As you work your way through the book, you may want to return to this chart to see where you are in the process.

B. When a Tenancy May Be Terminated With a 30-Day Notice

There are basically two types of residential tenancies. The first is a "fixed-term" tenancy, where the property is rented to the tenant for a fixed period of time, usually a year or more, and which is normally formalized with a written lease. During this period, the landlord may not raise the rent and may not terminate the tenancy except for cause, such as the tenant's failure to pay the rent or violation of other lease terms. This type of tenancy may not be terminated by a 30-day notice.

> **Negotiating With Tenants**
> *If a lease is in effect and for some important reason, such as your need to sell or demolish the building, you want the tenants out, you might try to negotiate with them. For example, offer them a month or two of free or reduced rent if they'll move out before their lease expires. Of course, any agreement you reach should be put in writing.*

The second type of tenancy is a "periodic tenancy," a tenancy for an unspecified time in which the rent is paid every "period"—month, week, every other week, etc. A "periodic tenancy" that goes from month to month may be terminated with a 30-day notice (subject to the two restrictions introduced earlier). If the rental period is shorter than one month, the notice period can be shorter, too. The point is that the notice must only be as long as the rental period.

Because the overwhelming majority of residential tenancies are month-to-month, we assume 30 days is the correct notice period for terminating a periodic tenancy using the procedures in this chapter. If you rent for a longer or shorter period, simply substitute your rental period whenever we use the term "30 days" or "month to month."

How do you tell if your tenancy is month to month? If you have been accepting monthly rent from your tenant without a written agreement or if you have a written rental agreement that either is noncommittal about a fixed term or specifically provides for 30 days' notice to terminate the tenancy, the tenancy is from month to month. It is also a month-to-month tenancy if you (or the owner from whom you purchased the property) continued to accept rent on a monthly basis from a tenant whose lease had expired.

CHECKLIST FOR 30-DAY NOTICE EVICTION

	Step	Earliest Time To Do It
☐	1. Prepare and serve the 30-day notice on the tenant.	Any time. Immediately after receipt of rent is best.
☐	2. Prepare the summons (or summonses, if there is more than one tenant) and complaint and make copies. (Chapter 6)	The 30th day after service of the 30-day notice is complete.
☐	3. File the complaint at the courthouse and have the summons(es) issued. (Chapter 6)	The first day after the notice period expires.
☐	4. Have the sheriff, marshal or a friend serve the summons and complaint. (Chapter 6)	As soon as possible after filing the complaint and having the summons(es) issued.
☐	5. Prepare Request for Entry of Default, Judgment, Declaration and Writ of Possession. (Chapter 7)	While you're waiting for five-day (or 15-day, if complaint not personally served) response time to pass.
☐	6. Call the court to find out whether or not tenant(s) have filed written response.	Just before closing on the fifth day after service of summons, or early on the sixth day. (If fifth day after service falls on weekend or holiday, count the first business day after that as the fifth day.)
☐	7. Mail copy of Request for Entry of Default to tenant(s), file original at courthouse. Also file Summons and Declaration, and have clerk issue judgment and writ for possession of the property. (Chapter 7)	Sixth day after service of summons and complaint. (Again, count first business day after fifth day that falls on weekend or holiday.)
☐	8. Prepare letter of instruction for, and give writ and copies to, sheriff or marshal. (Chapter 7)	As soon as possible after above step. Sheriff or marshal won't evict for at least five days after posting notice.
☐	9. Change locks after tenant vacates.	As soon as possible.

for Money Judgment

☐	10. Prepare Request for Entry of Default, Judgment and, if allowed by local rule, Declaration in Lieu of Testimony. (Chapter 7)	As soon as possible after property is vacant.
☐	11. Mail Request for Entry of Default copy to tenant, file request at courthouse. If Declaration in Lieu of Testimony allowed, file that too, and give clerk judgment and writ forms for money part of judgment. If testimony required, ask clerk for default hearing. (Chapter 7)	As soon as possible after above step.
☐	12. If testimony required, attend default hearing before judge, testify and turn in your judgment form for entry of money judgment. (Chapter 7)	When scheduled by court clerk.
☐	13. Apply security deposit to cleaning and repair of property, and to any rent not accounted for in judgment, then apply balance to judgment amount. Notify tenant in writing of deductions, keeping a copy. Refund any balance remaining. If deposit does not cover entire judgment, attempt to collect balance of judgment. (Chapter 9)	As soon as possible after default hearing. Deposit must be accounted for within two weeks after the tenant leaves.

C. Impermissible Reasons To Evict

A landlord can evict a tenant for no reason, but not for the wrong reason. This means you can't evict a tenant:

- because of race, marital status, religion, sex, having children, national origin, age or other arbitrary reasons (Unruh Civil Rights Act, Civ. Code §§ 51-53);

- if the tenant exercised the "repair-and-deduct" remedy (by deducting the cost of habitability-related repairs from the rent) within the past six months, unless the notice states a valid reason for terminating the tenancy;

- because of a characteristic not legitimately related to your operation of a successful rental business—sexual preference, for example (see *Volume 1*, Chapter 9); or

- because he complained about the premises to local authorities, exercised rights given to tenants by law, or engaged in behavior protected by the first amendment —for example, organizing other tenants. (See *Volume 1*, Chapter 15.)

If you evict for an illegal reason, or if it looks like you are trying to, your tenant can defend the unlawful detainer lawsuit or sue you later for damages. Generally, if any of the elements listed below are present, you should think twice about evicting with a 30-day notice that doesn't state a valid reason. Even though you state a valid reason, the tenant can still sue if she believes the eviction was illegally motivated. Conversely, even if you state no reason, your eviction will be upheld if you prevail over the tenant's defense. The main reason to state a valid reason (except in rent control areas where the reason must be stated) is to convince the tenant not to be paranoid.

Think twice about evicting with a 30-day notice when:

- The tenant is a member of a racial, ethnic or religious minority group;

- The tenant is gay;

- The tenant has children when your other tenants don't;

- The tenant has recently (say within a year) complained to the authorities about the premises;

- The tenant has recently (within six months) lawfully withheld rent;

- The tenant has organized a tenants' union;

- The tenant is handicapped;

- The tenant is elderly; or

- The tenant receives public assistance.

If none of these factors is present (and the premises are not covered by a rent control ordinance), you will probably have no problem using a 30-day notice, without specifying a reason, to terminate a tenancy.

Federal Housing Programs

"Section 8" refers to Section 8 of the United States Housing Act of 1937 (42 U.S.C. § 1437f), and "Section 236" refers to Section 236 of the National Housing Act of 1949 (12 U.S.C. § 1517z-1). Both are federal laws providing government housing assistance to low-income families. For additional information about the more stringent requirements for eviction from government-subsidized rentals, see the following cases: Appel v. Beyer (1974) 39 Cal. App. 3d Supp. 7; Gallman v. Pierce (1986, N.D. Cal.) 639 F. Supp. 472; Mitchell v. Poole (1988) 203 Cal. App. 3d Supp. 1; Gersten Companies v. Deloney (1989) 212 Cal. App. 3d 1119; and 24 C.F.R. §§ 450 and following, 882 and following.

D. Government Subsidy Requirements

If you receive rent or other subsidies from federal, state or local governments, you may evict only for certain reasons. Acceptable reasons for termination are usually listed in the form lease drafted by the agency or in the agency's regulations. If your tenants receive assistance from a local housing authority under a "Section 8" program or from the U.S. Department of Housing and Urban Development (HUD), you must state the reasons for termination in the 30-day notice. Allowable reasons for eviction are contained in the standard-form leases the housing authority or HUD requires the landlord to use.

E. Rent Control Ordinances

"Just cause" requirements for evictions severely limit the reasons for which landlords can evict tenants. Landlords are authorized to terminate a month-to-month tenancy only for the reasons specifically listed in the particular ordinance. Most just cause provisions also require that the reason be clearly and specifically stated on the notice (see Section G, below) as well as in a subsequent unlawful detainer complaint.

Cities That Require Just Cause for Eviction

Berkeley	Los Angeles
Beverly Hills	San Francisco
Cotati	Santa Monica
East Palo Alto	Thousand Oaks
Hayward	West Hollywood

If your property is in a city that requires just cause, the old rules for 30-day notice evictions simply do not apply. Even if an eviction is authorized under state law a stricter local rent control ordinance may forbid it. For example, San Francisco's rent control ordinance, which does not permit eviction of a tenant solely on the basis of a change in ownership, has been held to prevail over state law, which specifically allows eviction for this reason. (*Gross v. Superior Court* (1985) 171 Cal. App. 3d 265.)

EXAMPLE

You wish to terminate the month-to-month tenancy of a tenant who won't let you in the premises to make repairs, even though you have given reasonable notice (all ordinances consider this a just cause for eviction). You must give the tenant a 30-day notice that complies with state law and that also states in detail the reason for the termination, listing specifics, such as dates the tenant refused to allow you in on reasonable notice. If the tenant refuses to leave and you bring an unlawful detainer suit, the complaint must also state the reason for eviction (this is usually done by referring to an attached copy of the 30-day notice). If the tenant contests the lawsuit, you must prove at trial that the tenant repeatedly refused you access, as stated in the notice.

Before you start an eviction by giving a 30-day notice, you should check the Appendix, which lists the just cause requirements of each city with rent control, and a current copy of your ordinance. (For a more thorough discussion of rent control, see *Volume 1*, Chapter 4.) Do this carefully. If you are confused, talk to your local landlords' association or an attorney in your area who regularly practices in this field.

Although cities' ordinances differ in detail, the basic reasons that constitute "just cause" are pretty much the same in all of them. Most rent control ordinances allow the following justifications for terminating a month-to-month tenancy with a 30-day notice:

Don't Get Tripped Up by Rent Control Violations
Any violation of a rent control ordinance by you can be used by a tenant to avoid eviction—even if the part of the ordinance you violated has nothing to do with the basis for eviction. For example, in many "strict" rent control cities, as well as in Los Angeles, where ordinances require landlords to register their properties with rent boards, a landlord who fails to register all the properties in a particular building cannot evict any tenant in any of the units for any reason—even if that particular unit is registered. In these cities, a tenant could be months behind in the rent and destroying his apartment, but the landlord would be legally unable to evict because he hadn't registered some other apartment in the same building with the rent board.

Similarly, a landlord's minor violation, such as failing to keep a tenant's security deposit in a separate account (if required), can be used by a tenant to defend an eviction based on the tenant's repeated loud parties. Problems of this sort can be avoided if you comply with every aspect of your city's ordinance.

1. Nonpayment of Rent

Although you can use a 30-day notice to evict a tenant who doesn't pay the rent, you should almost always use a three-day notice (see Chapter 2) instead. A 30-day notice will delay the eviction, and you can't sue for back rent in your unlawful detainer action. (*Saberi v. Bakhtiari* (1985) 169 Cal. App. 3d 509, 215 Cal. Rptr. 359.) It is, however, arguable that if you use a 30-day notice based on nonpayment of rent, you deprive the tenant of her right to a conditional notice that gives her the chance to stay if she pays the rent. Although the 30-day notice gives more time, it's unconditional, unlike a three-day notice to pay rent or quit.

2. Refusal To Allow Access

If, following receipt of a written warning from you, the tenant continues to refuse you or your agent access to the property (assuming you give the tenant reasonable notice of your need to enter—see *Volume 1*, Chapter 13) to show it to prospective buyers or to repair or maintain it, you may evict the tenant.

Most ordinances require that tenants be given a written warning before their tenancy is terminated by notice. Thus, if the tenant refuses you entry, you should serve, at least three days before you give the tenant a 30-day notice, a written demand that the tenant grant access. Check your ordinance to make sure you comply with its requirements for such a notice. Before you begin an eviction on this ground, you should answer yes to all the following questions:

- Was your request to enter based on one of the reasons allowed by statute, such as to make repairs or show the property? (See *Volume 1*, Chapter 13, for more on this.)

- Did you give your tenant adequate time to comply with the notice?

- Did you send a final notice setting out the tenant's failure to allow access and clearly stating your intent to evict if access was not granted?

3. Relatives

A landlord who wants the premises to live in herself (or for her spouse, parent or child) may, under most circumstances, use a 30-day notice to ask the existing tenants to leave.

Some ordinances also allow landlords to evict tenants so that other relatives of the landlord (such as step-children, grandchildren, grandparents or siblings) may move in. Because some landlords have abused this reason for eviction—for example, by falsely claiming that a relative is moving in—most cities strictly limit this option by requiring the termination notice to include detailed information, such as the name, current address and phone number of the relative who will be moving in.

In addition, several rent control cities forbid the use of this ground if there are comparable vacant units in the building into which the landlord or relative could move. Some cities allow only one unit per building to be occupied this way, and most cities do not allow non-individual landlords (corporations or partnerships) or persons with less than a 50% interest in the building to use this reason. Los Angeles, West Hollywood and a few other cities go so far as to require landlords evicting for this reason to compensate the tenant who must move out. (See the Appendix.)

Finally, rent control ordinances and state law ordinances now provide for heavy penalties against landlords who use a phony-relative ploy. State law requires that in rent control cities that mandate registration, landlords who evict tenants on the basis of wanting to move a relative (or the landlord) into the property must have their relative actually live there for six continuous months. (Civ. Code § 1947.10.) If this doesn't happen, the tenant can sue the landlord in court for actual and punitive damages caused by the eviction. Typically, such suits are brought in Superior Court, with the tenant demanding well over the $25,000 minimum required to sue in that court.

If a court determines that the landlord or relative never intended to stay in the unit, the tenant can move back in. The court can also award the tenant three times the increase in rent she paid while living somewhere else and three times the cost of moving back in. If the tenant decides not to move back into the old unit, the court can award her three times the amount of one month's rent of the old unit and three times the costs she incurred moving out of it. The tenant can also recover attorney fees and costs. (Civ. Code § 1947.10.) A court awarded one San Francisco tenant $200,000 for a wrongful eviction based on a phony-relative ploy. (*Beeman v. Burling* (1990) 216 Cal. App. 3d 1586, 265 Cal. Rptr. 719.)

If you are planning to evict on the ground of renting the premises to a family member, you should answer yes to all the following questions:

- Are you an "owner" as that term is described in your ordinance for the purpose of defining who has the right to possession?

- If a relative is moving in, does he qualify under the ordinance?

- Will the person remain on the premises long enough to preclude a later action against you by the tenant?

- Does your notice provide the specific information required by the ordinance?

- Are you prepared to pay the tenant compensation, if required by your local ordinance?

4. Remodeling

A landlord who wants possession of the property to conduct remodeling or extensive repairs can use a 30-day notice to evict tenants in some circumstances. Because of the ease with which this ground for eviction can be abused, most cities severely limit its use. For instance, the Los Angeles ordinance requires that at least $10,000 or more per unit (depending on the size of the property) be spent on the repairs or remodeling before eviction on this ground is allowed, and some ordinances (for example, those in Berkeley and Santa Monica) allow this ground only where the repairs are designed to correct local health or building code violations. In some cities, the landlord, once the repairs are made, must give the evicted tenant the right of "first refusal" to re-rent the property. All cities with just cause eviction provisions require that the landlord obtain all necessary building and other permits before eviction. Finally, most cities allow the tenant to sue the landlord for wrongful eviction if the work isn't accomplished within a reasonable time (usually six months) after the tenant leaves.

If you plan to evict using this ground, you should answer yes to all the following questions:

- Is the remodeling really so extensive that it requires the tenant to vacate the property?

- Have you obtained all necessary permits from the city?

- Are you prepared to pay the tenant compensation if required by ordinance?

- Have you made all necessary arrangements with financing institutions, contractors, etc., in order to make sure the work will be finished within the period required by the ordinance?

- Have you met all other requirements of your local ordinance, such as giving proper notice to the tenant, offering the tenant the right to relocate into any vacant comparable unit or giving the tenant the opportunity to move back in once the apartment is remodeled?

5. Condominium Conversion or Demolition

A landlord may evict to permanently remove the property from the rental market by means of condominium conversion or "good faith" demolition (not motivated by the existence of the rent control ordinance). But termination of the tenancy by 30-day notice (which specifies the reason) is only the last step in a very complicated process. All cities allow this ground to be used only after the landlord has obtained all the necessary permits and approvals. Most cities have very stringent condominium-conversion or anti-demolition ordinances that require all sorts of preliminary notices to tenants. A state statute, the Ellis Act, allows this ground for eviction, but cities can (and do) restrict application of the law.

6. Violation of Rental Agreement

If the tenant violates a significant provision of the rental agreement, you can use a 30-day notice to initiate an eviction. This ground also justifies evicting with a three-day notice. (See Chapter 4.) As a general rule, however, you should use a 30-day notice. (See Section F, below.)

Violation of New Terms. Some cities prohibit eviction for violation of a rental agreement provision that was added to the original rental agreement, either by means of a notice of change in terms of tenancy or by virtue of a new rental agreement signed after the original one expired.

Even in places without rent control, judges are reluctant to evict based on breaches other than nonpayment of rent. First, the breach must be considered "substantial"—that is, very serious. Second, you should be able to prove the violation with convincing testimony from a fairly impartial person, such as a tenant in the same building who is willing to testify in court. If you're unable to produce any witnesses who saw (or heard) the violation, or who heard the tenant admit to it, forget it.

Before you begin an eviction on this ground, you should answer yes to the following questions:

- Was the violated provision part of the original rental agreement?
- If the provision was added later, does your ordinance allow eviction on this ground?
- Can you definitely prove the violation?
- Was the violated provision legal under state law and the ordinance? (See *Volume 1*, Chapter 2.)

7. Damage to the Premises

If the tenant is disturbing other tenants or seriously damaging the property, you can use a 30-day notice to initiate an eviction procedure. Under state law, a three-day notice to quit that doesn't give the tenant the option of correcting the problem may also be used. Some rent control cities (Berkeley, Cotati, East Palo Alto and Hayward) require that a landlord give the tenant a chance to correct the violation. (See Chapter 4.)

8. Illegal Activity on the Premises

If the tenant has committed (or, in some cities, been convicted of) serious illegal activity on the premises, a landlord may initiate an eviction by using a 30-day notice. This ground also justifies using a three-day notice. (See Chapter 4.) You should document the illegal activity thoroughly (see Chapter 4), keeping a record of your complaints to police and the names of the persons with whom you spoke. And although not required by ordinance, it's often a good idea to first give the tenant written notice to cease the illegal activity. If he fails to do so, the fact that you gave notice should help establish that there's a serious and continuing problem.

Drug-Dealing Tenants. As stated earlier, it is essential to do everything you can to evict any tenant who you strongly suspect is dealing illegal drugs on the property. A landlord who ignores this sort of problem can face severe liability and even lose his or her property!

F. Should You Use a Three-Day or 30-Day Notice?

As we have pointed out, some reasons for eviction under a 30-day notice, such as making too much noise or damaging the property, also justify evicting with a three-day notice, as described in Chapter 4. If you can evict a tenant by using a three-day notice, why give the tenant a break by using a 30-day notice? Simply because a tenant is more likely to contest an eviction lawsuit that accuses her of misconduct and gives her a lot less time to look for another place to live. In places where you don't have to show "just cause" to give a 30-day notice, you also avoid having to prove your reason for evicting (unless you must overcome a tenant's defense based on your supposed retaliation or discrimination).

Finally, if you base the three-day notice on trivial violations, such as a tenant's having a goldfish or parakeet contrary to a no-pets clause in the rental agreement, but you really want her out because she can't get along with you, the manager or other tenants, you are likely to lose your unlawful detainer suit. Judges are not eager to let a tenant be evicted, with only three days' notice, for a minor breach of the rental agreement or causing an insignificant nuisance or damage. If, on the other hand, you use a 30-day notice and rent in an area that does not require just cause to evict, you don't have to state a reason. In other words, by following this approach, you have one less significant problem to deal with.

G. Preparing the 30-Day Notice

A sample 30-Day Notice of Termination of Tenancy, with instructions, appears below. You will find a blank tear-out version in the forms section in the Appendix. As you can see, filling in the notice requires little more than setting out the name of the tenant, the address of the property, the date and your signature.

List the names of all adult occupants of the premises, even if their names aren't on the rental agreement.

As mentioned above, some rent control ordinances that require just cause for eviction require special additions to 30-day notices. For example, San Francisco's ordinance requires that every notice on which an eviction lawsuit is based tell the tenant that she may obtain assistance from that city's rent control board.

In addition, many rent control ordinances require that the reason for eviction be stated specifically in the 30-day notice (state law doesn't require any statement of a reason). For example, under most just cause provisions, a 30-day notice based on the tenant's repeated refusal to allow the landlord access to the property on reasonable notice must state at least the dates and times of the refusals. And for terminations based on wanting to move in a relative or remodel the property, extra notice requirements are specified in detail in the ordinance or in regulations adopted by the rent control board. Check the Appendix for general information, and be sure to get a current copy of your rent control ordinance and follow it carefully.

30-DAY NOTICE OF TERMINATION OF TENANCY

To: _____ | fill in tenant's name(s) | _____ ,

(name)

Tenant(s) in possession of the premises at

_____ | list street address, including apartment number | _____ ,

(street address)

City of _____ County of _____ , California.

YOU ARE HEREBY NOTIFIED that effective 30 DAYS from the date of service on you of this notice, the periodic tenancy by which you hold possession of the premises is terminated, at which time you are required to vacate and surrender possession of the premises. If you fail to do so, legal proceedings will be instituted against you to recover possession of the premises, damages and costs of suit.

_____

_____ | if you are in a rent-control city which requires that you | _____

_____ | state a reason for terminating a tenancy, insert it here | _____

_____

_____

Date: _____ | date of notice | | owner's or manager's signature | _____

Owner/Manager

| the instructions for completing the Proof of Service are the same as those described under the Three-Day Notice To Pay Rent or Quit (Chapter 2, Section B4) with one exception—service by certified mail may be used

·········· ········   ·········· ········

PROOF OF SERVICE

I, the undersigned, being at least 18 years of age, served this notice, of which this is a true copy, on _____ , one of the occupants listed above as follows:

☐ On _____ , 19____, I delivered the notice to the occupant personally.

☐ On _____ , 19____, I delivered the notice to a person of suitable age and discretion at the occupant's residence/business after having attempted personal service at the occupant's residence, and business if known. On _____ , 19____, I mailed a second copy to the occupant at his or her residence.

☐ On _____ , 19____, I posted the notice in a conspicuous place on the property, after having attempted personal service at the occupant's residence, and business, if known, and after having been unable to find there a person of suitable age and discretion. On _____ , 19____, I mailed a second copy to the occupant at the property.

☐ On _____ , 19____, I mailed the notice by certified mail addressed to the occupant at his or her place of residence.

I declare under penalty of perjury under the laws of the State of California that the foregoing is true and correct.

Dated: _____ , 19____   _____

Signature

S A M P L E

30-DAY NOTICE OF TERMINATION OF TENANCY

To: _____Rhoda D. Renter_____,
                             (name)

Tenant(s) in possession of the premises at

_____950 Parker Street_____,
                    (street address)

City of ___Palo Alto___ County of ___Santa Clara___, California.

YOU ARE HEREBY NOTIFIED that effective 30 DAYS from the date of service on you of this notice, the periodic tenancy by which you hold possession of the premises is terminated, at which time you are required to vacate and surrender possession of the premises. If you fail to do so, legal proceedings will be instituted against you to recover possession of the premises, damages and costs of suit.

_____

_____

_____

_____

_____

Date:___August 3, 19—___   *Lani Landlord*_____
                                  Owner/Manager

....

PROOF OF SERVICE

I, the undersigned, being at least 18 years of age, served this notice, of which this is a true copy, on _____, one of the occupants listed above as follows:

☐ On _____, 19____, I delivered the notice to the occupant personally.

☐ On _____, 19____, I delivered the notice to a person of suitable age and discretion at the occupant's residence/business after having attempted personal service at the occupant's residence, and business if known. On _____, 19____, I mailed a second copy to the occupant at his or her residence.

☐ On _____, 19____, I posted the notice in a conspicuous place on the property, after having attempted personal service at the occupant's residence, and business, if known, and after having been unable to find there a person of suitable age and discretion. On _____, 19____, I mailed a second copy to the occupant at the property.

☐ On _____, 19____, I mailed the notice by certified mail addressed to the occupant at his or her place of residence.

I declare under penalty of perjury under the laws of the State of California that the foregoing is true and correct.

Dated: _____, 19____   _____
                                        Signature

If your rental agreement has a provision reducing the amount of notice you have to give to as low as seven days (this is allowed under Civ. Code § 1946—see *Volume 1*, Chapter 2), you will have to modify our form slightly. Simply delete the "30" every place it appears and fill in the lesser number of days if you want to try to get the tenant out in a hurry.

You should not list the reason for the termination unless you are in a high-risk situation as described in Section B, or the local rent control ordinance or government regulation (for subsidized housing) requires it. If you do have to include the reason, you may wish to check with an attorney or other knowledgeable person in your area to make sure you state it properly and with specificity; this will help assure that your tenant cannot complain that the notice is too vague or void under local law.

H. Serving the 30-Day Notice

The law sets out detailed requirements for serving a 30-day notice on a tenant. If you don't comply with them, you could lose your unlawful detainer lawsuit.

1. When the 30-Day Notice Should Be Served

A 30-day notice can be served on the tenant on any day of the month. For example, a 30-day notice served on March 17 terminates the tenancy 30 days later on April 16. (Remember to count 30 days, regardless of whether the month has 28, 29 or 31 days.) This is true even if rent is paid for the period from the first to the last day of each month. There's one exception—if your lease or rental agreement requires notice to be served on a certain day, such as the first of the month.

The best time to serve the 30-day notice is shortly after you receive and cash a rent check. Assuming the tenant paid on time, this means the 30-day notice is given toward the beginning of the month or rental period, so that the last day of the tenancy will fall only one or two days into the next month. The advantage is that

you will already have the rent for almost all of the time the tenant can (legally) remain on the premises. If the tenant refuses to pay any more rent (for the day or two in the next month), you can just deduct it from the security deposit. (See Chapter 9.)

EXAMPLE

Tess is habitually late with the rent, usually paying on the third day after receiving your three-day notice. On October 2 you knock on Tess's door and ask for the rent. If you luck out and get her to pay this time, cash the check and then serve Tess with a 30-day notice. The last day of the tenancy will be November 1, and she'll owe you only one day's rent. You can deduct this amount from the deposit before you return it, assuming you give the tenant proper written notice of what you are doing.

Of course, if Tess doesn't pay her rent on the 2nd, you can resort to the usual three-day notice. If she still doesn't pay within three days, you can sue for nonpayment of rent as described in Chapter 2.

If you've already collected "last month's rent," you can serve the 30-day notice on the first day of the last month without worrying about collecting rent first. Do not, however, serve it so that the tenancy ends before the end of the period (the last month) for which you have collected rent. Accepting rent for a period beyond the date you set in the 30-day notice for termination of the tenancy is inconsistent with the notice and means you effectively cancel it. (See *Highland Plastics, Inc. v. Enders* (1980) 109 Cal. App. 3d Supp.1, 167 Cal. Rptr. 353.)

If you serve the 30-day notice in the middle of the month, your tenant may not be eager, when the end of the month comes around, to pay rent for the part of the next month before the tenancy ends. If this happens and you can't settle the issue by talking to your tenant, you can take the pro-rated rent for the last portion of a month out of the security deposit. (See Chapter 9.) You could also serve the tenant with a three-day notice to pay rent or quit for the pro-rated rent due, but we recommend against it. Using two notices increases the chances that you will make a procedural mistake. It complicates the eviction, increases hostility and probably won't get the tenant out any faster.

If you are giving less than 30 days' notice because your rental agreement allows it (see Section E, above), but you collect your rent once a month, be sure that the notice doesn't terminate the tenancy during a period for which you've already collected rent. For example, if you collected the rent for August on August 1, serving a seven-day notice any sooner than August 24 would improperly purport to end the tenancy before the end of the paid-for rental period, August 31.

2. Who Should Serve the 30-Day Notice

The 30-day notice may be served by any person over age 18. (See Chapter 2, Section C.) Although you can legally serve the notice yourself, it's often better to have someone else serve it. That way, if the tenant refuses to pay the rent and contests the eviction lawsuit by claiming he didn't receive the notice, you can present the testimony of someone not a party to the lawsuit who is more likely to be believed by a judge. Of course, you must weigh this advantage against any time, trouble or expense it takes to get someone else to accomplish the service and, if necessary, appear in court.

3. Whom To Serve

As with three-day notices, you should try to serve a copy of the 30-day notice on each tenant to whom you originally rented the property. (See Chapter 2, Section B.)

4. How To Serve the Notice on the Tenant

A 30-day notice may be served in any of the ways three-day notices can be served (see Chapter 2, Section B):

- By personal delivery to the tenant;
- By substituted service on another person, plus mailing; or
- By posting and mailing.

In addition, the 30-day notice can be served by certified mail. The statute does not require that it be sent return receipt requested. The return receipt gives you proof that the tenant received the notice, but it also entails a risk because a tenant can refuse the letter by refusing to sign the receipt. In any case, the Post Office gives you a receipt when you send anything by certified mail.

As with three-day notices, you should give the tenant an extra five days (in addition to the 30 days) when the 30-day notice is served by any method involving mailing. For this reason, it's best to take the time to serve the 30-day notice personally.

REMEMBER:
- Do not accept any rent whatsoever for any period beyond the day your tenant should be out of the premises under your 30-day notice.
- Accept only rent pro-rated by the day up until the last day of tenancy, or you'll void your 30-day notice and have to start all over again with a new one.
- Don't accept any rent at all if you collected "last month's rent" from the tenant, since that's what you apply to the tenant's last month or part of a month.
- Be sure the person serving the 30-day notice completes a Proof of Service at the bottom of an extra copy of the notice, indicating when and how the notice was served. (See Chapter 2, Section B.)

I. When To File Your Lawsuit

Once your 30-day notice is properly served, you must wait 30 days before taking any further action. If you file an unlawful detainer complaint prematurely, you will lose the lawsuit and have to start all over again. Here's how to figure out how long you have to wait.

- Service is complete when you personally serve the 30-day notice. It is also complete if you serve the notice by substituted service, certified mail or posting-and-mailing, five days after you deposit the notice in the mail and (except for certified mail) give the notice to a competent adult (or post it).

- If you serve more than one tenant with notices, but not all on the same day, start counting only after the last tenant is served.

- Do not count the day of service as the first day. The first day to count is the day after service of the notice was completed.

- The tenant gets 30 full days after service. Do not file your lawsuit until at least the 31st day after service is complete.

- If the 30th day is a business day, you may file your lawsuit on the next business day after that.

- If the 30th day falls on a Saturday, Sunday or legal holiday, the tenant can stay until the end of the next business day. You cannot file your suit on that business day, but must wait until the day after that.

EXAMPLE

You personally served Tanya with her 30-day notice on June 3 (the day after she paid you the rent). June 4 is the first day after service, and July 3 is the 30th day. But July 3 is a Sunday, and July 4 is a holiday. This means Tanya has until the end of the next business day, July 5, to vacate. The first day you can file your suit is July 6.

If you had served Tanya on June 3 using any other method of service, she would have an additional five days to leave, and you could file suit on July 11 (or later if July 10th were a Saturday, Sunday or holiday).

Once you have waited the requisite period, and the tenant has failed to leave, you can proceed to the next phase, which is filing an eviction complaint. We tell you how to do this in Chapter 6. ∎

Eviction for Lease Violations, Property Damage or Nuisance

This chapter is about evicting tenants who:

- engage in highly disruptive activity (for example, making unreasonable noise, creating a nuisance, threatening neighbors);

- destroy part or all of the premises;

- clearly violate the lease or rental agreement (for example, keeping a pet or subleasing without permission);

- make illegal use of the premises (for example, selling drugs); or

- fail to make a payment (other than rent) that is required under the lease or rental agreement (for example, late fee, security deposit upgrade, utility surcharge). (If you want to evict the tenant for nonpayment of rent, use Chapter 2.)

A. When To Use This Chapter

Surprising as it may seem, you may prefer to use a 30-day notice instead of the three-day notice allowed under these circumstances. Why would you want to take the slower route? First, if you use a three-day notice, you will have to prove your reason for eviction (the tenant's misconduct) in court, whereas with a 30-day notice you don't have to (except in cities with rent control that require just cause; see the Appendix). Second, a tenant who receives a three-day notice for misconduct is a lot more likely to defend the suit. He may want to vindicate his reputation, get back at you or simply want some additional time to move. By contrast, if you terminate the month-to-month tenancy with a 30-day notice, the tenant has time both to move and to cool off emotionally, and will probably exit quietly without finding it necessary to shoot a hole in your water heater.

Also, to use a three-day notice successfully, the problem you're complaining about must be truly serious. A judge will not order an eviction based on a three-day notice for minor rental agreement violations or property damage. For example, if you base a three-day notice eviction on the fact that your tenant's parakeet constitutes a

serious violation of the no-pets clause in the lease, or that one or two noisy parties or the tenant's loud stereo is a sufficient nuisance to justify immediate eviction, you may well lose. The point is simple. Any time you use a three-day notice short of an extreme situation, your eviction attempt becomes highly dependent on the judge's predilections, and therefore at least somewhat uncertain.

For these reasons, you should resort to three-day notice evictions based on something other than nonpayment of rent only when the problem is serious and time is very important.

Drug Dealing. If the tenant is dealing illegal drugs on the property, the problem is serious. A landlord who hesitates to evict a drug-dealing tenant (1) faces lawsuits from other tenants, neighbors and local authorities, (2) may wind up liable for tens of thousands of dollars in damages and (3) may even lose the property.

It's easier to evict drug-dealing tenants with a 30-day notice, especially in cities without rent control. However, if the tenant has a fixed-term lease (which can't be terminated with a 30-day notice), you will have no choice but to follow the procedures set forth in this chapter. You should start by getting other tenants, and neighbors, if possible, to document heavy traffic in and out of the tenant's home at odd hours. Under these circumstances, an attorney is recommended.

Checklist for Uncontested Non-Rent Three-Day Notice Eviction

Here are the steps involved in evicting on the grounds covered in this chapter, if the tenant defaults (doesn't contest the eviction). We cover some of the subjects (for example, filing a complaint and default judgments) in later chapters. As you work your way through the book you may want to return to this chart to see where you are in the process.

CHECKLIST FOR UNCONTESTED NON-RENT THREE-DAY NOTICE EVICTION

Step	Earliest Time To Do It
☐ 1. Prepare and serve the three-day notice on the tenant.	Any day the tenant is in violation of the lease, has damaged the property or has created a nuisance.
☐ 2. Prepare the summons (or summonses, if there is more than one tenant) and complaint and make copies. (Chapter 6)	When it's apparent the tenant(s) won't leave on time; don't sign and date it until the day indicated below in Step 3.
☐ 3. File the complaint at the courthouse and have the summons(es) issued. (Chapter 6)	The first day after the lease term or tenant's notice period expires.
☐ 4. Have the sheriff, marshal or a friend serve the summons and complaint. (Chapter 6)	As soon as possible after filing the complaint and having the summons(es) issued.
☐ 5. Prepare Request for Entry of Default, Judgment, Declaration and Writ of Possession. (Chapter 7)	While you're waiting for five-day (or 15-day, if complaint not personally served) response time to pass.
☐ 6. Call the court to find out whether or not tenant(s) have filed written response.	Just before closing on the fifth day after service of summons, or early on the sixth day. (If fifth day after service falls on weekend or holiday, count the first business day after that as the fifth day.)
☐ 7. Mail copy of Request for Entry of Default to tenant(s), file original at courthouse. Also file Summons and Declaration and have clerk issue judgment and writ for possession of the property. (Chapter 7)	Sixth day after service of summons and complaint. (Again, count first business day after fifth day that falls on weekend or holiday.)
☐ 8. Prepare letter of instruction for, and give writ and copies to, sheriff or marshal. (Chapter 7)	As soon as possible after above step. Sheriff or marshal won't evict for at least five days after posting notice.
☐ 9. Change locks after tenant vacates.	As soon as possible.

for money judgment

Step	Earliest Time To Do It
☐ 10. Prepare Request for Entry of Default, Judgment and, if allowed by local rule, Declaration in Lieu of Testimony). (Chapter 7)	As soon as possible after property is vacant.
☐ 11. Mail Request for Entry of Default copy to tenant, file request at courthouse. If Declaration in Lieu of Testimony allowed, file that too, and give clerk judgment and writ forms for money part of judgment. If testimony required, ask clerk for default hearing. (Chapter 7)	As soon as possible after above.
☐ 12. If testimony required, attend default hearing before judge, testify, and turn in your judgment form for entry of money judgment. (Chapter 7)	When scheduled by court clerk.
☐ 13. Apply security deposit to cleaning and repair of property, and to any rent not accounted for in judgment, then apply balance to judgment amount. Notify tenant in writing of deductions, keeping a copy. Refund any balance remaining. If deposit does not cover entire judgment, collect balance of judgment. (Chapter 9)	As soon as possible after default hearing. Deposit must be accounted for within two weeks of when the tenants vacate.

B. The Two Types of Three-Day Notices

Two kinds of three-day notices are covered here. The first is called a Notice To Perform Covenant or Quit and is like the three-day notice used for nonpayment of rent (Chapter 2) in that it gives the tenant the option of staying if he corrects his behavior within the three-day period. If he doesn't, then the tenancy is considered terminated. Most three-day notices fit into this category.

The other type of three-day notice simply tells the tenant to move out in three days. There is no option to correct the behavior. This kind of unconditional notice is allowed only in certain circumstances described in Section D, below.

We strongly recommend that you use the conditional notice if any guesswork is involved. The consequences of using the unconditional notice can be drastic if the judge later disagrees with you and thinks that the situation called for a conditional notice. In that event, the judge will rule that your unconditional three-day notice was void; you will lose the lawsuit, be liable for the tenant's court costs and attorney's fees and have to start all over again with a new notice.

C. Using the Three-Day Notice To Perform Covenant or Quit

In most situations, you'll use a conditional three-day notice, giving the tenant the option of correcting the violation or moving out.

1. When To Use a Conditional Notice

If a tenant who has violated a provision of the lease or rental agreement can correct her behavior, your three-day notice must give her that option. As mentioned, most lease violations are correctable. For instance:

- The tenant who violates a "no-pets" clause can get rid of the pet.

- The tenant who has failed to pay separate charges for utilities, legitimate late charges or an installment toward an agreed-on security deposit can make the payment.

- The tenant who violates a lease clause requiring him to allow you reasonable access to the property (on proper notice—see *Volume 1*, Chapter 13) can let you in.

The list of potentially correctable lease violations is endless. As a general rule, if the violation isn't of the type listed in subsection 2, below, it's probably correctable, and you should use a three-day notice giving the tenant the option of correcting the violation.

Rent control ordinances that require just cause for eviction (many don't) often dictate what kind of notice must be used. For example, Berkeley's ordinance allows eviction of a tenant who damages the property only after she's given a notice giving her a chance to stop and to pay for the damage. State law does not require the landlord to give any warning, but rather authorizes an unconditional three-day notice to quit in such a circumstance. These two sources of law can be reconciled by giving the tenant two notices—first, the warning or "cease and desist" notice required by the local ordinance, followed by an unconditional three-day notice to quit under state law. This can be very tricky, so if you're unsure about applicable eviction regulations or have any doubt about the validity of your grounds for eviction, a consultation with a landlord-tenant specialist will be well worth the price.

If you attempt to evict a tenant in violation of a city's ordinance, you may be facing more than an unsuccessful eviction. Depending on the circumstances and the city, the tenant may come back at you with a suit of her own, alleging any number of personal injuries—even if the tenant defaults or loses in the underlying eviction action. (*Brossard v. Stotter* (1984) 160 Cal. App. 3d

1067.) And, as always, if you are not in compliance with the entire ordinance, a tenant in an eviction lawsuit may successfully defend on that basis.

Also, some rent control cities preclude eviction for violations of a lease provision if the provision was added to the original agreement, either by means of a notice of change of terms in tenancy or by virtue of a new lease signed by the tenant after the previous one expired. In such cities, a landlord who, for example, rented to a tenant with a pet couldn't later change the terms of the rental agreement with a 30-day notice saying no pets are allowed, then evict for violation of that term after it goes into effect. (Los Angeles' ordinance specifically forbids just this sort of eviction.) This would allow the landlord without grounds for eviction to evade the just cause requirement by changing the terms to assure the tenant's breach. Even in cities that do permit eviction based on after-added clauses, the clauses still must be legal and reasonable. Also, every city's ordinance makes it illegal for a landlord to attempt to evade its provisions. An unreasonable change in the rental agreement that assures a tenant's breach will most likely be considered an attempt to circumvent any just cause requirement, and will not be enforced.

If your property is located in a rent control city which provides for just cause eviction (see Chapter 3, Section E), be sure to check the Appendix and a current copy of your ordinance for additional eviction and notice requirements that may apply.

Before using the violation-of-lease ground to evict a tenant, ask yourself the following questions:

- Was the violated provision part of the original lease or rental agreement?

- If the provision was added later, does a rent control ordinance in your city preclude eviction on this ground?

- If the violation is correctable (most are), does your three-day notice give the tenant an option to cure the defect?

- Does your city's rent control ordinance impose special requirements on the notice, such as a requirement that it state the violation very specifically, be preceded by a "cease-and-desist" notice, or include a notation that assistance is available from the rent board?

2. Preparing a Conditional Three-Day Notice

If you opt for the conditional notice, your three-day notice to perform the lease provision (often termed a covenant or promise) or quit should contain all of the following:

- The tenant's name. List the names of all adult occupants of the premises, even if they did not sign the original rental agreement or lease;

- The property's address, including apartment number if applicable;

- A very specific statement as to which lease or rental agreement provision has been violated, and how.

EXAMPLE

"You have violated the Rules and Regulations incorporated by paragraph 15 of the lease, prohibiting work on motor vehicles in the parking stalls, by keeping a partially dismantled motor vehicle in your parking stall."

- A demand that within three days the tenant either comply with the lease or rental agreement provision or leave the premises.

- A statement that you will pursue legal action or declare the lease or rental agreement "forfeited" if the tenant does not cure the violation or move within three days.

- The date and your (or your manager's) signature.

Two sample Three-Day Notices To Perform Covenant or Quit appear below. The instructions for completing the Proof of Service are the same as those described under the Three-Day Notice To Pay Rent or Quit. (See Chapter 2, Section B4.) A blank tear-out form is included in the forms section in the back of the book.

D. Using and Preparing an Unconditional Three-Day Notice To Quit

As noted above, under certain circumstances, the three-day notice need not give the tenant the option of correcting the problem. This is true in four kinds of situations:

1. The tenant has sublet all or part of the premises to someone else, contrary to the rental agreement or lease.

2. The tenant is causing a legal nuisance on the premises. This means that he is seriously interfering with his neighbors' ability to live normally in their homes, for example, by repeatedly playing excessively loud music late at night.

   If you are tempted to use this ground, be sure that you can prove the problems with convincing testimony from a fairly impartial person, such as a tenant in the same building who is willing to testify in court. If you're unable to produce any witnesses, forget it.

3. The tenant is causing a great deal of damage ("waste," in legalese) to the property. Forget about evicting on this ground for run-of-the-mill damage caused by carelessness. It will work only in extreme cases such as where a tenant shatters numerous windows, punches large holes in walls or the like. Again, you must be able to prove the damage convincingly.

Some rent control cities (for example, Berkeley, Cotati, East Palo Alto and Hayward) require that the tenant be given a written notice directing her to stop damaging the property and pay the estimated cost of repairs before you can evict using this ground. This requirement can be satisfied by either a Three-Day Notice To Perform Covenant or Quit, or a "cease and desist" notice followed by a Three-Day Notice To Quit.

S A M P L E

THREE-DAY NOTICE TO PERFORM COVENANT OR QUIT

To: ___Tillie D. Tenant_____,

                               (name)

Tenant(s) in possession of the premises at

___123-4th Street_____,

                       (street address)

City of ____Monterey_____, County of ___Monterey_____, California.

YOU ARE HEREBY NOTIFIED that you are in violation of the lease or rental agreement under which you occupy these premises because you have violated the covenant to:

___pay agreed installments of the security deposit in the amount_____

___of $50 per month on the first day of each month (in addition_____

___to the rent) until paid_____

in the following manner:

___failing to pay the $50 on the first day of the month of_____

___September, 19—_____

YOU ARE HEREBY REQUIRED within THREE (3) DAYS from the date of service on you of this notice to remedy the violation and perform the covenant or to vacate and surrender possession of the premises.

If you fail to do so, legal proceedings will be instituted against you to recover possession of the premises, declare the forfeiture of the rental agreement or lease under which you occupy the premises, and recover damages and court costs.

Date:____Sept. 25, 19—____ _____*Leo Landlord*_____

                                     Owner/Manager

....

PROOF OF SERVICE

I, the undersigned, being at least 18 years of age, served this notice, of which this is a true copy, on _____,
one of the occupants listed above as follows:

☐ On _____, 19____, I delivered the notice to the occupant personally.

☐ On _____, 19____, I delivered the notice to a person of suitable age and discretion at the occupant's residence/business after having attempted personal service at the occupant's residence, and business if known. On _____, 19____, I mailed a second copy to the occupant at his or her residence.

☐ On _____, 19____, I posted the notice in a conspicuous place on the property, after having attempted personal service at the occupant's residence, and business, if known, and after having been unable to find there a person of suitable age and discretion. On _____, 19____, I mailed a second copy to the occupant at the property.

I declare under penalty of perjury under the laws of the State of California that the foregoing is true and correct.

Dated: _____, 19____   _____

                                                     Signature

S A M P L E

THREE-DAY NOTICE TO PERFORM COVENANT OR QUIT

To: _____Lester Lessee_____ ,
(name)

Tenant(s) in possession of the premises at

_____123 Main Street, Apartment 4_____ ,
(street address)

City of _____San Jose_____ , County of _____Santa Clara__ , California.

YOU ARE HEREBY NOTIFIED that you are in violation of the lease or rental agreement under which you occupy these premises because you have violated the covenant to:

____refrain from keeping a pet on the premises_____

_____

_____

in the following manner:

____by having a dog and two cats on premises_____

_____

YOU ARE HEREBY REQUIRED within THREE (3) DAYS from the date of service on you of this notice to remedy the violation and perform the covenant or to vacate and surrender possession of the premises.

If you fail to do so, legal proceedings will be instituted against you to recover possession of the premises, declare the forfeiture of the rental agreement or lease under which you occupy the premises, and recover damages and court costs.

Date: ____November 6, 19–_____   *Linda Landlord*_____
Owner/Manager

....

PROOF OF SERVICE

I, the undersigned, being at least 18 years of age, served this notice, of which this is a true copy, on _____ , one of the occupants listed above as follows:

☐ On _____ , 19____, I delivered the notice to the occupant personally.

☐ On _____ , 19____, I delivered the notice to a person of suitable age and discretion at the occupant's residence/business after having attempted personal service at the occupant's residence, and business if known. On _____ , 19____, I mailed a second copy to the occupant at his or her residence.

☐ On _____ , 19____, I posted the notice in a conspicuous place on the property, after having attempted personal service at the occupant's residence, and business, if known, and after having been unable to find there a person of suitable age and discretion. On _____ , 19____, I mailed a second copy to the occupant at the property.

I declare under penalty of perjury under the laws of the State of California that the foregoing is true and correct.

Dated: _____ , 19____   _____
Signature

4. The tenant is using the property for an illegal purpose (running a house of prostitution, dealing drugs or operating a legitimate business clearly in violation of local zoning laws). You probably can't evict for minor transgressions such as smoking marijuana on the premises. It is unclear just how serious illegal activity must be to justify eviction; there are very few court decisions dealing with this question.

Because local police—or at least health department employees—may be interested in the tenant's illegal conduct, make sure to make appropriate complaints to them first. Keep a record of the dates and times of your complaints, and the name(s) of the person(s) with whom you spoke. And, although not required by ordinance, your record of having given the tenant written notice to cease the illegal activity should also help establish that there's a problem.

No rent control ordinance requires the tenant be given a chance to correct illegal use of property. Some cities, however, allow eviction on this ground only if the tenant is convicted of illegal activity. (See the Appendix.)

The notice must contain:

- The tenant's name. List the names of all adult occupants of the premises, even if they didn't sign the original lease or rental agreement.
- The property's address.
- A specific statement as to how and approximately when the tenant violated the rental agreement or lease in a way that can't be corrected—for example, if the tenant illegally sublet, created a nuisance, damaged the premises or illegally used the premises. This is the most important part of the notice, and must be drafted very carefully to clearly tell the tenant what she is doing wrong. Failure to be very specific regarding dates, times and conduct could render the notice void—another reason why a 30-day eviction or, at least, a conditional three-day notice is usually preferable.

Again, many rent control ordinances that provide for just cause for eviction require that the reason to use an unconditional three-day notice be stated even more specifically than is required under state law. Check your ordinance.

- A demand that the tenant leave the premises within three days.
- An unequivocal statement that the lease is forfeited and that you will take legal action to remove the tenant if she fails to vacate within three days.
- The date and your (or your manager's) signature.

Two sample Unconditional Three-Day Notices To Quit appear below. The instructions for completing the Proof of Service are the same as those described under the Three-Day Notice To Pay Rent or Quit. (See Chapter 2, Section B4.) A blank tear-out form is included in the back of this book.

E. Serving the Three-Day Notice (Either Type)

A three-day notice telling a tenant to either comply with a lease provision or vacate can be served any day the tenant is in violation of the lease, but not before. For example, if your tenant informs you of his intent to move in a pet Doberman in violation of the "no pets" clause in the lease, you can serve him with a conditional three-day notice only as soon as he gets the dog. You can't get the jump on him by anticipating the violation. The same is true of an unconditional Three-Day Notice To Quit. You can serve the notice any time after the tenant has illegally sublet, caused a nuisance, severely damaged the property or used it for an illegal purpose.

SAMPLE

THREE-DAY NOTICE TO QUIT
(IMPROPER SUBLETTING, NUISANCE, WASTE OR ILLEGAL USE)

To: ___Ronald Rockland_____ ,
    (name)

Tenant(s) in possession of the premises at

___1234 Diego Street, Apartment 5_____ ,
(street address)

City of ___San Diego_____ , County of _____San Diego_____ , California.

YOU ARE HEREBY NOTIFIED that you are required within THREE (3) DAYS from the date of service on you of this notice to vacate and surrender possession of the premises because you have committed the following nuisance, waste, unlawful use or unlawful subletting:

___You committed a nuisance on the premises by reason of loud boisterous___
___parties at which music was played at an extremely loud volume, and at___
___which intoxicated guests milled about outside the front door to the___
___premises and shouted obscenities at passersby every night from Febru-___
___ary 26th through 28th, 19—___

As a result of your having committed the foregoing act(s), the lease or rental agreement under which you occupy these premises is terminated. If you fail to vacate and surrender possession of the premises within three days, legal proceedings will be instituted against you to recover possession of the premises, damages and court costs.

Date: ___March 1, 19—_____   *Laura Landlord*_____
Owner/Manager

....

PROOF OF SERVICE

I, the undersigned, being at least 18 years of age, served this notice, of which this is a true copy, on _____ , one of the occupants listed above as follows:

☐ On _____ , 19____ , I delivered the notice to the occupant personally.

☐ On _____ , 19____ , I delivered the notice to a person of suitable age and discretion at the occupant's residence/business after having attempted personal service at the occupant's residence, and business if known. On _____ , 19____ , I mailed a second copy to the occupant at his or her residence.

☐ On _____ , 19____ , I posted the notice in a conspicuous place on the property, after having attempted personal service at the occupant's residence, and business, if known, and after having been unable to find there a person of suitable age and discretion. On _____ , 19____ , I mailed a second copy to the occupant at the property.

I declare under penalty of perjury under the laws of the State of California that the foregoing is true and correct.

Dated: _____ , 19____   _____
Signature

S A M P L E

THREE-DAY NOTICE TO QUIT
(IMPROPER SUBLETTING, NUISANCE, WASTE OR ILLEGAL USE)

To: ___Leslie D. Lessee_____ ,
(name)

Tenant(s) in possession of the premises at

___2468 Alameda Street_____ ,
(street address)

City of ___San Jose_____ , County of _____Santa Clara___ , California.

YOU ARE HEREBY NOTIFIED that you are required within THREE (3) DAYS from the date of service on you of this notice to vacate and surrender possession of the premises because you have committed the following nuisance, waste, unlawful use or unlawful subletting:

___You have unlawfully sublet a portion of the premises to another___

___person who now lives on the premises with you contrary to the___

___provisions of your lease.___

_____

As a result of your having committed the foregoing act(s), the lease or rental agreement under which you occupy these premises is terminated. If you fail to vacate and surrender possession of the premises within three days, legal proceedings will be instituted against you to recover possession of the premises, damages and court costs.

Date: ___March 3, 19—_____   _Mel Manager_____
Owner/Manager

....

PROOF OF SERVICE

I, the undersigned, being at least 18 years of age, served this notice, of which this is a true copy, on _____ , one of the occupants listed above as follows:

☐ On _____ , 19____ , I delivered the notice to the occupant personally.

☐ On _____ , 19____ , I delivered the notice to a person of suitable age and discretion at the occupant's residence/business after having attempted personal service at the occupant's residence, and business if known. On _____ , 19____ , I mailed a second copy to the occupant at his or her residence.

☐ On _____ , 19____ , I posted the notice in a conspicuous place on the property, after having attempted personal service at the occupant's residence, and business, if known, and after having been unable to find there a person of suitable age and discretion. On _____ , 19____ , I mailed a second copy to the occupant at the property.

I declare under penalty of perjury under the laws of the State of California that the foregoing is true and correct.

Dated: _____ , 19____   _____
Signature

1. When To Serve Notice

What happens if you've accepted rent for a whole month and then want to give your tenant a three-day notice? Should you wait a while? Here are some general rules about when to serve your tenants with three-day notices.

- Serve a conditional notice right after you receive the rent. That way, you won't be out the rent during the first month the eviction lawsuit is pending. It's perfectly reasonable to accept the rent for the month and then demand, for example, that the tenant get rid of her pet, anticipating that she will comply.

- Serve an unconditional notice as close as possible to the end of a rental period. If you serve the notice right after you've collected the rent in advance for a whole month, the tenant may claim that by accepting the rent (assuming you knew about the problem) you gave up your right to complain. However, if you can prove that you became aware of a noncorrectable violation only a few days after having accepted rent, don't worry. If you get the tenant out within the month for which the tenant has already paid rent, the tenant does not get a refund for the days he paid for but didn't get to stay. By breaching the lease or rental agreement, the tenant forfeited his right to occupy the premises, even though he'd already paid the rent.

- Never give a tenant an unconditional Three-Day Notice To Quit concurrently with a Three-Day Notice To Pay Rent or Quit. The two are contradictory, one telling the tenant he can stay if he pays the rent, the other telling the tenant to move no matter what.

2. Who Should Serve the Three-Day Notice

As with a Three-Day Notice To Pay Rent or Quit, anyone over 18 can serve the notice, including you. (See Chapter 2, Section C2.)

3. Whom To Serve

As with other three-day notices, you should try to serve a copy of the notice on each tenant to whom you originally rented the property. (See Chapter 2, Section C3.)

4. How To Serve the Notice

The three-day notice must be served in one of three ways:

- Personal service on the tenant;
- Substituted service and mailing; or
- Posting-and-mailing.

    You may not serve the notice by certified mail, which may be used only for 30-day notices terminating month-to-month tenancies. Chapter 2, Section C4, explains how to accomplish service.

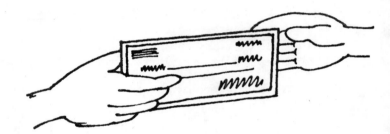

F. Accepting Rent After the Notice Is Served

With conditional three-day notices, don't accept any rent unless the tenant has cured the violation within three days—in which case you can't evict and the tenant can stay. If the tenant doesn't correct the violation within three days, don't accept any rent unless you want to forget about evicting for the reason stated in the notice.

    Don't accept rent after you've served an unconditional three-day notice unless you want to forget about the eviction. Acceptance of the rent will be considered a legal admission that you decided to forgive the violation and go on collecting rent rather than complain about the problem.

EXAMPLE

You collected $600 rent from Peter on March 1. On March 15, Peter threw an extremely boisterous and loud party that lasted until 3 a.m. Despite your warnings the next day, he threw an identical one that night. He did the same on the weekend of March 22-23. You served him an unconditional Three-Day Notice To Quit on the 25th of the month, but he didn't leave and you therefore have to bring suit. The rent for March is already paid, but you can't accept rent for April or you'll give up your legal right to evict on the basis of the March parties. However, you can get a court judgment for the equivalent of this rent in the form of "damages" equal to one day's rent for each day from April 1 until Peter leaves or you get a judgment.

G. When To File Your Lawsuit

Once you have properly served the notice you will need to wait for the appropriate number of days to pass before you take the next step, filing your lawsuit. Here is how to compute this period:

- Service is complete when you personally serve the three-day notice or, if you serve the notice by "substituted service" or "posting-and-mailing" service, five days after service.

   Los Angeles County Note. The court in *Highland Plastics Inc. v. Enders* (1980) 109 Cal. App. 3d Supp. 1, 167 Cal. Rptr. 353 ruled that service is complete after mailing and that you needn't wait five extra days. This ruling is binding only in Los Angeles County. We recommend that you not rely on it, even in Los Angeles, but instead allow an extra five days.

- If you serve more than one tenant with notices, but not all on the same day, start counting only after the last tenant is served.

- Do not count the day of service as the first day. The first day to count is the day after service of the notice was completed.

- Do not file your lawsuit on the third day after service is complete. The tenant must have three full days after service before you file suit.

- If the third day is a business day, you may file your lawsuit on the next business day after that.

- If the third day falls on a Saturday, Sunday or legal holiday, the tenant has until the end of the next business day to correct the violation (if the notice was conditional) or move. You cannot file your suit on that business day, but must wait until the day after that.

EXAMPLE

On November 11, Manuel personally served Maria with a conditional three-day notice at home. The first day after service is Friday the 12th, the second day is Saturday the 13th, and the third day is Sunday the 14th. Since the third day falls on a Sunday, Maria has until the end of the next business day—Monday the 15th—to correct the lease violation or leave. Only on the 16th can Manuel file suit.

   If Manuel tried unsuccessfully to serve Maria at home and at work and then resorted to substituted service, he would have to wait five extra days. Thus if on November 11 he gave the three-day notice to Maria's co-worker, with instructions to give it to her, and mailed another copy to Maria's home address, he would have to wait five days and then count three more days. He couldn't file suit until Monday, November 22.

   Once you have waited the requisite period, and the tenant has failed to leave (or correct the violation if your notice was conditional), you can proceed to the next phase, which is filing an eviction complaint. We tell you how to do this in Chapter 6. ■

5

Eviction Without a Three-Day or 30-Day Notice

There are just two situations in which you may file an eviction lawsuit against a tenant without first giving a written three-day or 30-day notice. They are:

- When the tenant refuses to leave after a fixed-term lease expires, and you haven't renewed it or converted it into a month-to-month tenancy by accepting rent after expiration of the lease term; and

- When your month-to-month tenant terminates the tenancy by giving you a 30-day notice, but then refuses to move out as promised.

Rent control ordinances requiring just cause for eviction in many cities limit evictions or add requirements for eviction. Be sure to check the Rent Control Chart in the Appendix and a copy of your city's rent control ordinance if your property is subject to rent control.

A. Lease Expiration

Unlike a month-to-month tenancy, a fixed-term tenancy ends on a definite date, stated in the lease. No further notice is necessary. However, unless you are careful you may find yourself inadvertently renewing the lease or converting it into a month-to-month tenancy. Here are the basic rules:

- If you simply continue to accept monthly rent after the termination date, the fixed-term tenancy is automatically converted to a month-to-month tenancy. (Civ. Code § 1945.) It must be terminated with a 30-day notice. (See Chapter 3.)

- If the lease has a renewal provision, your acceptance of rent may automatically operate to renew the lease for another full term.

EXAMPLE

Masao rented his house to Yuko under a six-month lease for January 1 through June 30. Although Masao assumed Yuko would leave on June 30, Yuko is still there the next day. When she offers Masao the rent on July 1, Masao accepts it, believing this is preferable to filing an eviction lawsuit, but tells Yuko she can stay only a month more. At the end of July, however, Yuko's lawyer tells Masao that Yuko is entitled to stay under her now month-to-month tenancy until and unless Masao terminates it with a proper 30-day notice. Masao gives Yuko a written 30-day notice on July 31, which means Yuko doesn't have to move until August 30.

In this example, Masao could have given Yuko a one-month extension without turning the tenancy into one from month to month. He need only have insisted that Yuko, as a condition of staying the extra month, sign a lease for a fixed term of one month, beginning on July 1 and ending on July 31.

1. Reminding the Tenant Before the Lease Expires

To avoid an inadvertent extension of the lease or its conversion into a month-to-month tenancy, it is always a good idea to inform a fixed-term tenant, in writing and well in advance, that you don't intend to renew the lease. While not required, such a notice will prevent a tenant from claiming that a verbal extension was granted. A fixed-term tenant who knows a month or two in advance that you want her out at the end of a lease term is obviously in a good position to leave on time. A tenant who realizes that the lease is up only when you refuse her rent and demand that she leave immediately is not. Your letter might look something like this:

November 3, 19____
950 Parker Street
Berkeley, CA 94710

Leo D. Leaseholder
123 Main St., Apt. #4
Oakland, CA 94567

Dear Mr. Leaseholder:

As you know, the lease you and I entered into on January 1 of this year for the rental of the premises at 123 Main Street, Apartment 4, Oakland, is due to expire on December 31, slightly less than two months from now.

I have decided not to extend the lease for any period of time, even on a month-to-month basis. Accordingly, I will expect you and your family to vacate the premises on or before December 31. I will return your security deposit to you in the manner prescribed by Section 1950.5 of the California Civil Code, within two weeks after you move out, if you will leave me your forwarding address.

Sincerely,

Lenny D. Landlord

The letter isn't a legally-required notice, but is just sent to show your intent to assert your right to possession of the property at the expiration of the lease. It doesn't have to be served in any particular way. It can be mailed first class. However, if you're afraid the tenant will claim she never received the letter, you may want to send it certified mail, return receipt requested.

2. Is the Tenancy for a Fixed Term?

If you want to evict a tenant who stays after her lease expires, the first question to ask yourself is whether or not the tenant actually did have a lease—or, more accurately, a fixed-term tenancy. Since the titles of standard rental forms are often misleading (a rental agreement may be called a "lease" or vice versa), you should look at the substantive provisions of the document if you are in doubt. (We discuss this in detail in *Volume 1*, Chapter 2.)

To summarize, if the agreement lists either a specific expiration date or the total amount of rent to be collected over the term, chances are it's a lease. For example, the sample lease in Volume 1 uses this language:

The term of this rental shall begin on _____, 19 ___, and shall continue for a period of _____ months, expiring on _____, 19 ____.

As discussed above (Section A), the big exception to the rule that no notice is required to end a fixed-term tenancy is when you have, by word or action, allowed the lease to be renewed, either for another full term (if there's a clause to that effect in the lease) or as a month-to-month tenancy (if you continued to accept monthly rent after the end of the term).

3. Must You Have a Reason for Not Renewing a Lease?

A landlord's reason for refusing to renew a lease is treated the same way as is a landlord's reason for terminating a month-to-month tenancy with a 30-day notice. (See Chapter 3, Section B.) The general rule is that (except in certain cities with rent control) you don't have to give a reason for refusing to renew the lease. (If you're in a rent control city that requires just cause for eviction, read Chapter 3, Section E.) However, your refusal may not be based on retaliatory or discriminatory motives. Laws against illegal discrimination apply to nonrenewal of fixed-term tenancies to the same extent they apply to termination of month-to-month tenancies.

In rent control cities with just cause ordinances, expiration of a fixed-term lease is generally not a basis for eviction, unless the tenant refuses to sign a new one on essentially the same terms and conditions. Most ordinances don't require you to give the tenant any specific kind of notice, although San Francisco, Thousand Oaks and West Hollywood require that the tenant be requested in writing to sign the new lease. (See the Appendix.)

The best practice is to personally hand the tenant a letter, at least 30 days before the lease expires, requesting that she sign the new lease (attached to the letter) and return it to you before the current one expires. Be sure to keep a copy of the letter and proposed new lease for your own records. Even if all this isn't required by your city, it will make for convincing documentation if the tenant refuses to sign and you choose to evict for this reason.

4. How To Proceed

You may begin an unlawful detainer suit immediately if:

- you conclude that your tenant's fixed-term tenancy has expired;

- you have not accepted rent for any period beyond the expiration date; and

- the tenant refuses to move.

Instructions on how to begin the suit are set out in Chapter 6.

B. Termination by the Tenant

You can also evict a tenant without written notice when the tenant terminates a month-to-month tenancy by serving you with a legally valid 30-day notice but refuses to leave after the 30 days. Again, if you accept rent for a period after the time the tenant is supposed to leave, you've re-created the tenancy on a month-to-month basis and cannot use this chapter.

If only one of several co-tenants (see *Volume 1,* Chapter 10) terminates the tenancy, the others may stay unless the tenant who signed the notice was acting on their behalf as well.

Because the tenant's notice may be unclear in this respect or may be invalid for other reasons (such as failure to give a full 30 days' notice), many landlords follow a tenant's questionable termination notice with a definite 30-day notice of their own. This avoids the problem of relying on a tenant's notice, rerenting the property and then finding, after the tenant has changed her mind and decided to stay, that the notice is not legally sufficient to terminate the tenancy.

If you choose not to serve your own 30-day notice and instead want to evict on the basis that the tenant has not vacated in accordance with her 30-day notice, proceed to Chapter 6 for how to file an unlawful detainer complaint. If you do decide to serve a 30-day notice of your own, turn to Chapter 3.

C. Checklist for Uncontested "No-Notice" Eviction

Here are the steps required in this type of eviction, assuming the tenant does not answer your unlawful detainer complaint (that is, the tenant defaults). At this point, much of the outline may not make sense to you, as you have not yet read the chapters on filing the unlawful detainer complaint, taking a default judgment, or enforcing the judgment. As you proceed through those chapters (or Chapter 8, if the tenant contests your action), you may want to return to this chapter to keep in touch as to where you are in the process.

CHECKLIST FOR UNCONTESTED NO-NOTICE EVICTION

Step	Earliest Time To Do It
☐ 1. Prepare the summons(es) and complaint and make copies. (Chapter 6).	When it's apparent the tenant(s) won't leave on time; don't sign and date it until the day indicated below, in Step 3.
☐ 2. File the complaint at the courthouse and have the summons(es) issued. (Chapter 6)	The first day after the lease term or tenant's notice period expires.
☐ 3. Have the sheriff, marshal or a friend serve the summons and complaint. (Chapter 6)	As soon as possible after filing the complaint and having the summons(es) issued.
☐ 4. Prepare Request for Entry of Default, Judgment, Declaration and Writ of Possession. (Chapter 7)	While you're waiting for five-day (or 15-day, if complaint not personally served) response time to pass.
☐ 5. Call the court to find out whether or not tenant(s) have filed written response.	Just before closing on the fifth day after service of summons, or early on the sixth day. (If fifth day after service falls on weekend or holiday, count the first business day after that as the fifth day.)
☐ 6. Mail copy of Request for Entry of Default to tenant(s), file original at courthouse. Also file Declaration and have clerk issue judgment and writ for possession of the property. (Chapter 7)	Sixth day after service of summons and complaint. (Again, count first business day after fifth day that falls on weekend or holiday.)
☐ 7. Prepare letter of instruction for, and give writ and copies to, sheriff or marshal. (Chapter 7)	As soon as possible after above step. Sheriff or marshal won't evict for at least five days after posting notice.
☐ 8. Change locks.	As soon as tenant vacates.

for money judgment

Step	Earliest Time To Do It
☐ 9. Prepare Request for Entry of Default, Judgment and, if allowed by local rule, Declaration in Lieu of Testimony. (Chapter 7)	As soon as possible after property is vacant.
☐ 10. Mail Request for Entry of Default copy to tenant, file request at courthouse. If Declaration in Lieu of Testimony allowed, file that too, and give clerk judgment and writ forms for money part of judgment. If testimony required, ask clerk for default hearing. (Chapter 7)	As soon as possible after above step.
☐ 11. If testimony required, attend default hearing before judge, testify and turn in your judgment form for entry of money judgment. (Chapter 7)	When scheduled by court clerk.
☐ 12. Apply security deposit to cleaning and repair of property, and to any rent not accounted for in judgment, then apply balance to judgment amount. Notify tenant in writing of deductions, keeping a copy. Refund any balance remaining. If deposit does not cover entire judgment, attempt to collect balance of judgment. (Chapter 9)	As soon as possible after default hearing. Deposit must be accounted for within two weeks after the tenant leaves. ■

Filing and Serving Your Unlawful Detainer Complaint

After you have legally terminated your tenant's tenancy by properly serving the appropriate termination notice (or the tenancy has ended because a lease expired or the tenant terminated it himself), you can begin an unlawful detainer lawsuit to evict the tenant. This chapter tells you how to prepare and file a complaint and summons, the documents that initiate your lawsuit.

A. How To Use This Chapter

The reason you're evicting (nonpayment of rent, for example) and the kind of notice you use to terminate the tenancy (Three-Day Notice To Pay Rent or Quit, for example) determine the actual wording of your unlawful detainer complaint. To keep you from getting confused, we label the parts of our discussion that apply to each type of eviction.

As you go through the instructions on how to fill out the complaint, simply look for the number of your "home" chapter (the one you used to prepare the termination notice) and start reading. You needn't pay any attention to the material following the other symbols.

Key to Symbols in this Chapter

❷ Evictions based on nonpayment of rent—Three-Day Notice To Pay Rent or Quit (Chapter 2)

❸ Evictions based on a 30-day notice (Chapter 3)

❹ Evictions based on lease violations, damage or nuisance—Three-Day Notice To Quit or Three-Day Notice To Perform Covenant or Quit (Chapter 4)

❺ Evictions based on termination of tenancy without notice (Chapter 5)

If a paragraph is relevant only to certain types of evictions, only the appropriate symbols will appear. In addition, we occasionally refer you to the chapter you started with (for example, Chapter 2 for evictions based on nonpayment of rent). We also alert you to the special requirements of rent control ordinances.

Okay, let's start.

B. When To File Your Unlawful Detainer Complaint

❷ ❸ ❹ If you terminated the tenancy with a three- or 30-day notice, you can file your unlawful detainer complaint when the notice period expires. You must be careful not to file prematurely. If you file before the notice period is over, there is no basis for the suit because the tenancy was never properly terminated, and if the tenant files a written response to your lawsuit, you will lose.

It is therefore very important to correctly calculate the length of the notice period. We explained how to do this in the chapter you started out in (for example, Chapter 2 for evictions based on nonpayment of rent, Chapter 3 for evictions based on a 30-day notice). If necessary, go back to the chapter covering your type of eviction and review how to determine when the notice period ends. Then return here for instructions on how to fill in and file your unlawful detainer complaint.

❺ If, as discussed in Chapter 5, the tenancy has already ended without a three- or 30-day notice, that is, if a lease has expired or the tenant terminated the tenancy with a proper notice to you, you may file your complaint at any time.

C. Where To File Suit

In most instances, you will file your unlawful detainer suit in municipal court for the judicial district in which the property is located. However, in some instances, you may be required to file your lawsuit in a justice court, if the property is located in a rural area.

The great majority of eviction lawsuits are brought in Municipal Courts. For this reason, all the examples and instructions in this book for preparing your lawsuit say "Municipal Court." If you use a justice court, just substitute "Justice" on your own forms.

1. Municipal and Justice Courts

Most counties are geographically divided into judicial districts, each of which is served by a local court. (Courts for California's seven largest counties are listed below.) In more densely-populated areas, this is called the municipal court, and in some rural areas the justice court. Municipal and justice courts serve exactly the same functions, and eviction procedures are the same—only the names are different.

The court located in the district where the property is located is the one in which you will have to file suit. Call the civil clerk of the local municipal or justice court for the judicial district in which your rental property is located to make sure you have the right court. You can find the court's address and phone number in the telephone book under "courts," "municipal court" or "justice court."

County	Judicial District	County	Judicial District
Alameda	Alameda Berkeley-Albany Fremont-Newark-Union City Livermore-Pleasanton-Dublin Oakland-Piedmont-Emeryville San Leandro-Hayward	Orange	Central Orange County (Santa Ana) North Orange County (Fullerton) Orange County Harbor (Newport Beach) South Court Annex (Laguna Hills) South Orange County (Laguna Nigel) West Orange County (Westminster)
Los Angeles	Alhambra Antelope (Lancaster) Beverly Hills Burbank Catalina Justice Court (Avalon) Citrus (W. Covina) Compton Culver (Culver City) Downey E. Los Angeles Glendale Inglewood Long Beach Los Angeles Los Cerritos (Bellflower) Malibu Newhall (Valencia) Pasadena Pomona Rio Hondo (El Monte) Santa Anita (Monrovia) Santa Monica South Bay (Torrance) Southeast (Huntington Park) Van Nuys Branch of L.A. Whittier	Sacramento San Diego San Francisco Santa Clara	Elk Grove Branch of South Sacramento Galt Branch of South Sacramento Walnut Grove Branch of South Sacramento Sacramento El Cajon Escondido Branch of N. County North County (Vista) San Diego South Bay (Chula Vista) Only one district for the City and County of San Francisco Gilroy Los Gatos Morgan Hill Palo Alto San Jose Santa Clara Sunnyvale

2. Small Claims Court

Until February 1992, landlords could in some circumstances use small claims court to evict a tenant. This is now illegal. (C.C.P. § 116.220.)

3. Superior Court

In addition to municipal or justice courts, each county has at least one superior court. The superior court hears eviction cases only if the rent and damages requested are more than $25,000. If you must file in superior court, see a lawyer.

D. Preparing the Summons

The first legal form that you'll need to start your lawsuit is the "summons." The summons is a message from the court to each defendant (person being sued). It states that you have filed a "complaint" (see Section E, below) against the defendant, and that if there is no written response to the complaint within five days, the court may grant you judgment for eviction and money damages.

A blank tear-out summons form is in the Appendix. You can use this form or a photocopy. If you use a photocopy, be sure that the front and back are in the same up-

side-down relation to each other as is the form in the back of this book. It is filled out in the same way no matter what the ground for the eviction you are using. Using a typewriter, fill it out as follows:

Step 1: "NOTICE TO DEFENDANT _____."

You should name as defendants the following individuals:

- All adults who live in the property, whether or not you made any agreement with them; and

- Any tenants who entered into the original rental agreement and have since sublet the property. (Such tenants are still legally in possession of the property through their subtenants.) If none of the original tenants is there, however, the current tenants are probably "assignees," not subtenants, and you shouldn't name the original tenants as defendants. (See *Volume 1*, Chapter 10, for more discussion of the subtenant/assignee distinction.)

It is not enough to name the person you think of as the "main" tenant. For example, if a husband and wife reside on the property and are listed as tenants in your lease, and the wife's brother also lives there, you must list all three as defendants. The sheriff or marshal will not evict any occupant not named as defendant who claims to have moved in before you filed suit. You may then have to go back to court to evict the person you forgot to sue. (Meanwhile, this person will be free to invite the evicted tenants back as "guests.")

Step 2: "YOU ARE BEING SUED BY PLAINTIFF _____."

Type in the name of the plaintiff, or person suing. Here are the rules to figure out who this should be:

1. If you are the sole owner of the property, you must be listed as plaintiff (but see rule (4), below).

2. If there are several owners, they don't all have to be listed—the co-owner who rented to the tenant, or who primarily deals with the manager, if there is one, should be listed.

3. The plaintiff must be an owner of the property (such as your spouse) or have some ownership interest, such as a lease-option. A non-owner manager or property management firm cannot be a plaintiff. (See C.C.P. § 367.) Some property managers and management companies have successfully brought unlawful detainer actions in their own behalf, without being called on it by a judge. Still, a competent tenant's attorney may raise this issue on occasion and win, perhaps even getting a judgment against the manager or management company for court costs and attorney's fees.

4. If the lease or rental agreement lists a fictitious business name (for example, "Pine Street Apartments") as the landlord, you cannot sue (either under that name or under your own name) unless the business name is registered with the county. (See Bus. & Prof. Code § 17910 and following.) If the name is registered, list it as the plaintiff if the property is owned by a partnership. If you own the property alone but use the business name, put your name followed by "dba Pine Street Apartments." (The dba means "doing business as.") If the name isn't registered, go down to the courthouse and get the process started. This involves filling out a form, paying a fee and arranging to have the name published.

EXAMPLE

John Johnson and Joan Smith, a partnership, own a five-unit apartment building they call "Whispering Elms." Their rental agreements list Whispering Elms as the landlord, and the name is properly registered with the county as a fictitious business name. They should enter "Whispering Elms" as the plaintiff.

EXAMPLE

Joan Smith owns the building herself, but her rental agreements list Whispering Elms as the landlord, and the name is on file with the county. The plaintiff in her eviction suit should be "Joan Smith, dba Whispering Elms."

5. If a corporation is the owner of the property, the corporation itself must be named as plaintiff and represented by an attorney. Even if you're president and sole shareholder of a corporation that owns the property, you cannot represent the corporation in court unless you're a lawyer. (Although C.C.P. § 87 seems

to allow this, this statute was declared unconstitutional in *Merco Construction Engineers, Inc. v. Municipal Court* (1978) 21 Cal. 3d 724, 147 Cal. Rptr. 631.)

Step 3: "The name and address of the court is _____."

Put the name and street address of the court, the county, and the judicial district in which your rental property is located. (See Section B, above.)

EXAMPLE

Your property is located in the City of Oakland, in Alameda County. Oakland is in the "Oakland-Piedmont-Emeryville" judicial district, whose municipal court is located at 600 Washington Street, Oakland. You should type in:

```
MUNICIPAL COURT OF CALIFORNIA,
COUNTY OF ALAMEDA
OAKLAND-PIEDMONT-EMERYVILLE DISTRICT
600 Washington Street
Oakland, CA 94607
```

Step 4: "CASE NUMBER _____."

Leave this space blank. The court clerk will fill in the case number when you file your papers.

Step 5: "Name, address, and telephone number of plaintiff's attorney or plaintiff without an attorney, is _____."

Place your name and mailing address along with a telephone number at which you can be reached.

Since your tenant will receive a copy of the summons, he will see this address (to which the tenant must mail a copy of any written response) and telephone number. You may prefer to list a business address or post office box and/or a business telephone number.

Do not fill out the rest of the summons—it is filled in later by the process server when she serves copies of the summons and complaint on each defendant. (See Section H, below).

S A M P L E

<table>
<tr><td colspan="2" align="center">**SUMMONS**
(CITACION JUDICIAL)</td><td>**UNLAWFUL DETAINER—EVICTION**
(PROCESO DE DESAHUCIO—EVICCION)</td></tr>
</table>

NOTICE TO DEFENDANT: *(Aviso a acusado)*

TERRENCE D. TENANT
TILLIE D. TENANT

YOU ARE BEING SUED BY PLAINTIFF:
(A Ud. le está demandando)

LENNY D. LANDLORD

FOR COURT USE ONLY
(SOLO PARA USO DE LA CORTE)

You have *5 DAYS* after this summons is served on you to file a typewritten response at this court. (To calculate the five days, count Saturday and Sunday, but do not count other court holidays.)	*Después de que le entreguen esta citación judicial usted tiene un plazo de 5 DIAS para presentar una respuesta escrita a máquina en esta corte. (Para calcular los cinco días, cuente el sábado y el domingo, pero no cuente ningún otro día feriado observado por la corte.)*
A letter or phone call will not protect you. Your typewritten response must be in proper legal form if you want the court to hear your case.	*Una carta o una llamada telefónica no le ofrecerá protección; su respuesta escrita a máquina tiene que cumplir con las formalidades legales apropiadas si usted quiere que la corte escuche su caso.*
If you do not file your response on time, you may lose the case, you may be evicted, and your wages, money and property may be taken without further warning from the court.	*Si usted no presenta su respuesta a tiempo, puede perder el caso, le pueden obligar a desalojar su casa, y le pueden quitar su salario, su dinero y otras cosas de su propiedad sin aviso adicional por parte de la corte.*
There are other legal requirements. You may want to call an attorney right away. If you do not know an attorney, you may call an attorney referral service or a legal aid office *(listed in the phone book)*.	*Existen otros requisitos legales. Puede que usted quiera llamar a un abogado inmediatamente. Si no conoce a un abogado, puede llamar a un servicio de referencia de abogados o a una oficina de ayuda legal (vea el directorio telefónico).*

The name and address of the court is: *(El nombre y dirección de la corte es)*

CASE NUMBER: *(Número del caso)*

Municipal Court of California, County of Los Angeles
Los Angeles Judicial District
110 North Grand Avenue, Los Angeles, CA 90012

The name, address, and telephone number of plaintiff's attorney, or plaintiff without an attorney, is:
(El nombre, la dirección y el número de teléfono del abogado del demandante, o del demandante que no tiene abogado, es)

LENNY D. LANDLORD   (213) 555-6789
12345 Angeleno St.
Los Angeles, CA 90010

DATE: Clerk, by _____, Deputy
(Fecha)   *(Actuario)*   *(Delegado)*

[SEAL]

NOTICE TO THE PERSON SERVED: You are served
1. ☐ as an individual defendant.
2. ☐ as the person sued under the fictitious name of *(specify)*:

3. ☐ on behalf of *(specify)*:

   under: ☐ CCP 416.10 (corporation)   ☐ CCP 416.60 (minor)
          ☐ CCP 416.20 (defunct corporation) ☐ CCP 416.70 (conservatee)
          ☐ CCP 416.40 (association or partnership) ☐ CCP 416.90 (individual)
          ☐ other:
4. ☐ by personal delivery on *(date)*:
       (See reverse for Proof of Service)

Form Adopted by Rule 982
Judicial Council of California
982(a)(11) [Rev. January 1, 1990]

SUMMONS — UNLAWFUL DETAINER

Code Civ. Proc., §§ 412.20, 1197

Eviction Postponement for Desert Storm Families. To prevent evictions of families of military reservists called to action in the Persian Gulf War, the California legislature passed a bill allowing veterans' families to postpone an eviction lawsuit.

To notify tenants of this law, landlords must now attach a second page to all unlawful detainer (eviction) summonses. The Summons—Unlawful Detainer Attachment informs dependents of military reservists called to active duty on account of the "Iraq-Kuwait Crisis" that they may delay eviction because of financial hardship. Landlords must attach this form to every summons, even if they are sure it does not apply, to avoid challenges and delays in the eviction process. (C.C.P. § 1167.6, Mil. & Vet. Code §§ 399.5, 800 and following, Stats. 1991, Ch. 49.)

A blank tear-out form is included in the forms section in the back of this book.

E. Preparing the Unlawful Detainer Complaint

In the unlawful detainer complaint, you allege why the tenant should be evicted. The complaint also formally requests a judgment for possession of the premises and any sums which you may be owed as back rent (in nonpayment of rent evictions), damages, court costs and attorney fees. The original of your unlawful detainer complaint is filed with the court. A copy is given to (served on) each defendant along with a copy of the summons. (See Section H, below.) Together, filing and serving the complaint and summons initiate the lawsuit.

To fill out the complaint correctly, you need to know whether or not your property is located in an area covered by rent control. To find this out, consult the list of rent control cities in the Rent Control Chart in the Appendix. Many rent control ordinances that require just cause for eviction require that the complaint (as well as the three- or 30-day notice) include a specific statement of reasons for the eviction. This requirement is satisfied by attaching a copy of the notice to the complaint and by making an allegation (that is, checking a box; see item 8.c, below) in the complaint that all statements in the notice are true. Some ordinances also require complaints to allege compliance with the rent control ordinance. If you don't comply with these requirements, the tenant can defend the unlawful detainer suit on that basis.

Although many of these specific rent control requirements are listed in the Appendix, we can't detail all the rent control ordinance subtleties, and we can't guarantee that your ordinance hasn't been changed since this book was printed. Therefore, it is absolutely essential that you have a current copy of your ordinance and rent board regulations at the ready when you're planning an eviction in a rent control city.

As with the summons, the unlawful detainer complaint is completed by filling in a standard form, which is fairly straightforward. But don't let this lull you into a false sense of security. If you make even a seemingly minor mistake, such as forgetting to check a box, checking one you shouldn't, or filling in wrong or contradictory information, it will increase the chances that your tenant can and will successfully contest the action, costing you time and money. Pay very close attention to the following instructions. This chapter includes directions on filling in each item of the complaint plus a completed sample form.

A tear-out form complaint is included in the Appendix. You can use this form or a two-sided photocopy. If you use a photocopy, be sure the two-sided photocopies you make have the front and back in the same seeming upside-down relation to one another as the forms in the back of this book, or a fussy court clerk may refuse to accept your papers for filing.

❷ ❸ ❹ ❺ At the top of the form, type your name, address and telephone number in the first box. Also cross out "Attorney For" at the bottom of the box and type in "Plaintiff Pro Per." Then fill in the name of the court, judicial district, county and court address (see Section D), the same as you put on the front of the Summons. Also, fill in the plaintiff's (your) and defendant's names. As with the Summons, leave blank the boxes entitled "FOR COURT USE ONLY" and "CASE NUMBER."

ATTORNEY OR PARTY WITHOUT ATTORNEY (NAME AND ADDRESS):	TELEPHONE:	FOR COURT USE ONLY
ATTORNEY FOR (NAME):		
Insert name of court, judicial district or branch court, if any, and post office and street address:		
PLAINTIFF:		
DEFENDANT:		
DOES 1 TO _____		
COMPLAINT—Unlawful Detainer	CASE NUMBER:	

In the space labeled "Does 1 to _____ ," put "5." This allows you to name more defendants later, if, for example, you find out the names of unauthorized occupants of the premises.

Item 1: Number of Pages

> 1. This pleading including attachments and exhibits consists of the following number of pages: _____

❷ ❸ ❹ List the total number of pages of the complaint. This will be at least three—the front and back of the complaint plus an attached copy of the three- or 30-day notice. (See item 8.a, below.) If a written rental agreement or lease is involved and you have a copy of it to attach to the complaint, count those pages too (counting each printed side of a piece of paper as a page). If you don't have a copy of the agreement, that's okay. It isn't necessary to attach it so long as the essentials—date, term, rent, due date, etc.—are stated as requested in items 6.a through 6.d, below.

❺ List the total number of pages of the complaint. This will be at least two—the front and back of the complaint. If a written rental agreement or lease is involved and you have a copy of it to attach to the complaint, include it too (counting each printed side of a piece of paper as a page). If you don't have a copy of the agreement, that's okay. It isn't necessary to attach it so long as the essentials—date, term, rent, due date, etc.—are stated as requested in items 6.a through 6.d, below.

Item 2: Plaintiff

---

2. a. Plaintiff is ☐ an individual over the age of 18 years.   ☐ a partnership.
                   ☐ a public agency.   ☐ a corporation.
                   ☐ other *(specify)*:
   b. ☐ Plaintiff has complied with the fictitious business name laws and is doing business under the fictitious name
        of *(specify)*:

---

❷ ❸ ❹ ❺ **Item 2.a:** State whether the plaintiff is an individual, a partnership or a corporation. If, as in most cases, the plaintiff is an adult individual—you— who is an owner of the property, type an X in the box next to the words "an individual over the age of 18 years."

Do not check the box next to the words "a partnership" unless you listed the partnership as the plaintiff on the summons (see Section D, Step 2, above).

Do not check the box next to the words "a corporation." Corporate landlords must be represented by an attorney—in which case you should not be doing the eviction lawsuit yourself (see Section D, above).

❷ ❸ ❹ ❺ **Item 2.b:** Type an X in the box if you included a fictitious business name when you identified the plaintiff in the summons (see Section D, Step 2, above). Type the fictitious business name in the space provided.

Item 3: Address of Property

---

3. Defendants named above are in possession of the premises located at *(street address, city and county)*:

---

❷ ❸ ❹ ❺ List the street address of the property, including apartment number if applicable, and the city and county in which it is located.

EXAMPLE

123 Main Street, Apartment 4, San Jose, County of Santa Clara.

Item 4: Plaintiff's Interest

---

4. Plaintiff's interest in the premises is ☐ as owner ☐ other *(specify)*:

---

❷ ❸ ❹ ❺ If you are an owner of the property, type an X in the box next to the words "as owner." If you have a lease-option on the property and rent it to the tenants, check the "other" box and type in "Lessor."

Item 5: Unknown Defendants

> 5. The true names and capacities of defendants sued as Does are unknown to plaintiff.

❷ ❸ ❹ ❺ You don't need to do anything here. This allegation applies only if there are unauthorized subtenants or long-term "guests" in the property, but you don't know their names. If you later learn the real name of a "John Doe," this allegation makes it easier for you to file an "amended" complaint, giving the correct name(s). Filing an amended complaint gets a bit tricky and if it is necessary, contact a lawyer to help you.

Item 6: Landlord and Tenant's Agreement

> 6. a. On or about *(date)*:   defendants *(names)*:
>
>   agreed to rent the premises for a ☐ month-to-month tenancy ☐ other tenancy *(specify)*:
>   at a rent of $_____ payable ☐ monthly ☐ other *(specify frequency)*:
>   due on the ☐ first of the month ☐ other day *(specify)*:
>   b. This ☐ written ☐ oral agreement was made with
>   ☐ plaintiff   ☐ plaintiff's predecessor in interest
>   ☐ plaintiff's agent   ☐ other *(specify)*:
>   c. ☐ The defendants not named in item 6.a. are
>   ☐ subtenants   ☐ assignees   ☐ other *(specify)*:
>   d. ☐ The agreement was later changed as follows *(specify)*:
>
>   e. ☐ A copy of the written agreement is attached and labeled Exhibit A.

❷ ❸ ❹ ❺ Item 6.a: This item calls for basic information about the terms of the tenancy.

On the first line (beginning with "On or about"), fill in the date on which you agreed to rent the property to your tenant. This is the date the agreement was made, not the date the tenant moved in. If a written lease or rental agreement is involved, the date should be somewhere on it. If it's an oral agreement and you can't remember the exact date, don't worry. The approximate date is okay.

Then, on the same line, fill in the names of the persons with whom you made the oral agreement or who signed a written agreement or lease. In the case of an oral agreement, list the name(s) of the person(s) with whom you or a manager or other agent originally dealt in renting the property. Don't worry if the list of people with whom the oral or written agreement was made does not include all the current adult occupants. Occupants who didn't make the original agreement are subtenants or assignees (see *Volume 1*, Chapter 10) and are accounted for in item 6.c (see below).

If some of the original tenants have moved out, they should still be listed in item 6.a, even though they are not named as defendants.

The boxes on the next line (beginning with the words "agreed to rent the premises for a") indicate the type of tenancy you and your tenant(s) originally entered into.

- If the tenancy was from month to month (see Chapter 3, Section A) check that box.

- If the tenancy was not originally month-to-month, type an X in the "other tenancy" box.

- For a fixed-term tenancy, type "fixed-term tenancy for _____ months," indicating the number of months the lease was to last.

- The "other tenancy" box can also be used to indicate periodic tenancies other than from month-to-month such as week-to-week tenancies.

- If the tenancy began for a fixed period (one year is common), but the term has expired and the tenancy is now month-to-month, indicate it as it originally was (fixed-term). You can note in item 6.d (see below) that the tenancy subsequently changed to month-to-month.

The next line in item 6.a (beginning with the words "at a rent of") has a space for you to fill in the amount of the rent when the tenant originally rented the premises. If the rent has increased since then, say so in item 6.d (see below). Next indicate how often the rent was payable (again, when the tenancy began; changes since then should be indicated in item 6.d). In the rare cases where the rent was not payable monthly, put an X in the "other" box and type in the appropriate period (for example, weekly, bi-monthly).

On the last line in this item, check "first of the month" if the rent was payable then. If it was payable on any other day (for example, on the 15th of each month, or every Monday), instead check the box next to "other day (specify):" and type in when the rent did come due.

❷ ❸ ❹ ❺ **Item 6.b:** This item tells whether the rental agreement or lease was oral or written and whether

you, an agent or a previous owner entered into it with the tenant. Check either the "written" box or the "oral" box on the first line. If there was a written agreement with the first tenants, but only an oral agreement with subsequent occupants, the latter are most likely subtenants under the written agreement. So you need only check the "written" box.

Also put an X in one of the four boxes below it. Check the box labeled "plaintiff" if you—the plaintiff—signed the written rental agreement or lease or made the oral agreement with the tenant. If a manager, agent or other person did this, check the box labeled "plaintiff's agent" instead. If the tenant was renting the property before you owned it, and you didn't have him sign a new rental agreement or lease, she is there because of some sort of agreement with the previous owner—in legalese, your "predecessor in interest"—and check that box.

❷ ❸ ❹ ❺ **Item 6.c:** If the occupants you're trying to evict are all named in item 6.a (because you entered into a written or oral rental agreement or lease with them), leave box c blank and go on to item 6.d.

If, however, some of the persons you named as defendants were not named in item 6.a (for example, adults who later moved in without your permission), check box c and one of the three boxes below it to indicate whether these defendants are "subtenants" or "assignees." (See *Volume 1*, Chapter 10, for a discussion of these terms.)

Here's a brief explanation:

Subtenants. If any of the original tenants listed in item 6.a still live in the premises with these defendants, check the "subtenants" box, because these people are essentially renting from the original tenants, not from you.

EXAMPLE

Larry rented to Tim and Twyla ten years ago. Tim and Twyla signed a month-to-month rental agreement which is still in effect (though Larry has increased the rent since then). Last year, Twyla moved out and Twinka moved in with Tim. Larry never had Twinka sign a new rental agreement.

What is the current status of Tim and Twinka? Tim is still renting from Larry under the old rental agreement, but Twinka is actually renting from Tim—even if she pays the rent to Larry herself. Twinka is a subtenant and should be listed under item 6.c. Tim and Twyla, the original tenants, are listed in item 6.a.

Assignees. On the other hand, if none of the original tenants live on the premises and you don't expect any of them to return, chances are that the current occupants are "assignees"—unless you had them sign or enter into a new rental agreement. An assignee is someone to whom the former tenants have, in effect, turned over all of their legal rights under the lease.

EXAMPLE

Lana rented one of her apartments to Toby and Toni five years ago. Three years ago, Toby and Toni left and, without telling Lana, had Toby's cousin Todd move in. Although Lana could have objected under the rental agreement clause prohibiting subletting and assignment, she didn't. She accepted rent from Todd, but never had Todd sign a new rental agreement, so he's an "assignee" of Toby's and Toni's. In this situation, Lana would name only Todd as defendant, but list Toby and Toni as the persons in item 6.a to whom she originally rented. (This is true even though item 6.a asks you to list "defendants." Toby and Toni aren't actually defendants, because they no longer live there; the form isn't perfectly designed for every situation.) In item 6.c, you should check the "assignees" box to indicate that Todd, not named in 6.a, is an assignee of the persons who are named.

❷ ❸ ❹ ❺ **Item 6.d:** Box d should be checked if there was a change in any of information provided in item 6.a since the original tenancy began. For instance, if the rent is higher now than it was at first, this is the place for you to say so, especially if your eviction is for nonpayment of rent and you are seeking unpaid rent. If there have been several rent increases, list them all, in chronological order.

EXAMPLE

Leon rented his property on a month-to-month basis to Teresa on January 1, 1991 for $800 per month. (This date and former rent amount should be listed in item 6.a.) On December 1, 1992, Leon gave Teresa a 30-day notice that her rent would be increased from $800 to $900, effective January 1, 1993. Leon should check box d under item 6 and after the words "The agreement was later changed as follows (specify):," type the following:

"On December 1, 1992, plaintiff notified defendant in writing that effective January 1, 1993 the rent would be increased to $900 each month."

EXAMPLE

Teresa's neighbor, Juan, moved into one of Leon's apartments on January 1, 1992. On December 1, Leon told Juan his rent would go from $650 to $700, effective January 1, 1993. However, Leon forgot to give Juan the required written 30-day notice (see *Volume 1*, Chapter 14). Still, Juan paid the increased rent for several months, beginning in January 1993. Even though Leon should have raised the rent with a written notice, Juan effectively "waived" or gave up his right to a written notice by paying the increase anyway. (Note: This may not be true in a rent control city, especially if the increased rent exceeds the legal rent for the property.) Now, in June 1993, Juan won't pay the rent (or move) and you have to sue him. Check box d under item 6 and type in the following:

"On December 1, 1992, plaintiff notified defendant that effective January 1, 1993, the rent due would be increased to $700 each month, and defendant agreed to and did pay the increased rent on its effective date."

Another common event that should be recorded in item 6.d is any change in the type of tenancy (for example, from a fixed-term lease to a month-to-month tenancy).

EXAMPLE

On June 1, 1991 you rented your property to Leroy for one year under a written lease. Leroy didn't leave on June 1, 1992, and paid you the usual rent of $600, which you accepted. Although the original tenancy was one for a fixed term, as should be indicated in item 6.a, it is now month-to-month. (See Chapter 5, Section A.) Check box d in item 6 and type the following:

"On June 1, 1992, after expiration of the lease term, defendant remained in possession and paid $600 rent, which plaintiff accepted, so as to continue the tenancy on a month-to-month basis."

Item 6.d should also be filled out for changes in the rental period (for example, from bimonthly to monthly) and changes in the date when the rent was due (for example, from the 15th of the month to the first). Simply put, item 6.d is your chance to bring the court up to date as to your current arrangements with your tenants.

You may find that there isn't enough space on the complaint form to type in all the required information for this item. If you can't fit it in with three typewritten lines that go right up against each margin, type the words "see attachment 6.d" and add all the necessary information on a sheet of white typing paper labeled "Attachment 6.d." This attachment is stapled to the complaint, along with the "Exhibit" copies of the lease/rental agreement and three-day or 30-day notice, discussed below. (Be sure to add one more page to the number of pages listed in item 1 if you do this.)

❷ ❸ ❹ ❺ Item 6.e: Put an X in this box if you have a copy of the tenant's rental agreement or lease. If so, attach a photocopy (not a signed duplicate) to the complaint. Write "EXHIBIT A" on the bottom of the copy. Be sure to add the correct number of pages (counting two printed sides of one page as two pages) to the number listed in item 1.

Attaching a copy of the rental agreement is not essential, so don't worry if you can't find one. It's a good practice, however, and if your tenant does contest the lawsuit, the judge who hears the case will be more favorably impressed with the way you put your complaint together if you do.

---

7. Plaintiff has performed all conditions of the rental agreement.

Item 7: Landlord's Compliance With Rental Agreement

❷ ❸ ❹ ❺ You need not fill in any boxes or add any statements to item 7. This allegation simply says that you've met all of your obligations under the written or oral rental agreement or lease. (If this isn't the case, the tenant may be able to successfully defend against your eviction action.) For example, if your lease requires you to make certain repairs, your use of this form—which must be signed under penalty of perjury—means that you allege you've done all the lease requires you to do.

Item 8: Notice

8. ☐ a. The following notice was served on defendant *(name)*:
      ☐ 3-day notice to pay rent or quit   ☐ 3-day notice to quit
      ☐ 3-day notice to perform covenant or quit   ☐ 30-day notice to quit
      ☐ other *(specify)*:
   b. The period stated in the notice expired on *(date)*:   and defendants failed
      to comply with the requirements of the notice by that date.
   c. All facts stated in the notice are true.
   d. ☐ The notice included an election of forfeiture.
   e. ☐ A copy of the notice is attached and labeled Exhibit B.

❷ ❸ ❹ Check the box immediately following the number 8 to indicate that a notice to quit was served on at least one of the tenants and fill in the name of the defendant to whom the notice was given. If you served more than one defendant, you will list the other names and method of service in item 9.b, below.

❺ Leave items 8 and 8.a through 8.e blank if your eviction is being brought under Chapter 5 of this book (that is, if no notice was given the tenant).

❷ **Item 8.a:** Check the first box, labeled "3-day notice to pay rent or quit."

❸ **Item 8.a:** Check the box labeled "30-day notice to quit."

❹ **Item 8.a:** Check either the box labeled "3-day notice to perform covenant or quit" (the conditional notice), or "3-day notice to quit" (the unconditional notice), depending on which type of notice you served.

❷ ❹ **Item 8.b:** List the date the period provided in your three-day notice expired. This is the third day, not counting the day the notice was served, after the three-day notice was personally served (8th day for substituted service), except that when the third (or 8th) day falls on a weekend or legal holiday, the last day is the next business day (see Chapter 2 or 4 for several detailed examples). If you used substituted service for your notice or are unsure of your notice's expiration date, return to your "home" chapter (Chapter 2 or 4) and compute the correct expiration date in accordance with our instructions.

❸ **Item 8.b:** List the date the period provided in your 30-day notice expired. This is the 30th day after the 30-day notice was personally served (don't count the day the notice was served), except that when the 30th day falls on a weekend or legal holiday, the last day is the next business day (see the detailed examples in Chapter 3 to get a better handle on this). If you used substituted service or are unsure of the proper expiration date, return to Chapter 3 and compute the proper expiration date in accordance with our instructions.

Don't File Until the 30 Days Have Expired. ❷ ❸ ❹ Be sure you do not file your papers with the court (see Section H) until after the date you indicate in item 8.b. Otherwise, the complaint will be premature, and you may lose the case and have to pay the tenant's court costs.

❷ ❸ ❹ **Item 8.c:** You don't need to fill in a box or add information on this one, which just says that everything in the notice you served (a copy of which you will attach to the complaint) is true.

❷ ❹ **Item 8.d:** Put an X in this box. This indicates that your three-day notice contained an "election of forfeiture"—legalese for a statement in the notice that the tenancy is ended if the notice is not obeyed. The form notices in this book include a forfeiture statement.

❸ **Item 8.d:** Leave this item blank, since 30-day notices do not require a notice of forfeiture.

❷ ❸ ❹ **Item 8.e:** Check this box. Label the bottom of your copy of the three- or 30-day notice "EXHIBIT B" (even if you don't have an Exhibit A), and remember to staple it to your complaint. This is essential.

Short Title

❷ ❸ ❹ ❺ At the top of the reverse side of the complaint is a large box labeled "SHORT TITLE." Put in the last name of the first plaintiff, a "v." and the last name of the first defendant listed on the summons and complaint. For example, if Leslie Smith and Larry Smith are suing Lester Jones and Teresa Brown, the short title of the case is "*Smith v. Jones.*" Leave the case number box blank.

Item 9: Service of Notice

9. ☐ a. The notice referred to in item 8 was served
       ☐ by personally handing a copy to defendant on *(date):*
       ☐ by leaving a copy with *(name or description):* , a person
       of suitable age or discretion, on *(date):* at defendant's ☐ residence
       ☐ business AND mailing a copy to defendant at his place of residence on *(date):*
       because defendant cannot be found at his residence or usual place of business.
       ☐ by posting a copy on the premises on *(date):* (☐ and giving a copy
       to a person residing at the premises) AND mailing a copy to defendant at the premises on
       (date):
       ☐ because defendant's residence and usual place of business cannot be ascertained OR
       ☐ because no person of suitable age or discretion can there be found.
       ☐ *(not for 3-day notice. See Civil Code section 1946 before using)* by sending a copy by certified or
       registered mail addressed to defendant on *(date):*
   b. ☐ Information about service of the notice on the other defendants is contained in attachment 9.

❷ ❸ ❹ Put an X in the box between the number 9 and letter a to indicate that a notice was served on your tenant.

❺ Leave items 9, 9.a and 9.b blank, since no notice was served on your tenant.

❷ ❸ ❹ **Item 9.a:** If the defendant listed in item 8.a was personally served with the notice, check the first box (next to the words "by personally handing a copy to defendant on (date):"), and type the date she was handed the notice. Then go on to item 9.b.

The second box in item 9.a, next to "by leaving a copy with...", should be checked instead only if you used "substituted service," that is, you gave the notice to someone at the tenant's home or workplace and mailed a second copy. On the same line, list the name (or physical description if name is unknown) of the person to whom the notice was given. On the next two lines, fill in the date you delivered the notice, whether the notice was served at the residence or business address, and the date the second copy was mailed to the residence address. Then go on to item 9.b.

If you had to resort to "posting and mailing" service because you couldn't find anyone at the defendant's home or place of employment, check the box next to the words "by posting a copy on the premises on (date):" and insert the date the notice was posted. Ignore the box by the words "and giving a copy to the person residing at the premises." Below that, list the date the copy of the notice was mailed to the residence address. Next, check one of the two boxes (in front of phrases beginning with "because") to indicate why you used posting-and-mailing service. In almost all residential cases you should check the second box, next to the phrase "because no person of suitable age or discretion can there be found." Leave blank the box next to the phrase "because defendant's residence and usual place of business cannot be ascertained"—after all, you always know the defendant's residence address in a residential eviction.

The last box in item 9.a, followed by the words *"not for three-day notice"* in parentheses, obviously should be used only if your eviction was preceded by a 30-day notice (Chapter 3), which you served by certified or registered mail.

❷ ❸ ❹ **Item 9.b:** If you had more than one defendant served with a copy of the notice, put an X in box 9.b. Staple to the complaint a separate piece of typing paper entitled "Attachment 9" to explain how service of the notice was made on the defendants not named in item 8.a. This attachment need only say something to the effect that "Defendant Tanya Tenant was personally served with the Three-Day Notice To Pay Rent or Quit (or 30-day notice) on July 31, 1992."

Item 10: Expiration of Lease

> 10. ☐   Plaintiff demands possession from each defendant because of expiration of a fixed term lease.

❷ ❸ ❹ Do not use this box. It does not apply in evictions based on three-day or 30-day notices.

❺ Check this box if you are proceeding under Chapter 5 on the grounds that your fixed-term lease expired. Do not check it if the reason for the eviction is that the tenant failed to vacate on time after serving you with a 30-day notice.

Item 11: Rent Due

> 11. ☐   At the time the 3-day notice to pay rent or quit was served, the amount of rent due was $ _____

❷ Put an X in box 11. At the end of the sentence following the box, put the amount of rent you demanded in the three-day notice.

Your complaint will be susceptible to a delaying motion if it ambiguously states that the rent due was something other than that stated on the attached three-day

notice, so do not under any circumstances list a different amount.

❸ ❹ ❺ Leave this box blank. It is solely for evictions based on a Three-Day Notice To Pay Rent or Quit (Chapter 2).

Item 12: Daily Rental Value

> 12. ☐ The fair rental value of the premises is $_____ per day.

❷ ❸ ❹ ❺ Check box 12 and list the daily pro-rated rent. This is the monthly rent divided by 30 or, if the rent is paid weekly, the weekly rent divided by seven. For example, if the rent is $450 per month, the daily rental value is $450/30, or $15. Round the answer off to the nearest penny if it doesn't come out even. This figure is the measure of the "damages" you suffer each day the tenant stays after the end of the rental period.

Item 13: Landlord's Right to Possession

> 13. Plaintiff is entitled to immediate possession of the premises.

❷ ❸ ❹ ❺ This sentence is just a legal statement that you're entitled to possession of the premises.

Item 14: Landlord's Right to Triple Damages

> 14. ☐ Defendants' continued possession is malicious, and plaintiff is entitled to treble damages. *(State specific facts supporting this claim in attachment 14.)*

❷ ❸ ❹ ❺ Check this box only if you want to claim that you are entitled to treble (triple) damages because the tenant is guilty of "malice," for example, trying to cheat you or deliberately damaging the property. We advise you to leave this box blank, as judges rarely award it and it gives your tenant an additional incentive to contest and delay your unlawful detainer. If you do check it, you will have to add another attachment to the complaint, listing specific acts of the tenant which you think show a malicious intent.

Rent vs. Damages

The difference between "rent" and "damages" is illustrated as follows: On February 1, Tim doesn't pay his landlord Lenny the monthly $450 rent. On February 6, Lenny serves Tim a three-day notice. After the three days have elapsed, and Tim still hasn't paid the rent, the tenancy is terminated. Lenny brings an unlawful detainer action to enforce that termination, and gets a judgment against Tim on March 10. Lenny is still entitled to the $450 rent for February, since it was all due as rent before the tenancy was terminated.

Since the termination of the tenancy was effective in February, Tim owes no "rent" as such for his stay during March. What Tim does owe Lenny for those ten days is money to compensate Lenny for being unable to re-rent the property during that time. Assuming that Lenny could have gotten the same rent from a new tenant, namely $450 per month or $15 per day, the "damages" for those ten days would be $150 in addition to the $450 rent, for total rent and damages of $600.

Item 15: Attorney Fees

> 15. ☐ A written agreement between the parties provides for attorney fees.

❷ ❸ ❹ ❺ Put an X in this box only if you have a written rental agreement or lease (a copy of which should be attached to the complaint—see item 6.e) and it has a clause specifically providing that you (or the prevailing party in a lawsuit) are entitled to attorney's fees. A clause referring only to "costs" or "court costs" isn't enough.

To be entitled to a court judgment for attorney's fees, you must also be represented by an attorney. Since you're representing yourself, you won't be entitled to attorney's fees even if you win. Still, you should fill in this part just in case your tenant contests the lawsuit and you later hire a lawyer.

Item 16: Rent Control

> 16. ☐ Defendants' tenancy is subject to the local rent control or eviction control ordinance of *(city or county, title of ordinance, and date of passage):*
>
> Plaintiff has met all applicable requirements of the ordinances.

❷ ❸ ❹ ❺ This box should be checked only if your property is subject to a local rent control law. When you put an X in this box, you declare under penalty of perjury that you have complied with all rent ceiling, registration and other applicable requirements under the ordinance. Be sure you have. If you haven't, or if you're not sure, do some research. (See *Volume 1*, Chapter 4.)

Once you're sure you are in compliance, type in the name of the city or county, the title of the ordinance and the date it went into effect. Much of this information is listed in the Rent Control Chart in the Appendix of this volume (as well as *Volume 1*, Chapter 4), but because rent control ordinances are constantly changing, you should also call the local rent control board for the latest information.

Item 17: Other Allegations

> 17. ☐ Other allegations are stated in attachment 17.

❷ ❸ ❹ This box does not have to be checked in cases based on three-day or 30-day notices.

❺ Check this box if you're suing a tenant who won't leave after having terminated a month-to-month tenancy by giving you at least 30 days' written notice. You'll have to add an extra paper titled "Attachment 17"

to the complaint. Using a blank sheet of typing paper, type a statement based on this model:

```
Attachment 17

    On ___(date)___, 19 ___, defendants
served plaintiff a written notice ter-
minating their month-to-month tenancy
no sooner than 30 days from the date of
```

service of the notice, for the termination to be effective on ___(date)___, 19 ___. That period has elapsed, and defendants have failed and refused to vacate the premises.

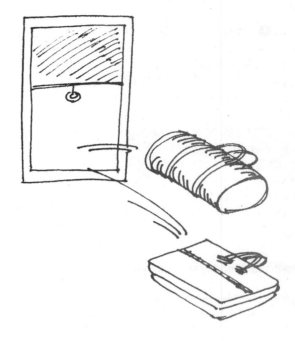

Extra Required Allegations. Some rent control cities require landlords to make additional allegations. For example, Berkeley requires landlords to allege that they are in compliance with the "implied warranty of habitability." Attachment 17 can also be used for this sort of required allegation. The landlord might allege, "Plaintiff is in full compliance with the implied warranty to provide habitable premises with respect to the subject property."

Item 18: Jurisdictional Limit of the Court

> 18. Plaintiff remits to the jurisdictional limit, if any, of the court.

❷ ❸ ❹ ❺ This statement just means you are not asking for more money than the court has power to give ($25,000 in municipal or justice court).

Item 19: Landlord's Requests

> 19. PLAINTIFF REQUESTS
>   a. possession of the premises.
>   b. ☐ costs incurred in this proceeding.
>   c. ☐ past due rent of $_____
>   d. ☐ damages at the rate of $_____ per day.
>   e. ☐ treble the amount of rent and damages found due.
>   f. ☐ reasonable attorney fees.
>   g. ☐ forfeiture of the agreement.
>   h. ☐ other (specify):

❷ Here you list what you want the court to grant. Put X's in boxes b, c, d and g. Also put an X in box f if your lease or rental agreement has an attorney fees clause (see item 15). Do not check box e (see item 14, above).

Fill in the amount of past due rent in the space provided following box c, again making sure this is the same amount stated in item 11 and the three-day notice. In the space following box d, put the same pro-rated daily rent amount you listed in item 12.

❹ Put X's in boxes b, d and g for evictions based on conditional three-day notices to perform covenant or quit or unconditional three-day notices. Don't check box c, since you can only collect back rent in evictions for nonpayment of rent. Don't check box e, for the reasons outlined in item 14, above. You may, however, put an X in box f if your lease or rental agreement has an attorney's fees clause (see item 15).

❸ ❺ Put X's in boxes b and d only. Don't check box c since it only applies in evictions for nonpayment of rent. Don't check box e for the reasons detailed in item 14, above. Don't check box g, which only applies in evictions based on three-day notices to quit (Chapters 2 and 4). You may, however, put an X in box f if your lease or rental agreement has an attorney's fees clause (see item 15). In the space following box d, put the same pro-rated daily rent amount you listed in item 12.

Verification and Plaintiff's Name and Signature

- _____
           (Type or print name)   (Signature of plaintiff or attorney)

VERIFICATION

(Use a different verification form if the verification is by an attorney or for a corporation or partnership.)
I am the plaintiff in this proceeding and have read this complaint. I declare under penalty of perjury under the laws of the State of California that this complaint is true and correct.

Date:

- _____
           (Type or print name)   (Signature of plaintiff)

                                                                    Page two

❷ ❸ ❹ ❺ The two lines side by side above the word "Verification" are the first of two places to sign and type the name(s) of the plaintiff(s). The name of each person who is listed on the complaint (and summons) as a plaintiff should be typed in the space to the left. Their signatures go on the space to the right. For more than one plaintiff, it's okay to either separate the names and signatures by commas, with all names on one line, or to list one above the other.

Here you state under penalty of perjury that all the allegations in the complaint are true. A name and signature—but only of one plaintiff even if there are several—is required here too. The plaintiff with the most knowl-edge about the matter should type her name and the date in the space to the left and sign in the space at the right.

❷ ❸ ❹ Be sure the date you sign is at least one day after the date in item 8.b of the complaint—the date the notice period legally expired.

If a partnership is named as plaintiff, the verification printed on the form must be modified. You can do this by using correction fluid to "white out" the line of instructions in parentheses just below the word "Verification," and typing over it "I am a partner of the partnership which is." Then, on the next line, white out the words "I am." The verification should then begin "I am a partner of the partnership which is the plaintiff in this proceeding...."

S A M P L E

	TELEPHONE:	FOR COURT USE ONLY
ATTORNEY OR PARTY WITHOUT ATTORNEY (NAME AND ADDRESS):		

LENNY D. LANDLORD   (213) 555-6789
12345 Angeleno Street
Los Angeles, CA 90010

~~ATTORNEY FOR (NAME)~~ XX Plaintiff in Pro Per

Insert name of court, judicial district or branch court, if any, and post office and street address:

MUNICIPAL COURT OF CALIFORNIA, COUNTY OF LOS ANGELES
Los Angeles Judicial District
110 N. Grand Avenue, Los Angeles, CA 90012

PLAINTIFF:

LENNY D. LANDLORD

DEFENDANT:

TERRENCE D. TENANT, TILLIE D. TENANT
   DOES 1 TO___5___

COMPLAINT— Unlawful Detainer	CASE NUMBER:

1. This pleading including attachments and exhibits consists of the following number of pages: 5
2. a. Plaintiff is [X] an individual over the age of 18 years. [ ] a partnership.
       [ ] a public agency. [ ] a corporation.
       [ ] other (specify):
     b. [ ] Plaintiff has complied with the fictitious business name laws and is doing business under the fictitious name
       of (specify):
3. Defendants named above are in possession of the premises located at (street address, city and county):
      6789 Angel Blvd., Apartment 10, Los Angeles, Los Angeles County
4. Plaintiff's interest in the premises is [X] as owner [ ] other (specify):

5. The true names and capacities of defendants sued as Does are unknown to plaintiff.
6. a. On or about (date): January 1, 1991 defendants (names): Terrence D. Tenant
                                                      Tillie D. Tenant
       agreed to rent the premises for a [X] month-to-month tenancy [ ] other tenancy (specify):
       at a rent of $___850___ payable [X] monthly [ ] other (specify frequency):
       due on the [X] first of the month [ ] other day (specify):
     b. This [X] written [ ] oral agreement was made with
         [X] plaintiff [ ] plaintiff's predecessor in interest
         [ ] plaintiff's agent [ ] other (specify):
     c. [ ] The defendants not named in item 6.a. are
         [ ] subtenants [ ] assignees [ ] other (specify):
     d. [X] The agreement was later changed as follows (specify): On May 31, 1992, plaintiff notified
   defendants in writing that effective July 1, 1992, the rent due would be
     e. [X] A copy of the written agreement is attached and labeled Exhibit A. $900.00 per month.
7. Plaintiff has performed all conditions of the rental agreement.
8. [X] a. The following notice was served on defendant (name): TERRENCE D. TENANT, TILLIE D. TENANT
       [X] 3-day notice to pay rent or quit [ ] 3-day notice to quit
       [ ] 3-day notice to perform covenant or quit [ ] 30-day notice to quit
       [ ] other (specify):
     b. The period stated in the notice expired on (date): August 8, 1992   and defendants failed
       to comply with the requirements of the notice by that date.
     c. All facts stated in the notice are true.
     d. [X] The notice included an election of forfeiture.
     e. [X] A copy of the notice is attached and labeled Exhibit B.
                              (Continued)

Form Approved by the
Judicial Council of California
Effective January 1, 1982
Rule 982.1(90)   **COMPLAINT— Unlawful Detainer**   CCP 425.12

LANDLORD'S LAW BOOK, VOLUME 2

SHORT TITLE:	CASE NUMBER:
LANDLORD v. TENANT	

COMPLAINT—Unlawful Detainer
Page two

9. ☒ a. The notice referred to in item 8 was served
   - ☒ by personally handing a copy to defendant on (date):   August 5, 1992
   - ☐ by leaving a copy with (name or description):   , a person
     of suitable age or discretion, on (date):   at defendant's ☐ residence
     - ☐ business AND mailing a copy to defendant at his place of residence on (date):
       because defendant cannot be found at his residence or usual place of business.
   - ☐ by posting a copy on the premises on (date):   (☐ and giving a copy
     to a person residing at the premises) AND mailing a copy to defendant at the premises on
     (date):
     - ☐ because defendant's residence and usual place of business cannot be ascertained OR
     - ☐ because no person of suitable age or discretion can there be found.
   - ☐ (not for 3-day notice. See Civil Code section 1946 before using) by sending a copy by certified or
     registered mail addressed to defendant on (date):
   b. ☐ Information about service of the notice on the other defendants is contained in attachment 9.

10. ☐ Plaintiff demands possession from each defendant because of expiration of a fixed term lease.
11. ☒ At the time the 3-day notice to pay rent or quit was served, the amount of rent due was $ ___900.00___
12. ☒ The fair rental value of the premises is $___30.00__ per day.
13. Plaintiff is entitled to immediate possession of the premises.
14. ☐ Defendants' continued possession is malicious, and plaintiff is entitled to treble damages. (State specific facts
    supporting this claim in attachment 14.)
15. ☒ A written agreement between the parties provides for attorney fees.
16. ☒ Defendants' tenancy is subject to the local rent control or eviction control ordinance of (city or county, title
    of ordinance, and date of passage): City of Los Angeles, Rent Stabiliation
    Ordinance, passed April 21, 1979

    Plaintiff has met all applicable requirements of the ordinances.
17. ☐ Other allegations are stated in attachment 17.
18. Plaintiff remits to the jurisdictional limit, if any, of the court.

19. PLAINTIFF REQUESTS
    a. possession of the premises.
    b. ☒ costs incurred in this proceeding.
    c. ☒ past due rent of $ _900.00_
    d. ☒ damages at the rate of $ __30.00__ per day.
    e. ☐ treble the amount of rent and damages found due.
    f. ☐ reasonable attorney fees.
    g. ☒ forfeiture of the agreement.
    h. ☐ other (specify):

LENNY D. LANDLORD   *Lenny D. Landlord*
. . . .
(Type or print name)   (Signature of plaintiff or attorney)

VERIFICATION
(Use a different verification form if the verification is by an attorney or for a corporation or partnership.)
I am the plaintiff in this proceeding and have read this complaint. I declare under penalty of perjury under the laws
of the State of California that this complaint is true and correct.

Date: August 10, 1992

LENNY D. LANDLORD   *Lenny D. Landlord*
. . . .
(Type or print name)   (Signature of plaintiff)

Page two

F.   Getting the Complaint and Summons Ready To File

Now that you have filled out the complaint, go through the instructions again and double-check each step, using the sample complaint form set out on the preceding few pages as a guide.

Finally, place the pages of the complaint in the following order:

1. Unlawful detainer complaint (front facing you, on top).

2. Exhibit A (copy of written rental agreement) if applicable.

3. Exhibit B (copy of three-day or 30-day notice) if notice was served.

4. Attachments, in numerical order if there are more than one. (For example, Attachment 9 goes after Exhibit B, and Attachment 17 goes after that.)

Fasten them with a paper clip for now.

Before you take the summons and complaint to court for filing and stamping, you need to:

- Make one copy of the complaint (together with attachments and exhibits) for your records, plus one copy to be served on each defendant. The original will be filed with the court. Make sure to copy both sides of the complaint, using a two-sided copying process if possible. Be sure that the front and back of the complaint you submit to the court are in the same upside-down relation to each other as is the form in the back of this book.

- Make two copies of the summons for each defendant and one for your records. For example, if you named three defendants in your complaint, make seven copies of the summons.

G.   Filing Your Complaint and Getting Summonses Issued

To file your unlawful detainer complaint, follow these steps:

Step 1: Take the originals and all the copies of the complaint and summons to the "civil" filing window of the municipal court (or justice court, if applicable—see Section C) at the courthouse and tell the clerk you want to file an unlawful detainer action.

Step 2: Give the clerk the original complaint to be filed with the court. Ask the clerk to "file-stamp" each of the copies of the complaint and give them back to you. He will rubber-stamp each of the copies with the date, the word "FILED" and a case number.

Step 3: Give the clerk one copy of the summons per defendant and ask him to "issue" a summons for each. The clerk will stamp the court seal on each of these summonses and fill in the date of issuance; these are now original summonses, and the clerk gives them back to you.

Step 4: Give the clerk the other copies of the summons, telling him they are copies to be "conformed." He will stamp them with the date, but not the court seal. Staple one of these summons copies to the front of each complaint copy. Both are to be served on the defendants at the same time. (The original summonses are returned to the clerk after the copies are served—see Section H, below.)

Step 5. Pay the municipal court filing fee of $80.

H.   Serving the Papers on the Defendant

After you've filed your unlawful detainer complaint and had the summonses issued, a copy of the summons and of the complaint must be served on each person you're suing. This is called "service of process," and it's an essential part of your lawsuit. The reason for this is simple—a person being sued is constitutionally entitled to be notified of the nature of the lawsuit against him and how he may defend himself.

The summons tells a defendant that he must file a written response to the allegations in your complaint within five days of the date of service or lose by "default." Unlike service of notices to quit, where service on one tenant is often considered service on others, each person sued must be separately served with copies of the summons and complaint.

If you don't follow service rules to the letter, you lose. For example, a "shortcut" service of summons and complaint, where the papers are given to the first person who answers the door at the property, instead of being properly handed to the defendant himself, is not valid. This is true even if the papers nevertheless are eventually given to the right person. (If the defendant cannot be found, the strict requirements of "substituted service"—discussed in subsection 4, below—including repeated attempts to personally serve, followed by mailing a second copy, must be followed.)

1. Who Must Be Served

Each defendant listed in the summons and complaint must be served. It doesn't matter that the defendants may live under the same roof or be married. If you don't serve a particular defendant, it's just as if you never sued her in the first place; the court can't enter a judgment against her, and she cannot be evicted when the sheriff or marshal comes later on. She not only will be allowed to stay, but may even be free to invite the evicted co-defendants back in as "guests." (Minor children are evicted along with their parents, without the necessity of naming them as defendants and serving them with complaints).

2. Service on Unknown Occupants (Optional)

If you don't serve copies of the summons and complaint on everyone residing in the property as of the date you filed the complaint, the eviction may be delayed even after you've gotten a judgment and arranged for the sher-

iff or marshal to evict. That's because occupants who weren't served with the summons and complaint were never really sued in the first place. After you get a court order for possession and the sheriff posts the property with a notice advising the occupants they have five days to move or be bodily evicted, the unserved occupants can file a Claim of Right to Possession with the sheriff and stop the eviction until you redo your lawsuit to get a judgment against them. (C.C.P. § 1174.3.) Coping with this problem is difficult, time-consuming and beyond the scope of this book, and a lawyer is almost a necessity.

How can you avoid this? State law gives you an option: A sheriff, marshal or registered process server, when serving the summons and complaint on the named defendants, can ask whether there are any other occupants of the property that haven't been named. If there are occupants who aren't named, the sheriff, marshal or registered process server can then serve each of them, too, with a blank Prejudgment Claim of Right to Possession form and an extra copy of the summons and complaint, and indicate this on the proof of service. The unnamed occupants have ten days from the date of service to file any Claim of Right to Possession; they can't file it later when the sheriff is about to evict. If anyone does file a claim, he or she is automatically added as a defendant. (The court clerk is supposed to do that and notify you of such by mail.) The person filing a claim then has five days to respond to the summons and complaint. If they don't, you can obtain a default judgment for possession (see Chapter 7) that includes the new claimant as well as the other named defendants.

With this optional procedure, an unknown occupant will be less likely to file such a claim, since the threat of eviction is not as immediate as when the sheriff offers this opportunity only days before the actual eviction. (C.C.P. §§ 415.46, 1174.25.) On the other hand, this optional procedure may not be necessary if you have no reason to believe there are occupants of the property whose names you don't know. Because only a sheriff, marshal or private process server can serve the papers when you follow this procedure, the eviction may be more costly or proceed more slowly. Also, if you use this option, you will have to wait ten days from service, rather than the usual five, to obtain a judgment that would include unnamed occupants.

If you want to have any unknown occupants served, you will need to make as many extra copies of the summons and complaint and claim form as you anticipate need to be served on unknown occupants. A blank Prejudgment Claim of Right to Possession form is included in the Appendix. Fill out the caption boxes at the top of the claim form as you have on your other court forms, and leave the rest of it blank. Your instructions to the process server, sheriff or marshal should include a statement something like this: "Enclosed are two additional sets of copies of summons and complaint, together with a blank Prejudgment Claim of Right to Possession form; please serve the same on any unnamed occupants of the premises pursuant to C.C.P. § 415.46. Please indicate this type of service on your proof of service."

3. Who May Serve the Papers

The law forbids you (the plaintiff) from serving a summons and complaint yourself, but any other person 18 or older and not named as a plaintiff or defendant in the lawsuit can do it. You can have a marshal or sheriff's deputy, a professional process server or just an acquaintance or employee serve the papers. (If you have a friend or employee serve the papers, have him read the part of this chapter on how to serve the papers and fill out the "proof of service" on the original summons.) However, if you use the optional procedure shown in Section 2, above, for serving a Claim of Right to Possession on any unnamed occupants, you must use a marshal or sheriff's deputy or registered process server. An ordinary individual cannot serve the Claim of Right to Possession.

What about having your spouse serve the papers? Although no statute or case law specifically disallows spouses not named in the complaint from serving papers for the named spouse, this isn't a good idea. Since spouses almost always share an ownership interest in real estate (even if the property is only in one spouse's name), a judge could rule, if the tenant contests service, that the

unnamed spouse is a "party" because he or she partly owns the property.

Some landlords prefer to have a marshal or deputy sheriff serve the papers to intimidate the tenant and give the impression, however false, that the forces of the law favor the eviction. Not all counties provide this service, however; and in those that do, sheriff's deputies and marshals are occasionally slow and sometimes don't try very hard to serve a person who is avoiding service by hiding or saying she is someone other than the defendant. To have a marshal or deputy serve the summons and complaint, go to the marshal's office or the civil division of the county sheriff's office, pay a $30 fee for each defendant to be served, and fill out a form giving such information as the best hours to find the defendant at home or work, general physical descriptions and so on.

Professional process serving firms are commonly faster and are often a lot more resourceful at serving evasive persons. They are also a little more expensive, but the money you'll save in having the papers served faster (and therefore in being able to evict sooner) may justify the extra expense. If you have an attorney, ask her to recommend a good process-serving firm, or check the Yellow Pages for process servers in the area where the tenant lives or works.

Marshals and Constables
Marshals are the enforcement officers for the municipal court. They serve court papers, enforce civil court judgments and physically evict tenants who refuse to leave the property following a judgment of eviction. Los Angeles County and some others have marshal's offices separate from sheriff's offices, but in many other counties—especially in Northern California—the sheriff is designated as the marshal. Justice courts call their marshals "constables."

4. How the Summons and Complaint Copies Are Served

If you use a sheriff, marshal or professional process server, you can skip this section.

There are only three ways to serve a defendant legally. Again, pay close attention to the rules for the method you use.

Remember that only copies of the summons, and not the originals with the court seals, should be served on the defendant. If you mistakenly serve the original, you'll have to prepare a "declaration of lost summons."

a. Personal Service

For personal service, the copy of the summons and of the complaint must be handed to the defendant by the server. The person serving the papers can't simply leave them at the defendant's workplace or in the mailbox. If the defendant refuses to take the paper, acts hostile or attempts to run away, the process server should simply put the papers on the ground as close as possible to the defendant's feet and leave. The person serving the papers should never try to force a defendant to take them—it's unnecessary and may subject the process server (or even you) to a lawsuit for battery.

Personal service of the papers is best; if you have to resort to either of the other two methods, the law allows the defendant an extra ten days (15 days instead of five) to file a written response to the complaint. It is therefore worthwhile to make several attempts at personal service at the defendant's home or workplace.

Before personally serving the papers, the process server must check boxes 1 and 4 on the bottom front of the summons copies to be served and fill in the date of service in the space following box 4. A sample is shown below. It's better for the process server to fill the information in on the summons copy in pencil before service—so it can be changed later if service isn't effected that way or on that date. This is also less awkward than doing it right there just as you've located the angry defendant.

Some individuals have developed avoidance of the process server into a high (but silly) art. It is permissible, and may be necessary, for the person serving the papers to use trickery to get the defendant to open the door or come out of an office and identify himself. One method which works well is for the process server to carry a wrapped (but empty) package and a clipboard, saying he has a "delivery" for the defendant and requires her signature on a receipt. The delivery, of course, is of the summons and complaint. If all else fails, your process server may have to resort to a "stakeout" and wait for the defendant to appear. It's obviously not necessary to serve the defendant inside his home or workplace. The parking lot is just as good.

DATE: (Fecha)	Clerk, by _____, Deputy (Actuario)　　　　　　　　　　　　　　　　　　(Delegado)

[SEAL]

NOTICE TO THE PERSON SERVED: You are served
1. [X] as an individual defendant.
2. [ ] as the person sued under the fictitious name of *(specify):*

3. [ ] on behalf of *(specify):*

under: [ ] CCP 416.10 (corporation)   [ ] CCP 416.60 (minor)
           [ ] CCP 416.20 (defunct corporation)   [ ] CCP 416.70 (conservatee)
           [ ] CCP 416.40 (association or partnership)   [ ] CCP 416.90 (individual)
           [ ] other:
4. [X] by personal delivery on *(date):*   8-12-92
        (See reverse for Proof of Service)

Form Adopted by Rule 982
Judicial Council of California
982(a)(11) [Rev. January 1, 1990]

SUMMONS — UNLAWFUL DETAINER

Code Civ. Proc., §§ 412.20, 1197

When serving more than one defendant, it's sometimes difficult to serve the remaining defendant after having served one. For example, if one adult in the family customarily answers the door and is served the papers, it's unlikely that she will cooperate by calling the other defendant to the door so that your process server can serve that person too. So, when one person answers the door, the process server should ask whether the other person is at home. Usually the defendant who answers the door will stay there until the other person comes to the door—at which time your process server can serve them both by handing the papers to each individual or laying them at their feet.

b. Substituted Service on Another Person

If your process server makes three unsuccessful attempts to serve a defendant at home, at times you would reasonably expect the defendant to be there, he can give the papers to another person at the defendant's home, workplace or usual mailing address (other than a U.S. Postal Service mailbox) with instructions to that person to give papers to the defendant.

If the papers are left at the defendant's home, they must be given to "a competent member of the household," who is at least 18 years old. In addition, the server must mail a second copy of the summons and complaint to the defendant at the place where the summons was left. (C.C.P. § 415.20(b).) This is called "substituted service."

There are two disadvantages to this method. First, several unsuccessful attempts to find the defendant have to be made and must be documented in a separate form (discussed below). The second disadvantage is that the law allows the defendant ten extra days (or 15 days) to respond to a summons and complaint served this way. So using this method instead of personal service means that the eviction will be delayed ten days.

In most instances, unless your process server can serve a defendant at home, it's better to get a professional process server to make substituted service. If you send a relative or friend to try to serve a tenant at work, you could regret it, as service at work is likely to create a lot

---

> *Post Office Boxes*
>
> *Thus, a tenant who is never home to be served (and no one ever answers the door at the tenant's home) cannot be served at a "usual mailing address" if that address happens to be a post office box at a U.S. Postal Service public post office. However, if the tenant rents a box at a private post office (such as Mailboxes, Etc.) and regularly uses that address and box, he may be served there by substituted service on the person in charge of the mail drop, followed by mailing a second copy of the summons and complaint (from a real U.S. Postal Service mailbox).*

---

of hostility. It may even prompt her to go out and get herself a lawyer, when she otherwise might have simply moved out.

EXAMPLE

You name Daily and Baily as defendants. When your process server goes to serve the papers, only Daily is home. He serves Daily personally. Baily, however, has to be served before you can get a judgment against him. Two more attempts to serve Baily fail, when Daily answers the door and refuses to say where Baily is. The process server uses the substituted service technique and gives Daily another set of papers—for Baily—and mails still another set addressed to Baily. Service is not legally effective until the tenth day after giving the papers to Daily and mailing a second copy of the papers to him. This means that you'll have to wait these ten days, plus the five day "response time" (Section I, below) for a total of 15 days, before you can take a default judgment against Baily.

Before serving the papers by substituted service, the process server should check box 3 on the bottom front of the summons copy and write in the name of the defendant served this way (not the person to whom the papers are given) after the words "On behalf of." Of the boxes below box 3 and indented, check the box labeled "other" and add "C.C.P. § 415.20" after it to indicate that substituted service was used. As with personal service, check box 4 and fill in the date of delivery of the papers. A sample is shown below.

The process server must then fill out the proof of service on the back of the original summons (see Section 5, below) and sign and date a declaration detailing her attempts to locate the defendant for personal service. This declaration is attached to the original summons. A sample is shown below.

c.   "Posting-and-Mailing" Service

Occasionally, a process server isn't able to use either personal or substituted service to serve a defendant with copies of the summons and complaint. For example, if your tenant lives alone and is deliberately avoiding service, and you don't know where he works (he's no longer at the job listed on his application several months ago), the law provides that your process server can post copies of the summons and complaint on his front door and mail a second set of copies.

As with substituted service, this "posting-and-mailing" method also gives the defendant an extra ten days to file a response with the court, and so ten more days (total of 15 days) before you can get a default judgment.

Posting and mailing can be more complicated than it looks, and we strongly recommend that you let a process server or a lawyer handle it. There are just too many ways to make a mistake, and if you do, your whole lawsuit will fail.

Before you can use posting and mailing, you must get written permission from a judge. Your process server must show that he has made at least two, and preferably three, unsuccessful attempts to serve the papers at reasonable times. For example, an attempt to serve an employed defendant at home at noon on a weekday, when she would most likely be at work, isn't reasonable. Attempts to serve at unreasonable hours may subject you to legal liability for invasion of privacy or intentional infliction of mental distress—another good reason to let someone experienced handle it. However, a sample form (Declaration for Order for Service of Summons and Complaint in Unlawful Detainer Action by Posting and Mailing) for getting permission from a judge for this type of service is shown below. Keep in mind, though, that this sample should be adapted to your own situation, in the "Declaration" and "Order" (the first two, and fourth, pages. (The legal argument, called Memorandum of Points and Authorities, on the third page, can be used without modifications.)

DATE: *(Fecha)*	Clerk, by _____, Deputy *(Actuario)* *(Delegado)*

[SEAL]

NOTICE TO THE PERSON SERVED: You are served
1. ☐ as an individual defendant.
2. ☐ as the person sued under the fictitious name of *(specify)*:
3. ☒ on behalf of *(specify)*: TILLIE D. TENANT

under:	☐ CCP 416.10 (corporation)	☐ CCP 416.60 (minor)
	☐ CCP 416.20 (defunct corporation)	☐ CCP 416.70 (conservatee)
	☐ CCP 416.40 (association or partnership)	☐ CCP 416.90 (individual)
	☒ other: C.C.P. SECTION 415.20	

4. ☒ by personal delivery on *(date)*: 8-15-92
(See reverse for Proof of Service)

Form Adopted by Rule 982
Judicial Council of California
982(a)(11) [Rev. January 1, 1990]

SUMMONS — UNLAWFUL DETAINER

Code Civ. Proc., §§ 412.20, 1197

SAMPLE

DECLARATION RE REASONABLE DILIGENCE FOR

SUBSTITUTED SERVICE OF SUMMONS ON INDIVIDUAL

I, SARAH SERVER, declare:

I am over the age of 18 years and not a party to this action.

On August 13, 19__, I served the summons and complaint on defendant Terrence Tenant by leaving true copies thereof with Teresa Tenant at the defendant's place of residence and mailing a second set of copies thereof addressed to defendant at his place of residence.

Prior to using substituted service to serve defendant Terrence Tenant, I attempted on the following occasions to personally serve him:

1. On August 10, 19__ at 5:30 P.M. I knocked on the front door of defendant's residence. A woman who identified herself as Teresa Tenant answered the door. I asked her whether I could see either Terrence or Tillie Tenant and she replied, "They're not at home."

2. On August 12, 19__ at 3:00 P.M. I went to defendant Terrence Tenant's place of employment, Bob's Burgers, 123 Main Street, Los Angeles, and was told that defendant Terrence Tenant had recently been fired.

3. On August 13, 19__ at 7:00 A.M. I again went to the defendant's home. Again, Teresa Tenant answered the door and said that Terrence Tenant was not home. I then gave her the papers for Terrence Tenant.

I declare under penalty of perjury under the laws of the State of California that the foregoing is true and correct.

DATED: August 13, 19__   *Sarah Server*
                                SARAH SERVER

SAMPLE

1	LENNY D. LANDLORD
2	12345 Angeleno St.
	Los Angeles, CA 90010
3	Phone: (213) 555-6789
	Plaintiff in Pro Per
4	
5	
6	
7	
8	MUNICIPAL COURT OF CALIFORNIA, COUNTY OF LOS ANGELES
9	LOS ANGELES JUDICIAL DISTRICT

10	LENNY D. LANDLORD,	)	Case No. 123456
11	Plaintiff,	)	DECLARATION FOR ORDER FOR
		)	SERVICE OF SUMMONS AND
12	v.	)	COMPLAINT IN UNLAFUL
13		)	DETAINER ACTION BY POSTING
14	TERRENCE D. TENANT,	)	AND MAILING; MEMORANDUM OF
	TILLIE D. TENANT	)	POINTS AND AUTHORITIES;
15		)	PROPOSED ORDER
16	Defendants.	)	[C.C.P. Section 415.45]

17

18   I, LENNY D. LANDLORD, declare:

19   1. I am the plaintiff herein. I have a cause of action in

20   unlawful detainer against defendants, in that they have failed and

21   refused to pay the rent to me for the month of August 1992, in the

22   sum of $900.00. On August 5, 1992 I caused to be served on them a

23   3-day notice to pay rent or quit demanding that rent, and they

24   have failed and refused to pay any rent or vacate the premises at

25   6789 Angel Boulevard, Apartment 10, Los Angeles, California.

26   Defendants agreed verbally in January 1991 to pay me monthly rent

27   in advance on the first day of each month, of $850.00 as rent for

28   the said premises, pursuant to a written agreement for a month-to-

month tenancy. The rent was increased to $900.00 effective
July 1, 1992, by 30-day notice. I have complied in all respects
with the Los Angeles Stabilization Ordinance Rent.

   2. The last time I saw defendants, or either of them, was on
August 5, 1992, when I gave them each the 3-day notice to pay
rent or quit.

   3. On August 10, 1992, at 5:30 p.m., I accompanied my
process server to the front door of defendants' residence. The
lights were on in the apartment and both defendants' cars were
parked outside. When my process server knocked, defendants'
daughter answered. She stated that her mother and father were not
home. I heard voices from inside the apartment, and noise from a
television set.

   4. On August 12, 1992 at 3:00 p.m., my process server went to
Tenant's place of employment, Bob's Burgers, 123 Main Street, Los
Angeles, and was told that defendant had been fired the week before.

   5. On August 13, 1992, at 7:00 a.m., my process server again
went to defendants' residence. Teresa Tenant answered the door
and said that neither Terrence nor Tillie Tenant was home. The
process server then gave Teresa Tenant the papers for Terrence
Tenant.

   6. A declaration of my process server as to the events
stated above in paragraphs 3,4, and 5 is attached.

> **NOTE:** *A separate declaration from the process server is required if you didn't accompany the process server on all his or her attempts, and so didn't observe all the events yourself.*

1   WHEREEORE, plaintiff prays for an order permitting service or

2 defendants TERRENCE D. TENANT and TILLIE D. TENANT by posting and

3 mailing pursuant to section 415.45 of the Code of Civil Procedure.

4 I declare under penalty of perjury under the laws of the State of

5 California that the foregoing is true and correct.

6 DATED: August 13, 1992

7   _____

8   LENNY D. LANDLORD, Plaintiff

9   MEMORANDUM OF POINTS AND AUTHORITIES

10   Under C.C.P. Section 415.45, a summons in an unlawful detainer

11 action may be served by posting and mailing, on appropriate order

12 of the court to that effect. Such an order may be issued by the

13 court in which the action is pending, "if upon affidavit it appears

14 to the satisfaction of the court in which the action is pending

15 that the party to be served cannot with reasonable diligence be

16 served" by personal or substituted service, and that a cause of

17 action in unlawful detainer exists against him.

18   Under subdivision (b) of the statute, the court should order

19 posting of the summons on the premises in a way that is most likely

20 to give the defendant actual notice. In the case of residential

21 premises, that method is simply posting on the front door to the

22 premises. The court should also direct that a second copy of the

23 summons and complaint be mailed by certified mail to the

24 defendant's last known address--in this case the street address of

25 the property.

26 DATED: August 13, 1992

27   _____

28   LENNY D. LANDLORD
                                     Plaintiff in Pro Per

1
2
3
4
5
6
7
8
9
10
11
12
13
14
15
16
17
18
19
20
21
22
23
24
25
26
27
28

ORDER

It appearing that a cause of action in unlawful detainer exists against defendants and that the defendants cannot with reasonable diligence be served by personal or substituted service,

IT IS HEREBY ORDERED that plaintiff may serve defendants TERRENCE D. TENANT and TILLIE D. TENANT with summons and complaint pursuant to C.C.P. Section 415.45 by posting copies of the same on the front door to the subject premises, at 6799 Angel Boulevard Apartment 10, Los Angeles, California, and by mailing a second set of copies thereof to the defendants at that address, by certified mail.

DATED: _August 13, 1992_

_____
JUDGE OF THE MUNICIPAL COURT

5. Filling Out the Proof of Service on the Original Summons

Once the process server has served the copies of the summonses, she must fill out the "proof of service" form on the back of each original summons. (Remember, there is one original summons for each defendant.) If you use a sheriff, marshal or registered process server, he or she should do this for you. So, even where two or more defendants are served at the same time and place by the same process server, two separate proofs of service—one on the back of each original summons—should be filled out. When this form is filled out and returned to the court clerk (see Chapter 7) it tells the clerk that the tenant received notice of the lawsuit, an essential element of your suit.

Here's how to fill out the Proof of Service:

In the box at the top of the form, fill in the plaintiff's and defendant's names, and leave blank the box entitled "case number."

Item 1: Put the words "summons and complaint" here. If a sheriff, marshal or registered process server served a Prejudgment Claim of Right to Possession using the optional procedure discussed in Section H2, above, that person will also list "Prejudgment Claim of Right to Possession."

Item 2.a: Type the name of the defendant for whom this summons was issued and on whom the copies were served.

Item 2.b: Check the box next to "party in item 2a," if the defendant was personally served; check the box next to "other" if he was served by substituted service. Remember, the process server must fill out the proof of service on a separate summons for each defendant.

Item 2.c: Type the address where the defendant (or the person given the papers by substituted service) was served.

Item 3: If the defendant was personally served, check box a and list the date and time of service on the same line in sub-items (1) and (2).

If the defendant was served by substituted service on another person, check box b and type the name of that other person in the space just below the same line; if you don't know the name of that person, insert the word "co-occupant," "co-worker," or whatever other word (such as "spouse of defendant") describes the relationship of the person to the defendant. Then, check the box in sub-item (1) or (2) to indicate whether the papers were left with this other person at the defendant's business or home. In sub-items (3) and (4), list the date and time the papers were given to this other person, and put a check next to the box at sub-item (5). Finally, check box c and indicate in sub-items (1) and (2) the date additional copies of the summons and complaint were mailed to the defendant (at the home or business address where the papers were left), and the city (or county, if mailed from an unincorporated area) from which the second set was mailed. Do not check sub-items (3) or (4), or box d. Be sure to attach the original Declaration Re Reasonable

PLAINTIFF: TERRENCE D. TENANT, TILLIE D. TENANT

DEFENDANT: LENNY D. LANDLORD

CASE NUMBER:

PROOF OF SERVICE

1. At the time of service I was at least 18 years of age and not a party to this action, and **I served copies** of the *(specify documents)*:

    Summons and Complaint

2. a. Party served *(specify name of party as shown on the documents served)*:

    TERRENCE D. TENANT

    b. Person served: [X] party in item 2a [ ] other *(specify name and title or relationship to the party named in item 2a)*:

    c. Address: 6789 Angel Blvd., Apt. 10
    Los Angeles, CA

3. I served the party named in item 2
    a. [X] **by personally delivering** the copies (1) on *(date)*: August 10, 1992 (2) at *(time)*: 7:30 A.M.
    b. [ ] **by leaving** the copies with or in the presence of *(name and title or relationship to person indicated in item 2b)*:

        (1) [ ] **(business)** a person at least 18 years of age apparently in charge at the office or usual place of business of the person served. I informed him or her of the general nature of the papers.
        (2) [ ] **(home)** a competent member of the household (at least 18 years of age) at the dwelling house or usual place of abode of the person served. I informed him or her of the general nature of the papers.
        (3) on *(date)*: (4) at *(time)*:
        (5) [ ] A **declaration of diligence** is attached. *(Substituted service on natural person, minor, conservatee, or candidate.)*
    c. [ ] **by mailing** the copies to the person served, addressed as shown in item 2c, by first-class mail, postage prepaid,
        (1) on *(date)*: (2) from *(city)*:
        (3) [ ] with two copies of the Notice and Acknowledgment of Receipt and a postage-paid return envelope addressed to me.
        (4) [ ] to an address outside California with return receipt requested. ← *(Attach completed form.)* ➤
    d. [ ] **by causing** copies to be mailed. A declaration of mailing is attached.
    e. [ ] **other** *(specify other manner of service and authorizing code section)*:

4. The "Notice to the Person Served" (on the summons) was completed as follows:
    a. [X] as an individual defendant.
    b. [ ] as the person sued under the fictitious name of *(specify)*:
    c. [ ] on behalf of *(specify)*:
        under: [ ] CCP 416.10 (corporation) [ ] CCP 416.60 (minor) [ ] other:
        [ ] CCP 416.20 (defunct corporation) [ ] CCP 416.70 (conservatee)
        [ ] CCP 416.40 (association or partnership) [ ] CCP 416.90 (individual)

5. **Person serving** *(name, address, and telephone No.)*:

    SARAH D. SERVER
    123 Serve Street
    Los Angeles, CA 90010
    (213) 555-1234

    a. **Fee** for service: $ 30.00
    b. [X] Not a registered California process server.
    c. [ ] Exempt from registration under B&P § 22350(b).
    d. [ ] Registered California process server.
        (1) [ ] Employee or independent contractor.
        (2) Registration No.:
        (3) County:

6. [ ] **I declare** under penalty of perjury under the laws of the State of California that the foregoing is true and correct.

7. [ ] I am a **California sheriff, marshal, or constable** and I certify that the foregoing is true and correct.

Date: August 10, 1992

▶ *Sarah D. Server*
        (SIGNATURE)

982(a)(11) [Rev. January 1, 1990]

PROOF OF SERVICE
(Summons—Unlawful Detainer)

Page two
Code Civ. Proc. § 417.10(f)

Diligence (see Section H4), signed and dated by the process server, to the summons.

If service by posting and mailing was used, after getting permission from a judge, check box e and type after the words "other (specify other manner of service and authorizing code section):" the words "C.C.P. § 415.45 pursuant to Court's order, by posting copies of summons and complaint on front door to premises at ___[list full street address]___ on ___[list date posted]___, 19__ and mailing copies thereof on ___[list date of mailing, or words "same date" if applicable]___ by certified mail addressed to defendant at that address."

Item 4: The boxes checked and information filled in for this item should be the same as those on Items 1 through 4 of the copies of the front of the summons; boxes a, b and c here correspond to boxes 1, 2, 3 and 4 on the bottom front of the summons.

- If personal service was used, check box a.
- If substituted service was used, check box c, and under this box check the "other" box and type after it "C.C.P. § 415.20." Also type in the defendant's name on line c.
- For posting-and-mailing service, check box a.

Items 5-7, Date and Signature: In the blank space below Item 5, list the home or business address and telephone number of the process server. At the right, next to "Fee for Service," list the amount you paid, if applicable, to the person who served the summons. Check box b to indicate that this person is not a registered process server. (If you do use a registered process server, they will fill out the Proof of Service for you.) Do not check box c unless the person who served the papers is an attorney or licensed private investigator, or an employee of either. Then, check box 6 and have the person who served the papers date and sign the Proof of Service at the bottom.

I.   What Next?

Your tenant has two choices after he is properly served with your summons and complaint: he can do nothing and lose automatically (in legalese, default), or he can fight the suit. He must decide what to do within five days (15 days if he wasn't personally served with the summons and complaint).

If the tenant doesn't file some kind of written response with the court within five days, you can get a default judgment by filing a few documents with the court. No court hearing is necessary. Chapter 7 tells you how to do this. ■

Taking a Default Judgment

If your tenant does not contest the unlawful detainer lawsuit by filing a written response to your complaint, you win the lawsuit almost automatically. The tenant is said to have "defaulted," and you are entitled to obtain a "default judgment" for possession of the property from the court clerk. Most unlawful detainer actions are uncontested and wind up as defaults. By submitting more papers and, where required, appearing before a judge, you can also obtain a separate default judgment for some or all of the money the tenant owes you.

You can obtain a default judgment if all of the following requirements are satisfied:

- the tenancy was properly terminated;

- the summons and complaint were properly served on all the tenants;

- at least five days (counting Saturday and Sunday but not other court holidays) have elapsed from the date the tenant was personally served with the summons and complaint (15 days if you used substituted service); and

- the tenants have not filed a written response to your complaint by the time you actually seek your default judgment.

This chapter tells you when and how you can obtain a default judgment. (Refer to the checklist in your "home" chapter for a step-by-step outline of the process.)

A. When Can You Take a Default?

If a defendant was personally served with the summons and complaint, the law gives her at least five days to respond to your unlawful detainer complaint. You can't take a default judgment until this response period has passed. You will have to wait at least six days before you can get a default judgment from the court clerk. This is because you don't count the day of service or court holidays, which include statewide legal holidays. You do count Saturday or Sunday, however, unless the fifth day falls on Saturday or Sunday.

A tenant who was served with the complaint and summons by substituted or posting-and-mailing service has an extra ten days to respond. Thus you must count 15 days from the date of mailing. If the 15th day falls on a weekend or legal state holiday, you must wait until after the next business day to take a default.

Because you don't want to give the tenant any more time to file a written response than you have to, you should be prepared to "take a default" against one or all of the defendants on the first day you can. If the defendant beats you to the courthouse and files an answer, you can't take a default.

How do you know whether or not the tenant has in fact defaulted? Although the tenant is supposed to mail you a copy of any response he files, he may not do so, or he may wait until the last day to file and mail you a copy. To find out if he has filed anything, call the court clerk on the last day of the response period, just before closing time. Give the clerk the case number stamped on the summons and complaint and ask if a response has been filed.

Most tenants don't file a written response. If no response has been filed, you can visit the courthouse when it opens the next day to obtain the default judgment.

If, however, you find to your dismay that the tenant or his lawyer has filed a response to your lawsuit, it will probably take you a few more weeks to evict. (Go to Chapter 8 on contested eviction lawsuits.)

EXAMPLE

Your process server personally served Hassan with the summons and complaint on Tuesday, August 2. You can take a default if Hassan doesn't file a response within five days, not counting the day of service. The first day after service is Wednesday, August 3, and the fifth day is August 7. Because August 7 falls on a Sunday, Hassan has until the end of Monday to file his response and prevent a default. If he hasn't filed by the end of that business day, you can get a default judgment against him the next day, Tuesday, August 9.

EXAMPLE

Angela is a co-defendant with Hassan, but neither you nor your process server can locate her at home or work. She is served by substituted service on August 7, when the papers are given to Hassan to give to her, and a second set of papers is mailed to her. She has 15 days to answer. The 15th day after the day of service is Monday, August 22. If she doesn't file a response by the end of the business day, you can take a default against her on August 23. (As a practical matter, you should probably wait until the 23rd to take Hassan's default too, since you won't get Angela out and the property back any sooner by taking Hassan's default first—and it's more paperwork.)

Don't Accept Rent Now. If you served the tenant with a Three-Day Notice To Pay Rent or Quit (Chapter 2), do not accept any rent from your tenant during (or even after) the waiting period (also called "response time") unless you want to allow him to stay. Your tenant already had his chance to pay the rent during the three-day period, and you don't have to accept it if it's offered after you file your suit. If you do, you will "waive," or give up, your right to sue, and the tenant can assert that as a defense in his answer. If you care more about getting your rent than getting the tenant out, you should at least insist that he pay all the rent plus the costs of your lawsuit, including any costs to serve papers. Don't be foolish enough to accept partial rent payment with a promise to pay more later. If you do, and it's not forthcoming, you will very likely have to start all over again with a new three-day notice and new lawsuit.

B. The Two-Step Default Judgment Process

As part of evicting a tenant, normally you will obtain two separate default judgments:

1. Default judgment for possession of property. It's fairly easy to get a judgment for possession of your property

on the day after the tenant's response time passes by simply filing your default papers with the court clerk.

2. Default judgment for any money you are entitled to. Getting a default judgment for back rent, damages and court costs you requested in your complaint is more time-consuming; you have to either go before a judge or submit a declaration setting forth the facts of the case. (See Section E.) And because the judge can only award you damages (pro-rated rent) covering the period until the date of judgment, your money judgment won't include any days after you get the judgment and before the tenant is actually evicted. (*Cavanaugh v. High* (1960) 182 Cal. App. 2d 714, 723, 6 Cal. Rptr. 525.) For example, a judgment cannot say, "$10 per day until defendant is evicted." Pro-rated daily damages end on the day of the money judgment. The actual eviction won't occur for at least a week after the possession default is entered unless, of course, the tenant leaves voluntarily before then.

For this reason, it's best to first get a clerk's default judgment for possession and then wait until the tenant leaves before you go back to court to get the money part of the judgment. If you do get the money part of the judgment before the tenant is evicted, you are still entitled to the pro-rated rent for the time between money judgment and eviction. You can deduct this amount from any security deposit the tenant paid you. This isn't quite as good as waiting, because it means less of the security deposit on rent will be available if the place is damaged or dirty. If you wait to enter the default as to rent until after the tenant leaves, you can get a judgment for the entire amount of rent due and still leave the deposit available to take care of cleaning and repairs. (See *Volume 1*, Chapter 20.)

C. Getting a Default Judgment for Possession

To obtain a default judgment for possession of the property, you must fill out and file three documents:

- a Request for Entry of Default;

- a Clerk's Judgment for Possession; and
- a Writ of Possession for the property.

Because you want to get your tenant out as fast as possible, you might as well prepare the default judgment forms during your five-day (or 15-day) wait. If the tenant files a response in the meantime, you won't be able to obtain a default judgment, and this work will be wasted. However, the time it takes to prepare these forms is not great. And because of the high percentage of cases that end in defaults, it's a worthwhile gamble.

If the tenant voluntarily moved out after being served with the summons and complaint, he still is required to answer the complaint within five days. Assuming he does not, you should still go ahead and get a money judgment for any rent owed, by skipping to Section E of this chapter.

1. Preparing Your Request for Entry of Default for Possession

Your request for the clerk to enter a default and a judgment for possession of the premises is made on a standard form called a "Request for Entry of Default." In it you list the names of the defendants against whom you're taking defaults and indicate that you want a "clerk's judgment" that says you are entitled to possession of the property.

If you're suing more than one occupant of the property, and they were all served with the summons and complaint on the same day, you can get a default judgment against them all the same day, by filing one set of papers with all their names on each form.

On the other hand, if you're suing more than one person and they were served on different days (or by different methods), each will have a different date by which he must respond. Your best bet is to prepare one set of papers with all the defaulting defendants' names on them, wait until the response time has passed for all defendants, and take all the defaults simultaneously.

You can fill out a separate set of papers for each defendant and take each defendant's default as soon as the waiting period for each defendant has passed, but there's nor-

mally no reason to, unless the tenants with later response times have already moved out or there is something special about the tenants with earlier response times (for example, they have potential retaliation or discrimination claims) that makes it advisable to take their default as soon as possible and get them out of the case. More paperwork is involved, and a default judgment against one tenant won't usually help you get the property back any sooner—you still have the others to deal with.

A sample Request for Entry of Default form is shown below. You will find a blank form in the Appendix; more are available from the clerk's office.

On the front of the form, fill in the caption boxes (name, address, phone, name and address of the court, name of plaintiff and defendants and case number) just as they are filled out on the complaint. Put X's in the boxes next to the words "ENTRY OF DEFAULT" and "CLERK'S JUDGMENT". Then fill in the following items:

Item 1.a: Enter the date you filed the complaint. This should be stamped in the upper right corner of your file-stamped copy of the complaint.

Item 1.b: Type your name; you're the plaintiff who filed the complaint.

Item 1.c: Put an X in the box next to "c" and type in the names of all the defendants against whom you are having the defaults entered.

Item 1.d: Leave this box blank.

Item 1.e: Put X's in boxes e and (1). This tells the clerk to enter judgment for possession of the property. If you used the optional procedure in Chapter 6, Section H2 (Service on Unknown Occupants), by which a sheriff, marshal or registered process server served a Prejudgment Claim of Right to Possession on unnamed occupants, also check the box next to the words: "Include in the judgment all tenants, subtenants ... in compliance with C.C.P. § 415.46." Leave boxes (2) and (3) blank.

Items 2a-2f: Because you're only asking for possession of the property at this point, don't fill in any dollar amounts. Just type "possession only" in the "Amount" and "Balance" columns.

SAMPLE

ATTORNEY OR PARTY WITHOUT ATTORNEY *(Name and Address)* :	TELEPHONE NO.:	FOR COURT USE ONLY

ATTORNEY OR PARTY WITHOUT ATTORNEY *(Name and Address)* :

    Lenny D. Landlord   (213) 555-6789
    12345 Angeleno St.
    Los Angeles, CA 90010

ATTORNEY FOR *(Name)* : In Pro Per

Insert name of court and name of judicial district and branch court, if any:

MUNICIPAL COURT OF CALIFORNIA, COUNTY OF LOS
ANGELES, LOS ANGELES JUDICIAL DISTRICT

PLAINTIFF:
LENNY D. LANDLORD

DEFENDANT:
TERRENCE D. TENANT
TILLIE D. TENANT

REQUEST FOR (Application)	[X] ENTRY OF DEFAULT [X] CLERK'S JUDGMENT [ ] COURT JUDGMENT	CASE NUMBER: A 12345 B

1. TO THE CLERK: On the complaint or cross-complaint filed
   a. On *(date)*: August 10, 1992
   b. By *(name)*: Lenny D. Landlord
   c. [X] Enter default of defendant *(names)*:
       Terrence D. Tenant
       Tillie D. Tenant

   d. [ ] I request a court judgment under CCP 585(b), (c), 989, etc. *(Testimony required. Apply to the clerk for a hearing date, unless the court will enter a judgment on an affidavit under CCP 585(d).)*

   e. [X] Enter clerk's judgment
     (1) [X] For restitution of the premises only and issue a writ of execution on the judgment. CCP 1174(c) does not apply. (CCP 1169) [ ] Include in the judgment all tenants, subtenants, named claimants, and other occupants of the premises. The Prejudgment Claim of Right to Possession was served in compliance with CCP 415.46.
     (2) [ ] Under CCP 585(a). *(Complete the declaration under CCP 585.5 on the reverse (item 3).)*
     (3) [ ] For default previously entered on *(date)*:

2. **Judgment to be entered**

	Amount	Credits Acknowledged	Balance
a. Demand of complaint	$	$	$
b. Statement of damages (CCP 425.11) *(superior court only)**	possession only		possession only
(1) Special	$	$	$
(2) General	$	$	$
c. Interest	$	$	$
d. Costs *(see reverse)*	$	$	$
e. Attorney fees	$	$	$
f. TOTALS	$	$	$

   g. **Daily damages** were demanded in complaint at the rate of: $ 30.00   per day beginning *(date)*: 9/1/92

Date: August 16, 1992

.....Lenny D. Landlord.....   ▶ *Lenny D. Landlord*
    (TYPE OR PRINT NAME)   (SIGNATURE OF PLAINTIFF OR ATTORNEY FOR PLAINTIFF)

* *Personal injury or wrongful death actions only.*

FOR COURT USE ONLY	(1) [ ] Default entered as requested on *(date)*: (2) [ ] Default NOT entered as requested *(state reason)*:

                      By: _____

(Continued on reverse)

Form Adopted by the
Judicial Council of California
982(a)(6) [Rev. September 30, 1991*]

REQUEST FOR ENTRY OF DEFAULT
(Application to Enter Default)

Code of Civil Procedure, §§ 585-587, 1169

*See note on reverse.

SHORT TITLE:	CASE NUMBER:
LANDLORD v. TENANT	A 12345 B

3. [X] **DECLARATION UNDER CCP 585.5** *(Required for clerk's judgment under CCP 585(a))* This action

   a. [ ] is [X] is not   on a contract or installment sale for goods or services subject to CC 1801, etc. (Unruh Act).

   b. [ ] is [X] is not   on a conditional sales contract subject to CC 2981, etc. (Rees-Levering Motor Vehicle Sales and Finance Act).

   c. [ ] is [X] is not   on an obligation for goods, services, loans, or extensions of credit subject to CCP 395(b).

4. **DECLARATION OF MAILING (CCP 587)** A copy of this Request for Entry of Default was

   a. [ ] **not mailed** to the following defendants whose addresses are **unknown** to plaintiff or plaintiff's attorney *(names)*:

   b. [X] **mailed** first-class, postage prepaid, in a sealed envelope addressed to each defendant's attorney of record or, if none, to each defendant's last known address as follows:

     (1) Mailed on *(date)*:   (2) To *(specify names and addresses shown on the envelopes)*:

     August 16, 1992   Terrence D. Tenant
                                       6789 Angel St., #10
                                       Los Angeles, CA 90010

     August 16, 1992   Tillie D. Tenant
                                       6789 Angel St., #10
                                       Los Angeles, CA 90010

I declare under penalty of perjury under the laws of the State of California that the foregoing items 3 and 4 are true and correct.

Date: August 16, 1992

Lenny D. Landlord   ▶   *Lenny D. Landlord*
....
       (TYPE OR PRINT NAME)   (SIGNATURE OF DECLARANT)

5. **MEMORANDUM OF COSTS** *(Required if judgment requested)* **Costs and Disbursements** are as follows (CCP 1033.5):

   a. Clerk's filing fees . . . . $

   b. Process server's fees . . . . $

   c. Other *(specify)*: . . . . $

   d. . . . . $

   e. **TOTAL** . . . . $

   f. [ ] Costs and disbursements are waived.

I am the attorney, agent, or party who claims these costs. To the best of my knowledge and belief this memorandum of costs is correct and these costs were necessarily incurred in this case.

I declare under penalty of perjury under the laws of the State of California that the foregoing is true and correct.

Date:

                                        ▶
....
       (TYPE OR PRINT NAME)   (SIGNATURE OF DECLARANT)

6. [X] **DECLARATION OF NONMILITARY STATUS** *(Required for a judgment)* No defendant named in item 1c of the application is in the military service so as to be entitled to the benefits of the Soldiers' and Sailors' Civil Relief Act of 1940 (50 U.S.C. Appen. § 501 et seq.).

I declare under penalty of perjury under the laws of the State of California that the foregoing is true and correct.

Date: August 16, 1992

      Lenny D. Landlord   ▶   *Lenny D. Landlord*
....
       (TYPE OR PRINT NAME)   (SIGNATURE OF DECLARANT)

*NOTE: Continued use of form 982(a)(6) (Rev. July 1, 1988) is authorized until June 30, 1992, *except* in unlawful detainer proceedings.

982(a)(6) [Rev. September 30, 1991*]   **REQUEST FOR ENTRY OF DEFAULT**   Page two
                                (Application to Enter Default)

Item 2.g: Type the daily rental value, listed in items 12 and 19.d of the complaint, in the space with the dollar sign in front of it. Then, if your complaint is based on nonpayment of rent, enter the date that follows the rental period for which rent is demanded. If your complaint is based on a 30-day termination notice, enter the date that follows the 30th day.

EXAMPLE

May Li's $600 June rent was due on June 1. On June 7, you served her a Three-Day Notice To Pay Rent or Quit, which demanded the rent for the entire month. Monthly rent of $600 is equivalent to $20 per day. List this amount in item 2.g. Then, since the last day of the rental period for which you demanded the $600 rent was June 30th, type in the next day, July 1. That is the date the pro-rated daily "damages" begin, at $20 per day.

EXAMPLE

You terminated Mortimer's month-to-month tenancy by serving a 30-day notice on September 10. The 30th day after this is October 9. The day after that, October 10, is the day you are entitled to pro-rated daily rent. Since Mortimer's monthly rent was $750, the dollar figure is $750/30, or $25 per day.

Enter the date you'll be filing the default papers with the court and type in your name opposite the place for signature.

Item 3: Put an X next to Item 3 and check the boxes next to the words "is not" in items a, b and c. (This is a general-purpose form, and none of these items applies to unlawful detainer lawsuits. Even so, many clerks insist that these items be checked, and doing so is easier than arguing.)

Item 4: Check box 4.b. (You don't check box 4.a because obviously you know the tenant's most recent address—at your property.) Then, type the date you'll mail the defendants their copies, and their mailing address, under headings (1) and (2). Below that, again type in the date you'll be filing the papers, and your name opposite the place for signature.

Item 5: Leave this entire item blank. You'll list your court costs when you file for your money judgment after the tenant is evicted (Section E, below).

Item 6: If none of the defendants against whom you're taking a default judgment is on active duty in the U.S. armed forces (the Reserves and National Guard don't count), Put an X in box b. Then, simply enter the date you'll file the papers and type your name opposite the place for you to sign.

If any of the defendants is in the military, no default can be taken against him until a judge appoints an attorney for him. That procedure is fairly complicated and beyond the scope of this chapter. See an attorney if a person you're suing is in the military and refuses to leave after you've served him with the summons and complaint. (Soldiers' and Sailors' Civil Relief Act of 1940, 50 U.S.C. § 520.) Some landlords take the expedient shortcut of complaining to their military tenant's commanding officer about nonpayment of rent or other problem. This often works a lot faster than the legal process.

Make two copies of the completed (but unsigned) form. Don't sign the Request for Entry of Default until you actually go down to the courthouse to file the papers and have mailed a copy to the defendant (see Section 4 below).

2. Preparing the Clerk's Judgment for Possession of the Premises

The judgment form provides the legal basis for issuance of a Writ of Possession, the document authorizing the sheriff or marshal to evict the tenant. You will present it to the clerk with the Request for Entry of Default.

Unlike the summons, complaint and request for entry of default forms, there is no standard statewide judgment form. Some courts allow you to prepare your own judgment form, while others require you to use their version, which the clerk will give you if you ask. We have drafted a form which is prepared in the same style and format as other standard statewide forms in the hope that the clerk will be less inclined to inconvenience you by insisting you use hard-to-get "local forms." Also included are the local judgment forms used in Santa Clara and Los Angeles counties, along with instructions. Blank copies of all three forms are in the Appendix.

After you fill out the form, make one copy for your records.

In any event, the judgment form will be easy to fill out. You enter the information (such as your name, address, court location, case number, names of plaintiff and defendants) that you listed in the big boxes at the top of the complaint and Request for Entry of Default.

The only other information you'll need to add to the Clerk's Judgment for Possession form is:

- The name(s) of the defendants against whom you're getting the default judgment,

- The date the default judgment is to be entered (the date you'll go to the courthouse to take the default), and

- The address of the property.

If you used the optional procedure in Chapter 6, Section H2, to have a Prejudgment Claim of Right to Possession served on unnamed occupants by a sheriff, marshal or registered process server, check "does" box next to the wording about the judgment including tenants, subtenants, named claimants, if any, and any other occupants of the premises. Otherwise, check the "does not" box.

3. Preparing the Writ of Possession

The final form you need to evict is the Writ of Possession. (The name of the pre-printed form you'll use is a Writ of Execution. It's a multi-purpose one for use as a writ of "possession," ordering the sheriff or marshal to put you in possession of real property or as a writ of "execution" that requests enforcement of a money judgment.) Like the summons, the writ of possession is "issued" by the court clerk, but you have to fill it out and give it to the clerk with the other default forms (see subsection 4 below). The clerk will issue the writ as soon as court files contain the judgment for possession. The original and copies of the writ of possession are given to the sheriff or marshal, who then "executes" the judgment by evicting the tenants against whom you obtained the judgment.

The Appendix includes a blank copy of the Writ of Execution (Writ of Possession) form. The usual information goes in the big boxes at the top of the writ form—your name, address and phone number, the name and address of the court, the names of plaintiffs and defendants, and the case number. Also put X's in the box next to the words "Judgment Creditor" in the top large box and in the boxes next to the words "POSSESSION OF" and "Real Property" as shown. Fill out the rest of the writ according to these instructions:

Item 1: Type the name of the county in which the property is located. The sheriff or marshal (or constable in justice court districts) of that county will perform the eviction.

Item 2: Nothing need be filled in here.

Item 3: Put an X in the box next to the words "Judgment creditor" and type your name and the names of any other plaintiffs. You are "judgment creditors" because you won the judgment.

Item 4: Type in the names of up to two defendants and list the residence address. If you got a judgment against more than two persons, check the box next to the words "additional judgment debtors on reverse." List the other names and address in the space provided in item 4 on the back of the form.

SAMPLE

ATTORNEY OR PARTY WITHOUT ATTORNEY *(Name and Address)* TELEPHONE NO:	FOR COURT USE ONLY
ATTORNEY FOR *(Name)*	
Insert name of court and name of judicial district and branch court, if any:	
PLAINTIFF: DEFENDANT:	

CLERK'S JUDGMENT FOR RESTITUTION OF PREMISES—UNLAWFUL DETAINER	CASE NUMBER:

In this action, the defendant(s) hereinafter named, having been regularly served with summons and copy of complaint, having failed to appear and answer the complaint within the time allowed by law, and the default of said defendant(s) having been entered, upon application of plaintiff(s) pursuant to C.C.P. Section 1169, the Clerk entered the following judgment:

Judgment is hereby entered that plaintiff(s) _____
have and recover from defendant(s) _____
the restitution and possession of the premises situated in the County of _____,
State of California, described as follows:

_____

_____

This judgment

☐ does (if Prejudgment Claim of Right to Possession served per C.C.P. Section 415.46)

☐ does not

include all tenants, subtenants, named claimants, and other occupants of the premises.

Judgment entered on _____ _____, Clerk

Judgment Book _____ Page_____ By _____, Deputy Clerk

NP	**CLERK'S JUDGMENT FOR RESTITUTION OF PREMISES —UNLAWFUL DETAINER**	Code of Civil Procedure, § 1169

SAMPLE

MUNICIPAL COURT OF CALIFORNIA, COUNTY OF SANTA CLARA

NAME OF MUNICIPAL OR JUSTICE COURT DISTRICT AND ADDRESS	FOR COURT USE ONLY

NAME OF MUNICIPAL OR JUSTICE COURT DISTRICT AND ADDRESS
MUNICIPAL COURT SANTA CLARA COUNTY JUDICIAL DISTRICT
SANTA CLARA FACILITY
1095 Homestead Road, Santa Clara, California 95050

TITLE OF CASE *(ABBREVIATED)*
Plaintiff:

> list plaintiff's and defendant's names

Defendant(s):

NAME, ADDRESS, AND TELEPHONE NUMBER OF SENDER

> list your name, address and phone number

CASE NUMBER

> case number

UNLAWFUL DETAINER
DEFAULT JUDGMENT
BY CLERK
FOR POSSESSION OF REAL
PROPERTY, ONLY

> list names of defaulting defendant(s)

The defendant(s) _____
having been regularly served with summons and copy of complaint, having failed to appear and answer said complaint within the time allowed by law, and the default of said defendant(s) having been duly entered; upon application of plaintiff to the Clerk for JUDGMENT.

It is adjudged the plaintiff(s) [plaintiff's name(s)] ——— [list names of defaulting defendants] ———
have and recover from defendant(s) _____
the restitution and possession of those certain premises situated in the County of Santa Clara, State of California, and more particularly described as follows:

> list complete address of property

This judgment [ ] does [ ] does not include all tenants, subtenants, named claimants, and other occupants of the premises.

> check the "does" box if you had a Prejudgment Claim of
> Right of Possession served. Otherwise, check "does not" box

I hereby certify this to be a true copy of the Judgment in the above action entered on ___ _____

_____

Judgment entered on _____ [clerk will fill in] ------------------------------ , Clerk

Judgment Book _____ Page _____ By _____ , Deputy Clerk

UNLAWFUL DETAINER DEFAULT JUDGMENT BY CLERK
(For Possession of Real Property, Only)

Pos. Record Catalog #607A

S A M P L E

This space for court clerk costs

list your name, address and phone number

| JUDGMENT
DEFAULT BY
CLERK
UNLAWFUL DETAINER | **IN THE MUNICIPAL COURT OF**
judicial district .... **JUDICIAL DISTRICT**
COUNTY OF LOS ANGELES, STATE OF CALIFORNIA
court address | Case Number
case number |

plaintiff's name(s)

Plaintiff(s)   v.   Defendant(s)

The defendant(s) _____ list names of defaulting defendant(s) _____

_____ having been served with a copy of the summons and complaint and having failed to answer complaint of plaintiff(s) within the time allowed by law and default of said defendant(s) having been entered, upon application of plaintiff(s) the clerk entered the following judgment:

Plaintiff(s) ____ plaintiff's name(s) _____

recover from defendant(s) ____ list names of defaulting defendant(s) _____

the restitution and possession of those premises situated in the County of Los Angeles, State of California, and more particularly described as: ____ list complete address of property _____

   This judgment ☐ does ☐ does not include all tenants, subtenants, named claimants, and other occupants of the premises.

check the "does" box if you had a Prejudgment Claim of Right of Possession served. Otherwise, check "does not" box

clerk will fill in

Deputy Clerk

I certify the foregoing Judgment was entered in the Judgment Book on

.... ,Copy filed.
CLERK OF THE ABOVE NAMED COURT

By .... clerk will fill in ....
                     Deputy

JUDGMENT — DEFAULT BY CLERK

UNLAWFUL DETAINER

76J752 CI-24 (5) (New - 1/ 83) PS 2- 83   1169ccp

Item 5: Fill in the date the judgment will be entered. If nothing goes wrong, this should be the date you take the papers down to the courthouse.

Item 6: Nothing need be filled in here.

Item 7: Only box a, next to the words "has not been requested," should be checked.

Item 8: Leave box 8 blank—it does not apply here.

Item 9: Put an X in box 9. On the back side of the form, at item 9, check boxes 9 and 9a and enter the date the complaint was filed. Then, if you used the optional procedure in Chapter 6, Section H2 (Service on Unknown Occupants), by which a sheriff, marshal or registered process server served a Prejudgment Claim of Right to Possession on unnamed occupants, put an X in box (1). Otherwise, put an X in Box (2), and list the daily rental value of the property in Item 9a(2)(a)—the same as in Item 12 of the complaint. For Item 9a(2)(b), call the court clerk for a future date (two to three weeks away), in case a person not named in the writ filed a post-judgment Claim of Right to Possession, and list that date in the space provided. Under e, list the complete street address, including apartment number if any, city and county of the property.

Items 10-20: These items apply only when you get a money judgment, and should not be filled in on this writ, which reflects only a judgment for possession of the property. (Later, after you have a default hearing before a judge and get a money judgment, you will fill out another writ (of execution) and fill in items 10-20—see Section E, below.) Instead, simply type the words "POSSESSION ONLY" next to item 11. Type "0.00" (zero) next to items 18 and 19.

You should make one copy of the writ of possession for your own records and three copies per defendant to give to the sheriff or marshal.

4. Filing the Forms and Getting the Writ of Possession Issued

On the day after the response period ends, after you have made sure no answer was filed (see Section A, above), mail a copy of the Request for Entry of Default to the tenant(s) at the property's street address. Then sign your name on the three places on the original. (Technically, if you sign this form before you mail the copy to the tenant(s), you will be committing perjury, because in one of the places on the form you state under penalty of perjury that a copy was mailed—before you signed.)

Then take the following forms to the courthouse:

1. the original summons for each defendant, with the proof of service on the back completed and signed by the process server (see Chapter 6),

2. the original plus at least two copies of the Request for Entry of Default,

3. the original plus at least one copy of the Judgment for Possession, and

4. the original plus three copies per defendant of the Writ of Possession.

Give the court clerk the originals and copies of all the forms you've prepared. Tell the clerk that you're returning completed summonses in an unlawful detainer case and that you want him to:

1. enter a default judgment for possession of the premises, and

2. issue a writ of possession.

He will file the originals of the summonses, the Request for Entry of Default and the Judgment, but will hand you back the original writ, stamped. The clerk should also file-stamp and hand back to you any copies you give him. You will have to pay a small fee for issuance of the writ.

In Los Angeles County, you must fill out a special "local" form before the clerk will issue you a Writ of Possession. This form is called an "Application for Issuance of Writ," and is filled out as shown below; a blank copy is included in the Appendix. Other large counties may require you to use their own similar form.

S A M P L E

ATTORNEY OR PARTY WITHOUT ATTORNEY *(Name and Address)*:	TELEPHONE NO.:	FOR RECORDER'S USE ONLY

Recording requested by and return to:

LENNY D. LANDLORD (213) 555-6789
1234 Angeleno St.
Los Angeles, CA 90010

ATTORNEY FOR [X] JUDGMENT CREDITOR [ ] ASSIGNEE OF RECORD

NAME OF COURT: MUNICIPAL COURT OF CALIFORNIA
STREET ADDRESS: COUNTY OF LOS ANGELES
MAILING ADDRESS: 110 N. Grand Avenue
CITY AND ZIP CODE: Los Angeles, CA 90012
BRANCH NAME: LOS ANGELES JUDICIAL DISTRICT

PLAINTIFF: LENNY D. LANDLORD

DEFENDANT: TERRENCE D. TENANT
TILLIE D. TENANT

WRIT OF
[ ] EXECUTION (Money Judgment)
[X] POSSESSION OF [ ] Personal Property [X] Real Property
[ ] SALE

CASE NUMBER:

FOR COURT USE ONLY

A 12345 B

1. **To the Sheriff or any Marshal or Constable of the County of:**
Los Angeles
You are directed to enforce the judgment described below with daily interest and your costs as provided by law.

2. **To any registered process server:** You are authorized to serve this writ only in accord with CCP 699.080 or CCP 715.040.

3. *(Name):* Lenny D. Landlord
is the [X] judgment creditor [ ] assignee of record
whose address is shown on this form above the court's name.

4. **Judgment debtor** *(name and last known address)*:

Terrence D. Tenant
6789 Angel St., Apt. 10
Los Angeles, CA 90010

Tillie D. Tenant
6789 Angel St., Apt. 10
Los Angeles, CA 90010

[ ] additional judgment debtors on reverse

5. **Judgment entered on** *(date)*: Aug 16, 1992
6. [ ] **Judgment renewed on** *(dates)*:

7. **Notice of sale** under this writ
a. [X] has not been requested.
b. [ ] has been requested *(see reverse)*.
8. [ ] Joint debtor information on reverse.

[SEAL]

9. [X] See reverse for information on real or personal property to be delivered under a writ of possession or sold under a writ of sale.
10. [ ] This writ is issued on a sister-state judgment.
POSSESSION ONLY
11. Total judgment . . . . $
12. Costs after judgment (per filed order or memo CCP 685.090) . $
13. Subtotal *(add 11 and 12)* . . . . . $
14. Credits . . . . $
15. Subtotal *(subtract 14 from 13)* . $
16. Interest after judgment (per filed affidavit CCP 685.050) . . . . . . $
17. Fee for issuance of writ . . . . . . $
18. Total *(add 15, 16, and 17)* . . . . $ 0.00
19. Levying officer: Add daily interest from date of writ *(at the legal rate on 15)* of . . . . $ 0.00

20. [ ] The amounts called for in items 11–19 are different for each debtor. These amounts are stated for each debtor on Attachment 20.

Issued on *(date)*:

Clerk, by _____, Deputy

— NOTICE TO PERSON SERVED: SEE REVERSE FOR IMPORTANT INFORMATION —

(Continued on reverse)

Form Approved by the Judicial Council of California EJ-130 [Rev. September 30, 1991*]

WRIT OF EXECUTION

Code of Civil Procedure, §§ 699.520, 712.010, 715.010
*See note on reverse.

S A M P L E

SHORT TITLE:	CASE NUMBER:
LANDLORD v. TENANT	A 12345 B

Items continued from the first page:

4. ☐ **Additional judgment debtor** *(name and last known address)*:

7. ☐ **Notice of sale** has been requested by *(name and address)*:

8. ☐ **Joint debtor** was declared bound by the judgment (CCP 989–994)
    a. on *(date)*:   a. on *(date)*:
    b. name and address of joint debtor: b. name and address of joint debtor:

    c. ☐ additional costs against certain joint debtors *(itemize)*:

9. ☒ *(Writ of Possession or Writ of Sale)* **Judgment** was entered for the following:
    a. ☒ Possession of real property: The complaint was filed on *(date)*: August 10, 1992 *(Check (1) or (2))*:
        (1) ☐ The Prejudgment Claim of Right to Possession was served in compliance with CCP 415.46.
                The judgment includes all tenants, subtenants, named claimants, and other occupants of the premises.
        (2) ☒ The Prejudgment Claim of Right to Possession was NOT served in compliance with CCP 415.46.
                (a) $ 30.00   was the daily rental value on the date the complaint was filed.
                (b) The court will hear objections to enforcement of the judgment under CCP 1174.3 on the following
                      dates *(specify)*: Sept. 18, 1992
    b. ☐ Possession of personal property
        ☐ If delivery cannot be had, then for the value *(itemize in 9e)* specified in the judgment or supplemental order.
    c. ☐ Sale of personal property
    d. ☐ Sale of real property
    e. Description of property:

        6789 Angel St., #10
        Los Angeles, CA 90010

— NOTICE TO PERSON SERVED —

WRIT OF EXECUTION OR SALE.   Your rights and duties are indicated on the accompanying Notice of Levy.
WRIT OF POSSESSION OF PERSONAL PROPERTY.   If the levying officer is not able to take custody of the property, the levying
officer will make a demand upon you for the property. If custody is not obtained following demand, the judgment may be enforced
as a money judgment for the value of the property specified in the judgment or in a supplemental order.
WRIT OF POSSESSION OF REAL PROPERTY.   If the premises are not vacated within five days after the date of service on the
occupant or, if service is by posting, within five days after service on you, the levying officer will remove the occupants from
the real property and place the judgment creditor in possession of the property. Personal property remaining on the premises will
be sold or otherwise disposed of in accordance with CCP 1174 unless you or the owner of the property pays the judgment creditor
the reasonable cost of storage and takes possession of the personal property not later than 15 days after the time the judgment
creditor takes possession of the premises.
► *A Claim of Right to Possession form accompanies this writ (unless the Summons was served in compliance with CCP 415.46).*

---

* *NOTE:* Continued use of form EJ-130 (Rev. Jan. 1, 1989) is authorized until June 30, 1992, *except* if used as a Writ of Possession of Real Property.

S A M P L E

MUNICIPAL COURT OF CALIFORNIA, LOS ANGELES COUNTY	COURT USE ONLY
LOS ANGELES _____ JUDICIAL DISTRICT	
ADDRESS: 110 N. Grand Avenue Los Angeles, CA 90012	
PLAINTIFF: LENNY D. LANDLORD	
DEFENDANT: TERRENCE D. TENANT TILLIE D. TENANT	

APPLICATION FOR ISSUANCE OF WRIT OF:

☐ POSSESSION   ☐ SALE   ☐ OTHER _____

CASE NUMBER
A 12345 B

I, the undersigned, say: I am _____ ✗✗✗✗✗✗✗✗✗✗✗✗✗✗✗
Judgment Creditor in the above-entitled action and that the following judgment was:

(check if applicable)

☒ entered on __August 16, 1992__ .

☐ renewed on _____ .

In favor of the Judgment Creditor as follows (name and address):

Lenny D. Landlord
1234 Angeleno St.
Los Angeles, CA 90010

against the Judgment Debtor(s) as follows (name and address):

Terrence D. Tenant, Tillie D. Tenant
6789 Angel St., Apt. 10
Los Angeles, CA 90010

for the amount of: $___N/A___ Principal

$___N/A___ Accured Costs

$___N/A___ Attorney Fees

$___N/A___ Interest

$___N/A___ TOTAL

and the possession of the premises located at: ___6789 Angel St., Apt. 10___
___Los Angeles, California___

The daily rental value of the property as of the date the complaint was filed is:

$_30.00_____ .

It is prayed that a writ as checked above be issued to the County of Los Angeles.
The writ will be directed to ___Los Angeles County Marshal--Los Angeles___ .
(Law Enforcement Agency and Location)

I declare under the penalty of perjury under the laws of the State of California
that the foregoing is true and correct.

Executed on___Aug. 16, 1992___ at ___Los Angeles___ , California.

Lenny D. Landlord
Signature

APPLICATION FOR WRIT OF POSS/SALE   712.010 CCP

D. Having the Sheriff Evict

Once the court clerk issues the writ of possession and gives you the original (plus stamped copies), you are responsible for taking it to the sheriff or marshal (or constable in justice court districts), who will carry out the actual eviction. You can get the sheriff's location from the court clerk.

Take the original of the writ of possession, plus three copies for each defendant you're having evicted, to the office of the marshal or civil division of the sheriff's office (whichever your county has). You will be required to pay a $75 fee, which is recoverable from the tenant. (See Section E, below.) You must also fill out a set of instructions telling the sheriff or marshal to evict the defendants. Usually the sheriff has a particular form of instructions, but you can prepare the instructions in the form of a signed letter. A sample letter is shown below.

Letter of Instructions for Sheriff or Marshal

> August 18, 1992
> 12345 Angeleno St.
> Los Angeles, CA 90010
>
> Los Angeles County Marshal
> Civil Division
> 210 W. Temple
> Los Angeles, California 90012
>
> Re: Landlord v. Tenant
> Los Angeles County Municipal Court
> Los Angeles District, Case No. A-12345-B
>
> Please serve the writ of execution for possession of the premises in the above-referenced action on Terrence D. Tenant and Tillie D. Tenant and place the plaintiff in possession of the premises at 6789 Angel Street, Apartment 10, Los Angeles, California.
>
> Sincerely,
>
> Lenny D. Landlord

Within a few days (or weeks, in large urban areas) a deputy sheriff or marshal will go to the property and serve the occupants (either personally or by posting and mailing) with a five-day eviction notice that says in effect, "If you're not out in five days, a deputy will be back to throw you out." (Many sheriffs and marshals will specify the next business day if the fifth day falls on a weekend or holiday.) In most cases, tenants leave before the deadline. If the property is still occupied after five days, call the marshal's or sheriff's office to ask that the defendants be physically evicted. Most sheriff's or marshal's offices don't automatically go back to perform the eviction, so it's up to you to call.

You should meet the sheriff or marshal at the property to change the locks. If you think the ex-tenant will try to move back into the premises, you may wish to supervise, to make sure he really moves his things out. If he tries to stay there against your wishes or to re-enter the premises, he is a criminal trespasser, and you should call the police.

If you did not have the Prejudgment Claim of Right to Possession forms served (as discussed in Chapter 6, Section H), the sheriff or marshal will not physically remove a person who:

- was not named as a defendant in your suit; and

- claims that he was in possession of the premises when you filed your suit, or had a right to be in possession before you filed your suit.

For example, if you rented to a husband and wife, sued and served them both with summonses and complaint, and got judgments against them both, the sheriff or marshal will refuse to evict the wife's brother who says he moved in months ago at her invitation, even though the rental agreement had a provision prohibiting this. (The optional procedure in Chapter 6, Section H2 is a sort of preventative medicine to make sure that such unknown occupants can't wait to do this until the sheriff comes, and must do it early in the proceeding.)

If an unknown occupant does make a claim when the sheriff shows up to evict, the eviction of that person (and perhaps of the defendants you named, if the unnamed one invites them back as "guests") will be delayed until a later hearing where the person must show why he should not be evicted too. This involves procedures that are beyond the scope of this book. See an attorney if you encounter this problem. (We discuss hiring and working with lawyers in *Volume 1*, Chapter 8.)

As for the tenant's belongings, the deputy who carries out the eviction will not allow the tenants to spend hours moving their belongings out, nor will their possessions be placed on the street. Rather, the tenant will be allowed to carry out one or perhaps a few armloads of possessions. The remainder will be locked in the unit. Of course, you should change the locks or the tenant may just go right back in. This does not mean you have a right to hold the tenant's possessions for ransom until the back rent is paid. Doing that is illegal and could subject you to

a lawsuit. You only have the right to insist on "reasonable storage charges" equal to 1/30th of the monthly rent for each day, starting with the day the deputy sheriff or marshal performs the eviction, as a condition of releasing the property.

Don't be too insistent on this, though. You don't want to have to store a bunch of second-hand possessions on the property and be unable to rent the premises to a rent-paying tenant, nor do you particularly want to front moving and storage charges to have the belongings hauled off to a storage facility. (See *Volume 1*, Chapter 21, for a detailed discussion of what you can legally do with a tenant's abandoned property.) Given this reality, it's amazing how many landlords and tenants who've been at each other's throats can suddenly be very reasonable and accommodating when it comes to arranging for the tenant to get his locked-up belongings back.

E. Getting a Money Judgment for Rent and Costs

Once the tenants have moved out of the premises, you should seek a judgment for the money they owe you. Although a court clerk can give you a judgment for possession of the premises, a money judgment for the rent and court costs (including filing, process server, writ and sheriff's fees) has to be approved by a judge at a "default hearing." You must also prepare a Request for Entry of Default (the same form you used earlier, filled out differently) and a Judgment form.

Unlawful detainer money judgments against tenants are notoriously difficult to collect (we discuss collection procedures, as well as the likelihood of success, in Chapter 9). So why bother getting a judgment? First, you've done most of the work already, and there isn't much more involved. Second, the law gives you ten years to collect (and another ten years if you renew your judgment), and you may someday find the tenant with some money; having a judgment ready will make it easier to collect if and when that happens.

1. Determining Rent, Damages and Costs

The first step is figuring out how much money you're entitled to. You won't know for sure how much this is until the tenant leaves. Use the following guidelines and worksheets.

❷ NONPAYMENT OF RENT CASES

You are entitled to:

- **Overdue rent.** This is the amount of rent you demanded in the three-day notice.

EXAMPLE

You served your three-day notice on August 3 for $450 rent due on the 1st and covering August 1 to 31. You got a default judgment for possession on the 16th, and your default hearing is scheduled for August 23. You are entitled to judgment for the entire $450 rent for August, even if the tenant leaves before the end of the month.

> **Get What You're Due**
> Some judges believe that you're not entitled to the rent for the entire month if you get your judgment before the month is up. This is wrong; rent payable in advance accrues and is due in its entirety for the whole period, without pro-ration on a daily basis. See Friedman v. Isenbruck (1952) 111 Cal. App. 2d 326, 335, 224 P. 2d 718; and Rez v. Summers (1917) 34 Cal. App. 527, 168 P. 156.

Leases. A tenant who was evicted while renting under a fixed-term lease is legally liable to you for the balance of the rent on the lease, less what you can get from a replacement tenant. (See Volume 1, Chapter 2.) However, you have to bring a separate lawsuit to recover this amount. The judgment in an unlawful detainer is limited to the rent the tenant owed when served with a three-day notice, plus pro-rated daily rent up until the date of judgment.

- **Damages.** If, after you obtained a default judgment for possession, the tenant stayed past the end of the period for which rent was due, you are entitled to an additional award of "damages at the rate of reasonable rental value" for each day the tenant stayed beyond the initial rental period. You specified the reasonable daily rental value (1/30th of one month's rent) in items 12 and 19.d of the complaint.

EXAMPLE

You were a little too patient and didn't serve your three-day notice until the 17th of August. You got a default judgment for possession on the 28th, and your tenant was evicted on September 4. You are entitled to a judgment for the $450 rent for August. In addition, you're entitled to pro-rated daily damages for each of the four days in September the tenant stayed, at the rate of 1/30th of $450 or $15 for each, or $60. The total is $510.

- **Your court costs.** This does not include things like copy fees or postage, but does include fees you had to pay court clerks, process servers and the sheriff or marshal.

You cannot get a judgment in this proceeding for the costs of repairing or cleaning the premises, but you can deduct them from the security deposit. (If you collected "last month's rent," you cannot use that money toward cleaning and damages, see Volume 1, Chapter 5.) If the deposit won't cover cleaning and repair costs, you'll have to go after the difference in a separate suit in small claims court, or municipal court if the costs are high enough to justify it.

You do not need to credit the security deposit when you seek your money judgment. If there is anything left over after you pay for cleaning and repairs, the balance is credited against the judgment after you obtain it, not before. (For more information on how to itemize and return security deposits, see Volume 1, Chapter 20.)

EXAMPLE

Lola obtained a judgment for $680, including rent, pro-rated damages and court costs. She holds her tenant's $400 security deposit. The cost of cleaning and repairing is $200, and Lola subtracts this from the deposit; the remaining $200 of the deposit is applied against the $680 judgment, so that the tenant owes Lola $480 on the judgment.

WORKSHEET #1
Calculating Amount of Judgment:
Eviction Based on Nonpayment of Rent

Overdue Rent:

(amount demanded in three-day notice) $_____

Damages:

_____ days x $ _____ (daily rental value) = $_____

Court Costs:

$_____ filing fee

$_____ process server

$_____ writ fee

$_____ sheriff's or marshal's fee $_____

TOTAL $_____

❸ 30-DAY NOTICE CASES

You are entitled to:

• Pro-rated daily "damages" at the daily rental value for each day the tenant stayed beyond the 30-day notice period. You are not entitled to judgment for any rent or damages that accrued before the 30 days passed. You can, however, deduct this amount from the security deposit; see Chapter 9. The daily rental value is listed in items 12 and 19.d of the complaint.

• Court costs, including your filing, service of process, writ and sheriff's or marshal's fees.

EXAMPLE

You served Jackson, whose $600 rent is due on the 15th of each month, with a 30-day termination notice on May 1. This means he is required to leave on May 31. He refuses to leave on the 31st and refuses to pay the $320 pro-rated rent, due on the 15th, for the period of May 15 through 31 (1/30 of the $600 monthly rent, or $20/day, for 16 days). On June 1, you sue on the 30-day notice, and finally get Jackson out on June 25. In this kind of unlawful detainer suit, you are entitled to judgment for pro-rated daily "damages" only for the period of June 1 (the day after he should have left under the 30-day notice) through June 25 (the day he left), for a total of $250, and your court costs. To be paid for the other 15 days, you'll have to either sue him in small claims court (usually not worth the trouble) or deduct it from any security deposit he paid.

❹ LEASE VIOLATION CASES

You are entitled to:

• "Damages," pro-rated at the rate of 1/30 the monthly rent (you listed this figure in items 12 and 19.d of the complaint) for each day beyond the expiration of the three-day notice period that the tenant stayed and for which you haven't already been paid in the form of rent, and

• Court costs—filing, service and writ fees.

The amount of your money judgment may be quite small, and you may get a judgment only for your court costs, particularly if you accepted the regular monthly rent in advance for the month during which you served the three-day notice.

EXAMPLE

Say you accepted the regular monthly rent of $500 from Ron when it was due the first of the month. Two weeks later, Ron begins having loud parties. You give Ron a written warning, but it continues. On the 16th, at the urging of all your other tenants who threaten to move, you give Ron an unconditional three-day notice to quit.

Ron doesn't move, and you file suit on the 20th and take a default judgment for possession on the 26th. The marshal posts a five-day eviction notice on the 28th, giving Ron until the third of the next month before he gets the boot. Ron leaves on the second, so you're out only two days' pro-rated rent or "damages" at the reasonable rental value of $16.67 per day (1/30th x $500 per month), for a grand total of $33.34 plus court costs.

If Ron had misbehaved earlier, and you had served the three-day notice only a few days after that, having collected rent on the first of the month, you might even have gotten Ron out before the end of the month. In that case, your judgment would have been for court costs only. Ron isn't entitled to a pro-rated refund for the last few days of the month for which he paid but didn't get to stay, since he "forfeited" his rights under the rental agreement or lease—including any right to stay for days prepaid.

❺ NO-NOTICE CASES

You are entitled to:

- Pro-rated daily "damages" at the daily rental value (you listed this figure in items 12 and 19.d of the complaint) for each day beyond the date of termination of tenancy (either the date the lease expired or the termination date of the 30-day notice the tenant gave you); and

- Court costs, including filing, service and writ fees.

EXAMPLE

Hilda sued Sally, whose six-month lease expired June 30. Even if Sally hadn't paid all the $600 rent for June, Hilda would be entitled only to pro-rated daily damages (rental value per day) of $20 ($600/30) per day for each day beyond June 30 that Sally stayed in possession of the premises. So, if Hilda got Sally out by July 25, Hilda would be entitled to damages of 25 x $20, or $500, plus costs.

Past Due Rent. You cannot seek past due rent unless the three-day notice was based on nonpayment of rent. So, if Sally hadn't paid all her rent when it was due in early June, Hilda should have used a three-day notice and the eviction procedure in Chapter 2.

WORKSHEET #2

Calculating Amount of Judgment:
Eviction Based on 30-Day Notice, Violation of Lease or No Notice

Damages:

_____ days x $ _____ (daily rental value) = $_____

Court Costs:

$_____ filing fee

$_____ process server

$_____ writ fee

$_____ sheriff's or marshal's fee $_____

                        TOTAL $_____

2. Preparing the Request for Entry of Default (Money Judgment)

You must complete a second Request for Entry of Default to get your money judgment. A sample is shown below.

Fill in the caption boxes the same way you did for the first Request for Entry of Default form (Section C, above). This time, though, put an X only in the box next to the words "court judgment." Do not put an X in any other box, not even the "Entry of Default" box, since the defendant's default has already been entered. Then fill in the numbered items as follows:

Items 1.a and 1.b: Enter the date you filed the complaint and your name, just as you did in the first Request for Entry of Default.

Item 1.c: Leave this box blank. The clerk already entered the defaults of the defendants when you filed your first Request for Entry of Default.

Item 1.d: Put an X in this box. This asks the clerk to schedule a "default hearing" in front of a judge. (Some courts instead accept a written declaration that says what you'd say in front of the judge. See subsection 3 below.)

Item 1.e: Leave these boxes blank. This is only for a clerk's judgment, and the clerk can't enter a money judgment in an unlawful detainer case.

SAMPLE

ATTORNEY OR PARTY WITHOUT ATTORNEY *(Name and Address)*:	TELEPHONE NO.:	FOR COURT USE ONLY
LENNY D. LANDLORD 12345 Angeleno St. Los Angeles, CA 90010	(213) 555-6789	

ATTORNEY FOR *(Name)*: In Pro Per

Insert name of court and name of judicial district and branch court, if any:

MUNICIPAL COURT OF CALIFORNIA, COUNTY OF LOS ANGELES, LOS ANGELES JUDICIAL DISTRICT

PLAINTIFF:
LENNY D. LANDLORD

DEFENDANT:
TERRENCE D. TENANT
TILLIE D. TENANT

REQUEST FOR (Application)	☐ ENTRY OF DEFAULT ☐ CLERK'S JUDGMENT ☒ COURT JUDGMENT	CASE NUMBER: A 12345 B

1. TO THE CLERK: On the complaint or cross-complaint filed
   a. On *(date)*: August 10, 1992
   b. By *(name)*: Lenny D. Landlord
   c. ☐ Enter default of defendant *(names)*:

   d. ☒ I request a court judgment under CCP 585(b), (c), 989, etc. *(Testimony required. Apply to the clerk for a hearing date, unless the court will enter a judgment on an affidavit under CCP 585(d).)*
   e. ☐ Enter clerk's judgment
      (1) ☐ For restitution of the premises only and issue a writ of execution on the judgment. CCP 1174(c) does not apply. (CCP 1169) ☐ Include in the judgment all tenants, subtenants, named claimants, and other occupants of the premises. The Prejudgment Claim of Right to Possession was served in compliance with CCP 415.46.
      (2) ☐ Under CCP 585(a). *(Complete the declaration under CCP 585.5 on the reverse (item 3).)*
      (3) ☐ For default previously entered on *(date)*:

2. Judgment to be entered

	Amount	Credits Acknowledged	Balance
a. Demand of complaint	$ 1,260.00	$ 0.00	$ 1,260.00
b. Statement of damages (CCP 425.11) *(superior court only)**			
(1) Special	$	$	$
(2) General	$	$	$
c. Interest	$ 0.00	$ 0.00	$ 0.00
d. Costs *(see reverse)*	$ 188.50	$ 0.00	$ 188.50
e. Attorney fees	$ 0.00	$ 0.00	$ 0.00
f. TOTALS	$ 1,448.50	$ 0.00	$ 1,448.50

   g. **Daily damages** were demanded in complaint at the rate of: $ 30.00 per day beginning *(date)*: 9/1/92

Date: September 12, 1992

Lenny D. Landlord
....
(TYPE OR PRINT NAME)

▶ *Lenny D. Landlord*
(SIGNATURE OF PLAINTIFF OR ATTORNEY FOR PLAINTIFF)

* *Personal injury or wrongful death actions only.*

FOR COURT USE ONLY	(1) ☐ Default entered as requested on *(date)*: (2) ☐ Default NOT entered as requested *(state reason)*: By: _____

(Continued on reverse)

Form Adopted by the
Judicial Council of California
982(a)(6) [Rev. September 30, 1991*]

REQUEST FOR ENTRY OF DEFAULT
(Application to Enter Default)

Code of Civil Procedure, §§ 585-587, 1169
*See note on reverse.

SAMPLE

SHORT TITLE:	CASE NUMBER:
LANDLORD v. TENANT	A 12345 B

3. [X] **DECLARATION UNDER CCP 585.5** *(Required for clerk's judgment under CCP 585(a))* This action
   a. [ ] is [X] is not   on a contract or installment sale for goods or services subject to CC 1801, etc. (Unruh Act).
   b. [ ] is [X] is not   on a conditional sales contract subject to CC 2981, etc. (Rees-Levering Motor Vehicle Sales and Finance Act).
   c. [ ] is [X] is not   on an obligation for goods, services, loans, or extensions of credit subject to CCP 395(b).

4. **DECLARATION OF MAILING (CCP 587)** A copy of this Request for Entry of Default was
   a. [ ] **not mailed** to the following defendants whose addresses are **unknown** to plaintiff or plaintiff's attorney *(names)*:

   b. [X] **mailed** first-class, postage prepaid, in a sealed envelope addressed to each defendant's attorney of record or, if none, to each defendant's last known address as follows:

   (1) Mailed on *(date)*:   (2) To *(specify names and addresses shown on the envelopes)*:

   September 12, 1992   Terrence D. Tenant
                                        6789 Angel St., #10
                                        Los Angeles, CA 90010

   September 12, 1992   Tillie D. Tenant
                                        6789 Angel St., #10
                                        Los Angeles, CA 90010

I declare under penalty of perjury under the laws of the State of California that the foregoing items 3 and 4 are true and correct.

Date: September 12, 1992

Lenny D. Landlord   ▶   *Lenny D. Landlord*
....
(TYPE OR PRINT NAME)   (SIGNATURE OF DECLARANT)

5. **MEMORANDUM OF COSTS** *(Required if judgment requested)* **Costs and Disbursements** are as follows (CCP 1033.5):
   a. Clerk's filing fees . . . . $ 80.00
   b. Process server's fees . . . . $ 30.00
   c. Other *(specify)*: . . writ fee . . . . $ 3.50
   d. Sheriff's eviction fee . . . $ 75.00
   e. **TOTAL** . . . . $ 188.50
   f. [ ] Costs and disbursements are waived.

   I am the attorney, agent, or party who claims these costs. To the best of my knowledge and belief this memorandum of costs is correct and these costs were necessarily incurred in this case.

   I declare under penalty of perjury under the laws of the State of California that the foregoing is true and correct.

Date: September 12, 1992

Lenny D. Landlord   ▶   *Lenny D. Landlord*
....
(TYPE OR PRINT NAME)   (SIGNATURE OF DECLARANT)

6. [X] **DECLARATION OF NONMILITARY STATUS** *(Required for a judgment)* No defendant named in item 1c of the application is in the military service so as to be entitled to the benefits of the Soldiers' and Sailors' Civil Relief Act of 1940 (50 U.S.C. Appen. § 501 et seq.).

   I declare under penalty of perjury under the laws of the State of California that the foregoing is true and correct.

Date: September 12, 1992

Lenny D. Landlord   ▶   *Lenny D. Landlord*
....
(TYPE OR PRINT NAME)   (SIGNATURE OF DECLARANT)

NOTE: Continued use of form 982(a)(6) (Rev. July 1, 1988) is authorized until June 30, 1992, *except* in unlawful detainer proceedings.

982(a)(6) [Rev. September 30, 1991*]   **REQUEST FOR ENTRY OF DEFAULT**   Page two
                                              (Application to Enter Default)

Items 2a-f: In the line entitled "a. Demand of complaint," list in the "Amount" column the total of rent plus pro-rated daily damages for any days the tenant stayed beyond the end of the rental period, as calculated above in subsection 1.

For example, in the rent nonpayment example in subsection 1 above, where the tenant didn't pay the August rent and stayed until September 4th, the past due rent (for August) is $450, and the damages are $60 (four September days at $15—1/30th of $450), for a total of $510. This sum goes in the "Amount" column.

Don't list anything next to lines b, b(1) or b(2) entitled "Statement of Damages." This does not apply to unlawful detainer cases.

Next to "c. Interest" and "e. Attorney fees," enter "0.00." Next to "d. Costs," enter the total of the filing fee, the process server's fee for serving all the defendants and other court costs tallied in item 5. (See below.) Total these amounts at item 2.f. Under the "Credits Acknowledged" column, list all amounts and the total as "0.00," since the defendant has not paid you anything. Don't include the security deposit. Finally, under "Balance," list the same amounts as under the "Amount" column.

Item 2.g: List the same pro-rated daily rent amount and the same date from which you are asking for pro-rated daily damages, as you did in the original Request for Entry of Default. Then, fill in the date you'll be filing the default papers with the court, type your name opposite the place for signature and sign the form.

Item 3: Fill in this item exactly the same as you did in the original Request for Entry of Default.

Item 4: Fill in this item exactly as you did in the first Request for Entry of Default, checking box b and entering the date of mailing of this second one to the defendant's address. (Even though the defendant has moved now, after eviction, that's still his address as last known to you, and it could be forwarded.) Mail copies to the tenants and put "ADDRESS CORRECTION AND FORWARDING REQUESTED" on the envelopes. This will help you locate them when you go to collect your money judgment. (See Chapter 9.)

Item 5: This is where you total your court costs. List the clerk's filing fee and your process server's fee in items 5.a

and b. In item 5.c, "Other," type in "writ fee" and add the cost of the writ of possession. Below that, in item d, add the sheriff's eviction fee. Total these items at item 5.e. This total should also be listed on item 2.d on the front.

Item 6: Date and sign the Declaration of Non-Military Status the same way you did on the original Request for Entry of Default.

3. Preparing a Declaration as to Rent, Damages and Costs

Some courts let you or require you to prepare a written declaration under penalty of perjury in lieu of testifying before a judge at a default hearing. The judge simply reads the declaration's statements about rent, damages and court costs, and awards you a judgment without a hearing. In the Central District of Los Angeles County, you must use a declaration; default hearings are not held. If you want to get your money judgment this way rather than attending a default hearing, call the court and ask whether or not it accepts declarations in lieu of testimony in unlawful detainer default cases. If you'd rather testify in person, or if the court doesn't allow declarations, proceed to subsection 4, below.

There is no standard form for the declaration. However, the one we set out in the Appendix should do the job for month-to-month tenancies. Some samples are shown below for a Declaration in Support of Default Judgment form. If you do your own declaration, prepare it on typed, double-spaced 8-1/2" x 11" legal (pleading) paper with the numbers down the left-hand side. You can copy the blank sheet of pleading paper in the Appendix.

Evictions based on violation of a lease provision or causing a nuisance. Such an eviction results in the tenant's "forfeiture" of the right to stay for a period for which he already paid rent. In cases like this, judges are more reluctant to find in your favor, even in a default situation, so you have to be very specific and detailed in your testimony. You must explain how the tenant committed a "material" (serious) breach of the lease, illegally sublet, or committed a nuisance. Otherwise, a judge could rule that the eviction was unfounded, even though you got the tenant out with a Clerk's Judgment and Writ of Possession.

SAMPLE

```
1  Name: LENNY D. LANDLORD
2  Address: 12345 Angeleno St.
   Los Angeles, CA 90010
3  Phone: (213) 555-1234
   Plaintiff in Pro Per
4
5
6
7
8      MUNICIPAL COURT OF CALIFORNIA, COUNTY OF ___LOS ANGELES___
9              ___LOS ANGELES___ JUDICIAL DISTRICT
10
11 LENNY D. LANDLORD_____  )  Case No. A-12345-B___
                                      )
12      Plaintiff,                    )  DECLARATION IN SUPPORT
   v.                                 )  OF DEFAULT JUDGMENT
13 TERRENCE D. TENANT , et al._____  )  FOR RENT, DAMAGES, AND
                                      )  COSTS
14      Defendant(s).                 )
                                      )  (C.C.P. SECS. 585(a), 1169)
15 _____)
16
17     I, the undersigned, declare:
18     1. I am the plaintiff in the above-entitled action and the
   owner of the premises at ___6789 Angel Boulevard, Apartment 10___,
19 City of ___Los Angeles___, County of ___Los Angeles___, California.
20     2 On _____August 1_____, 19_92_, defendant(s) rented
21 the premises from me pursuant to a written/oral [cross out one] agreement
22 under which the monthly rent was $__900.00__ payable in advance
23 on the ___first___ day of each month.
24     3. The terms of the tenancy [check one]:
25         (x) were not changed; or
26         ( ) were changed, effective _____, 19__, in that
27 monthly rent was validly and lawfully increased to $_____ by
28
```

( ) agreement of the parties and subsequent payment of
such rent; or

( ) **[month-to-month tenancy only]** service on defendant(s) of a written
notice of at least 30 days, setting forth the increase in rent.

4. The reasonable rental value of the premises per day, i.e.,
the current monthly rent divided by 30, is $ 30.00 .

5. Pursuant to the agreement, defendant(s) went into
possession of the premises.

6. On   August 3 , 19 92 , defendant(s) were in
default in the payment of rent in the amount of $ 900.00 , and I
caused defendant(s) to be served with a written notice demanding
that defendant(s) pay that amount or surrender possession of the
premises within three days after service of the notice.

7. Defendant(s) failed to pay the rent or surrender
possession of the premises within three days after service of the
notice, whereupon I commenced this action, complying with any
local rent control or eviction protection ordinance applicable,
and caused summons and complaint to be served on each defendant.
Defendant(s) have failed to answer or otherwise respond to the
complaint within the time allowed by law.

8. Defendant(s) surrendered possession of the premises on
  September 9 , 19 92 , after entry of a clerk's judgment for
possession and issuance of a writ of execution thereon.

9. The rent was due for the rental period of August 1 , 1992
through   August 31 , 19 92 . After this latter date, and until
defendant(s) vacated the premises, I sustained damages at the
daily reasonable rental value of $ 30.00 , for total damages of
$ 270.00 .

10. I have incurred filing, service, and writ fees in the total amount of $ 188.50 in this action.

11. If sworn as a witness, I could testify competently to the facts stated herein.

I declare under penalty of perjury under the laws of the State of California that the foregoing is true and correct.

DATED: September 12   , 19 92

Lenny D. Landlord
Plaintiff in Pro Per

DECLARATION: VIOLATION OF LEASE

```
 1    Name: LORNA D. LANDLADY
      Address: 3865 Oak St.
 2    Anaheim, CA
      Phone: (818) 555-1234
 3    Plaintiff in Pro Per

 4

 5

 6

 7

 8            MUNICIPAL COURT OF CALIFORNIA, COUNTY OF ORANGE

 9            CENTRAL ORANGE COUNTY JUDICIAL DISTRICT

10
      LORNA D. LANDLADY              )   Case No. 5-0368
11                                   )
          Plaintiff,                 )   DECLARATION IN SUPPORT
12    v.                             )   OF DEFAULT JUDGMENT
                                     )   FOR DAMAGES AND COSTS
13    TERESA A. TENANT , et al.      )
                                     )
14        Defendant(s).              )   (C.C.P. SECS. 585(a), 1169)
                                     )
15    _____)

16
          I, the undersigned, declare:
17
          1. I am the plaintiff in the above-entitled action and the
18
      owner of the premises at 15905 Lafayette Street, Apartment 202,
19
      City of Anaheim, County of Orange, California.
20
          2 On September 1, 1992, defendant(s) rented the premises from
21
      me pursuant to a written one-year lease under which the monthly
22
      rent was $900.00 payable in advance on the first day of each month.
23
      The terms of the agreement have not been changed.
24
          3. Pursuant to the agreement, defendants went into possession
25
      of the premises.
26
          4. Defendants last paid rent on March 1, 1993, for March.
27
          5. On March 14 Teresa began having loud parties that would
28
```

1 begin around noon and last until about 4 a.m. On the 14th, my

2 other tenants began to complain and threaten to move. I went to

3 the apartment above, and the floor was vibrating from all the

4 noise. I knocked at Teresa's door, but apparently no one could

5 hear the knocking, with the music as loud as it was. Finally, I

6 just walked in, found Teresa, and asked her to turn down the

7 music. She did, but she turned it back up when I left. The same

8 thing happened the next two days.

9   6. On March 16th, I caused defendant to be served with a

10 three-day notice to perform covenant or quit. She had another

11 party on the 18th and didn't leave on the 19th, so I filed suit on

12 the 20th.

13   7. I obtained a default judgment for possession on March 28,

14 1993.

15   8. Defendant moved out on the second day of April.

16   9. The damages for the period I didn't receive rent were

17 equal to the pro-rated daily reasonable rental value of $20.00 per

18 day, which for two days is $40.00. My court costs have been $80.00

19 for the filing fee, $30.00 process server's fees, $3.50 for

20 issuance of the writ of possession, and $75.00 to have the sheriff

21 evict, for a total of $188.50

22   10. If sworn as a witness, I could testify competently to the

23 facts stated herein.

24   I declare under penalty of perjury under the laws of the State

25 of California that the foregoing is true and correct.

26 DATED: April 15, 1993

27   *Lorna D. Landlady*

                       Plaintiff in Pro Per

28

SAMPLE DECLARATION: 30-DAY NOTICE

```
 1    Name: LINDA D. LANDLADY
      Address: 459 Rose St.
 2    Berkeley, CA 94710
      Phone: (510) 555-1234
 3    Plaintiff in Pro Per

 4

 5

 6

 7

 8        MUNICIPAL COURT OF CALIFORNIA, COUNTY OF ALAMEDA

 9         OAKLAND-PIEDMONT-EMERYVILLE COUNTY JUDICIAL DISTRICT

10
      LINDA D. LANDLADY_____    )  Case No. __5-0258__
11                                        )
           Plaintiff,                     )  DECLARATION IN SUPPORT
12    v.                                  )  OF DEFAULT JUDGMENT
                                          )  FOR DAMAGES AND COSTS
13    THAD TENANT , et al._____  )
                                          )
14         Defendant(s).                  )  (C.C.P. SECS. 585(a), 1169)
                                          )
15    _____    )

16
           I, the undersigned, declare:
17
           1. I am the plaintiff in the above-entitled action and the
18
      owner of the premises at _____950 Parker Street_____, City
19
      of ___Oakland___, County of ____Alameda____, California.
20
           2 On ___February 1___, 19_92_, defendant(s) rented the premises
21
      from me pursuant to a written/oral [cross out one] agreement for a month-
22
      to-month tenancy at a monthly rent of $_400.00_.
23
           3. The terms of the tenancy [check one]:
24
           (x) were not changed; or
25
           ( ) were changed, effective _____, 19___,
26
      in that the monthly rent was validly and lawfully increased to
27
      $_____ by ( ) agreement of the parties and subsequent
28
```

1 payment of such rent; or

2   ( ) **[month-to-month tenancy only]** service on defendant(s) of a

3 written notice of at least 30 days, setting forth the increase in

4 rent.

5   4. The reasonable rental value of the premises per day, i.e.,

6 the current monthly rent divided by 30, is $ _13.33_ .

7   5. Pursuant to the agreement, defendant(s) went into

8 possession of the premises.

9   6. On __August 30_, 19_92_, I served defendant with a written

10 30-day termination notice.

11   7. Defendant was still in possession of the property 31 days

12 later on ___September 30___, 19__92_, and stayed until

13 ___October 20___, 19__92_ when the sheriff evicted him/her/them

14 pursuant to a clerk's judgment for possession and issuance of a

15 writ of execution.

16   8. I sustained damages at the daily reasonable rental value

17 of $_13.33__ for _21_ days between ___September 30___, and

18 ___October 20___, for a total of $ 279.93.

19   9. I have incurred filing, service, and writ fees in the

20 total amount of $_188.50_ in this action.

21   10. If sworn as a witness, I could testify competently to the

22 facts stated herein.

23   I declare under penalty of perjury under the laws of the

24 State of California that the foregoing is true and correct.

25 DATED:__October 31___, 19_92_

26   *Linda D. Landlady*

27   Plaintiff in Pro Per

28

4. Preparing the Proposed Judgment

You should prepare a proposed judgment for the judge to sign. That way, you'll be able to simply hand the form to the judge to sign right after the hearing, instead of going home to prepare the judgment and going back to court to leave it for his signature.

Most courts have their own judgment forms, and many require their use. Ask the clerk if the court has a particular printed form for an unlawful detainer default judgment. Most forms have spaces for listing the names of the parties, case numbers, names of defendants against whom the default is taken, the address of the property, dollar amounts for rent/damages and costs, as well as a place for the judge to sign. Be sure to fill in this information in the appropriate blanks and read it over to make sure it makes sense. Sample forms for three California counties (Los Angeles, Santa Clara and San Diego) appear below.

SORRY, BUT I NEVER RENT TO ANIMALS

5. Submitting Your Papers and/or Going to the Default Hearing

Make one copy of the proposed money judgment for your records, and one copy of the Request for Entry of Default for yourself plus one for each defendant. Mail a copy of the Request for Entry of Default to each tenant, and sign the proof of mailing on the back of the original. If you are submitting a declaration, also make a copy of it. You need to mail each defendant only a copy of the Request for Entry of Default, not a copy of any declaration or proposed judgment.

If you're submitting a declaration, give the original and copies of the Request for Entry of Default and the declaration to the court clerk, who should file the originals and rubber-stamp the copies and return them to you. Also give her the original and copy of the proposed judgment, which she will hold on to for submission to the judge. After a few days, the judge should sign the original, and the clerk will file it and return your copy to you. (To avoid another trip to the courthouse, give the clerk a self-addressed, stamped envelope in which to mail your copy of the judgment.) Once you get the judgment, you will be ready to proceed to Chapter 9 to have the sheriff or marshal collect it.

If you are going to appear before a judge at a default hearing, file only the Request for Entry of Default and ask the court clerk to set a hearing date. In most counties, hearings are held on certain days and times during the week. The defendant is not allowed to participate in the hearing, and therefore is not given any notice of it—she missed the chance to fight by not answering the complaint within the time allowed.

On the day of the default hearing, take the original and copy of the proposed judgment and go to court a few minutes early. If you're lucky, you may see another landlord testifying before your case is called. When the clerk or judge calls your case, go forward and say to the judge something like, "Good morning, your honor, I'm Lenny D. Landlord appearing in pro per." The clerk will swear you in as your own witness. Some judges prefer that you take the witness stand, but others will allow you to present your case from the "counsel table" in front of the judge's bench.

SAMPLE

IN THE MUNICIPAL COURT OF

MINUTES AND DE-
FAULT JUDGMENT

...... judicial district ......JUDICIAL DISTRICT
COUN........ELES, STATE OF CALIFORNIA

CASE NUMBER

case number

court address

court dept.
number and
name of judge;
you may leave
this blank and
fill it in later

plaintiffs' name(s)   vs   defendants' name(s)

Plaintiff(s)   Defendant(s)

In Division ....●......, Honorable ....●................................., Judge Presiding.

Court convened on . [date of default hearing] ....; and the following proceedings were had:

Plaintiff(s) not appearing . [list any plaintiff not appearing at the hearing] ....

the defendant(s) [list names of defaulting defendants] ....

having been served with summons and copy of complaint, having failed to answer complaint of plaintiff(s) within the
time allowed by law and default of said defendant(s) having been entered, plaintiff(s) applied to the court for judgment.

check
applicable
box

☐ Affidavit or declaration of . [your name] .... under 585.5 C.C.P. having been filed.

☐ Witness(es) sworn for plaintiff(s): ... [your name] ......

Exhibit(s) received in evidence for plaintiff(s): ....

The court, after having considered the evidence,

list rent and pro-rated
damages (if any) separately

found the amount of rent due the plaintiff(s) to be $.........●........ , and assessed the damages for the
unlawful detainer at $ ....●.......... and determined that said sums should not be trebled, ordered
the following judgment: It is adjudged that on the complaint,

plaintiff(s) .... [list names of plaintiffs and defaulting defendants] .... recover from

defendant(s) ....

☐ the restitution and possession of those premises situated in the County of Los Angeles, State of California, and more
particularly described as: .... [list complete address of property] ....

and the sum of $ ......●........... , and $ ......●............ attorney fees, with costs as provided by law in the sum of
$.................... , and that the lease or agreement under which the aforesaid property is held be, and the same is
hereby declared fo [list total rent and damages and costs]

☐ the possession of the following described personal property, to wit: ....

or its value, which is fixed at $ .... in case possession of said personal property cannot be had and
in either event the sum of $....................damages $ .... attorney fees, and $....................
interest with costs as provided by law in the sum of $ .... ,

☐ the sum of $ .... , $ .... , attorney fees,

and $ .... interest with costs as provided by law in the sum of $ ....

The foregoing minutes are correct and the judgment conforms to the decision of the court.

.... [clerk will fill in] .... Deputy Clerk

i certify the foregoing Judgment was entered in the Judgment Book on

.... , Copy filed.   CLERK OF THE ABOVE NAMED COURT

By .... [clerk will fill in] eputy

[clerk will fill in]

MINUTES AND DEFAULT JUDGMENT

76M416K6-C i 40—(5)(Rev. 6/82 PS-10-82   C.C.P.585, 585.5, 664, 668, 1033½, 1161-1174

SAMPLE

MUNICIPAL COURT OF CALIFORNIA, COUNTY OF SANTA CLARA

NAME OF MUNICIPAL OF JUSTIC COURT DISTRICT AND ADDRESS	FOR COURT USE ONLY
list court address	
TITLE OF CASE *(ABBREVIATED)*	
list first plaintiff and defendant names	
NAME, ADDRESS, AND TELEPHONE NUMBER OF SENDER	
your name, address and phone number	CASE NUMBER
	case number

UNLAWFUL DETAINER
DEFAULT JUDGMENT

list names of defaulting defendants

The defendant(s) .... having been regularly served with summons and copy of complaint, having failed to appear and answer said complaint within the time allowed by law, and the default of said defendant(s) having been duly entered, and after having heard the testimony and considered the evidence, or pursuant to affidavit on file herein, the Court ordered the following JUDGMENT:

It is ordered and adjuged the plaintiff(s) list plaintiff's name(s) have and recover from defendant(s)... list names of defaulting defendants the restitution and possession of those certain premises situated in the County of Santa Clara, State of Cali-

list total rent and damages and costs

articularly described as follows: list complete address of property

and the sum of $................... rent, and $.................... damages for unlawful detainer, making a total amount of $..........................., plus $........0......... attorney fees, with costs as provided by law in the sum of $................. and that said lease or agreement under which the aforesaid property is held be, and it is hereby declared forfeited.

list "zero (0)"

.... days stay of execution.

list date of default hearing

Dated:..   leave blank

                                                                                                         ....
                                                                                                         Judge of the Municipal Court

I hereby certify this to be a true copy of the Judgment in the above action rendered on ....
....

Judgment entered on ....   clerk will fill in   ...., Clerk

Minute Book.............................. Page...........................   By..., Deputy Clerk

UNLAWFUL DETAINER DEFAULT JUDGMENT

CCP 585, 664, 668, 1033½, 1174

SAMPLE

NAME AND ADDRESS OF ATTORNEY: TELEPHONE NO   For Court use only:

list your name, address and phone number

MUNICIPAL COURT OF CALIFORNIA, COUNTY OF SAN DIEGO

list judicial district and court address

PLAINTIFF: (ABBREVIATED)

list first plaintiff and defendant names

DEFENDANT: (ABBREVIATED)

JUDGMENT BY DEFAULT BY COURT—UNLAWFUL DETAINER   CASE NUMBER   case number

list names of defaulting defendants

In this action the Defendant (s), ...
having been regularly served with summons and copy of complaint, having failed to appear and answer
the complaint of Plaintiff (s) within the time allowed by law, and the default of said Defendant (s)
having been duly entered, upon application of Plaintiff (s) to the Court, and

☐ after having heard the testimony and considered the evidence,

fill in applicable box   ☐ a declaration under CCP 585 (4), in lieu of testimony, having been considered the Court
ordered the following judgment: list names of defaulting defendants
That Plaintiff (s) do have and recover from Defendant (s) ....

the restitution and possession of those certain premises situated, lying and being in the City and County
of San Diego, State of California, and is described as follows,

list complete address of property

And that the lease or agreement under which said property is held be, and the same is hereby
forfeited.

It is further ordered that plaintiff (s) recover from said Defendant (s) the sum of:

Damages $ list total rent plus damages

Attorney fees $ −0−

Interest $ −0−

Costs $ list costs and total judgment

Total $

Done in open Court this date: date of default hearing   blank

_____
Judge of Said Court

CLERK OF COURT

By _____ blank _____ , Deputy

SDM(14 (Rev. 5-75)   **JUDGMENT BY DEFAULT BY COURT—UNLAWFUL DETAINER**   CCP 585

You should be prepared to testify to the same kinds of facts that go into written declarations (see subsection 3 above). Lenny Landlord's testimony should go something like this:

"My name is Lenny D. Landlord. On January 1, 1991, I rented my premises at 5789 Angel Street, Apartment 10 to Terrence and Tillie Tenant, the defendants in this proceeding. They signed a rental agreement for a month-to-month tenancy. I have a copy of the rental agreement, which I wish to introduce into evidence as Exhibit No. 1. The rent agreed on was $850 per month, but on May 31, 1992, I gave the defendants a 30-day notice that the rent would be increased to $900 per month effective July 1, 1992. This amount of rent was paid in July 1992, but on August 1 the defendants failed to pay the rent for August. On August 3 I served Tillie Tenant with a three-day notice to pay rent or quit. I have a copy of the three-day notice which I wish to introduce into evidence as Exhibit No. 2. They didn't pay the rent and were still in possession on August 8, and I filed this lawsuit on August 9. They left the premises on August 25, but I believe I'm entitled to the rent for all of August."

If Lenny's tenants hadn't been evicted until, say, September 10, Lenny's last sentence would instead be something like:

"They left the premises on September 9, so I sustained damages at the daily reasonable rental value rate of $30 for nine days, for damages of $270, in addition to the $900 contract rent, for total rent and damages of $1,170."

Finally, Lenny might want to add the following testimony about his court costs:

"My court costs have been $80 for the filing fee, $30 process server's fee for serving both defendants, $3.50 for issuance of the original writ of possession, and $75 to have the marshal post the eviction notice, for a total of $188.50."

If you need to call another witness such as an agent who entered into the rental agreement on your behalf or a person who served the three-day notice, tell this to the judge and have that person testify.

The judge may ask you a question or two, but probably won't if you've been thorough. He will then announce the judgment that you should get possession of the property (in effect repeating the part of the judgment you got from the clerk) plus a specified amount of rent/damages plus costs. Don't be afraid to ask the judge to specify the dollar amount of the court costs. (That way you'll have judgment for them without having to file another form called a "Memorandum of Costs.") Also, don't be afraid to politely differ with the judge ("Excuse me, your honor, but...") as to the dollar amount of the rent/damages if you're sure you calculated the amount correctly. Especially if the judge awarded only part of the rent for the first month the tenant didn't pay—you're entitled to the entire amount of unpaid rent that came due at the beginning of the month even if the tenant left before the month's end.

Once the judge gives judgment in your favor, hand the judgment form with the correct amounts filled in to the courtroom clerk, and ask him to file-stamp and return a copy to you. We discuss how to collect the money part of the judgment in Chapter 9. ■

Contested Cases

Read this chapter only if the tenant has filed a response to your unlawful detainer complaint. This chapter outlines how a contested unlawful detainer suit is resolved, either by settlement between the parties or at a trial. The purpose is to give you a solid idea of how a typical case is likely to proceed. We do not, and cannot, provide you with the full guidance necessary to handle all contested unlawful detainer cases to a successful conclusion. But we believe that an overview of the process is necessary whether you hire a lawyer or decide that your particular situation is simple enough that you can do it yourself.

If the tenant has not filed a response to your unlawful detainer complaint, and you have waited at least five days, you are entitled to seek a default judgment, a procedure that is described in detail in Chapter 7.

A. What Is Involved in a Contested Eviction Case

Your tenant can complicate your life enormously simply by filing one or two pieces of paper with the court and mailing copies to you. If the tenant files a written response to your unlawful detainer complaint (whether it is in the form of a motion, demurrer or answer), you will have to fill out some additional documents and probably appear in court one or more times. All of this will require that you be very much on your toes. As a general rule, judges will not evict a tenant unless every legal "t" and "i" has been scrupulously crossed and dotted. In a contested case, some or all of the following may occur:

- If you or your process server erred in some particular of service, you may have to start from scratch by serving the tenant with a new notice to quit and/or a new summons and complaint.

- If the tenant convinces the judge that the complaint you filed is deficient in some particular, you may have

to redraft your complaint one or more times, without any guidance from the judge.

- If your tenant accuses you, you may have to defend against such charges as:

  1. You illegally discriminated against the tenant (for example, the tenant is gay, the tenant is Latino);

  2. The premises were legally uninhabitable;

  3. Your eviction is in retaliation against the tenant for complaining to the health authorities or organizing other tenants; or

  4. Your eviction is in violation of the local rent control ordinance.

- You may have to disclose large amounts of business and sometimes personal information to the tenant by answering written questions under oath (interrogatories), producing documents and allowing the tenant to inspect the premises.

- You may have to appear before a judge (or jury) to argue your case.

- Even if you win, your tenant may be entitled to remain on the premises because of a hardship.

- Even if you win, if you have evicted your tenant for the wrong reasons, you may be setting yourself up for a lawsuit for wrongful eviction.

- If you lose, you're back to the drawing board and will owe the tenant court costs (and perhaps attorney's fees, if the tenant was represented by an attorney) and maybe some damages as well.

B. Should You Hire an Attorney?

Clearly, you may be in for a good deal of trouble if your tenant contests your suit. Does this mean you should simply give up and hire a lawyer? At the very least, once you become aware of the tenant's response (and assuming you have not already filed for a default judgment), you should seriously consider locating and hiring an attorney experienced in landlord/tenant matters. Without knowing the particulars of a given contested case, it is impossible to predict whether or not you can safely handle it on your own.

Unless you are extremely experienced in these matters, you should always turn the case over to a lawyer if the tenant:

- Is represented by a lawyer;

- Makes a motion or files a demurrer (these terms are explained in Sections D and F, below);

- Demands a jury trial; or

- Alleges any of the following defenses in his answer (discussed in Section G, below):

  1. Violation of a rent control ordinance;

  2. Discriminatory eviction;

  3. Retaliatory eviction; or

- Requests extensive pre-trial disclosure of information that you feel would be harmful to disclose.

Understandably, you may be reluctant to turn the case over to a lawyer when you've taken it this far on your own. We're reluctant to recommend lawyers, too. The whole point of this book, after all, is to equip you to handle your unlawful detainer suit yourself. Unfortunately, we can't anticipate and prepare you to deal with every possible defense a tenant's lawyer may throw at you, or for that matter even predict what the tenant will raise in a motion. In short, once you find yourself facing a contested unlawful detainer suit, getting experienced help may be your best, and in the long run most cost-efficient, bet.

C. How To Settle a Case

You may negotiate a settlement with a tenant before or even during trial. Although it may not seem true in the heat of battle, it is our experience that considering the usually unpalatable alternative of a trial, it is very often in your economic interest to reach a settlement short of trial. That's why most unlawful detainer cases are settled without a trial.

1. Why Settle?

Why is a reasonable—or sometimes even a somewhat unreasonable—settlement better than fighting it out in court? Aside from the possibility that your tenant might win the lawsuit (as well as a judgment against you for court costs and attorney's fees), the time and trouble entailed in going to court often mean you are better off compromising. Even landlords who plow forward to trial and ultimately "win" a court judgment commonly suffer a larger out-of-pocket loss than if they would have compromised earlier. For example, a tenant who refuses to pay the $500 rent on the first of the month will be able to stay anywhere from four to six weeks before having to leave if he properly contests an unlawful detainer case. This means that if the tenant loses the case and is evicted after six weeks, the landlord loses $750 rent in the meantime, plus court costs approaching $100. If the landlord hires a lawyer, he'll be out at least another several hundred dollars, and probably a good deal more if a full scale trial develops. Although these amounts will be added to the judgment against the tenant, the truth is that a great many such judgments are uncollectable. (See Chapter 9.)

Given this unhappy reality, the landlord is usually ahead of the game by accepting a reasonable compromise, even if the tenant gets an unfairly favorable result. Depending on the situation, this may mean that a tenant who has violated a lease or rental agreement provision is allowed to stay on if all past due rent is paid. Or if the tenant is simply impossible to have around over the long term, the landlord may want to enter into a written settlement agreement under which the tenant agrees to leave within a few weeks in exchange for the forgiveness of some or even all the rent that will have accrued through that time.

No matter what sort of deal you make, if it involves the tenant moving out, it should be in writing, and should provide you with an immediate eviction remedy should the tenant refuse to keep his part of the bargain.

EXAMPLE

When Dmitri fails to pay his rent of $500 on May 1, Ivan serves him with a three-day notice. When that runs out without Dmitri paying the rent, Ivan sues Dmitri for an eviction order and the $500. Dmitri contests the suit with an Answer that alleges Ivan breached the implied warranty of habitability by not getting rid of cockroaches. Ivan believes this is nonsense because he maintains the building very well, but does concede that the building is old and that tenants have had occasional problems with bugs and rodents. At trial, Ivan will attempt to prove that Dmitri's poor housekeeping caused the cockroaches and that Dmitri never complained about them before filing his answer. Both Ivan and Dmitri think they will win at trial, but each is sensible enough to know he might lose and that a trial will certainly take up a lot of time, money and energy. So they (or their lawyers) get together and hammer out a settlement agreement. Dmitri agrees to give Ivan a judgment for possession of the property, effective July 1, and Ivan agrees to drop his claim for back rent.

2. What Kind of Agreement Should You Make?

Broadly speaking, there are two ways to resolve a contested landlord-tenant dispute. The first is discussed above and is called a "written settlement agreement."

The other is termed a "stipulation for judgment." Both should be in writing and set out the terms under which the dispute will be settled (for example, how much money will be paid by whom, when the tenant will leave).

The difference is that under a stipulation for judgment, the tenant agrees that the landlord is entitled to an unlawful detainer judgment on a certain date if he (the tenant) doesn't comply with his end of the stipulation. In a settlement agreement, however, the tenant typically agrees to vacate the premises in exchange for the landlord's promise to dismiss the lawsuit when he leaves, but does not agree to a judgment. Clearly, the stipulation favors the landlord, and the settlement agreement favors the tenant, because if the tenant does not live up to the settlement agreement, the landlord will have to revive the lawsuit which has been put on hold. When a stipulation is used, however, the landlord needs only enforce the judgment if the tenant violates its terms.

How To Negotiate With a Tenant

Here are some thoughts on negotiating with a tenant you are trying to get out:

• Be courteous, but don't be weak. If you have a good case, let the tenant know you have the resources and evidence to fight and win if you can't reach a reasonable settlement.

• Don't get too upset about how the tenant is using the system to get undeserved concessions out of you; don't be so blinded by moral outrage that you reject workable compromises. At this point you want to balance the costs of a settlement against the costs of fighting it out and choose the less expensive alternative. If this sometimes means that a rotten tenant gets a good deal, so be it. The alternative, your getting an even worse deal from California's court system, is even less desirable.

For advice on negotiating techniques, see Getting to Yes: Negotiating Agreements Without Giving In, by Fisher and Ury, of the Harvard Negotiation Project (Penguin).

Unless you agree to let the tenant stay in exchange for cash paid immediately, your written stipulation for judgment should provide that you may enter a "judgment for possession of the premises at (street address)," which is "stayed" until about a week before the tenant's promised moving date. If you accept only the tenant's written promise to leave, and she doesn't leave as promised, you will have to go back to court to get a judgment.

If the tenant insists on a settlement agreement (under which she promises to leave in exchange for your dismissing the case afterward), at least be sure that there is a fair trade-off—such as you getting an immediate substantial payment of cash; a mere judgment for money can be hard to collect.

Avoid agreements under which the tenant promises to pay past due rent in future installments. Even if the agreement says you get a judgment for possession if the tenant fails to pay the installment, you'll still have to file papers and go back to court to get a judgment for this amount of the unpaid installments.

A sample Stipulation for Judgment form is shown below, as is a sample judgment (Judgment Pursuant to Stipulation), to be signed by the judge. The purpose of these forms is to make it clear what you and the tenant agreed to, and to allow you to obtain a judgment if the tenant fails to abide by its terms. A Stipulation for Judgment is basically a contract settling a lawsuit, which can be enforced in the lawsuit itself, without having to file another suit to enforce the contract. The stipulation should be signed by you and by the tenant (and her attorney, if any). You should also give the tenant or her attorney a copy of the proposed judgment. Both forms must be typed double-spaced on 8-1/2" x 11" legal (pleading) paper with numbers down the left hand side. You can copy the blank sheet of pleading paper in the Appendix.

Take the original and two copies each of the stipulation and proposed judgment to the courthouse for filing. The court clerk should file the stipulation and return your file-stamped copies right away. However, the clerk will wait until after the judge signs the proposed judgment to file it and stamp those copies. If you give the clerk a self-addressed stamped envelope, he will mail the signed judgment copies to you. Finally, as a courtesy to the tenant or her attorney, you should mail copies of the file-stamped judgment and stipulation to her.

D. The Tenant's Written Response to an Unlawful Detainer Complaint

Sooner or later you will receive a copy of the tenant's written response to your unlawful detainer complaint. This response can take several forms. Let's discuss these in the order of their likelihood, assuming the tenant has a lawyer or is well-informed about responding to unlawful detainer complaints.

1. Motions as Responses to an Unlawful Detainer Complaint

A tenant can object to something in your summons or complaint by filing a response which, rather than answering the complaint allegations, simply asserts that the complaint isn't technically up to snuff. It is common for tenants to bring these types of issues to the attention of the court (and thus obtain delay) in the form of a request called a "motion." A motion is a written request that a judge make a ruling on a particular issue, before any trial occurs. Once a motion (or motions) are filed with the court, the case will automatically be delayed by several weeks because the tenant doesn't have to respond to the substance of your complaint until the procedural questions raised in the motion (or motions) are cleared up.

For example, a tenant (or her attorney) could file a motion to "quash service of summons," in which the judge is asked to state that the summons wasn't properly served, and to require the landlord to serve it again, properly. A court hearing to consider the merits of the motion will normally be held between one and two weeks after filing.

Or a tenant who believes a landlord's request for triple rents and damages isn't backed up by enough allegations of ill-will on the tenant's part can make a motion to have the judge "strike" (consider as deleted) the request for triple rents and damages from the unlawful detainer complaint.

S A M P L E

```
 1   Name:
     Address:
 2
     Phone:
 3   Plaintiff in Pro Per

 4

 5

 6

 7

 8       MUNICIPAL COURT OF CALIFORNIA, COUNTY OF _____

 9       _____ JUDICIAL DISTRICT

10
     _____  )  Case No. _____
11                                            )
             Plaintiff,                       )  STIPULATION FOR JUDGMENT
12   v.                                       )
                                              )
13   _____         )
                                              )
14   _____         )
                                              )
15           Defendant(s).                    )
                                              )
16   _____         )

17       Plaintiff _____ and

18   defendant(s) _____

19   hereby agree to settle the above-entitled unlawful detainer action

20   for possession of the real property at _____

21   _____, City of _____

22   County of _____, California, hereinafter

23   described as the "premises," on the following terms and conditions:

24       1. Defendant(s) agree to vacate the premises on or before

25   _____, 19___. Plaintiff shall therefore have a

26   judgment for possession of those premises. The judgment may issue

27   immediately, but execution on the judgment is to be stayed until

28   _____, 19___.
```

1   2. Defendants shall pay to plaintiff the sum of $_____,

2   as full payment of the rent for the following period:

3   _____, 19____ through _____, 19____.

4   This sum shall be paid as follows: (Check one)

5   ( ) Immediately, on signing this stipulation;

6   ( ) On or before _____, 19____; should defen-

7   dants fail to pay this sum as promised, plaintiff shall be en-

8   titled, on ex parte application to the Court, to a judgment or

9   amended judgment for that sum and for immediate possession of the

10   premises, with no stay of execution thereon.

11   3. The tenant's security deposit of $_____ shall be

12   handled as follows (Check one:)

13   ( ) Treated according to law;

14   ( ) Applied as follows: _____

15   _____.

16   In addition, plaintiff and defendants agree to waive all

17   claims or demands that each may have against the other for any

18   transaction directly or indirectly arising from their landlord/

19   tenant relationship, and further agree that this stipulation not

20   be construed as reflecting on the merits of the dispute.

21

22   DATED:_____, 19____   DATED:_____, 19 ___

23   _____   _____

24   Plaintiff in Pro Per   Defendant/Attorney
                                         for Defendant

25

26

27

28

SAMPLE JUDGMENT PURSANT TO STIPULATION

```
 1 │ Name:
   │ Address:
 2 │
   │ Phone:
 3 │ Plaintiff in Pro Per
 4 │
 5 │
 6 │
 7 │
 8 │   MUNICIPAL COURT OF CALIFORNIA, COUNTY OF _____
 9 │   _____ JUDICIAL DISTRICT
10 │
   │   _____  )  Case No. _____
11 │                                )
   │      Plaintiff,                )  JUDGMENT PURSUANT
12 │   v.                           )  TO STIPULATION
   │                                )
13 │   _____  )
   │                                )
14 │   _____  )
   │                                )
15 │      Defendant(s).             )
   │   _____  )
16 │
17 │      Pursuant to stipulation by and between plaintiff and
18 │ defendant(s),
19 │      IT IS HEREBY ORDERED AND ADJUDGED AS FOLLOWS:
20 │ Plaintiff _____ shall have judgment against
21 │ defendant(s) _____
22 │ for restitution and possession of the real property at
23 │ _____,
24 │ City of _____, County of
25 │ _____, California.
26 │      ( )  [Check, if applicable] Execution thereon shall be stayed until
27 │ _____, 19___.
28 │
```

```
1        ( )  [Check, if applicable] Plaintiff shall also have judgment against
2    defendants in the sum of $_____.
3
4    DATED:_____, 19____      _____
5                                          JUDGE OF THE MUNICIPAL COURT
6
7
8
9
10
11
12
13
14
15
16
17
18
19
20
21
22
23
24
25
26
27
28
```

To have any motion heard by a judge, a tenant files a set of typewritten papers. The first paper is a "notice of motion," which notifies you of the date and time the motion will be heard and summarizes the basis ("grounds") for the motion. The second paper is a short legal essay called a memorandum of points and authorities, stating why the tenant should win the motion. Motions sometimes also include a "declaration" in which the tenant states, under penalty of perjury, any relevant facts—for example, that the tenant wasn't properly served with the summons.

From the landlord's point of view, the worst thing about a tenant's motion is not that the judge might grant it, but that it can delay the eviction for at least several weeks, during which the tenant will not be paying rent. This is true even if the tenant loses the motion. Motions generally can be heard no sooner than 20 days after the tenant files the motion papers and mails copies of them to the landlord. (C.C.P. §§ 1177 and 1005, Rules 325 and 329, Calif. Rules of Court.) One exception is motions to quash, which under C.C.P. § 1167.4(a) must be heard no later than seven days after filing.

Before the hearing, the landlord should file a written response arguing that the tenant's motion should be denied. The judge will read both sides' papers in advance and will allow limited discussion by each side at the hearing, perhaps asking a few questions. The judge then rules on the motion. If the motion is denied, the judge will require the tenant to file an answer to the complaint within five days.

Here is a brief discussion of the kinds of motions commonly filed in unlawful detainer cases.

a. The Motion To Quash

Officially called a "motion to quash summons or service of summons," this motion alleges some defect in the summons or the way it was served. (If the defect is in the way it was served on one tenant, only that tenant may make this kind of motion.) If the judge agrees, the case is delayed until you have a new summons served on the tenant. Typical grounds for a tenant's motion to quash, based on defective service, are:

- the summons was served on one defendant but not the other;
- the wrong person was served;
- no one was served;
- the process server didn't personally serve the summons as claimed in the proof of service (and instead mailed it, laid it on the doorstep or served it in some other unauthorized manner); or
- you, the plaintiff, served the summons.

Grounds based on a defect in the summons itself include:

- the wrong court or judicial district is listed; or
- the complaint requests sums not awardable in an unlawful detainer action, such as pre-termination rent in a 30-day notice case, utility charges or late security deposit installments; this makes the case a regular civil action in which a different summons giving more than five days to respond is necessary. (*Greene v. Municipal Court* (1975) 51 Cal. App. 3d 446; *Castle Park No. 5 v. Katherine* (1979) 91 Cal. App. 3d Supp. 6; *Saberi v. Bakhtiari* (1985) 169 Cal. App. 3d 509.)

If the motion to quash is based on allegations that can logically be responded to by your process server, he will have to appear at the hearing on the motion to testify to when, where and how the papers were served. For instance, if the tenant's motion to quash states that the summons and complaint were "served" solely by first class mail (which is not permitted), you would need your process server to testify as to how the papers were, in fact, served. Before the hearing, you should file with the court clerk the Proof of Service (on the back of the original summons) that the process server filled out.

If you encounter a motion to quash, you will need the assistance of an attorney unless, of course, you are able to interpret and contest the tenant's motion papers and know how to file and serve your response papers and argue the motion in a court hearing.

b. Motion To Strike

A "motion to strike" asks the judge to "strike" (delete) all or part of a complaint. For example, if your unlawful detainer complaint asks for treble rent and/or damages without alleging any specific facts that tend to show the tenant's malicious intent, the tenant may make a motion to strike the treble rent/damages request from the complaint. If the judge grants the motion, it doesn't mean that the judge or clerk goes through your complaint and crosses out the part objected to, but the case is treated as if that had been done.

Motions to strike are heard no sooner than 20 days after the tenant files the motion, which means that, win or lose on the motion, you lose three weeks.

Other defects in the complaint that might subject it to a tenant's motion to strike include:

- a request for attorneys' fees, if you don't allege a written rental agreement or lease that contains an attorneys' fees clause;

- a request for pro-rated daily damages at the reasonable rental value without an allegation of the daily rental value;

- a request for something not awardable in an unlawful detainer action (see motions to quash, above); or

- your failure to "verify" (sign under penalty of perjury) the complaint (this could result in a successful motion to strike the entire complaint).

How you should respond to a motion to strike depends on the part of your complaint objected to, but in most cases you can shorten the delay caused by the motion by simply filing and serving an "amended complaint" that corrects your errors. After that, you must make a motion to be allowed to file another amended complaint. (C.C.P. § 472.) Telling you how and when to file an amended complaint is beyond the scope of this book. However, you can only amend the complaint once without special permission from the judge. If you do this, you render the motion to strike moot and should be able to proceed with your unlawful detainer without waiting for a hearing.

Assuming there is a hearing on the motion to strike, the judge will decide whether or not to strike the material the tenant objects to. Once this is done, the tenant has to file an answer within the time allowed by the judge, usually five days.

You may get a default judgment if the answer isn't filed by that time, (See Chapter 7.)

2. Demurrers

A "demurrer" is a written response to an unlawful detainer complaint that claims that the complaint (or the copy of the three-day or 30-day notice attached to it) is deficient in some way. When a tenant files a demurrer, he is really saying, "Assuming only for the purpose of argument that everything the landlord says in the complaint is true, it still doesn't provide legal justification to order me evicted.". When this is the case, it's usually because the complaint (including attachments) itself shows that the landlord has not complied with the strict requirements for preparation and service of the three-day or 30-day notice. For example, if the attached three-day notice doesn't demand that the tenant pay a specific dollar amount of rent or leave within three days, it's obvious from the complaint alone that the tenancy has not been properly terminated, and that the tenant therefore should win.

Typical objections directed to the attached three-day or 30-day notice by a demurrer include:

- not stating the premises' address, or stating an address different from that alleged elsewhere in the complaint;

- stating an amount of rent more than that alleged elsewhere in the complaint as past due;

- demanding sums other than rent, such as late charges, where the notice clearly indicates this; or

- alleging that the notice was served before the rent became past due.

Objections directed at the unlawful detainer complaint itself include:

- failure to check boxes containing essential allegations, such as compliance with rent control or just cause eviction ordinances; or
- allegation of contradictory statements.

Demurrers can often be more technical than motions to quash or strike. If a successful demurrer is based on a defect in the three-day or 30-day notice attached to the complaint, you could wind up not only having the eviction delayed, but also with a judgment against you for court costs and attorney's fees. It is for this reason (and because we simply can't predict the content of any particular demurrer) that we tell you to consult an attorney if you are faced with one.

3. The Tenant's Answer

Sooner or later, if you adequately respond to any motions or demurrer filed by the tenant, the tenant will be required to respond to the substance of your complaint. This response is called the "answer." It will finally let you know what aspects of your case the tenant plans to contest and what other arguments, if any, the tenant plans to advance as to why she thinks you should lose (called "affirmative defenses").

Like your unlawful detainer complaint, the tenant's answer is usually submitted on a standard fill-in-the-boxes form. (It can also be typed from scratch on 8-1/2" x 11" paper with numbers in the left margin, but this is increasingly rare.) A typical answer is shown below.

Here is what you need to pay attention to in the tenant's answer.

a. The Tenant's Denial of Statements in the Complaint

The first part of the answer with which you must concern yourself is item 3. Here, the defendant denies one or more of the allegations of your complaint. If box 3.a is checked, this means that the tenant denies everything you alleged.

At trial, you will have to testify to everything you alleged in the complaint: ownership, lease or rental agreement existence, rent amount, rent overdue, service of three-day notice, refusal to pay rent, etc.

If box 3.b is checked, the space immediately below should indicate which, if any, of your allegations is denied, either by specific reference to the numbered allegation paragraphs in your complaint or in a concise statement. At trial, you will be required to offer testimony or other evidence as to any of your allegations the tenant denies.

For example, in the sample answer below, Terrence and Tillie Tenant deny the allegations of paragraphs "6.d, 8.a, 8.b, 9.a, 11, 12, and 13" of Lenny Landlord's complaint. This means Lenny has to go back and look at his complaint to see exactly what Terrence and Tillie are denying. He would find that the allegations denied are:

SAMPLE

ATTORNEY OR PARTY WITHOUT ATTORNEY (NAME AND ADDRESS):	TELEPHONE:	FOR COURT USE ONLY

ATTORNEY OR PARTY WITHOUT ATTORNEY (NAME AND ADDRESS):   TELEPHONE:

TERRENCE D. TENANT, TILLIE D. TENANT (213) 555-6789
P.O. Box 12345
Los Angeles, CA 90010

ATTORNEY FOR (NAME): Defendants

Insert name of court, judicial district or branch court, if any, and post office and street address:

MUNICIPAL COURT OF CALIFORNIA, COUNTY OF LOS ANGELES
LOS ANGELES JUDICIAL DISTRICT
100 North Grand Avenue
Los Angeles, CA 90012

PLAINTIFF:

LENNY D. LANDLORD

DEFENDANT:

TERRENCE D. TENANT, TILLIE D. TENANT

ANSWER— Unlawful Detainer	CASE NUMBER: A-12345-B

1. This pleading including attachments and exhibits consists of the following number of pages: __2__

2. Defendants *(name):* Terrence D. Tenant, Tillie D. Tenant

   answer the complaint as follows:

3. **Check ONLY ONE of the next two boxes:**

   a. ☐ Defendant generally denies each statement of the complaint. *(Do not check this box if the complaint demands more than $1,000.)*

   b. ☒ Defendant admits that all of the statements of the complaint are true EXCEPT:

      (1) Defendant claims the following statements of the complaint are false *(use paragraph numbers from the complaint or explain):*

         6.d, 8.a, 8.b, 9.a, 11, 12 and 13

         ☐ Continued on Attachment 3.b.(1).

      (2) Defendant has no information or belief that the following statements of the complaint are true, so defendant denies them *(use paragraph numbers from the complaint or explain):*

         ☐ Continued on Attachment 3.b.(2).

4. AFFIRMATIVE DEFENSES

   a. ☒ *(nonpayment of rent only)* Plaintiff has breached the warranty to provide habitable premises. *(Briefly state the facts below in item 4.k.)*

   b. ☐ Plaintiff waived, changed, or canceled the notice to quit. *(Briefly state the facts below in item 4.k.)*

   c. ☐ Plaintiff served defendant with the notice to quit or filed the complaint to retaliate against defendant. *(Briefly state the facts below in item 4.k.)*

   d. ☐ Plaintiff has failed to perform his obligations under the rental agreement. *(Briefly state the facts below in item 4.k.)*

   e. ☐ By serving defendant with the notice to quit or filing the complaint, plaintiff is arbitrarily discriminating against the defendant in violation of the constitution or laws of the United States or California. *(Briefly state the facts below in item 4.k.)*

   f. ☐ Plaintiff's demand for possession violates the local rent control or eviction control ordinance of *(city or county, title of ordinance, and date of passage):*

      (Briefly state the facts showing violation of the ordinance in item 4.k.)

      (Continued)

Form Approved by the
Judicial Council of California
Effective January 1, 1982
Rule 982.1(95)

ANSWER—Unlawful Detainer

CCP 425.12

SHORT TITLE: LANDLORD V. TENANT	CASE NUMBER: A-12345-B

ANSWER—Unlawful Detainer   Page two

g. ☐ Plaintiff accepted rent from defendant to cover a period of time after the date stated in paragraph 8.b. of the complaint.

h. ☐ *(nonpayment of rent only)* On *(date):*   defendant offered the rent due but plaintiff would not accept it.

i. ☐ Defendant made needed repairs and properly deducted the cost from the rent, and plaintiff did not give proper credit.

j. ☐ Other affirmative defenses. *(Briefly state below in item 4.k.)*

k. FACTS SUPPORTING AFFIRMATIVE DEFENSES CHECKED ABOVE *(Identify each item separately.)*

Plaintiff is in violation of the implied warranty to provide habitable premises in that he failed and refused, after repeated demand, to repair the following defects of the premises: (1) a defective heater which provides heat intermittently, (2) a bathroom toilet that will not flush, (3) a leaky roof that allows rain to enter, and (4) a severe cockroach infestation. As a result, the reasonable rental value of the premises is only $200.00 per month or $6.66 per day.

☐ Continued on Attachment 4.k.

5. OTHER STATEMENTS
   a. ☐ Defendant vacated the premises on *(date):*
   b. ☒ Defendant claims a credit for deposits of $ 300.00
   c. ☒ The fair rental value of the premises in item 12 of the complaint is excessive *(explain):*

   d. ☐ Other *(specify):*

6. DEFENDANT REQUESTS
   a. that plaintiff take nothing requested in the complaint.
   b. costs incurred in this proceeding.
   c. ☐ reasonable attorney fees.
   d. ☐ other *(specify):*

_____   *Terrence D. Tenant*
(Type or print name)   _____
                                        (Signature of defendant or attorney)

_____   *Tillie D. Tenant*
(Type or print name)   _____
                                        (Signature of defendant or attorney)

(Each defendant for whom this answer is filed must be named in item 2 and
must sign this answer unless represented by an attorney.)

VERIFICATION

(Use a different verification form if the verification is by an attorney or for a corporation or partnership.)

I am the defendant in this proceeding and have read this answer. I declare under penalty of perjury under the laws of the State of California that this answer is true and correct.

Date:
     August 15, 1992
     TILLIE D. TENANT   *Tillie D. Tenant*
.... _____
     (Type or print name)   (Signature of defendant)

                                                            Page two

- that Lenny changed the rental agreement by increasing the rent (complaint item 6.d);

- that a three-day notice to pay rent or quit was served (item 8.a);

- that the notice expired on August 8 (item 8.b);

- that any such notice was served on the date Lenny indicated (item 9.a);

- that the rent due was $900 (item 11);

- that the fair rental value is $30 per day (item 12); and

- that Lenny is entitled to possession of the premises (item 13).

This means that Lenny will, at the very least, have to have the person who served the three-day notice testify in court that she in fact served it. Lenny, himself, will have to testify about when he last received the rent and how much the tenants owed when the notice was served.

b.   The Tenant's Affirmative Defenses

If none of the boxes in item 4 of the answer are checked, skip this discussion and go directly to subsection c, below.

In addition to responding to the landlord's statements in the complaint, the tenant is entitled to use the answer to make some of his own. These statements (in item 4 of the answer) are called "affirmative defenses." The tenant checks the boxes next to any applicable defenses and explains the relevant facts in some detail in item 4.k (on the reverse).

If an affirmative defense is proved by the tenant to the satisfaction of a judge, the tenant wins, even if everything you said in the unlawful detainer complaint is true. The duties imposed on you by law, the breach of which can give rise to these defenses, are discussed in detail in *Volume 1*. In Section E, below, we discuss when you may need an attorney to help you handle a defense, and, if you decide to go it alone, how you will need to respond at trial.

If you are still representing yourself, but upon inspecting the answer (item 4) discover that an affirmative defense is being raised, now is the time to start looking for help. You should at least consult an attorney to assess the probable strength of the tenant's case—even if you think the affirmative defense is untrue or just a bluff. We are reluctant to advise a consultation with a lawyer solely because an affirmative defense is raised by the tenant. However, please understand that by making such a response, the tenant is warning you that he has something in mind that may torpedo your case. If you proceed on your own and later are unable to handle the defense, all your hard work up to this point may go down the drain.

Here is a brief description of each affirmative defense that may be raised in the answer.

Item 4.a: Breach of Warranty of Habitability

In suits based on nonpayment of rent, this defense asserts that the tenant should be excused from paying all the rent because of your failure to keep the place in good repair. (See *Volume 1*, Chapter 11.) Technically, the habitability defense should not be raised in suits based on reasons other than nonpayment of rent. If a tenant does assert it improperly, you should object at trial.

Item 4.b: Waiver or Cancellation of Notice To Quit

If the landlord acted in a way that was somehow inconsistent with the three- or 30-day notice, the notice may effectively be cancelled. For example, if your three-day notice complained about the rent not being paid on the first of the month, but you'd accepted it on the fifth every month for the past year, you might have given up or "waived" the right to complain. Another example would be your acquiescing for several months to the tenant's breach of the "no-pets" lease clause and then serving the tenant with a Three-Day Notice To Perform Covenant or Quit that says the tenant must get rid of the pet or leave within three days. Item 4.b might also be checked if the tenant claims you accepted or agreed to accept rent later than the notice deadline. (See Chapter 2, Section D, for a discussion of the consequences of accepting rent after serving a three-day notice; and Chapter 3, Section H, regarding acceptance of rent following service of a 30-day notice terminating a month-to-month tenancy.)

Item 4.c: Retaliation

This alleges that your true reason for serving a notice—usually a 30-day notice terminating a month-to-month tenancy—was to retaliate for the tenant's exercise of some legal right. Retaliation is often claimed by tenants who have complained to local government authorities about housing conditions, or who have attempted to organize your other tenants. (See *Volume 1*, Chapter 15.)

Item 4.d: Failure To Perform Your Obligations

In a suit based on a three-day notice, the tenant can allege that you failed to live up to your part of the rental agreement or lease. This defense is seldom applicable, however, since very few landlord-written rental agreements and leases require the landlord to do anything other than provide a space for the tenant to rent. Many tenants who complain about housing conditions incorrectly check this box, even though the issue should actually be raised as a breach of the implied warranty of habitability (box 4.a).

Item 4.e: Discrimination

This defense refers to discrimination prohibited under state and federal law. (See *Volume 1*, Chapter 9, for a discussion of this complex topic.)

Item 4.f: Violation of Rent Control Ordinance

Many rent control ordinances not only limit the amount of rent you may charge, but also have "just cause eviction" provisions that limit your freedom to terminate a month-to-month tenancy. Your tenant can defend the lawsuit based on your failure to comply with any aspect of the ordinance, including:

1. Property registration requirements,

2. Rent limits, or

3. Special requirements for three-day or 30-day eviction notices.

Cities that require registration of rents (Berkeley, Santa Monica, Cotati, East Palo Alto, Los Angeles, Palm Springs, Thousand Oaks and West Hollywood) must limit the sanctions against landlords who are in "substantial compliance" with a rent control law and made only a good-faith mistake in calculating rent or registering property with the local rent control agency. (Civ. Code § 1947.7.) The statute appears to apply only to sanctions imposed by local rent control agencies, however. You should still expect to have your complaint dismissed if it is based on a three-day notice that demanded an amount of rent that was illegal under a rent control ordinance.

Item 4.g: Acceptance of Rent

If you accepted rent for a period beyond the termination date in a three or 30-day notice, you may have revoked that notice. For example, if rent is due in advance on the first of each month, and you gave your tenant a 30-day notice on June 15, the tenancy terminates on July 15. By accepting a full month's rent on July 1, however, you accepted rent for the period through July 31, well beyond the termination date of the 15th, and you impliedly revoked the 30-day notice.

In many instances, this defense is identical to the "waiver and cancellation" defense (Item 4.b, above), and the tenant can check either or both defenses.

Item 4.h: Refusal of Rent

If you gave the tenant a Three-Day Notice To Pay Rent or Quit, you must accept rent offered during the three-day notice period. This defense is occasionally used when a tenant's offer of a check is rejected by the landlord during the three-day period because of a requirement that payment be made by cash or money order—usually, after a few bounced checks. As long as you insisted on being paid by cash or money order well before the time that the tenant insists on using the check (and can document this), you should be able to beat this defense. (See *Volume 1*, Chapter 3.)

This point is often mistakenly raised by tenants when landlords properly refuse rent after the applicable notice period expired. Once the judge understands that the rent was offered only after the three-day period, and not before, you should prevail.

Item 4.i: Repair-and-Deduct Defense

As discussed in *Volume 1*, Chapter 11, state statute forbids an eviction within six months after the exercise of the tenant's "repair-and-deduct" rights unless the notice to quit states a valid reason for the eviction and the landlord proves the reason in court if the tenant contests it. Even if you think the tenant's deduction was improper, be prepared to prove a valid reason (under the repair-and-deduct statute) for the eviction.

Item 4.j: Other Affirmative Defenses

Although items 4.a through 4.i list the most common defenses, an imaginative tenant's attorney may use item 4.j to describe additional defenses. (This ability of tenants' attorneys to introduce strange theories into the most mundane case is a large part of the reason we advise you to consider hiring an attorney if one appears for the tenant.) As with the listed defenses, the facts specific to any defense checked here must be listed in item 4.k, below.

Item 4.k: Specific Facts Relating to the Defenses

Under item 4.k on the reverse of the answer, the tenant is supposed to explain the affirmative defense boxes checked. No special language or format is necessary, and almost any brief, factual statement will do. These statements are supposed to give you an idea of what the defendant is going to try to prove at trial. At trial, the defendant may testify only to subjects he brought up in the answer.

c.　Other Things in the Answer

Item 5 on the back of the answer form has spaces for miscellaneous "other statements." If the tenant has given up possession of the property before filing his answer (item 5.a), for instance, the case will be treated as a regular civil lawsuit. You and the tenant can then ask for things not allowed in an unlawful detainer action, but the case won't get to trial as fast as an unlawful detainer suit normally would. (Civ. Code § 1952.3.) An unlawful detainer suit is a special "summary" (expedited) procedure with shorter response times, and more restrictions on the issues that may be raised, than regular suits.

Item 5.b has a space for the tenant to allege a credit for her security deposit. Since you don't have to credit or refund the tenant's security deposit until two weeks after the tenant vacates the property (see *Volume 1*, Chapter 20), and since the answer must be filed within five days of your serving the complaint on the tenant—who was still in the property—the tenant's use of this statement is improper unless she has already moved out, and you can object at trial.

In item 5.c, the tenant can state that the pro-rated daily "fair rental value" you alleged is too high (usually because of a habitability defense).

Finally, item 6.a allows the tenant to request attorney's fees. This is proper only if the written rental agreement or lease has an attorneys' fees clause. Because of the restrictions on unlawful detainer suits, there is really nothing else the tenant can properly ask for here.

E. Responding to the Answer

If the tenant has simply denied your allegations, not raised any defenses of his own and is not represented by an attorney, you are still on pretty firm ground as far as going ahead on your own is concerned. The next step is getting a trial date.

1. The Memorandum To Set Case for Trial

Like almost everything else in the legal system, the trial on your now-contested unlawful detainer complaint will not happen automatically. You have to ask for it in a form known as a "Memorandum To Set Case for Trial" (also sometimes called a "memo to set" or an "at-issue memorandum"). This form differs from county to county, and many courts require you to use the local form, which can be obtained from the court clerk. A sample Los Angeles form is shown below.

The forms all require pretty much the same information. In addition to the names of the parties and case number, the form will have spaces for you to list the type of case, whether the case has "preference" for trial, whether a jury trial is requested, and how long the trial will take. A copy of the form should be mailed to the tenant(s) or their attorney at the address indicated on their answer. Most forms include a "Proof of Service" portion to indicate this was done.

The most important information to include is that yours is an unlawful detainer case, which has "preference" for trial over regular civil cases, which normally have to wait anywhere from three months to well over a year to get to trial. Trial in an unlawful detainer case must be held no more than 20 days after you file your memo to set. Some forms ask you to list the statute giving preference; for unlawful detainer actions, this is C.C.P. § 1179a.

If the Tenant Has Moved Out. If the tenant who has filed an Answer moves out before you file your Memorandum To Set Case for Trial, you can still ask the court to set the case for trial. You would normally do this if you want to get a judgment against the tenant for rent and court costs. However, the case becomes a "regular civil action" without "preference" (Civ. Code § 1952.3), and you should not state your case has preference for trial setting. The court will then set it for trial much more slowly.

Do not request a jury trial. Jury trials are procedurally much more complex than trials before judges, and it is easy to get in way over your head. Also, the party requesting a jury trial has to deposit jury fees (about $200/day) with the court in advance. All you want is a simple trial, lasting no more than a few hours at most, in front of a judge. Your estimated time for trial should be anywhere from one hour, for a simple case where the tenant has failed to assert any affirmative defenses, to two hours in cases involving fairly complicated issues like alleged rent control violations, discriminatory or retaliatory evictions, or breach of the warranty to provide habitable premises.

Make two photocopies and have a friend mail one to the tenant (or his attorney) at the mailing address indicated in the upper left corner of the answer. Fill out the proof-of-service portion of the form and have your friend sign it, indicating that he mailed the copy, and take the original and one copy to the courthouse. The court clerk will file the original and stamp the copy for your records.

The court will hold on to your Memorandum To Set Case for Trial for up to five days to give the tenant a chance to file a "Countermemo To Set." This gives the tenant the opportunity to also list unavailable dates and dispute any of the information you listed. (Rule 507(c), California Rules of Court.) Then the clerk will set the case for trial on a date no more than 20 days after the date you filed your Memorandum, and will notify you by mail of the date, time and place of the trial.

SAMPLE

Name, address and telephone no. of attorney(s)

   LENNY D. LANDLORD   (213) 555-6789
12345 Angeleno St.
Los Angeles, CA 90010

Attorney(s) for Plaintiff in Pro Per

This space for court clerk only

Memorandum to Set

Case for Trial

IN THE MUNICIPAL COURT OF
LOS ANGELES .... **JUDICIAL DISTRICT**
COUNTY OF LOS ANGELES, STATE OF CALIFORNIA

Case Number

A 12345 B

LENNY D. LANDLORD   vs.   TERRENCE D. TENANT, TILLIE D. TENANT

(Plaintiff(s))   Defendant(s)

I hereby represent to the court that this case is at issue, and request that it be set for trial.
Nature of the case: unlawful detainer action
Jury trial is not demanded. Time necessary for trial: 2 hours
    (is or is not)   (estimate carefully)
This case is entitled to legal preference in setting. unlawful detainer - CCP 1179a
    (is or is not)   (is so, state reasons)

The following dates are NOT acceptable to me: All dates acceptable

Names, addresses and telephone number of attorneys for other parties, or of parties appearing in person:
    Terrence D. Tenant, Tillie D. Tenant   (213) 555-6789
P.O. Box 12345
Los Angeles, CA 90010

Dated August 16, 1992   *Lenny D. Landlord*
                                (Note: Must be signed by attorney or party requesting setting)

DECLARATION OF SERVICE BY MAIL

I, the undersigned, say: my business address is 123 Main St., #4, Los Angeles, CA
             (business/residence)

I am over the age of eighteen years, not a party to the above-entitled action, and at the time of mailing, was employed or resided

in the County where said mailing occurred.

On August 16, 1992 I served the foregoing document by depositing a copy thereof, enclosed in separate,

sealed envelope(s), with the postage thereon fully prepaid, in the United States mail at Los Angeles
                                         (city or postal area)

, County of Los Angeles , California, each of which envelopes was addressed

respectively as follows:
    Terrence D. Tenant   Tillie D. Tenant
P.O. Box 12345   P. O. Box 12345
Los Angeles, CA 90010   Los Angeles, CA 90010

Executed on August 16, 1992 , at , California.
          (date)   (place)

I declare under penalty of perjury that the foregoing is true and correct. *Fred Friend*
                                               Declarant

Space below for court clerk only

The above-entitled case has been set for jury/court trial in
MASTER CALENDAR Division

on   at   M.

Entered on calendar by
Entered in register by
Requesting party notified

MEMORANDUM TO SET CASE FOR TRIAL

76M169–Ci 25–(4)–(Rev. 8/79) PS 7/91

Rules for the Municipal Courts, Rule 507(a) (b)
Also see local court rules.

2. Summary Judgment

As soon as you've served and filed the Memorandum To Set Case for Trial, you may want to make a pre-trial motion of your own to request a summary judgment—a judgment without an actual trial. To be eligible for a summary judgment, you must convince a judge that there is no real dispute about the facts in the case—that is, you and the tenant are only really arguing over the legal issues. If the judge agrees, she can issue a judgment on the spot. (C.C.P. § 1170.7.) Not only do you save the effort of preparing for trial, but it also allows you to significantly shorten the time you have to wait to get a judgment and get your tenant out.

This section shows you how to make a summary judgment motion in a rent nonpayment case (Chapter 2), using the form provided in the forms section in the back of the book. If your eviction is on any ground other than for nonpayment of rent, you will need the assistance of an attorney to pursue this remedy. The potential variation in the facts makes it impossible to accurately show you how to draft your papers without producing what would amount to another book.

You must pay a $100 filing fee to the court clerk when you file this kind of motion. (This is in addition to the $80 fee you paid to file the case.) This may well be worth the price because if you file this motion quickly after the tenant files her answer, you could get the tenant evicted one to two weeks sooner than if you waited for the court to set the case for trial. Also, this motion will save you the time and effort involved in a trial. Finally, the $100 filing fee for this motion will be added to the money judgment you will get against the tenant.

Here is an overview of how a summary judgment proceeding works.

The first step is to obtain a motion hearing date at least five days away. Then type the motion papers, which include a notice of motion for summary judgment, your declaration under penalty of perjury stating the basic facts of the case from your perspective, and a brief legal essay stating why the motion should be granted. Copies of these papers must be served on the tenant at least five days before the hearing, the originals filed with the court, and a motion fee paid to the clerk. At the hearing, you or your lawyer appear. You don't bring witnesses to testify at this stage because you are only dealing with questions of law, not questions of fact. The important things have already been done, including the written declarations and argument you filed earlier. In most cases, if the tenant doesn't respond to your motion with his own written declaration contradicting yours, the judge is required to grant the motion, so that you win your case without trial—and sooner. If you lose the motion, you have not really lost anything but some time and $100. You will still be able to present your full case at the trial.

EXAMPLE

Your declaration says that you rented your property to Terrence and Tillie Tenant, that the rent was $900 per month due on the first, and that they didn't pay on the first of August. It also states that on August 5, you served them with a three-day notice and they still didn't pay or leave. Tillie and Terrence can defeat your motion by filing their own declaration saying that the rent wasn't $900, or that they paid the rent, that they never received the notice or that you failed to repair serious defects in the property after they notified you of them.

If you decide you want to try to speed up your case by requesting a summary judgment, carefully read the following instructions.

If you believe that you and your tenant disagree significantly over the facts, or you are not sure that a summary judgment will work and therefore want to wait for the trial rather than engage in yet another procedure, skip to Section F.

Our instructions assume that the tenant is not represented by an attorney. If she is, you will probably want to consult one and may want to arrange to be represented. Our instructions do not cover how you should proceed if an attorney has appeared for the tenant.

Step 1: Select a Date for Hearing on Your Motion

First, find out when the court hears motions. Some of the larger courts hear them on several different days of the week, while smaller courts have their "law and motion" day once a week. Call or visit the court clerk and tell her you're a plaintiff in an unlawful detainer case and wish to have a summary judgment motion heard. (You may have to remind the clerk that, unlike motions in regular cases, summary judgment motions in unlawful detainer cases are heard on just five days' notice, according to C.C.P. § 1170.7.) Ask what dates and times are available.

In some counties you can choose a date over the phone. In others, the clerk won't schedule your motion hearing on the court calendar until you file your "Notice of Motion" (Step 2, below).

Pick the earliest date that is at least five days after the day you'll be able to have the motion papers personally served on the tenant. If the court has a policy that only a certain number of cases can be heard at each session, remind the clerk that the case is an unlawful detainer case entitled to priority.

Step 2: Prepare the Papers

If you think you've already been run through the mill on the paperwork required to do a "simple" eviction, it's time to grit your teeth and prepare for some more. Even the most simple request to a court, including your summary judgment motion papers, must be submitted on typed, double-spaced, 8-1/2" x 11" legal pleading paper with the numbers down the left hand side. You can copy the blank sheet of pleading paper in the Appendix. The papers consist of three parts, which can be combined into one document. These are:

1. A "Notice of Motion," which tells the tenant where, when and on what legal grounds you're making the motion;

2. A "Declaration" in which you and/or someone else states the pertinent facts under penalty of perjury; and

3. A "Memorandum of Points and Authorities" (usually referred to simply as "points and authorities"), a short legalistic statement that explains why the facts stated in the declaration legally entitle you to judgment.

Below are provided instructions and sample completed forms demonstrating how to draft each of these documents. Fill-in-the-blanks forms are included in the Appendix.

Step 3: Photocopy the Papers

Once you've prepared and signed your summary judgment motion papers, make a set of photocopies for each tenant who has answered the complaint, plus one for your files. For instance, if three tenants have answered the complaint, you will need at least four photocopies.

Step 4: Have the Papers Served

Because of the short (five-day) notice given the tenant, you must have the papers personally served on each tenant or on another person over 18 at the tenant's home. Unlike service of the summons, service on an adult at the tenant's residence—or on an employee in the office of

S A M P L E

```
1   Name:
    Address:        [list your mailing address and phone number]
2
    Phone:
3   Plaintiff in Pro Per
4
5
6
7
8   MUNICIPAL COURT OF CALIFORNIA, COUNTY OF _____ [list county] _____
9   _____ [list judicial district here] _____ JUDICIAL DISTRICT
10
         [your name]
11  _____ )  Case No. ____ [case number] ____
                                      )
12       Plaintiff,                   )  NOTICE OF MOTION FOR
    v.                                )  SUMMARY JUDGMENT;
13       [defendants' names]          )  PLAINTIFF'S DECLARATION;
    _____  )  POINTS AND AUTHORITIES
14                                    )  (C.C.P. 437C, 1170.7)
         Defendant(s).                )
15  _____ )  Hearing Date:
                                         Time:
16                                       Courtroom:    [list hearing date, time
                                                        and courtroom number]
17
18  TO DEFENDANTS ____ [defendants' names] _____
19       AND THEIR ATTORNEY OF RECORD:
20       PLEASE TAKE NOTICE that on _____, 19___
21  at _____ __.M in the above-entitled Court, at
22  _____ [list court address and city] _____,
23  City of _____, California, the above-named
24  plaintiff will move the Court for an Order granting summary
25  judgment for possession of the subject premises herein, rent,
26  damages, and costs in the above-entitled action.
27       This motion is made on the ground that defendants' defense has
28  no merit and there exists no triable issue of fact as to
```

1 plaintiff's cause of action, plaintiff having established that

2 defendants are guilty of unlawfully detaining the subject premises

3 following nonpayment of the rent due, service of a 3-day notice to

4 pay rent or quit, and failure to pay the rent or vacate the

5 premises within the time given in the said notice.

6   This motion is based on this notice, the declaration of

7 plaintiff attached hereto, the points and authorities attached

8 hereto, the pleadings, records, and files herein, and on such

9 argument as may be presented at the hearing on the motion.

10 DATED: _____[date]_____, 19___

11   _____[your signature]_____

                                Plaintiff in Pro Per

12

13   DECLARATION OF PLAINTIFF

14   I, the undersigned, declare:

15   1. I am the plaintiff in the within action and the owner of

16 the subject premises located at ___[list premises's address, city and county]___

17 _____, City of _____,

18 County of _____, California.

19   2. On ___[date premises rented]___, 19___, defendant(s) rented th[e] [cross one out]

20 from me pursuant to a written/oral agreement. The monthly rent was

21 $___[monthly rent]___ payable in advance on the day of each month, the

22 reasonable rental value of the premises per day being $_____[monthly rent divided by 30]

23   3. Pursuant to the agreement, defendant(s) went into

24 possession of the premises. [date defendants served with 3-day notice]   [rent due when 3-day notice served]

25   4. On _____, 19___, defendant(s) were in default

26 in the payment of rent in the amount of $_____, and I served

27 defendant(s) ___[list names of defendants]_____

28 _____

1 with a written notice demanding that defendant(s) pay that amount

2 or surrender possession of the premises within three days of

3 service of the said notice. A true copy of that notice is

4 attached to the complaint herein as Exhibit "B" thereto.

5   5. Prior to my service of the said three-day notice,

6 defendant(s) had not notified me of any substantial defect in the

7 premises relating to the tenantability or habitability thereof.

8   6. Defendant(s) failed to pay the said rent or surrender

9 possession of the said premises within three days of service of

10 the said notice, whereupon I commenced the instant action,

11 complying with all applicable rent control and/or eviction

12 protection ordinances. Defendant(s) still remain in possession of

13 the premises.

14   7. This rent was due for the rental period of

list period covered by rent demanded in 3-day notice

15 _____, 19___ through _____, 19___.

16 After this latter date and to the present, I sustained damages at

17 the daily reasonable rental value indicated above in paragraph 2

if applicable, list total pro-rated rent after period; if none, list zero (0)

18 for total damages in the amount of $_____, and total rent and

19 damages in tne amount of $_____.

total unpaid rent in 3-day notice plus pro-rated rent

20   8. I have incurred service and filing fees in the total

list court costs amount

21 amount of $_____ in the within action.

22   9. If sworn as a witness, I could testify competently to the

23 facts stated herein.

24   I declare under penalty of perjury under the laws of the

25 State of California that the foregoing is true and correct.

26 DATED: _____, 19___

27

date and sign _____

28   Plaintiff in Pro Per

**you don't have to fill in
anything on this page**

POINTS AND AUTHORITIES

I. PLAINTIFF'S MOTION FOR SUMMARY JUDGMENT IS PROPERLY BEFORE THE COURT.

In an unlawful detainer action a motion for summary judgment may be made on five days' notice. C.C.P. Sec. 1170.7. The time limits imposed by subdivision (a) of section 437c, as well as the requirement in subdivision (b) of a separate statement of material facts not in dispute, are not applicable to summary judgment motions in unlawful detainer actions. C.C.P. Sec. 437c(n). In all other respects, the motion is required to be granted on the same terms and conditions as a summary judgment motion under C.C.P. Sec. 437c, and such a motion must be decided solely on the affidavits or declarations filed. Ibid, subd. (c).

II. PLAINTIFF HAS ESTABLISHED THE PRIMA FACIE ELEMENTS OF AN UNLAWFUL DETAINER ACTION FOR NONPAYMENT OF RENT.

Under section 1162(2) of the Code of Civil Procedure, a tenant or subtenant is guilty of unlawful detainer.

> When he continues in possession . . . after default
> in the payment of rent . . . and three days' notice,
> in writing requiring its payment, stating the amount
> which is due, or possession of the property, shall
> have been served on him . . . .

Elements other than default in rent, service of the notice, the expiration of three days without payment, and the continuance in possession include the existence of a landlord-tenant relationship (<u>Fredricksen v. McCosker</u> (1956) 143 Cal. App. 2d 114) and proper contents of the notice (<u>Wilson v. Sadleir</u> (1915) 26 Cal. App. 357, 359)incorporation of proper notice is sufficient)). Plaintiff's declaration establishes all these elements, so that plaintiff is entitled to summary judgment.

III. DEFENDANT(S) CANNOT PREVAIL UNDER A DEFENSE OF BREACH OF THE IMPLIED WARRANTY OF HABITABILITY.

Under the rule of <u>Green v. Superior Court</u> (1974) 10 Cal. 3d 616, the California Supreme Court held that in an unlawful detainer action founded on nonpayment of rent, the tenant could assert as a defense that the landlord breached an implied warranty to keep the premises habitable. The Court cited with approval the case of <u>Hinson v. Delis</u> (1972) 26 Cal. App. 3d 62 in this regard. In <u>Hinson</u>, the tenant sued the landlord in a regular civil action for breach of this implied warranty. After the trial court ruled in favor of the landlord, the Court of Appeal reversed, holding that there existed such a warranty in the law, as to which, "The tenant must also give notice of alleged defects to the landlord and allow a reasonable time for repairs to be made." <u>Hinson</u> at p. 70. When the <u>Green</u> court held that the warranty of habitability established by the <u>Hinson</u> court could be asserted by the tenant as a defense to an unlawful detainer action, as well as a basis for suit by the tenant, it did not modify or remove this requirement of notice by the tenant to the landlord of the alleged defects by which the tenant seeks to withhold rent. Therefore, the notice requirement also applies where the defense is asserted by the tenant in an unlawful detainer action.

Plaintiff's declaration establishes that defendant(s) failed to give plaintiff notice of the alleged defects in the premises. Unless a triable issue of fact exists in this regard, defendant(s) cannot assert this defense, as a matter of law.

DATED: _____, 19____

| date and sign |

_____
Plaintiff in Pro Per

```
 1                        PROOF OF SERVICE
 2          I the undersigned, declare:
 3          I am over the age of 18 years and not a party to the within
 4     action.
 5          On   September 5   , 19 92 , I served the within Notice of
 6     Motion for Summary Judgment, Declaration of Plaintiff, and Points
 7     and Authorities on defendant(s) by delivering true copies thereof
 8     to each such defendant, or other person not less than 18 years of
 9     age, at defendants' residence address of
10        6789 Angel Blvd., Apt. 10                                    ,
11     City of        Los Angeles       , California, between 8:00 A.M.
12     and 6:00 P.M.
13          I declare under penalty of perjury under the laws of the
14     State of California that the foregoing is true and correct.
15     DATED:   September 5   , 19 92     Fred Friend
16                                        Name: FRED FRIEND
17
18
19
20
21
22
23
24
25
26
27
28
```

the tenant's attorney, if the tenant is represented—is sufficient, and the time for the tenant to respond is not extended by the fact that he did not receive them personally. (C.C.P. § 1011.)

As with a summons, you can't serve the papers yourself, but must have a friend or other disinterested person over 18 do it for you. Since service can be made on any adult who answers the door at the tenant's residence, all the tenants named as defendants can be served at the same time this way, provided one copy for each defendant is given to the person answering. The person serving the papers then fills out the proof of service on the originals, before they are filed with the court.

Step 5: File the Papers

Finally, you must file the original motion papers, including proof of service, with the court clerk as soon as possible after the copies are served on the tenant. The clerk should file the originals and file-stamp and return any copies to you. She will also place the motion hearing "on

calendar" (if that wasn't done when you called earlier), and ask you to pay a motion fee of about $100.

Step 6: Prepare the Proposed Order and Judgment

While you're waiting the five or more days until the hearing, you should prepare a proposed order granting your motion and a proposed judgment for the judge to sign. This allows you to hand the judge the necessary papers to sign right at the hearing if he grants your motion. If you don't have the judgment ready for the judge to sign, a delay of several days might result from your having to run home, type the papers, bring them back to court and get them to the judge for signature. Once signed, you can take them to the clerk and get the actual eviction rolling, using the procedures in Section I of this chapter.

Instructions and samples for your proposed order granting the motion and the resulting judgment are shown below.

Step 7: Prepare the Writ of Execution

Chapter 7 shows how to prepare a writ of execution for possession of the property after getting a default judgment for possession. Chapter 9 shows how to fill out another writ of execution for the money part of the judgment after the tenant leaves. If you win a summary judgment motion, however, you get both parts of the judgment—money and possession of property—at the same time. You need only one writ of execution. Refer to both sets of instructions in Chapters 7 and 9 to fill in the appropriate information on the writ of execution. A sample is shown below.

Step 8: Argue Your Motion in Court

The evening before the hearing, you should sit down, try to relax and review the points stated in your motion papers. On the day of the hearing, try to get to the courtroom a little early. At the entrance, there may be a bulletin board with a list of the cases to be heard that morning. If your case isn't listed, check with the clerk.

S A M P L E

```
1   Name:
    Address:        [list your mailing address and phone number]
2
    Phone:
3   Plaintiff in Pro Per
4
5
6
7
8       MUNICIPAL COURT OF CALIFORNIA, COUNTY OF _____ [list county]
9       _____ [list judicial district here] _____ JUDICIAL DISTRICT
10          [your name]
11      _____ ) Case No. _____ [case number]
                                     )
12          Plaintiff,               ) ORDER GRANTING MOTION
        v.                           ) FOR SUMMARY JUDGMENT
13          [defendants' names]      )
14      _____ )
                                     )
15          Defendant(s).            )
16      _____ )
            [list date and courtroom in
            which your hearing will be held]
17          Plaintiff's motion for summary judgment came on for hearing in
18      Department _____ of the above-entitled Court on
            [if defendants didn't
            appear, insert "not"]
            _____, 19___ , said plaintiff appearing in pro
20      per and defendant(s) _____ appearing by
                                                 [insert defendants' attorney's name; if no attorney,
                                                 type "in pro per" and cross out "by"]
21      The matter having been argued and submitted,
22          IT IS HEREBY ORDERED that plaintiff's motion for summary
23      judgment for restitution of the premises the subject of this
                                                 [list anticipated rent/damages judge should award]
24      action, rent and damages in the sum of $_____, and costs
25      of suit be, and the same is, granted.
26      DATED: _____, 19___
27      _____
            [leave date and signature lines blank for judge to fill in]  JUDGE OF THE MUNICIPAL COURT
28
```

S A M P L E

1	Name: LENNY D. LANDLORD
	Address: 12345 Angeleno St.
2	Los Angeles, CA 90010
	Phone: (213) 555-6789
3	Plaintiff in Pro Per

1   Name: LENNY D. LANDLORD
      Address: 12345 Angeleno St.
2   Los Angeles, CA 90010
      Phone: (213) 555-6789
3   Plaintiff in Pro Per

4

5

6

7

8   MUNICIPAL COURT OF CALIFORNIA, COUNTY OF ____LOS ANGELES____

9   ____LOS ANGELES_____ JUDICIAL DISTRICT

10

11   _LENNY D. LANDLORD_____) Case No. __A-12345-B__

)

12   Plaintiff,   ) PROPOSED ORDER

   v.   ) GRANTING MOTION FOR

13   ) SUMMARY JUDGMENT

  TERRENCE D. TENANT, TILLIE D. TENANT)

14   )

     Defendant(s).   )

15 _____)

16

17   Plaintiff's motion for summary judgment came on for hearing

18 in Department _____12_____ of the above-entitled Court on

19 _____September 9_____, 1992_ , said plaintiff appearing in pro per

20 and defendant(s)   not   appearing ~~byx~~ in pro per

21 The matter having been argued and submitted,

22   IT IS HEREBY ORDERED that plaintiff's motion for summary

23 judgment for restitution of the premises the subject of this

24 action, rent and damages in the sum of $___1,120.00___, and costs

25 of suit be, and the same is, granted.

26 DATED: _____, 19___

27   _____

                       JUDGE OF THE MUNICIPAL COURT

28

S A M P L E

1	Name:
	Address: ┌─ list your mailing address and phone number ─┐
2	
	Phone:
3	Plaintiff in Pro Per
4	
5	
6	
7	
8	MUNICIPAL COURT OF CALIFORNIA, COUNTY OF [list county] _____
9	_____ [list judicial district here] _____ JUDICIAL DISTRICT
10	[your name]
11	_____) Case No. [case number] _____
	)
12	Plaintiff,) JUDGMENT
	v.)
13	[defendants' names])
	_____)
14	)
	_____)
15	Defendant(s).)
	_____)
16	The motion of plaintiff for summary judgment having been
17	granted,
18	IT IS HEREBY ORDERED AND ADJUDGED that plaintiff have and
19	recover from defendant(s) ┌ [list names of defendants] _____
20	_____
21	possession and restitution of the real property located at
22	___ [list address, city and county of property] ___, City of _____,
23	County of _____, California, rent and damages
24	in the sum of $_____, plus costs of suit in the sum of
25	$_____ for the total sum of $___ [fill in rent/damages amount and total amount after adding costs]
26	DATED: _____, 19___
27	_____
	JUDGE OF THE MUNICIPAL COURT
28	

S A M P L E

1	Name: LENNY D. LANDLORD
	Address: 12345 Angeleno St.
2	Los Angeles, CA 90010
	Phone: (213) 555-6789
3	Plaintiff in Pro Per
4	
5	
6	
7	MUNICIPAL COURT OF CALIFORNIA, COUNTY OF ____LOS ANGELES____
8	_____LOS ANGELES_____ JUDICIAL DISTRICT
9	
10	__LENNY D. LANDLORD_____) Case No. __A-12345-B__
	)
11	Plaintiff,) JUDGMENT
	v.)
12	)
	TERRENCE D. TENANT, TILLIE D. TENANT)
13	)
	Defendant(s).)
14	_____)
15	
16	The motion of plaintiff for summary judgment having been
17	granted,
18	IT IS HEREBY ORDERED AND ADJUDGED that plaintiff have and
19	recover from defendant(s) ___Terrence D. Tenant and_____
20	Tillie D. Tenant_____
21	possession and restitution of the real property located at
22	_6789 Angel Boulevard, Apt. 10_, City of ___Los Angeles____,
23	County of ___Los Angeles_____, California, rent and damages
24	in the sum of $__1,120.00__, plus costs of suit in the sum of
25	$110.00_ for the total sum of $__1,230.00__.
26	DATED: _____, 19___
27	_____
	JUDGE OF THE MUNICIPAL COURT
28	

ATTORNEY OR PARTY WITHOUT ATTORNEY *(Name and Address)*.	TELEPHONE NO.:	FOR RECORDER'S USE ONLY

☐ Recording requested by and return to:

LENNY D. LANDLORD   (213) 555-6789
12345 Angeleno St.
Los Angeles, CA 90010   Plaintiff in Pro Per

☐ ATTORNEY FOR   ☐ JUDGMENT CREDITOR   ☐ ASSIGNEE OF RECORD

NAME OF COURT: MUNICIPAL COURT OF CALIFORNIA
STREET ADDRESS: COUNTY OF LOS ANGELES,
MAILING ADDRESS: 110 N. Grand Ave.
CITY AND ZIP CODE: Los Angeles, CA 90012
BRANCH NAME: LOS ANGELES JUDICIAL DISTRICT

PLAINTIFF: LENNY D. LANDLORD

DEFENDANT: TERRENCE D. TENANT
TILLIE D. TENANT

WRIT OF

☒ **EXECUTION (Money Judgment)**
☒ **POSSESSION OF** ☐ **Personal Property**
                ☒ **Real Property**
☐ **SALE**

CASE NUMBER:
A 12345 B
FOR COURT USE ONLY

1. **To the Sheriff or any Marshal or Constable of the County of:** Los Angeles

You are directed to enforce the judgment described below with daily interest and your costs as provided by law.

2. **To any registered process server:** You are authorized to serve this writ only in accord with CCP 699.080 or CCP 715.040.

3. *(Name)*: Lenny D. Landlord
is the ☒ judgment creditor ☐ assignee of record
whose address is shown on this form above the court's name.

4. **Judgment debtor** *(name and last known address)*:

Tillie D. Tenant
6789 Angel St., #10
Los Angeles, CA 90010

Terrence D. Tenant
6789 Angel St., #10
Los Angeles, CA 90010

☐ additional judgment debtors on reverse

5. **Judgment entered on** *(date)*: Sept. 9, 1992
6. ☐ **Judgment renewed on** *(dates)*:

7. **Notice of sale** under this writ
   a. ☒ has not been requested.
   b. ☐ has been requested *(see reverse)*.
8. ☐ Joint debtor information on reverse.

[SEAL]

9. ☒ See reverse for information on real or personal property to be delivered under a writ of possession or sold under a writ of sale.
10. ☐ This writ is issued on a sister-state judgment.
11. Total judgment . . . . $ 1,120.00
12. Costs after judgment (per filed order or memo CCP 685.090) . $ .00
13. Subtotal *(add 11 and 12)* . . . . . $ 1,120.00
14. Credits . . . . $ 1,120.00
15. Subtotal *(subtract 14 from 13)* . $
16. Interest after judgment (per filed affidavit CCP 685.050) . . . . . . $ 0.00
17. Fee for issuance of writ . . . . . . $ 3.50
18. Total *(add 15, 16, and 17)* . . . . $ 1,123.50
19. Levying officer: Add daily interest from date of writ *(at the legal rate on 15)* of . . . . $ 0.17

20. ☐ The amounts called for in items 11–19 are different for each debtor. These amounts are stated for each debtor on Attachment 20.

Issued on *(date)*:

Clerk, by _____ , Deputy

— NOTICE TO PERSON SERVED: SEE REVERSE FOR IMPORTANT INFORMATION —

(Continued on reverse)

Form Approved by the
Judicial Council of California
EJ-130 [Rev. September 30, 1991*]

WRIT OF EXECUTION

Code of Civil Procedure, §§ 699.520, 712.010, 715.010
*See note on reverse.

SHORT TITLE:	CASE NUMBER:
— LANDLORD V. TENANT	A 12345 B

Items continued from the first page:

4. ☐ **Additional judgment debtor** *(name and last known address)*:

7. ☐ **Notice of sale** has been requested by *(name and address)*:

8. ☐ **Joint debtor** was declared bound by the judgment (CCP 989–994)
    a. on *(date)*:   a. on *(date)*:
    b. name and address of joint debtor: b. name and address of joint debtor:

    c. ☐ additional costs against certain joint debtors *(itemize)*:

9. ☒ *(Writ of Possession or Writ of Sale)* **Judgment** was entered for the following:
    a. ☒ Possession of real property: The complaint was filed on *(date)*: August 10, 1992 *(Check (1) or (2))*:
        (1) ☐ The Prejudgment Claim of Right to Possession was served in compliance with CCP 415.46.
                The judgment includes all tenants, subtenants, named claimants, and other occupants of the premises.
        (2) ☒ The Prejudgment Claim of Right to Possession was NOT served in compliance with CCP 415.46.
           (a) $ was the daily rental value on the date the complaint was filed.
           (b) The court will hear objections to enforcement of the judgment under CCP 1174.3 on the following
                 dates *(specify)*:
    b. ☐ Possession of personal property
          ☐ If delivery cannot be had, then for the value *(itemize in 9e)* specified in the judgment or supplemental order.
    c. ☐ Sale of personal property
    d. ☐ Sale of real property
    e. Description of property:

        6789 Angel St., #10
        Los Angeles, CA 90010

— NOTICE TO PERSON SERVED —

WRIT OF EXECUTION OR SALE. Your rights and duties are indicated on the accompanying Notice of Levy.
WRIT OF POSSESSION OF PERSONAL PROPERTY. If the levying officer is not able to take custody of the property, the levying officer will make a demand upon you for the property. If custody is not obtained following demand, the judgment may be enforced as a money judgment for the value of the property specified in the judgment or in a supplemental order.
WRIT OF POSSESSION OF REAL PROPERTY. If the premises are not vacated within five days after the date of service on the occupant or, if service is by posting, within five days after service on you, the levying officer will remove the occupants from the real property and place the judgment creditor in possession of the property. Personal property remaining on the premises will be sold or otherwise disposed of in accordance with CCP 1174 unless you or the owner of the property pays the judgment creditor the reasonable cost of storage and takes possession of the personal property not later than 15 days after the time the judgment creditor takes possession of the premises.
► *A Claim of Right to Possession form accompanies this writ (unless the Summons was served in compliance with CCP 415.46).*

---

* *NOTE*: Continued use of form EJ-130 (Rev. Jan. 1, 1989) is authorized until June 30, 1992, *except* if used as a Writ of Possession of Real Property.

EJ 130 (Rev. September 30, 1991*)   **WRIT OF EXECUTION**   Page two

Try to find out whether or not the tenant has filed a written response to your motion. The fact that you didn't receive a copy of any response in the mail doesn't prove anything, because the law seems to allow the tenant to file a response at any time before the hearing. If the tenant appears at the hearing, it won't hurt to walk up and ask if he filed a response to your papers. If the answer is yes, ask for a copy. Also, if you can fight your way through all the attorneys clustered around the courtroom clerk, ask her to check the file to see if there's a response. If there is, ask to see it. Assuming the judge doesn't have the file in her chambers, the clerk will hand it to you. If the tenant has filed a response to your motion, the papers should be at the top of the papers in the file, just above your motion papers. Look for any "declaration" or "affidavit" that contradicts your declaration. If there isn't one, you will probably win the motion by default. On the other hand, if the tenant has submitted a declaration, the judge will most likely have to rule that there is a "triable issue of fact" presented by the tenant's papers and that summary judgment is therefore improper. The judge will not attempt to decide at this time which side's statements are true—that's the trial's function. The fact that there is a contradiction is enough to defeat your motion and necessitate a trial.

When your case is called, step forward. Some judges prefer to ask questions, but others prefer that the person bringing the motion (you) start talking first. If the tenant has not filed a declaration, you should politely point out to the judge that:

- C.C.P. § 1170.7 requires the judge to grant a summary judgment motion in an unlawful detainer case on the same basis as in regular civil cases under § 437c; and

- C.C.P. § 437c requires the judge to rule based only on what the declarations or affidavits of the parties say, not what the tenant says at the hearing; and therefore

- If the tenant hasn't filed a declaration, your motion should be granted, regardless of what arguments the tenant advances.

Say this in your own words, and don't be nervous. If the tenant has filed papers in response to your motion, be prepared to point out that the tenant's declaration doesn't contradict yours (if this is so), or perhaps even that the tenant's papers aren't in the proper legal form of a declaration under penalty of perjury (if that's correct). If the tenant tries to file the papers right there at the hearing, and you haven't received copies, you should let the judge know and ask to see what the tenant is filing. You may want to ask the judge to pass your case for a few minutes while you review the response.

After the tenant or his lawyer has had a chance to argue his side, the judge will either rule on the motion or take the matter "under submission." (In some cases, the judge will grant a one-week continuance or postponement to a tenant who states a credible defense but hasn't come up with a written declaration.) If the judge denies the motion, you will have to wait until trial to get a judgment. If the judge grants the motion, present your proposed order and judgment for him to sign. Once that's done, you can have the clerk issue a writ of execution, which is then forwarded to the sheriff to begin the eviction. (See Chapter 7, Section C4.)

F.   Other Pre-Trial Complications

Between the time you file a Memorandum To Set Case for Trial and the date set for trial, the tenant may file legal documents requiring action on your part. They can include the following:

1.   Countermemo To Set/Jury Demand

Many tenants think it is in their interest to demand a jury trial. They are often right. Not only does this delay scheduling of the case, but (in certain areas) it sometimes guarantees an audience more receptive to the tenant's arguments and less skeptical than a case-worn judge.

The tenant can ask for a jury trial with a document called a "jury demand" or in a "counter-memorandum," a response to your Memorandum To Set. There is normally nothing you can do to avoid a jury trial if the tenant demands it and pays the jury fees in advance.

If a jury trial is demanded, it is wise for you to seek legal representation. In a jury trial, a complex set of rules governs what evidence the jury may hear. It's very difficult for a nonlawyer to competently deal with these rules. In a trial before a judge without a jury, things are much simpler because judges, who know the rules themselves, just disregard evidence that it is improper for them to consider.

2. Discovery Requests

One of the biggest surprises to many nonlawyers about the legal system is that in all civil cases, including eviction lawsuits, each side has the right to force the other side to disclose, before trial, any relevant information it has about the case. Discovery is most often initiated by lawyers, not by tenants representing themselves, and if your tenant is represented by a lawyer, you may want to be too (see Section B, above). This following brief discussion of discovery techniques is just to give you an overview.

a. Depositions

In very rare instances, a tenant's lawyer may mail you a document that instructs you to show up at the lawyer's office and answer questions under oath about the case at a "deposition." The tenant's lawyer's questions and your responses to them are taken down by a court reporter. Any of your answers can be used against you later at trial. You must pay the court reporter a fairly hefty fee for a copy of the transcript, typically about a dollar for each double-spaced page; if you win the lawsuit, this sum is recoverable in the judgment as a court cost.

The rules on the types of questions the lawyer is allowed to ask are fairly complicated. The basic rule is that you must answer any question that might lead the tenant's lawyer to the discovery of relevant evidence. Your refusal to answer a proper question or to attend a deposition after proper notification can be punished by a

court-ordered fine, if the other side requests it, or, in extreme cases, by dismissal of your case.

b. Interrogatories and Requests for Admissions

Another far more common way the tenant may obtain relevant information is to mail you questions called "interrogatories." They may be typed or may be entered on a standard form provided by the court clerk. You are required to answer all interrogatories within 35 days if they're mailed to you (30 days if they are personally served), or by five days before trial, whichever comes first. As with depositions, the rules about the type of questions you have to answer are fairly technical, but basically you have to respond to all questions that might lead the other side to relevant information.

"Requests for Admissions" are something like interrogatories, but instead of having to make a possibly detailed response to a particular question, you have only to admit or deny statements put to you by the other side.

Because admission or denial of a key statement can be used against your position in court, you must be very careful in answering each request. Your failure to answer (or to answer on time) is equivalent to admitting that all the statements are true. This can be extremely damaging, if not fatal, to your case.

c. Requests To Produce and/or Inspect

A third discovery device is the "Request To Produce and/or Inspect." This is a written request that you produce specified documents, books or other records for inspection and copying by the other party, on a certain date and time. The party receiving the notice usually makes photocopies and mails them, rather than waiting for the other party or attorney to show up to inspect the records.

You must respond within five days, and produce the documents for actual inspection within ten days. Again, the rules on the type of material that can be requested this way are technical, but generally any records which can lead to relevant information can be sought.

If the tenant seeks to have you produce sensitive or confidential business records that you do not believe are directly relevant to the proceeding, see a lawyer.

So far we have assumed that the discovery was initiated by the tenant. However, you can also use discovery to obtain information relating to the tenant's defense of the case. While this is not normally necessary, there are always exceptional cases. For example, you might want the tenant claiming a bogus habitability defense to admit she didn't complain to you or anyone else about the condition of the property until after you insisted on receiving the rent. Unfortunately, the special skills involved in properly drafting interrogatories and requests for admissions and in conducting depositions are beyond the scope of this book.

If you think you need to utilize discovery to find out more about the tenant's defense, consult an attorney.

G. Preparing for Trial

Preparing a case for trial, and handling the trial itself, are both very difficult subjects to handle in a self-help law book. Few eviction cases go to trial, but each case has its own unpredictable twists and turns that can greatly affect trial preparation and tactics. Simply put, there is no way for us to guide you step-by-step through this process. For this reason, we believe you will probably elect to bring a lawyer into the case, assuming you are still doing it yourself, to assist with the preparation for and conduct of the trial.

Here we provide you with a basic overview of what needs to be done for and at the trial so that you will know what to expect and better be able to assist your lawyer.

If the tenant filed an answer to your complaint, and the court has set the case for trial but you think the tenant has moved out and might not show up for trial, prepare for trial anyway. First, the tenant might not have actually moved out, and you're safer waiting to get a judgment before retaking possession (unless, of course, you've settled the case and the tenant has returned the keys). Second, unless you and the tenant have settled the case, you'll still want to get the money part of the judgment. Third, if you don't show for trial—and the tenant does—the tenant will win and be entitled to move back in and to collect costs from you.

1. What You Have To Prove at Trial

What you must prove at trial obviously depends on the issues raised in your complaint and the tenant's answer. For example, the testimony in a case based on nonpayment of rent where the tenant's defense is that you failed to keep the premises habitable will be very different from that in a case based on termination of a month-to-month tenancy by 30-day notice where the tenant denies receiving the notice.

All contested evictions are similar, however, in that you, the plaintiff, have to do two things in order to win. First, you have to establish the basic elements of your case; this means you have to present hard evidence (usually through documents or live testimony) of the basic facts that would cause the judge to rule in your favor if the tenant didn't present a defense. If you don't produce evidence on every essential factual issue contested by the tenant in his answer, the tenant can win the case by pointing this out to the judge right after you "rest" your case. This is done by the tenant making a "motion for judgment" after you have presented your evidence and closed your case.

The second thing you have to do is provide an adequate response to any rebuttal or defense the tenant presents. For example, the tenant may say he didn't have to pay the rent because you didn't fix the leaky roof, overflowing toilet or defective water heater. You should counter with whatever facts relieve you of this responsibility. This might be that you kept the premises habitable or that the tenant didn't tell you about the defects until well after you began to ask about the late rent. (See *Volume 1*, Chapter 11, on the landlord's duty to keep the property habitable.)

2. Elements of Your Case

If the tenant has denied everything in your complaint, you will have to prove your case. To give you some idea of what is required, we set out the legal elements that must be proved for various types of eviction below. Also remember that if the tenant has admitted an element, you don't have to prove it. For example, if the tenant's answer admits that your allegations in paragraph 9 of the complaint are true, and you alleged in that paragraph that the tenant was served with a three-day notice on a certain date, you don't have to present testimony to prove it.

Okay, now find the symbol representing your type of eviction and review the elements that you will have to prove.

❷ **Eviction for Nonpayment of Rent**

- You, your agent, or the person from whom you purchased the property (or her agent) rented the property to the tenant pursuant to an oral or written agreement.
- The monthly rent was a certain amount.
- The tenant got behind in the rent, so that she owed a certain amount.
- The tenant was properly served with a Three-Day Notice To Pay Rent or Quit.
- The notice demanded that the tenant pay the exact amount of rent due or leave within three days.
- The tenant neither paid the amount demanded in the notice nor left within three days (plus any extensions allowed if the third day fell on a weekend or holiday).
- The tenant is still in possession of the property.
- You have complied with any applicable rent control or just cause eviction ordinances and regulations.

❸ **Eviction for Termination of Month-to-Month Tenancy**

- You, your agent, etc., rented the property to the tenant.
- The tenancy is month-to-month, having either started out that way or having become month-to-month after a fixed-term lease expired.
- If a local rent control or eviction ordinance requires "just cause" for terminating a month-to-month tenancy, that the reason you give for termination is true, and that you've complied with all aspects of the ordinance and any applicable regulations.
- The tenant was served with a written notice requiring that he leave, and giving him at least 30 days to do so.
- The 30-day (or longer) period has expired, and the tenant is still in possession of the property.

❹ **Eviction for Violation of Lease/Nuisance/Waste**

- You, your agent, etc., rented the property to the tenant.

- The lease or rental agreement contains a valid clause requiring the tenant to do something (for example, pay a security deposit installment by a certain date) or to refrain from doing something (like having pets or subletting the property), and the tenant has violated the clause; or

- The tenant seriously damaged the property, used it unlawfully or created a legal nuisance.

- The tenant was served with a three-day notice demanding that she vacate the property within that time, or, if the violation was correctable, that the tenant correct it within that time.

- The tenant neither vacated the property nor corrected the problem (if correctable) after the three days, plus any extensions.

- The tenant is still in possession of the property.

- You have complied with applicable rent control or just cause eviction ordinances or regulations.

3. Assessing and Countering the Tenant's Defenses

If the tenant raised any affirmative defenses in his answer, you must be ready to counter them at trial.

As we have emphasized, trying to assess and counter these defenses can be extremely risky unless you are experienced in doing so. Even if you otherwise feel competent to conduct your own trial, you should bring in a lawyer to help you with this aspect of the case. (See Section B, above.)

a. Habitability Defense

The "habitability defense" is commonly raised in evictions for nonpayment of rent. If the tenant's answer states that his rent payment was partly or entirely excused be-cause you kept the property in poor repair, you should first read Chapter 11 in Volume 1, on landlords' duties to keep rental property in good repair. If in fact you haven't properly maintained the property, the tenant may win the lawsuit. To win, the tenant must prove to the judge that you "breached" (violated) a "warranty," which is implied by law, to provide the tenant with "habitable" (reasonably livable) premises in exchange for the rent. You don't have to prove that you properly maintained the property; rather, the tenant has to prove to the judge's satisfaction that you didn't make needed repairs.

To establish that you breached the implied warranty of habitability, the tenant must prove that:

- You failed to provide one or more of the minimum "tenantability" requirements, including waterproofing, a working toilet, adequate heating and electricity, and hot and cold running water. (Civ. Code § 1941.1);

- The defects were serious and substantial;

- The tenant or some other person (such as a health department inspector) notified you (or your manager) about the defect before you served the three-day notice to pay rent; and

- You failed to make repairs within a reasonable time.

Once the tenant makes the showing described above, you must show a valid excuse for allowing the deficiency to continue. If you can convince the judge that the problems the tenant is complaining about are either non-habitability-related (such as old interior paint, carpets or drapes) or minor (dripping but working faucets, cracked windows, etc.), or that the tenant didn't complain until receiving the three-day notice, you will have knocked one or more holes in the tenant's habitability defense.

If the tenant produces evidence showing that you failed to make required repairs within 60 days after receiving written notice to do so from a health department or other official following an inspection of the property by that person, the burden shifts to you to show that you had a good reason for not making the repair. (See *Volume 1*, Chapter 11.) (Civ. Code § 1941.3.)

b. Other Defenses

Other defenses tenants often raise include:

- Discrimination on the basis of race, sex, or children (see *Volume 1*, Chapter 9);

- Retaliation for the tenant's exercise of a legal right such as complaining to the building inspector or organizing other tenants (see *Volume 1*, Chapter 15);

- The landlord's breach of an express promise to make repairs, or other misconduct. or

- Failure to comply with the requirements of a local rent control ordinance (see Volume 1, Chapter 4, and your "home" chapter—either Chapter 2, 3, 4 or 5—in this volume).

4. Preparing the Judgment Form

When you go to trial you should have a judgment form ready for the judge to sign if she rules in your favor. Some courts have their own forms; others let you use your own. Below are sample judgment forms from San Diego and San Francisco, and a Nolo judgment form, which should be acceptable in most places. Call the clerk of the court to find out what form you must use. The Appendix includes a blank copy of Nolo's Judgment After Trial Form.

H. The Trial

As the plaintiff, you have the burden of proving to the judge (or jury if it's a jury trial) that you are entitled to the relief requested in your complaint. You present your case first.

Much of your case will consist of two types of evidence: your testimony, and documents which you offer to prove one or more of your points. In addition, you may want to bring in witnesses.

Once you have met your "burden of proof," it is the tenant's turn. To defeat your case the tenant must offer testimony and/or documents to:

- Convince the judge (the jury, if it's a jury trial) that your proof on one or more issues was wrong or deficient; or

- Prove that one of her affirmative defenses is valid.

After the tenant has put on her case, you will have an opportunity to rebut the tenant's case. After your rebuttal, both you and the tenant can summarize your cases. The case is then submitted to the judge or jury for its verdict. If you win, you will be entitled to evict the tenant unless the tenant appeals the verdict and obtains a stay of the eviction pending the appeal. Also, it is possible for the tenant to request a new trial and an order barring the eviction because of hardship.

Now let's take a minute to go into a little more detail on the procedures outlined above.

1. The Clerk Calls the Case

The trial begins when the clerk calls your case by name, usually by calling out the last name of the parties (for example, in the case of *Lenny D. Landlord v. Terrence and Tillie Tenant*, "*Landlord v. Tenant*"). As mentioned, since you're the plaintiff, you present your case first, when the judge asks you to begin.

2. Last-Minute Motions

Before you begin your case, the tenant may make a last-minute motion, perhaps for a continuance or postponement of the trial, or to disqualify the judge. A party to a lawsuit is allowed to disqualify one judge—even at the last minute—simply by filing a declaration under penalty of perjury that states a belief that the judge is prejudiced. (C.C.P. § 170.6.) Unlawful detainer defendants frequently use this procedure to disqualify judges notoriously unsympathetic to tenants' defenses or sometimes just to delay things. Landlords rarely use this procedure, even against somewhat pro-tenant judges, due to their desire to get the trial moving.

It isn't too likely that the judge will agree to postpone the trial. If the tenant disqualifies the judge, however, the case must be transferred to another judge or postponed if no other judge is available.

Another frequent last-minute motion is one to "exclude witnesses." If you or the tenant so requests, witnesses (but not parties) will be required to leave the courtroom until it's their turn to testify. This prevents witnesses from patterning their testimony after other witnesses on their side they see testify. If you are your only witness and the tenant comes in with a string of friends to testify to what a slumlord you are, you can at least minimize the damage by insisting that each be kept out while the others testify. Remember, however, that a motion to exclude works both ways. If you ask the judge to exclude the tenant's witnesses, your witnesses must also wait in the corridor.

The Courtroom

Unlawful detainer trials are conducted in courtrooms that look much like those on television. In addition to the judge, a clerk and bailiff are normally present. They sit at tables immediately in front of the judge's elevated bench, or slightly off to the side. The clerk's job is to keep the judge supplied with the necessary files and papers and to make sure that the proceedings flow smoothly. A clerk is not the same as a court reporter, who keeps a word-by-word record of the proceedings. In most municipal courts, a reporter is not present unless either party insists on (and pays for) one. The bailiff, usually a uniformed deputy sheriff or marshal, is present to keep order.

Courtrooms are divided about two-thirds of the way toward the front by a sort of fence known as "the bar." The judge, court personnel and lawyers use the area on one side of the bar, and the public, including parties and witnesses waiting to be called, sits on the other side. You're invited to cross the bar only when your case is called by the clerk, and any witnesses you have may do so only when you call them to testify. You then come forward and sit at the long table (the one closest to the empty jury box) known as the "counsel table," facing the judge.

---

3. Opening Statements

Both you and the tenant have a right to make an opening statement at the start of the trial. Chances are that the judge has heard many cases like yours, so that an opening statement would be a fruitless exercise. If you do make a statement, keep it very brief. Say what you're going to prove, but don't start proving it, and above all, don't argue all the points. Here's what an opening statement in a nonpayment of rent case might sound like:

"Your honor, this is an unlawful detainer action based on nonpayment of rent. Mr. Tenant's answer admits the fact of the lease, and that the monthly rent is $550, due on the first of the month, but denies everything else. I will testify to my receipt of previous rents, so that the balance due the day the three-day notice was served was $850. I will also testify that I served the three-day notice to pay rent or quit on Mr. Tenant, who was never home or at work went I went there, by posting a copy of it on the door and mailing a second copy to his home, and that later when I called him he admitted having received it. Finally, I will testify that he didn't pay the rent within three days after that, and of course, is still in possession."

4. Presenting Your Case

There are two ways you can offer testimony to prove the disputed elements of your case. The most common is to testify yourself.

As you may know from old Perry Mason episodes, parties to lawsuits usually testify in response to questions posed by their own lawyer. This is called "direct examination" (as opposed to "cross-examination," when the other side asks you questions). If you represent yourself this is done by simply recounting the relevant facts.

Your testimony should be very much like that you would give at a default hearing. (See Chapter 7, Section E.) If the tenant's answer admits certain of your allegations, such as the basic terms of the tenancy or service of the three-day or 30-day notice, you can leave that part out, having noted in your opening remarks that it's not disputed.

S A M P L E

```
 1   Name:
     Address:    [ list your mailing address and phone number ]
 2
     Phone:
 3   Plaintiff in Pro Per
 4
 5
 6
 7
 8       MUNICIPAL COURT OF CALIFORNIA, COUNTY OF _____ [ list county ] _____
 9       _____ [ list judicial district here ] _____ JUDICIAL DISTRICT
10
11       ___ [ your name ] _____ )  Case No. __ [ case number ] __
                                                    )
12          Plaintiff,                              )  JUDGMENT AFTER TRIAL
     v.                                             )
13                                                  )
14       ___ [ defendants' names ] _____   )
                                                    )
15          Defendant(s).                           )
     _____          )
16
17       The above-entitled cause came on for trial on
18   _____ [ list date of trial ] _____, 19___ in courtroom No.____ of the
19                                   [ list name of trial judge and courtroom number ]
     above-entitled Court, the Hon. _____
20
21   presiding, plaintiff appearing in pro per and defendant(s)
         [ indicate whether defendants or their attorneys—or no one—showed up at trial ]
22   _____
23       ( ) not appearing
24       ( ) appearing in pro per
25
26       ( ) appearing by attorney(s): _____.
27       Jury trial having been waived, and the Court having heard the
28   testimony and considered the evidence,
```

1
2
IT IS HEREBY ORDERED AND ADJUDGED that the above-entitled

3
plairtiff have and recover from the said defendant(s) possession

4
of the real property described as _____ list property address, city and county _____

5
_____,

6
City of _____, County of _____,

7
California, rent and damages in the sum of $_____, and

8
9
costs in the sum of $_____. list total rent/damages amount and total including costs

10
DATED: _____, 19____

11
                            _____
                            JUDGE OF THE MUNICIPAL COURT

12
13
leave date and signature lines blank for judge to sign

14
15
16
17
18
19
20
21
22
23
24
25
26
27
28

S A M P L E

```
 1   Name: LENNY D. LANDLORD
     Address: 12345 Angeleno St.
 2   Los Angeles, CA 90010
     Phone:  (213) 555-6789
 3   Plaintiff in Pro Per

 4

 5

 6

 7

 8      MUNICIPAL COURT OF CALIFORNIA, COUNTY OF ____LOS ANGELES_____

 9         _____LOS ANGELES_____  JUDICIAL DISTRICT

10

11   ____LENNY D. LANDLORD_____  )  Case No. __A-12345-B__
                                           )
12        Plaintiff,                       )  JUDGMENT AFTER TRIAL
     v.                                    )
13                                         )
     TERRENCE D. TENANT, et al.,           )
14   _____     )
                                           )
15        Defendant(s).                    )
     _____     )

16

17      The above-entitled cause came on for trial on

18   _____September 20,_____, 19_92_ in courtroom No._25_ of the

19
     above-entitled Court, the Hon. __Julia Judge_____
20
     presiding, plaintiff appearing in pro per and defendant(s)
21
      Terrence D. Tenant and Tillie D. Tenant_____
22
23        ( ) not appearing
24
          (x) appearing in pro per
25
          ( ) appearing by attorney(s): _____.
26
27      Jury trial having been waived, and the Court having heard the
28   testimony and considered the evidence,
```

1   IT IS HEREBY ORDERED AND ADJUDGED that the above-entitled

2 plaintiff have and recover from the said defendant(s) possession

3 of the real property described as   6789 Angel Blvd., Apt. 10

4

5 _____,

6 City of   Los Angeles   , County of   Los Angeles   ,

7 California, rent and damages in the sum of $ 1,120.00 , and

8 costs in the sum of $ 110.00 .

9

10 DATED: _____, 19___

11   _____

                                 JUDGE OF THE MUNICIPAL COURT

12

13

14

15

16

17

18

19

20

21

22

23

24

25

26

27

28

S A M P L E

<table>
<tr>
<td>NAME AND ADDRESS OF ATTORNEY:

PAULA PLAINTIFF
123 Sunshine Street
La Jolla, CA

Plaintiff in Pro Per</td>
<td>TELEPHONE NO.:

(619) 555-1234</td>
<td>For Court use only:</td>
</tr>
</table>

MUNICIPAL COURT OF CALIFORNIA, COUNTY OF SAN DIEGO
SAN DIEGO JUDICIAL DISTRICT
220 W. Broadway, San Diego, California 92101

PLAINTIFF (ABBREVIATED)

PAULA PLAINTIFF

DEFENDANT (ABBREVIATED)

DARLENE DEFENDANT

JUDGMENT AFTER TRIAL BY COURT UNLAWFUL DETAINER	CASE NUMBER 12345

This cause came on regularly for trial on ....January 15, 1992.........., at ..2:00 P....... before Judge ...Adam Adjudicator... plaintiff(s) appearing by attorney ...XXXX....in pro per... and defendant(s) appearing by attorney ...XXXX.......in pro per.. and a jury trial having been duly waived, the Court having heard the testimony and considered the evidence, and findings ..not................. having been requested, ..., the Court ordered the following Judgment: that plaintiff(s) .....Paula Plaintiff... recover from defendant(s) ....Darlene Defendant..

the restitution and possession of those certain premises situated, lying and being in the City and County of San Diego, State of California, and is described as follow:
......456 Renter Court, San Diego, California...

And that the lease or agreement under which said defendant(s) hold(s) said premises, be and the same is hereby declared forfeited, void and of no effect.

It is further Ordered that said plaintiff(s) recover from said defendant(s) the sum of

$.............550.00.....Damages,

$....................00.....Attorney fees

together with $............110.00.....Costs

Date:...

Entered in Judgment Book No. ....

Page................................

on ....

_____
Judge of Said Court

CLERK OF COURT

By _____, Deputy

JUDGMENT AFTER TRIAL BY COURT—UNLAWFUL DETAINER

SDMC 11 (Rev. 5-75)   CCP 664

S A M P L E

MCF 38
6 - 76
Name, Address, and Telephone No. of Attorney(s)
PRISCILLA PROPERTYOWNER
123 Prudence Place
San Mateo, CA
Tel: (415) 555-1234
~~Attorney(s)~~ for XX Plaintiff in Pro Per

JUDGMENT AFTER TRIAL BY COURT	IN **THE MUNICIPAL COURT** OF THE CITY AND COUNTY OF SAN FRANCISCO, STATE OF CALIFORNIA	Case Number SF-12345

PRISCILLA PROPERTYOWNER ....   vs.   .... TED TENANT

.............**Plaintiff(s)**...........   ....**Defendant(s)**...........

In Dept. ____15____, Honorable _____Julius Judge_____, **Judge Presiding.**

This cause came on regularly for trial on October 10, 1992

Plaintiff(s)   appearing by attorney(s)   in pro per

Defendant(s)   appearing by attorney(s)   Aaron Arnold

and a jury trial having been duly waived, the Court having heard the testimony and considered the evidence, and findings not **having been requested**

THE COURT ORDERED THE FOLLOWING JUDGMENT.

   It is adjudged that Priscilla Propertyowner

recover from

            Ted Tenant possession of the premises at 456 Main Street, City
            and County of San Francisco, and

        $600.00 principal $0 attorney fee $0 interest $110.00 costs

                                                      Approved:

                                         ....
                                                      Judge of the Municipal Court
Date entered: ....   I certify this to be a true copy of
                                                            the judgement on file in the judgement
Entered in Judgement Bk. Vol.............Page ....   book.

Clerk of the Municipal Court,   **Clerk of the Municipal Court,**

By ....   By ....
                                        Deputy   **Deputy**

After you've finished testifying, the tenant or her lawyer may cross-examine you. The general rule is that you, like any other witness, can be cross-examined on anything relating to your testimony on direct examination. You should respond courteously, truthfully and as briefly as possible. Contrary to popular myth, you don't have to give a "yes" or "no" answer to any question for which it would be inappropriate. You have a right to explain and expand on your answer in detail if you feel it's necessary. For example, the question, "Have you stopped pocketing security deposits?" is best answered by, "I have never 'pocketed' a deposit," rather than by "yes" or "no."

Don't appear hostile toward the person doing the cross-examining; it could hurt your case. If you have a lawyer, he has the right to object to any question that is abusive or irrelevant. If you are representing yourself and consider a question to be particularly awful, ask the judge if you have to answer it.

EXAMPLE
After you've finished testifying, the tenant begins cross-examining you with, "Ms. Landlord, didn't you remember my telling you I couldn't pay the rent because I lost my job?" Since the issue of the tenant's hardship isn't a legal defense to failure to pay rent, it's legally irrelevant, and your lawyer should say, "Your honor, I object to this question as irrelevant." The judge should "sustain" this objection, meaning you don't have to answer.

If the case is tried by a judge, objections on the ground of relevancy are often overruled by the judge, who figures her training equips her to sort out the wheat from the chaff when decision time comes around. This discrepancy between legal rules and the real world is one example among thousands of why doing your own trial is not advised.

Another way to prove part or all of the disputed elements of your case is by questioning the tenant at the start. The law allows you to call the defendant as a witness before you or any of your own witnesses testify. (Evid. Code § 776.)

Handled properly, the tenant will testify truthfully, if reluctantly, so as to establish most or all of the basic elements of your lawsuit, even if he denied these elements in the answer. Here's an example of such an exchange:

Landlord: Mr. Tenant, you rented the premises at 123 State Street, Los Angeles, from me, didn't you?

Tenant: Yes.

Landlord: And that was in March 1992, correct?

Tenant: Yes.

Landlord: I'd like to show you a copy of this document entitled "Rental Agreement," attached as Exhibit "A" to the complaint. This is your signature here at the bottom, isn't it?

Tenant: Well . . . yeah.

Landlord: You paid the monthly rent of $550 until August 1992, didn't you?

Tenant: Well yeah, but in July I got laid off, and . . .

Landlord: Please just answer the question, Mr. Tenant.

Tenant: Yeah.

Landlord: And you didn't pay the $550 rent in August 1992, did you?

Tenant: Well, no.

Landlord: And I'd like to show you a copy of this document entitled "3-Day Notice To Pay Rent or Quit" attached as Exhibit "B" to the complaint. You told me on August 5 when I phoned you that you received the notice, didn't you?

Tenant: Yeah.

Landlord: And you, in fact, did receive it, correct?

Tenant: Yes.

Landlord: And you're still living in the premises, aren't you?

Tenant: Yes.

Landlord: I have no further questions, your honor.

You should also call other witnesses to testify about basic elements of your case that you were unable to cover, or that will likely be disputed by the tenant (such as service of a three-day notice served by a person other than yourself). After the clerk swears your witness in, he may only answer questions asked by you, unless the judge allows narrative testimony and the tenant doesn't object.

5. The Tenant's Case

After you and your witnesses have testified and been cross-examined, it's the tenant's turn to present evidence to contradict you on any of the elements of your case or to present defenses. He can testify himself and/or call other persons (even you) to testify.

After the tenant and any of his witnesses have testified, your lawyer may cross-examine them on any issue raised in their testimony.

6. Your Rebuttal

You now have a second chance to testify and to have any witnesses testify, to respond to denials or points raised by the tenant in his defense. This is called the "rebuttal" phase of the trial. The rules are the same as those for your earlier testimony, with one important difference. The only subjects you may go into on rebuttal are those addressed by the tenant or his witnesses. The purpose is to rebut what they said, not to raise other issues. For example, this is the time to testify that the problems the tenant complains about are fairly minor or that he never asked you to make repairs until after you served a three-day notice. Again, the tenant may cross-examine you and your witnesses.

7. Closing Arguments

After both sides have presented their testimony, each is allowed to make a brief closing argument to the judge. The plaintiff goes first.

8. The Judge's Decision

After the closing statements, the judge decides the case. Some judges do not announce their decision in court, but rather take the case "under submission" or "under advisement." This may mean that the judge wants to think the matter over before deciding. If this happens, you will be notified of the result by mail.

If the judge announces a decision in your favor, you should produce your prepared judgment form for the judge to sign, fill in the dollar amount awarded and hand it to the clerk.

I. The Writ of Execution and Having the Sheriff or Marshal Evict

To have the clerk issue a writ of execution after trial, simply hand the original writ form to the court clerk after the judgment is signed and pay a writ issuance fee. (See Chapter 7, Sections C and D for instructions on how to fill out the writ form and what happens before and during the eviction.) The writ will be for both the money and possession parts of the judgment. A sample writ for both the possession and money parts of the judgment (following a summary judgment) is shown in Chapter 7, Section D2. A writ to enforce a judgment obtained after trial is filled out the same way. Take the original and copies of the writ to the sheriff or marshal (or constable, in justice court districts), along with appropriate instructions for evicting. (See Chapter 7, Section D.) We discuss collecting the money part of the judgment in the next chapter.

After the sheriff or marshal has evicted the tenant and turned possession of your property back over to you, you may find yourself stuck with property the tenant has left behind. You should not simply throw away or otherwise dispose of the property, nor should you refuse to return it because the tenant won't pay what he owes you. You do have the right to insist the tenant pay reasonable storage charges, and to hold onto the property if the tenant won't pay that. However, most of the time doing so isn't worth the trouble, and you'll be happier just to get rid of the stuff by turning it over to the tenant, no strings attached. If you wind up with property the tenant won't reclaim, you will have to hold onto it for at least 18 days, notify the tenant by mail that she can pick up the property, and auction it off if it's worth more than $300. (C.C.P. § 1174.) We discuss this at length in *Volume 1*, Chapter 21.

J. Appeals

The losing party can appeal the judgment of the municipal or justice court to the "Appellate Department" of the superior court for the county within 30 days of the date of the judgment.

On appeal, you or the tenant may argue only issues of law, not fact. For example, the tenant may argue that the trial court erred in refusing to hear evidence on the tenant's retaliation defense, since he was behind in the rent. This is a legal issue. But the tenant may not argue that the judge or jury was wrong in believing that you didn't retaliate against the tenant for calling the health department. This is an issue of fact. Similarly, you could argue on appeal that the judge erred in ruling your three-day notice was invalid because it didn't list all the tenants' names—an issue of law. But you couldn't argue that the judge shouldn't have believed the tenant who claimed never to have received the three-day notice—an issue of fact.

Appeals are very technical and time-consuming. You should contact a lawyer before undertaking an appeal.

1. Appeals by the Landlord

It very seldom makes sense for a landlord to appeal a tenant's victory. Landlords who lose unlawful detainer cases generally do so because of rulings on factual issues; for example, the judge rules that the landlord didn't properly maintain the premises or had illegal retaliation in mind when he gave the tenant a 30-day notice. As we saw above, an appeals court will not reconsider the factual rulings made by the trial judge, and an appeal of this sort of ruling is a waste of time. When landlords do lose cases on legal issues that might be argued on appeal, it is usually for technical reasons, such as the three-day notice not being in the correct form. In these cases, it usually makes more sense for the landlord, instead of filing an appeal that will likely take at least three months, to go back and correct the mistake. For example, the landlord would prepare and serve a new, proper three-day notice and begin a new unlawful detainer lawsuit.

2. Appeals by the Tenant

Most appeals of unlawful detainer judgments are by tenants, and many of these appeals seem designed to prolong the tenant's stay as long as possible. Filing an appeal, however, does not automatically "stay" (delay) enforcement of your judgment for possession of the property and rent. However, a tenant who files an appeal can ask the court for a stay pending the appeal if he is willing to pay the rent during the period of the stay.

The appeal is initiated when the tenant files a notice of appeal in the trial court. This is a simple one-page document which says nothing more than that the tenant appeals the judgment. After the tenant files the notice of appeal, he can obtain a stay only by filing a motion, which must be heard by the same judge who ruled against him. Trial judges routinely deny requests for stays and will grant them only if the tenant appears to be basing the appeal on a genuine legal issue, rather than simply stalling for time. If a tenant files a motion for a stay, you should receive written notice to appear in court to oppose the motion. In any event, a judge who grants a stay is required to order that as a condition of the stay, the tenant must pay the monthly rent to the court. (C.C.P. § 1176(a).)

Whether or not a stay is granted, the tenant must prepare more documents. First, she must pay a court reporter to prepare a transcript of the trial proceedings, or file a narrative "proposed statement" of what occurred at trial. After that, the case is transferred to the appellate court, and the tenant files a "brief," her argument about why the trial judge erred. At each stage, you will be notified by mail and required to file papers of your own in response. ■

Collecting Your Money Judgment

After you obtain a judgment for possession of property in your unlawful detainer action, you also are awarded at least some amount of money (if only for court costs). Unfortunately, having a judgment for the payment of money is not the same as having the money itself. It is unlikely that the ex-tenant you have just evicted will be both able and willing to pay you just because you converted your legal right to be paid into a formal court order.

Nothing will happen—that is, you won't get paid—unless you pursue your claim. In fact, a judgment for money is really little more than a sort of court-sanctioned hunting license, good for ten years (and renewable for subsequent ten-year periods), that allows you to use certain techniques to collect the debt. This chapter shows you a few of those techniques.

For a much more thorough guide to finding assets, devising a collection plan and collecting your judgment, see *Collect Your Court Judgment*, by Scott, Elias and Goldoftas (Nolo Press).

Collecting from Co-Tenants. For convenience, we talk about judgments in this chapter as if they were against only one person. Many times, though, a landlord will get a money judgment against two or more people, usually co-tenants under the same rental agreement. You have the right to pursue all the debtors or just the one(s) who have assets to seize until you collect the entire amount. This is because all the debtors are said to be "jointly and severally" liable to you.

EXAMPLE

Because the two tenants you sued for nonpayment of rent, Larry and Moe, were co-tenants under the same written lease, you obtained a judgment against both of them. Since Larry is unemployed, you garnished Moe's wages and eventually collected the entire amount from him. This is okay; the fact that Moe wound up paying it all is between him and Larry.

A. Collection Strategy

Before you start trying to collect the money the tenant owes you, take a minute to assess your chances of success and devise a strategy for proceeding.

1. Your Chances of Collecting

Some assets are easier to grab than others. Generally, you should try to go after assets in this order:

- the tenant's security deposit
- the tenant's paycheck or bank account
- the tenant's personal property (car, furniture).

In general, if you can't collect from the tenant's pay or bank account, you're probably out of luck. Most of the tenant's personal possessions are probably exempt, by law, from being seized to pay a court judgment.

Second, the sale of personal property, including vehicles, will often net you less than the expenses you'll have to front the sheriff for storage and auction costs. In other words, you'll wind up losing money.

2. Using a Collection Agency

You may have many better things to do—like running your rental business—than tracking down nonpaying tenants you've managed to evict. If you feel debt collection isn't worth the time it takes, or if your attempts at attaching wages or bank accounts are unsuccessful, you might consider turning the judgment over to a collection agency.

Generally, collection agencies take as their fee 50% of what they collect. They do, however, typically pay fees for sheriffs or marshals, so you're not out money if you don't collect. The fee you pay a collection agency is not recoverable from the debtor. For example, if a collection agency collects a $1,000 judgment for you, pocketing $500, you get $500, but you have to give the judgment debtor full credit for the $1,000 that was collected. (This is important to know because after the judgment is paid, you must file a form called an "Acknowledgment of Satisfaction of Judgment" that says the judgment is paid off; see Section H, below.)

Professional collection agencies would like to have you believe that only they have recourse to secret sources of information that will lead to the whereabouts or assets of a person who owes you money. This isn't true; anyone with a little ingenuity and energy can become a "skip tracer." In fact, once you learn the tricks, you will most likely tackle the task with more dedication and commitment and may well do a better job than any professional skip tracer.

B. Using the Tenant's Security Deposit

As mentioned, your best chance to collect the judgment lies in the security deposit the tenant put up when he moved in. If there's anything of the deposit left over after making legitimate deductions for repairs and cleaning (see *Volume 1*, Chapter 20), you can apply it to the judgment. If the judgment is fully covered by the deposit, you're home free.

EXAMPLE

You collected an $800 security deposit from Maurice when he moved in in January. When he didn't pay his $500 rent in September, you moved quickly, got a judgment for possession and had him evicted before the end of the month. Your court costs were $180. Maurice left a broken window that cost you $30 to repair and left the carpet very dirty, necessitating professional cleaning at a cost of $75. You got a judgment of $680 (unpaid rent plus costs). You're entitled to deduct $105 for repairs and cleaning from the deposit. This leaves $695 to apply to a judgment of $680, so you will be fully compensated. The money left over after that must be promptly returned to Maurice, using the procedures outlined in *Volume 1*, Chapter 20.

EXAMPLE

In January, Francesca paid you a security deposit of $450, an amount equal to one month's rent. Because of her repeated loud parties, you gave Francesca a 30-day notice on April 5, terminating her tenancy effective May 5. Francesca refused to pay the rent for the five days in May and also refused to leave. You brought an unlawful detainer action, finally getting her evicted on May 30. You got a judgment for $375 pro-rated "damages" for the days she stayed after the 5th (25 days at $15/day), plus $140 court costs, for a total of $515. After deductions for cleaning and damages ($123 for carpet cleaning and furniture repair), and the five days' rent not reflected in the judgment (5 x $15, or $75), only $252 of Francesca's security deposit remains to apply toward the judgment. You can try to have the sheriff or marshal collect the rest of the judgment as explained in the rest of this chapter.

Remember that you must still send the tenant an itemized statement showing what you did with the security deposit, even if there's nothing left of it to return to him. If you use all or part of the security deposit to satisfy your judgment, you must include this fact in your accounting to the tenant. (See *Volume 1*, Chapter 20.) In the likely event the tenant leaves without telling you where she can be found, you will be relieved of liability if you mail the statement to the address at the property you just evicted her out of. If the tenant left a forwarding address at the post office, the mail will be forwarded.

C. Finding the Tenant

Skip this section if you know where the ex-tenant works, lives or banks.

If you can't find where your ex-tenant banks, works or lives, however, you'll have to start the collection process by finding the tenant. This involves doing a little investigation before you prepare any more paperwork.

1. Post Office Records

Very often, a person who moves notifies the Postal Service of the new address. If your former tenant has done this, you can obtain the new address by asking the Post Office; the charge is $1.00 if you mail in a request. Or, just mail to the tenant's last mailing address—which, of course, is the address of the property you rented to him—an envelope with your return address and "FORWARD-ING AND ADDRESS CORRECTION REQUESTED" in large bold letters at the bottom. If the tenant has given a new address, the Postal Service will send you a form, postage due about 30¢, listing the tenant's new address. If the tenant hasn't left a forwarding address, the envelope will simply be delivered to the address indicated.

2. Telephone Records

A tenant may also leave a forwarding number with the phone company, which you can get by calling the old number. Or call directory assistance to check for a current listing. If you only have the number, you can get an address through a reverse directory. Many public libraries have such reverse directories.

3. Credit Reports

For a small fee, a credit bureau will sell you a tenant's credit report, which should contain the tenant's new address if she applied for credit since leaving your rental address. The three largest credit bureaus are TRW, Equifax, and Trans Union—one or more should be listed in your telephone Yellow Pages under Credit Reporting Agencies. To get a credit report, you will need to provide the tenant's name, old address (the place the tenant rented from you), date or year of birth and Social Security number. If the credit bureau does not have the tenant's current address, ask the bureau to put the tenant's name on its locate list. If the tenant applies for new credit, the locate list should spot the tenant and give her new address.

4. Voter Registration Records

Every California county has a Registrar of Voters who maintains records of all registered voters in the county. Visit the Registrar of Voters for the county in which your property is located and ask if the former tenant is registered. If he is, ask for his address. If no such voter is listed, or if the only address listed is the old one, try an adjacent county.

Unfortunately, voter registration records are seldom updated, and many people don't bother to vote except in presidential elections. One major exception seems to be in cities with large and activist student populations, such as Berkeley, Santa Monica and San Francisco. Thus you probably aren't going to get a new address using this technique until six months or so after the tenant has moved. You may get lucky if the tenant happens to move around the time of a presidential election.

5. Double-Checking the Tenant's New Address

Once you have what you think is the debtor's new address, double-check it by calling the County Assessor and asking for the name and mailing address of the owner of the property at that address. Ask the owner or manager to confirm that the tenant lives there, or pay a visit yourself to see if the tenants' vehicles are parked there or if the tenant's name is on an apartment mailbox. You should identify yourself as the tenant's former landlord who wants to locate him to provide an accounting of the security deposit.

6. Getting the Tenant's Business Address

You may be able to locate a self-employed tenant through a state or local government licensing agency. The state licenses many types of occupations and professions, and most cities and counties impose "business license" taxes. If you think your ex-tenant is self-employed in a particular city, or in an unincorporated area of a county, call the Business License Department of the city or county and ask.

Also, all persons who own businesses in names other than their own last names, or in names that suggest additional owners, are required to file a Fictitious Business Name Statement in each county where they do business. If they don't, they may be prevented from using the courts to collect business debts. For example, John Jones would file a fictitious business name statement if he operated his business under the name of Speedy Auto Repair, or Jones and Sons Auto Repairs, but not if he called it simply Jones' Auto Repair. The County Clerk for each county maintains records of fictitious business names by owner as well as by name of business. You can check them for a few dollars. However, don't be disappointed if the information relevant to your ex-tenant is out-of-date.

Dealing with state licensing agencies may also get results. Many professions and occupations in California are licensed by state agencies that require their members to keep their business addresses current. There are state regulatory agencies for, among others:

accountants
architects
attorneys
auto dealers and repair shop owners
barbers
bar owners
chiropractors
contractors
cosmetologists
dentists
doctors
electronic repair shop owners
engineers
employment agencies
family counselors
geologists
insurance agents
medical technicians
nurses
optometrists
psychiatrists
real estate brokers and agents
social worker technicians
teachers
veterinarians

A complete listing of all regulatory agencies can be found by going to your local library and checking the Sacramento telephone directory under the State of California listings. A telephone call or letter to the appropriate agency in Sacramento (or sometimes a regional office in Los Angeles, San Francisco, San Jose, San Diego or Fresno) may yield the tenant's business address.

D. Locating the Tenant's Assets

If you already know where the tenant banks or works, skip to Section E.

It doesn't make much sense to prepare papers and pay filing fees for papers to collect the money part of the judgment until you locate property of the tenant that can be legally taken ("levied on") by the sheriff or marshal to apply to the judgment. The first sources of funds you should try to locate are the tenant's bank accounts and his paycheck.

1. The Rental Application

If you used a good rental application (like the one in the back of *Volume 1*), the tenant's bank accounts and employer should be listed on it. Of course, one or both may have changed since the application was prepared. If you keep copies of your tenant's rent checks (or you have the original of a bounced check), you may have more recent information. You may also be able to get that information from your bank, although you may be charged a search fee.

2. The Judgment Debtor Examination

Suppose you know your ex-tenant has money in a checking account, but you don't know which bank or branch. Or perhaps you know where she lives, but not where she works and has a paycheck to garnish. Wouldn't it be nice if you could get her to sit down and answer all your questions? Happily, you can, if you know where your former tenant lives or works. You do this by going to court to conduct a "judgment debtor's examination."

The judgment debtor's examination is a proceeding in which a person against whom an unpaid judgment is entered (a "judgment debtor") is ordered to show up in court at a certain date and time to answer, under oath, your questions about income and assets. The only requirements for using this procedure are that the debtor lives or works no more than 150 miles from the courthouse, and that you not have taken a debtor's examination in the past four months. There are exceptions to these requirements. If the debtor lives more than 150 miles from the courthouse, you may schedule an examination at a closer court. If you've conducted a debtor's exam within the last 120 days, you can submit an affidavit explaining why you need to hold another exam so soon. If he fails to show or refuses to answer legitimate questions about his financial affairs, he can be fined or even (rarely) jailed for a few days.

a. Getting a Court Date

In order to have the court issue the Order of Examination (the court order that tells the tenant to come to court for the examination), fill out a form called "Application and Order for Appearance and Examination." Once the judge has approved and signed it, the form serves as the order itself. A copy of the form is included in the forms section of the book. You can use it or a photocopy.

Before you begin filling out the form, call the clerk of the court where you obtained a judgment. Find out in what courtroom or department debtor's examinations are held and ask the clerk to set a date and time for the debtor's examination. Many courts schedule debtor examinations on a particular day of the week. Some allow you to pick a convenient date yourself. Ask for a date at least four weeks away, to allow you some time to have the debtor served with the order. The debtor must be served personally at least ten days before the debtor's examination. Once you've obtained a date and time, fill out the form in the following manner:

Caption Boxes: List your name, address, phone number, court name and location, and case title and number in the boxes at the top of the form, in the same way as on the complaint and other court forms. Just below the spaces for the names of the parties, put "X's" in the boxes next to "ENFORCEMENT OF JUDGMENT" and "Judgment Debtor."

The Order: The first portion of the form below the caption boxes is the "Order to Appear for Examination," the part addressed to the debtor. List the debtor's name in item 1. In item 2, put an X in box "a" only. Below that, list the date and time for the examination, as well as the courtroom (or "department") number you got from the court clerk. If the address of the court is the same as that in the caption box (it usually is), check the box next to the words "shown above." If for some reason the court at which the examination is to take place has an address different from that on the caption, list that address instead.

S A M P L E

ATTORNEY OR PARTY WITHOUT ATTORNEY *(Name and Address):*	TELEPHONE NO.:	FOR COURT USE ONLY

ATTORNEY OR PARTY WITHOUT ATTORNEY *(Name and Address):*   TELEPHONE NO.:

Lenny D. Landlord   (213) 555-6789
12345 Angeleno St.
Los Angeles, CA 90010

ATTORNEY FOR *(Name):*   Plaintiff in Pro Per

NAME OF COURT: Municipal Court of California
STREET ADDRESS: County of Los Angeles
MAILING ADDRESS: 110 N. Grand Ave.
CITY AND ZIP CODE: Los Angeles, CA 90012
BRANCH NAME: Los Angeles Judicial District

PLAINTIFF: Lenny D. Landlord

DEFENDANT: Terrence D. Tenant, Tillie D. Tenant

APPLICATION AND ORDER FOR APPEARANCE AND EXAMINATION

[X] ENFORCEMENT OF JUDGMENT   [ ] ATTACHMENT (Third Person)
   [X] Judgment Debtor   [ ] Third Person

CASE NUMBER:

A-12345-B

ORDER TO APPEAR FOR EXAMINATION

1. TO *(name):*   Terrence D. Tenant, Tillie D. Tenant
2. YOU ARE ORDERED TO APPEAR personally before this court, or before a referee appointed by the court, to
   a. [X] furnish information to aid in enforcement of a money judgment against you.
   b. [ ] answer concerning property of the judgment debtor in your possession or control or concerning a debt you owe the judgment debtor.
   c. [ ] answer concerning property of the defendant in your possession or control or concerning a debt you owe the defendant that is subject to attachment.

Date: November 1, 1992   Time: 9:00 A.M. Dept. or Div.: 3   Rm.:
Address of court [X] shown above [ ] is:

3. This order may be served by a sheriff, marshal, constable, registered process server, or the following specially appointed person *(name):*

Date: ▶ _____
                      (SIGNATURE OF JUDGE OR REFEREE)

This order must be served not less than 10 days before the date set for the examination.

IMPORTANT NOTICES ON REVERSE

APPLICATION FOR ORDER TO APPEAR FOR EXAMINATION

1. [X] Judgment creditor   [ ] Assignee of record   [ ] Plaintiff who has a right to attach order
   applies for an order requiring *(name)* Terrence D. Tenant, Tillie D. Tenant to appear and furnish information to aid in enforcement of the money judgment or to answer concerning property or debt.
2. The person to be examined is
   [X] the judgment debtor
   [ ] a third person (1) who has possession or control of property belonging to the judgment debtor or the defendant or (2) who owes the judgment debtor or the defendant more than $250. An affidavit supporting this application under CCP §491.110 or §708.120 is attached.
3. The person to be examined resides or has a place of business in this county or within 150 miles of the place of examination.
4. [ ] This court is **not** the court in which the money judgment is entered or *(attachment only)* the court that issued the writ of attachment. An affidavit supporting an application under CCP §491.150 or §708.160 is attached.
5. [ ] The judgment debtor has been examined within the past 120 days. An affidavit showing good cause for another examination is attached.

I declare under penalty of perjury under the laws of the State of California that the foregoing is true and correct.

Date: October 10, 1992
Lenny D. Landlord

Lenny D. Landlord

....   ▶ _____
(TYPE OR PRINT NAME)   *(SIGNATURE OF DECLARANT)*

Form Approved by the
Judicial Council of California
AT-138, EJ-125 (New July 1, 1984)

**APPLICATION AND ORDER
FOR APPEARANCE AND EXAMINATION**
(Attachment—Enforcement of Judgment)

CCP 491.110, 708.110, 708.120
Post Record Catalog # AT-138

Leave item 3 blank unless you want someone besides the sheriff or a registered process server to serve the order on the ex-tenant. If you want someone else to serve the order (this must be an adult who isn't a party in the case), put that person's name in item 3. Leave the date and signature blank; the judge will complete them.

The Application: The second part of the form, below the order, is the application for issuance of the order. In item 1, put an X in the box next to the words "Judgment creditor" (you), and fill in the ex-tenant's name in the blank. In item 2, put an X in the first box, before the words "judgment debtor" (tenant) only. Fill in the date and your name and sign the application.

Make at least three copies of the form, being sure to copy both sides. (The reverse contains important warnings to the debtor about failure to appear as ordered, and the order is void without this information.) Take the original and the copies to the court clerk, who will have the original signed by the judge and file it. You can either pick up the file-stamped copies later or give the clerk a self-addressed, stamped envelope to mail the copies to you. One of these copies must be personally served on the debtor.

b. Having a Copy Served on the Debtor

You must make arrangements to have the Order of Examination served on the debtor. Unlike most other legal documents, an Order of Examination must be served by a sheriff, marshal or registered private process server unless you listed someone else's name in item 3 of the Order. As a general rule, private process servers are faster and more aggressive. Give the process server the debtor's home or business address as well as the best time to serve him. Make sure the process server understands that service must be completed at least ten days before the date of the examination.

About two weeks before the hearing, call the process server to see if the Order of Examination has been served. If it has, make sure the process server has filed a Proof of Service with the court. (Most process servers have their own form for this.) Or, have the process server give you the filled-out form, and file it with the court yourself. The Proof of Service should be filed at least five days before the date of the examination. Some courts cancel the debtor's examination if you don't file the Proof of Service on time; check with your court if you're running late. If the process server has been unable to serve the paper at least ten days before the hearing, you'll have to call the court clerk to ask that the examination be taken "off calendar" and to get a new date at least two to three weeks off. Unless the court will let you change the date, you'll have to prepare and submit a new application form, with the new date, and try again.

c. What To Ask at the Examination

The form Questionnaire for Judgment Debtor in the back of the book gives some sample questions to ask the debtor. Go through them carefully before the hearing and ask only those that apply. Use a photocopy of the form to list the answers to the questions. Don't feel intimidated by the length of this questionnaire; many questions will not apply.

On the day of the examination, appear in court prepared to meet the debtor. If she doesn't show, the judge may reschedule the examination or issue a "bench warrant" for her arrest. To have a bench warrant issued, you will have to complete a form and return it to the court with a fee of $20 to have the sheriff or marshal serve it.

When your case is called, you and the debtor should come forward. The debtor will be ordered to take an oath and answer your questions about her income or assets. The two of you will probably be directed to a spare room or some part of the courthouse, perhaps just the benches down the hall (or seats right in the courtroom if it isn't being used for something else). Should the debtor refuse to give you straight answers, tell her you're going back to the courtroom to ask the judge to order her to answer. If she refuses to come back to the courtroom for this, or simply wanders off, you can ask the judge to order the bailiff to bring her back—or issue an arrest warrant if she skips out altogether.

Important. There is one question you don't want to overlook: "Do you have any money with you today?" If the answer is "no," you have the right to insist that the debtor show you his empty wallet to make sure. If the debtor has money, you can ask the judge to order that it be turned over to you on the spot. The judge has the power to order the debtor to do this, but may allow the debtor to keep some of it for essentials. If the debtor has a checkbook and knows the balance in the account, you may even be able to get the judge to order him to write you a check—which you should cash at his bank immediately after the hearing. If you put it in your account, chances are the debtor's account will be closed before the check can be presented for collection.

Once you've found out where the former tenant banks or works, you're ready to go after his bank account or paycheck. Section E tells you how.

E. Garnishing Wages and Bank Accounts

This section describes your next step—how to prepare the proper documents to give to the sheriff or marshal. These are:

- a Writ of Execution, and
- written instructions to the sheriff or marshal (or, if you're going after wages, an Application for Earnings Withholding Order).

Once you start emptying a tenant's bank account or garnishing his wages, you may have only to wait a few weeks before the money from the marshal or sheriff comes in the mail.

1. Preparing the Writ of Execution

The Writ of Execution for the money part of the judgment allows the sheriff or marshal to take all the money out of the tenant's bank savings or checking account (up to the amount of the judgment, of course) or to order an employer to take up to 25% out of the tenant's paycheck.

Once issued by the court, the Writ of Execution remains valid for 180 days.

You prepare the Writ of Execution for a money judgment in the same manner as the Writ of Possession of the premises (see Chapter 7, Section C), with the following exceptions:

Check the "EXECUTION (MONEY JUDGMENT)" box, rather than the "POSSESSION OF" and "Real Property" boxes in the top part of the form.

In item 1, fill in the county in which the levy will take place, regardless of what county the judgment was entered in.

Leave all of item 9 blank.

In item 11, list the total judgment that was awarded as rent, damages and costs.

Item 12 is filled in as zero ("0.00"), since it refers to certain costs incurred to collect a judgment. You must file special papers to be entitled to receive post-judgmental costs.

In item 13, fill in the same amount that you listed for item 11.

In item 14, credit should be given for any payments made by the tenant toward the judgment. Be sure to apply any amount of the security deposit left over after deducting for cleaning, damages, and any rent not reflected in the judgment. (See *Volume 1*, Chapter 20.)

After subtracting any partial payments and other credits, fill in the balance in item 15.

Fill in "0.00" in item 16. Again, you must file special papers with the court before you're entitled to receive post-judgmental interest.

In item 17, enter $3.50, the fee for issuance of this writ of execution (the fee for the issuance of the first writ, for possession, should be included in the judge's award of costs).

Add the amounts in items 15-17 together, putting the sum in item 18.

Finally, calculate the daily interest on the judgment at the rate of 10 percent. (This can add up, since it may take a long time to collect the judgment.) Multiply the amount in item 15 by 0.10 to get the yearly interest, then divide this amount by 365 to get the daily interest amount. List this amount in item 19.

A sample money judgment Writ of Execution is shown below.

When your writ is filled out, make four copies (remember to copy the back side) and ask the court clerk to open the file, check the judgment and issue the Writ of Execution. After collecting the $3.50 writ-issuance fee from you, the clerk will stamp the original writ with the date and a court seal, stamp the copies with the date (but not the court seal), and hand you back both the original and copies. The original and three copies are given to the sheriff or marshal. Keep one copy for your records.

2. Bank Accounts

Before you waste the fees you'll have to pay the sheriff, call the ex-tenant's bank and ask if there's money in the account.

Although banks are forbidden to tell you specifically how much money an individual has in her checking account, virtually all banks will respond to a telephone request as to whether a particular check is good. For example, if you call the bank and ask whether your "$100 check from Skelly Jones, Account No. 123-45678, is good," a bank employee will normally answer yes or no.

To get cash in a bank account, start by calling the sheriff or marshal in the county in which the account is located. Make sure that the office serves bank levies; in a few counties, you must hire a registered process server. Give the original and three copies of the writ of execution to the sheriff, marshal or registered process server, along with the necessary fee (about $40 as of this writing, but call ahead to get the exact amount) and a letter or filled-out "instructions" form. Most sheriff's or marshal's departments have their own form, which they like you to use. If you use a simple letter, it should look like the one below.

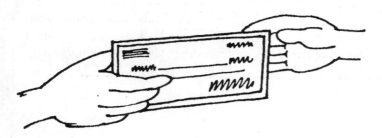

Sample Instructions to Sheriff for Writ of Execution

September 15, 1992

Lenny Landlord
12345 Angeleno St.
Los Angeles, CA 90010

Los Angeles County Sheriff
111 N. Hill St.
Los Angeles, California 90012

Re: Lenny Landlord v. Terrence D. Tenant and Tillie D. Tenant
Los Angeles County Municipal Court
No. A-12345-B

Enclosed are the original and three copies of a Writ of Execution issued by the municipal court, and a check in the amount of $40. Please levy on all monies of the judgment debtors Terrence D. Tenant and Tillie D. Tenant at the West Los Angeles branch of First National Bank, 123 First Street, Los Angeles, California.

Sincerely,

Lenny D. Landlord

After the sheriff, marshal or process server serves the necessary papers on the bank, the bank will hold the money for ten days, then pay it over to the county sheriff or marshal. After a few more weeks, the sheriff or marshal will forward the money to you, provided the tenant hasn't filed a "Claim of Exemption." (See Section G, below.)

ATTORNEY OR PARTY WITHOUT ATTORNEY *(Name and Address)*:	TELEPHONE NO.:	FOR RECORDER'S USE ONLY

☐ Recording requested by and return to:

LENNY D. LANDLORD   (213) 555-6789
12345 Angeleno St.
Los Angeles, CA 90010   Plaintiff in Pro Per

☐ ATTORNEY FOR   ☐ JUDGMENT CREDITOR   ☐ ASSIGNEE OF RECORD

NAME OF COURT: MUNICIPAL COURT OF CALIFORNIA
STREET ADDRESS: COUNTY OF LOS ANGELES
MAILING ADDRESS: 110 N. Grand Ave.
CITY AND ZIP CODE: Los Angeles, CA 90012
BRANCH NAME: LOS ANGELES JUDICIAL DISTRICT

PLAINTIFF: LENNY D. LANDLORD

DEFENDANT: TERRENCE D. TENANT
TILLIE D. TENANT

WRIT OF

☒ **EXECUTION (Money Judgment)**
☐ **POSSESSION OF** ☐ **Personal Property**
                    ☐ **Real Property**
☐ **SALE**

CASE NUMBER:

A-12345-B

FOR COURT USE ONLY

1. **To the Sheriff or any Marshal or Constable of the County of:** Los Angeles

   You are directed to enforce the judgment described below with daily interest and your costs as provided by law.

2. **To any registered process server:** You are authorized to serve this writ only in accord with CCP 699.080 or CCP 715.040.

3. *(Name)*: Lenny D. Landlord
   is the ☒ judgment creditor ☐ assignee of record
   whose address is shown on this form above the court's name.

4. **Judgment debtor** *(name and last known address)*:

   Tillie D. Tenant
   6789 Angel St., #10
   Los Angeles, CA 90010

   Terrence D. Tenant
   6789 Angel St., #10
   Los Angeles, CA 90010

   ☐ additional judgment debtors on reverse

5. **Judgment entered on** *(date)*: Sept. 9, 1992
6. ☐ **Judgment renewed on** *(dates)*:

7. **Notice of sale** under this writ
   a. ☒ has not been requested.
   b. ☐ has been requested *(see reverse)*.
8. ☐ Joint debtor information on reverse.

9. ☐ See reverse for information on real or personal property to be delivered under a writ of possession or sold under a writ of sale.
10. ☐ This writ is issued on a sister-state judgment.
11. Total judgment . . . . $ 1,120.00
12. Costs after judgment (per filed order or memo CCP 685.090) . $ 0.00
13. Subtotal *(add 11 and 12)* . . . . . $ 1,120.00
14. Credits . . . . $
15. Subtotal *(subtract 14 from 13)* . $ 1,120.00
16. Interest after judgment (per filed affidavit CCP 685.050) . . . . . . $ 0.00
17. Fee for issuance of writ . . . . . . $ 3.50
18. Total *(add 15, 16, and 17)* . . . . $ 1,123.50
19. Levying officer: Add daily interest from date of writ *(at the legal rate on 15)* of . . . . $ 0.17
20. ☐ The amounts called for in items 11–19 are different for each debtor. These amounts are stated for each debtor on Attachment 20.

[SEAL]

Issued on *(date)*:	Clerk, by _____, Deputy

— NOTICE TO PERSON SERVED: SEE REVERSE FOR IMPORTANT INFORMATION —

(Continued on reverse)

Form Approved by the
Judicial Council of California
EJ-130 [Rev. September 30, 1991*]

WRIT OF EXECUTION

Code of Civil Procedure, §§ 699.520, 712.010, 715.010
*See note on reverse.

3. Wages

The law allows you to have the sheriff or marshal order the judgment debtor's employer to withhold up to 25% of her wages each pay period to satisfy a judgment. (If the person has a very low income, the amount you can recover can be considerably less than 25%. Also, you may have to wait in line if other creditors got to the employer first.) So if you know where your ex-tenant works (and he doesn't quit or declare bankruptcy when you start garnishing his paycheck), you may be able to collect the entire judgment though it may take a while before all the money dribbles in. There's one exception: The federal government, except the Postal Service and Federal Housing Administration, will not cooperate with a garnishment of employees' wages.

Like double-checking on bank accounts, it's a good idea to check to see if the debtor is still employed before paying fees to the sheriff or marshal. You can easily check on whether a tenant is employed at a particular business. Call the personnel department and simply state that you'd like to "verify the employment of Emmett Employee." If the tenant no longer works there, ask to speak to his former supervisor or someone in that person's department, who may have been contacted by a more recent employer following through on a reference. Also, people who once worked together sometimes keep in touch for years afterwards. You'll get the most information if you assume a polite, friendly approach. If you're asked why you need the information, you can truthfully say that you're the ex-tenant's former landlord and that you need his new address so you can send him an accounting of his security deposit.

To initiate a wage garnishment, start by completing an "Application for Earnings Withholding Order," available in the forms section in the back of the book. A completed sample is shown below. On the Application for Earnings Withholding Order, list your name and the usual information about the court name and address, the names of the parties, and the case number in the boxes at the top of the form. In the box at the upper right hand corner, list the name and address of the office of the sheriff or marshal. Be sure also to enter the name of the county where the debtor is employed below these boxes, just before item 1.

List your name in item 1, and the names and addresses of the debtor and his employer in the boxes below that. You must provide the employer's street address; a mailing address isn't enough. Below the box at the right for the employee/debtor's name and address is a space for her social security number, if known.

Put an X in box 2.a to indicate that the funds are to be paid to you. In item 3.a, list the date the judgment was entered. Leave item 3.b blank unless for some reason you aren't owed the full amount listed in the Writ of Execution. Check item 6.a if this is your first wage garnishment. Or check the appropriate boxes in item 6.b to reflect previous wage garnishment attempts you have made. Finally, type your name and sign twice at the bottom, listing the date as well.

Call the sheriff or marshal for the county in which the judgment debtor works and find out if they serve wage garnishments, or whether you must use a registered process server. Also, find out the fee for a wage garnishment. Forward the original and three copies of the Writ of Execution, a check for the required fee, a letter of instructions and the completed Application for Earnings Withholding Order.

S A M P L E

ATTORNEY OR PARTY WITHOUT ATTORNEY *(Name and Address)*:	TELEPHONE NO.	LEVYING OFFICER *(Name and Address)*:

Lenny D. Landlord   (213) 555-6789
12345 Angeleno St.
Los Angeles, CA 90010

ATTORNEY FOR *(Name)*:   Plaintiff in Pro Per

NAME OF COURT, JUDICIAL DISTRICT OR BRANCH COURT, IF ANY:
Municipal Court of California, County of Los
Angeles, Los Angeles Judicial District

PLAINTIFF:
    Lenny D. Landlord

DEFENDANT:
    Terrence D. Tenant, Tillie D. Tenant

APPLICATION FOR EARNINGS WITHHOLDING ORDER (Wage Garnishment)	LEVYING OFFICER FILE NO.:	COURT CASE NO.: A-12345-B

TO THE SHERIFF OR ANY MARSHAL OR CONSTABLE OF THE COUNTY OF Los Angeles
OR ANY REGISTERED PROCESS SERVER

1. The judgment creditor *(name)*: Lenny D. Landlord

   requests issuance of an Earnings Withholding Order directing the employer to withhold the earnings of the judgment debtor (employee).

    Name and address of employer   Name and address of employee

    Ernie Employer   Terrence D. Tenant
    123 Business Lane   6789 Angel Blvd., Apt. 10
    Los Angeles, CA   Los Angeles, CA 90010

                                   Social Security Number *(if known)*: 555-12-3456

2. The amounts withheld are to be paid to
    a. ☐ The attorney (or party without an attorney) named at the top of this page.
    b. ☐ Other *(name, address, and telephone)*:

3. a. Judgment was entered on *(date)*: September 6, 1992
    b. Collect the amount directed by the Writ of Execution unless a lesser amount is specified here:
       $

4. ☐ The Writ of Execution was issued to collect delinquent amounts payable for the **support** of a child, former spouse, or spouse of the employee.

5. ☐ Special instructions *(specify)*:

6. *(Check a or b)*
    a. ☒ I have not previously obtained an order directing this employer to withhold the earnings of this employee.
       —OR—
    b. ☐ I have previously obtained such an order, but that order *(check one)*:
          ☐ expired at least 10 days ago.
          ☐ was terminated by a court order, but I am entitled to apply for another Earnings Withholding Order under the provisions of Code of Civil Procedure section 706.105(h).
          ☐ was ineffective.

    Lenny D. Landlord   ▶ *Lenny D. Landlord*
    (TYPE OR PRINT NAME)   *(SIGNATURE OF ATTORNEY OR PARTY WITHOUT ATTORNEY)*

I declare under penalty of perjury under the laws of the State of California that the foregoing is true and correct.

Date: October 10, 1992

    Lenny D. Landlord   ▶ *Lenny D. Landlord*
    (TYPE OR PRINT NAME)   *(SIGNATURE OF DECLARANT)*

Form Adopted by the Judicial Council of California 982.5(1) [Rev. January 1, 1985]	**APPLICATION FOR EARNINGS WITHHOLDING ORDER** (Wage Garnishment)	CCP 706.121 Post Record Catalog #982.5(1)

Sample Instructions to Marshal for Application for Earnings Withholding Order

---

October 10, 199_

Lenny Landlord
12345 Angeleno St.
Los Angeles, CA 90010

Office of the Marshal
Los Angeles Judicial District, Los
Angeles County
110 N. Grand Avenue
Los Angeles, CA 90012

Re: Landlord v. Tenant
Los Angeles Municipal Court Case No.
A-12345-B

Enclosed is an Application for
Earnings Withholding Order, an
original and three copies of a Writ
of Execution from the Municipal
Court for the Los Angeles Judicial
District, and a check for $20.00.
Please levy on the wages of Terrence
D. Tenant, who is employed at Ernie
Employer, 123 Business Lane, Los
Angeles, California.

Sincerely,

Lenny D. Landlord

The original goes to the sheriff or marshal of the county in which the employer is located or to a registered process server, if required by county policies. Send along the original and three copies of the Writ of Execution and the appropriate fee. The fee varies from county to county, so call the marshal or sheriff's civil division to find out the amount.

The debtor's wages should be levied on until you are paid in full unless:

- the debtor successfully claims an exemption (see Section G, below)
- someone else already has effected a wage garnishment
- your garnishment is supplanted by a support order (e.g., the IRS)
- the debtor stops working at that place of employment, or
- the debtor declares bankruptcy. (See Chapter 10 for your options if the tenant declares bankruptcy.)

F.   Seizing Other Property

Although it's not likely to be worth the time and trouble, you may want to try to seize property of the debtor if you haven't gotten the whole judgment paid yet.

1.   Motor Vehicles

To find out whether it is worth the time and trouble to have the tenant's vehicle seized and sold at an auction to pay off the judgment, first find out its market value. Go to your local library and check the most recent edition of the *Kelly Blue Book* (published monthly), or check newspaper want ads for the price of similar vehicles. If the value isn't at least $2,000, forget it. Even if the vehicle is paid off, the owner/debtor is legally entitled to the first $1,200 of the proceeds. Sheriff's storage and sales charges, which you'll have to pay for up front, will run at least $300, and likely more.

If the "legal owner" of the vehicle is the bank or finance company that loaned the money to buy the vehicle, the situation is even worse. If you have the car sold, the legal owner (who normally has the right to repossess if payments aren't made) is entitled to be paid what it is owed out of the proceeds of the sale. This amount is called the "payoff figure"; it may well equal, or even exceed, the sale value of the vehicle. If it does, a levy and sale of a debtor's vehicle will net you no money and you'll be out substantial costs. Here are a few examples:

EXAMPLE

You have a judgment against your former tenant Skip, the owner of a 1990 Chevrolet with a book value of $5,000. The DMV informs you, in its response to your Vehicle Registration Information Request, that the legal owner is General Motors Acceptance Corp. in San Jose. You call GMAC, giving the owner's name, license plate number and V.I.N. (serial) number (if you have it), and ask for a "payoff figure." They tell you it's $3,500. This means that even if the vehicle is sold for $4,500 at a sheriff's auction, GMAC will get the first $3,500. Since Skip is entitled to the $1,200 exemption, the remaining $1,000 will go to him, and you'll get nothing. Moreover, you'll be out the $300 you fronted to the sheriff for service, storage and sales costs.

EXAMPLE

The legal owner of Darlene's 1991 Honda is Household Finance. Household Finance tells you the payoff figure is $3,000. The book value of the vehicle is $7,000, but at a sheriff's auction it might not net more than $5,000, leaving only $2,000 after the legal owner is paid off. Subtract the $1,200 exemption that goes to Darlene, and that leaves you with $800—less any storage and sale costs you've paid. Of course, if your auction sale price of $5,000 was overly optimistic—and the car only netted $4,000—you would get nothing and be out the costs of storage and sale.

As the above examples show, levying on a vehicle can actually cost you money. Most owners of new autos owe more on them than they could sell them for at an auction. By the time the loan is paid off, the auction value of the vehicle is fairly low, and might not be enough over $1,200 to be profitable for you. As a general rule, you should forget about having the debtor's vehicle seized and sold unless its fair market value is at least $2,000 to $3,000 above what the debtor still owes on it.

If you decide it's worthwhile, give the original and at least two copies of the Writ of Execution to the sheriff or marshal, along with your letter or other written instructions requesting a levy on defendant's automobile. Be sure to give the description and license number of the vehicle and say where and when it can be found on a street or other public place (the sheriff cannot go into a private garage or warehouse). You will also need to give

the sheriff or marshal a check for the total amount of the fees and deposit for towing and storage; check to find out how much this will be.

Instructions to Sheriff for Levying on a Vehicle

November 1, 199_

Cruz Creditor
123 Market Street
Monterey, California

Monterey County Sheriff
P.O. Box 809
Salinas, CA 93902

Re: Creditor v. Debtor
    Monterey Judicial District
    Monterey County
    Case No. 2468-C

As instructed yesterday by a member of your office staff, I am enclosing a deposit check for $300 and an original and three copies of a writ of execution in the above-entitled case.

Please levy on the automobile of judgment debtor Dale Debtor; the vehicle is a 1992 Cadillac El Dorado sedan, license number 1SAM123. It is normally parked in front of the debtor's residence address of 12345 East Main Street, Salinas, California. Please call me at (408) 555-5678 if you have any questions.

Sincerely,

Be patient, because the whole process could easily take several months. First, it may take up to several weeks for the sheriff or marshal to arrange for a tow truck to be present when the vehicle is available and not locked in a garage. Second, once it's picked up, it will take at least a month to auction it off (unless the debtor redeems the vehicle by paying off the judgment, which sometimes happens). Finally, once the sheriff gets the money from the auction, he will hold it for about another month after paying off the towing and storage charges and any loan.

Identifying the Legal Owner of a Vehicle
You may be able to identify the legal owner of your ex-tenant's vehicle by filing a Vehicle Registration Information Request with the DMV. But before the DMV releases that information, it allows the ex-tenant the opportunity to object to having the information released. Since most debtors won't let the DMV release information to you, a debtor's examination may be a better bet. (See Section D2, above.)

---

2. Other Personal Property

As mentioned, most of your tenant's personal property is probably protected from creditors. Here is a list of statutorily exempt property. (All references are to the California Code of Civil Procedure.)

- Motor vehicles, up to a net equity (market value less payoff) of $1,200 (§ 704.010)

- Household items, including furniture, appliances and clothing that are "ordinarily and reasonably necessary" (§ 704.020)

- Materials to be used for repair or maintenance of a residence (§ 704.030)

- Jewelry, heirlooms and artworks, up to a net value of $2,500 (§ 704.040)

- Health aids (§ 704.050)

- Tools used in a trade or business, up to a net value of $2,500 for each spouse in business (§ 704.060)

- 75% of wages or up to 30 times the federal minimum wages (currently $4.25 an hour or $127.50 per week), whichever is greater (§ 704.070)

- Social Security direct-deposit bank, S&L or credit union accounts (§ 704.080)

- Jail or prison inmate's trust account, up to $1,000 (§ 704.090)

- Life-insurance policy equity, up to $4,000 for each spouse, and life insurance policy benefits "reasonably necessary" for support of debtor and family (§ 704.100)

- Retirement benefits paid by a public entity (§ 704.110)

- Vacation credits payable to a public employee (§ 704.113)

- Private retirement benefits necessary for support of debtor and family (§ 704.115)

- Unemployment, disability and strike benefits (§ 704.120)

- Health or disability insurance benefits (§ 704.130)

- Personal injury or wrongful death damages necessary for support of debtor and family (§§ 704.140, 704.150)

- Workers' compensation benefits (§ 704.160)

- Welfare benefits and aid from charitable organizations (§ 704.170)

- Relocation benefits paid by government entity (§ 704.180)

- Student financial aid (§ 704.190)

- Burial plots (§ 704.200)

- Bank account and cash traceable to an exempt asset (§ 703.080)

- Business licenses, except liquor licenses (§§ 695.060, 708.630)

3. Real Estate

Don't overlook the possibility that the ex-tenant owns or might purchase real estate. Putting a lien on real estate is simple and inexpensive, and it will likely get you results if the debtor wants to sell or refinance the property. The process is explained in *Collect Your Court Judgment*, by Scott, Elias and Goldoftas (Nolo Press).

G. If the Debtor Files a Claim of Exemption

There are several legal maneuvers a debtor can use to delay or even stop the collection process. The most common is the filing, with the sheriff or marshal, of a simple form known as a Claim of Exemption. In it, a debtor claims that the bank account, paycheck or property being subjected to garnishment is legally exempt from execution to satisfy a judgment.

For example, an ex-tenant whose bank account is attached might claim that the funds in the account consist entirely of funds that are exempt by law, such as welfare or certain Social Security payments. Another exemption commonly claimed is that the debtor has insufficient funds to provide for "ordinary necessities" of life. A judgment debtor may not claim this type of exemption if the debt was itself incurred to pay for necessities of life—like rent. What this means in practice is that it's improper for your ex-tenant to claim a hardship exemption to avoid paying a judgment for rent. However, if the tenant attempts to claim this exemption anyway (easy to do on the standard fill-in-the-blank exemption forms), you have the burden of pointing out to a judge that the debtor can't claim a "necessities of life" exemption if the money you're seeking was for nonpayment of rent. If you do nothing, the tenant will be able to claim the exemption and get back any seized property or prevent a wage garnishment.

If the sheriff or marshal notifies you that the debtor has filed a Claim of Exemption, you will have to respond with a few forms of your own. If you do nothing in the face of a Claim of Exemption filed by a debtor, the sheriff

or marshal will automatically treat the wages or bank account attached as legally exempt. Your response depends on what the tenant's Claim of Exemption states. If you want to oppose a tenant's claim, see *Collect Your Court Judgment*, by Scott, Elias & Goldoftas (Nolo Press). A good general discussion of exemption law is contained in *Money Troubles: Legal Strategies To Cope With Your Debts*, by Robin Leonard (Nolo Press).

H. Once the Judgment Is Paid Off

You may be pleasantly surprised to find that through deposit credits, wage garnishments, bank account seizures, or a combination of these, your judgment is in fact paid off entirely, including interest and costs. This may take a long time, but after that, the judgment is said to be "satisfied" (even if you aren't). When this happens, you are legally required to fill out a form called an Acknowledgment of Satisfaction of Judgment and file it with the court, so that the court records no longer reflect an unpaid judgment against your ex-tenant. A sample filled-out form is shown below. A tear-out version is included in the Appendix. Note that the form must be notarized before you file it with the court.

SAMPLE

ATTORNEY OR PARTY WITHOUT ATTORNEY *(Name and Address)*:   TELEPHONE NO.:   FOR RECORDER'S OR SECRETARY OF STATE'S USE ONLY

fill in caption boxes and case number

ATTORNEY FOR *(Name)*:

NAME OF COURT:
STREET ADDRESS:
MAILING ADDRESS:
CITY AND ZIP CODE:
BRANCH NAME:

PLAINTIFF:

DEFENDANT:

indicate whether judgment completely or partially paid

ACKNOWLEDGMENT OF SATISFACTION OF JUDGMENT   CASE NUMBER:
☐ FULL   ☐ PARTIAL   ☐ MATURED INSTALLMENT

check box a and box (1) if judgment is paid in full

Satisfaction of the judgment is acknowledged as follows *(see footnote* before completing)*:   FOR COURT USE ONLY

a. ☐ Full satisfaction
  (1) ☐ Judgment is satisfied in full.
  (2) ☐ The judgment creditor has accepted payment or performance other than that specified in the judgment in full satisfaction of the judgment.

check box b) if judgment is partially paid

b. ☐ Partial satisfaction
    The amount received in partial satisfaction of the judgment is
    $

c. ☐ Matured installment
    All matured installments under the installment judgment have been satisfied as of *(date)*:

2. Full name and address of judgment creditor:

type your name and address

3. Full name and address of assignee of record, if any: **type "N/A"**

4. Full name and address of judgment debtor being fully or partially released:

type tenant's name and address

5. a. Judgment entered on *(date)*:   **fill in date of judgment**
    ☐ (1) in judgment book volume no.:   (2) page no.:
  b. ☐ Renewal entered on *(date)*:
    ☐ (1) in judgment book volume no.:   (2) page no.:

ask court clerk if judgment entered in judgment book, and fill in volume and page number

6. ☐ An ☐ abstract of judgment ☐ certified copy of the judgment has been recorded as follows *(complete all information for each county where recorded)*:

          COUNTY   DATE OF RECORDING   BOOK NUMBER   PAGE NUMBER

leave items 6 and 7 blank

7. ☐ A notice of judgment lien has been filed in the office of the Secretary of State as file number *(specify)*:

NOTICE TO JUDGMENT DEBTOR: If this is an acknowledgment of full satisfaction of judgment, it will have to be recorded in each county shown in item 6 above, if any, in order to release the judgment lien, and will have to be filed in the office of the Secretary of State to terminate any judgment lien on personal property.

Date: **sign and date form** ▶

_____
(SIGNATURE OF JUDGMENT CREDITOR OR ASSIGNEE OF CREDITOR OR ATTORNEY)

*The names of the judgment creditor and judgment debtor must be stated as shown in any Abstract of Judgment which was recorded and is being released by this satisfaction. A separate notary acknowledgment must be attached for each signature.

Form Approved by the
Judicial Council of California   **ACKNOWLEDGMENT OF SATISFACTION OF JUDGMENT**   CCP 724.060, 724.120, 724.250
EJ-100 [Rev. July 1, 1983][Cor. 7/84]   Post Record Catalog # EJ-100

When a Tenant Files for Bankruptcy

If a tenant files for bankruptcy, all legal proceedings against him—including an eviction lawsuit—must cease until the bankruptcy court says otherwise. (11 U.S.C. § 362.) This is called the "automatic stay." Any creditor who violates the stay—that is, attempts to collect from the person who declared bankruptcy ("debtor," in legalese) or pursues a legal proceeding—can, and probably will, be fined by the bankruptcy court. The bankruptcy court might agree to remove ("lift") the automatic stay for a creditor who can show that the stay is not serving its intended purpose of freezing the debtor's assets. Getting the court to lift the stay, however, takes time and is fairly complicated.

Because filing for bankruptcy stops dead an eviction, some tenants, attorneys and typing services (especially in the Los Angeles area) file last-minute bankruptcies to delay eviction, rather than to erase unmanageable debt burdens or set up repayment plans. Because a debtor can begin a bankruptcy case by filing just three or four pages of documents (a legitimate bankruptcy filer must file the rest of the forms within 14 days), filing a bankruptcy petition simply to stave off an eviction is extremely easy.

Kinds of Bankruptcy

A tenant can file for different kinds of bankruptcy. The most common are "Chapter 7," which erases debts completely, and "Chapter 13," which lets a debtor repay a portion of his debts over three to five years. A tenant may also file for Chapter 11 (a repayment plan for people with debts over $450,000) or Chapter 12 (a repayment plan for farm owners). The word "chapter" refers to a particular chapter of the Bankruptcy Code, Title 11 of the U.S. Code, the federal laws that govern bankruptcy.

A. When the Tenant Can File for Bankruptcy

A tenant can file for bankruptcy at any time—when you serve a three-day notice, after you've filed an unlawful detainer action or just moments before the sheriff or mar-

shal comes out to evict. Most commonly, a tenant who files for bankruptcy to delay an eviction will do so after you've obtained an eviction judgment but before the sheriff or marshal pays a visit. If the sheriff or marshal attempts to evict a tenant who claims to have filed for bankruptcy, the sheriff or marshal must halt the eviction.

If a tenant has filed for Chapter 13 bankruptcy—which can take three to five years—the tenant's bankruptcy may have started long before you rented to her. The tenant may inform you, the municipal court where you file the unlawful detainer action, or the sheriff or marshal of the bankruptcy only as the eviction date approaches.

Regardless of when you find out about a pending bankruptcy case, you must stop all legal actions. You may proceed only if the bankruptcy court lifts the automatic stay.

B. Landlord Options When a Tenant Files for Bankruptcy

What can you do if a tenant files for bankruptcy? There are two options:

1. Ignore the Automatic Stay

If your rental property is in Los Angeles, Orange, Ventura, San Bernadino or Santa Barbara County, you may choose to ignore the automatic stay and continue your case in municipal court—but only if the following conditions are met:

- the tenancy is month-to-month, and
- the rent is not unusually below market rate.

You have this option because these counties are in the Central District of California of the U.S. federal court system, and the Central District Bankruptcy Court has ruled that a landlord whose tenant's tenancy is month-to-month, and who seeks eviction (as opposed to seeking a probably-uncollectible judgment for rent), may disregard the automatic stay. (*In re Smith* (C.D. Cal. 1989) 105 B.R. 50.) Even so, you will still need to convince the municipal court, or the sheriff or marshal who is to perform the eviction, that the automatic stay doesn't apply. Section C, below, discusses how to pursue this option.

2. Ask the Court To Lift the Stay

You can file a motion in bankruptcy court to have the automatic stay lifted. This is your only option if:

- your tenant's tenancy is not month-to-month, or
- your property is not located in one of the California counties listed above, or
- you don't think the municipal court will let you proceed with the eviction.

This procedure involves preparing several legal forms and can take several weeks between the time you file your motion and the time the bankruptcy court lets you proceed with the eviction. See Section D for information on filing a motion in bankruptcy court to have the stay lifted.

C. Going Ahead Despite the Automatic Stay (Los Angeles, Orange, Ventura, San Bernadino or Santa Barbara County Only)

To understand how and whether to pursue this option—assuming your meet the conditions outlined above—requires a little explanation.

1. Why You Can Ignore the Stay in Some Circumstances

The main purpose of the automatic stay is to freeze the debtor's assets. It's the bankruptcy court's job to fairly distribute the debtor's assets to creditors. It can't do that if one creditor can use a state-court procedure—like eviction— to grab the debtor's assets ahead of the bankruptcy court. A debtor's lease—that is, the right to rent real estate from a landlord under the terms of a lease agreement—may be a valuable asset that the bankruptcy court orders to be sold, with the proceeds distributed to the bankruptcy debtor's creditors.

EXAMPLE

Herman is a tenant under a lease with three of its five years remaining. His monthly rent is $1,000, despite the fact that the going monthly rental rate for similar property is $1,500. Herman files for bankruptcy. The court declares the lease an asset with a value of $18,000 ($500 per month times the remaining 36 months).

On the other hand, a tenancy that may be terminated by the landlord for any reason on 30 days' notice is worth almost nothing, even if the rent is below market rate. Why? Because the tenancy can be terminated on 30 days' notice, the tenant does not have the benefit of a below-market rate for any definite period. Since the tenancy can be terminated after a month's notice, its value is, at most, the difference between actual and fair-market rental for only one month.

The *In re Smith* decision says that a residential month-to-month tenancy is not a valuable asset that the bankruptcy court needs to hold on to. If a landlord seeks only to evict the tenant, and not collect past due rent, the automatic stay does not apply.

So according to this court decision, you can ignore the automatic stay if you seek to evict a month-to-month tenant without requesting back rent if your property is located in the Central District of California of the U.S. federal court system.

2. Dangers of Ignoring the Stay

In practice, going ahead with the eviction may not be a good idea. First, the opinion that allows it is from a bankruptcy trial court, not a bankruptcy appeals court. That means *In re Smith* is not legally binding on other bankruptcy judges, (even other judges in the Central District). A bankruptcy judge who disagreed with the opinion could interpret your actions as a deliberate and intentional violation of the automatic stay. The tenant or his bankruptcy lawyer could then ask the bankruptcy court to order you to refrain from proceeding with the eviction and ask that you be fined, probably for the amount of the tenant's attorney's fees.

If that were to happen, you could argue that you relied in good faith on *In re Smith* and that the bankruptcy court should follow it because it makes sense, but the decision is up to the judge.

Second, you may run into problems with the municipal court bureaucracy. Once a tenant files for bankruptcy, the municipal court clerk or judge, or a sheriff or marshal, will most likely refuse to proceed until you get the bankruptcy court to lift the automatic stay.

If you run into that kind of obstacle, you can go to the bankruptcy court and file a motion to have the stay lifted (see Section D, below) or try to proceed in municipal court. If the refusal came from a court clerk or the sheriff or marshal, consider submitting to the municipal court judge a document like the one shown below, called an "Ex Parte Application for Order to Proceed With Eviction Notwithstanding Defendant's Bankruptcy." If the municipal court judge refused to proceed with the eviction, however, it's unlikely that she'll change her mind even if you submit the Ex Parte Application.

Watch What You Say in Your Court Papers. Keep in mind that the sample below is just an example, which you must adapt to your particular situation. The sample states that the landlord believes that the tenant has filed bankruptcy just to avoid eviction. You can legitimately make this claim if the tenant filed for bankruptcy only after you began the eviction lawsuit—unless you happen to know the tenant filed for bankruptcy because of many other debts. Remember that you are signing the document under penalty of perjury.

3. How To File and Serve the Ex Parte Application

After you have prepared your Ex Parte Application, attach a copy of *In re Smith* (found in the Appendix), labelled "Appendix A," to it. You will need to prepare the

Application on pleading paper. (Make copies of the blank sheet of pleading paper—the 8-1/2" x 11" paper with the numbers down the left side—in the Appendix.) Also prepare and attach a Proof of Service by Mail (a blank copy is in the Appendix), as shown below. Have a friend over the age of 18 mail copies of your Ex Parte Application to the tenant's eviction-defense attorney, if any; if the tenant does not have an eviction-defense attorney, mail the copies to the the tenant and to his or her bankruptcy attorney. Their addresses should be listed on the Proof of Service by Mail, which your friend should then sign.

Then take the original Ex Parte Application, with two copies, to the municipal court clerk. The clerk will take the form but not file-stamp it. Because it includes a proposed order for the judge to sign, the clerk cannot file the form until the judge signs it. Ask the clerk when and how you will learn whether or not the judge signed the order.

4. How To Proceed

If the judge does sign the Ex Parte Application, the clerk will then file it. Then, you can proceed with the eviction as if the tenant had not filed for bankruptcy. If you are still in court, obviously the judge won't give you any grief about proceeding. If you have already obtained a judgment for possession, ask the clerk for a certified copy of the Ex Parte Application and Order and give it to the sheriff or marshal with a note to proceed with the eviction.

If the judge refuses to sign the order, look into asking the bankruptcy court to lift the stay (Section D, below).

S A M P L E

1	LENNY D. LANDLORD
2	12345 Angeleno St.
	Los Angeles, CA 90010
3	Tel: (213) 555-6789
4	Plaintiff in Pro Per

MUNICIPAL COURT OF CALIFORNIA, COUNTY OF LOS ANGELES

LOS ANGELES JUDICIAL DISTRICT

LENNY D. LANDLORD,   )   Case No. A-12345-B
)
        Plaintiff,   )   EX PARTE APPLICATION FOR
v.   )   ORDER TO PROCEED WITH
)   CASE NOTWITHSTANDING
TERRENCE D. TENANT,   )   DEFENDANT'S BANKRUPTCY;
)   PROPOSED ORDER
        Defendant.   )
_____)

        I, LENNY D. LANDLORD, declare:

        I am the plaintiff in this case. I am informed and believe

that defendants have filed a bankruptcy proceeding for the purpose

of delaying eviction pursuant to any judgment by this Court for

possession of the real property which is the subject of this

unlawful detainer action, namely that at 6789 Angel Boulevard,

Apartment 10, Los Angeles, California.

        As indicated in Item 6.a of the verified complaint on file in

this case, defendants' tenancy is a residential month-to-month

tenancy. A state court proceeding to obtain and execute on a

judgment for possession of a month-to-month residential tenancy is

not stopped by bankruptcy's automatic stay under 11 U.S.C. § 362.

(In re Smith (C.D. Cal 1989) 105 B.R. 50; a copy is attached to

1 this Application as Appendix A.) I do not seek a money judgment in

2 this case, but only a judgment for possession of the premises.

3   WHEREFORE, I request that the Court issue the Order set forth

4 below, directing the clerk and sheriff or marshal to proceed with

5 all aspects of prosecution and execution of judgment for possession

6 of the real property which is the subject of this unlawful detainer

7 action. I seek this Order because I believe the clerk, sheriff or

8 marshal may decline to proceed as required by law without it.

9   I declare under penalty of perjury under the laws of the State

10 of California that the foregoing is true and correct.

11 DATED: August 15, 1992

12   *Lenny D. Landlord*
                                Lenny D. Landlord

13

14

15

16

17

18

19

20

21

22

23

24

25

26

27

28

ORDER

It appearing from the within declaration that the tenancy for the premises that is the subject of the within-entitled unlawful detainer action is a residential month-to-month tenancy, and it therefore appearing that based on the decision of the U.S. Bankruptcy Court in In re Smith (C.D. Cal. 1989) 105 B.R. 50 that the automatic bankruptcy stay under 11 U.S.C. § 362 is not violated by obtaining and enforcing a judgment for possession of such premises,

IT IS HEREBY ORDERED that the within action is not subject to stay on account of defendants' having filed a petition in bankruptcy, and that the clerk, sheriff or marshal may execute any judgment for possession of the real property at 6789 Angel Boulevard, Apartment 10, Los Angeles, California, notwithstanding any bankruptcy filing by defendants.

DATED: _____, 19____

_____
JUDGE OF THE MUNICIPAL COURT

PROOF OF SERVICE BY MAIL

My address is _____123 Main Street_____,

_____Los Angeles_____, California.

On _____August 15_____, 19_92_, I served the within:

_Ex Parte Application for Order to Proceed with Case_____

_Notwithstanding Defendant's Bankruptcy and Proposed Order_____

by depositing true copies thereof, enclosed in separate, sealed

envelopes, with the postage thereon fully prepared, in the United

States Postal Service mail in _____Los Angeles_____ County,

addressed as follows:

    Terrence D. Tenant
    Tillie D. Tenant
    6789 Angel Boulevard, Apt. 10
    Los Angeles, CA 90010

I am, and was at the time herein-mentioned mailing took

place, a resident of or employed in the County where the mailing

occurred, over the age of eighteen years old and not a party to

the within cause.

I declare under penalty of perjury under the laws of the

State of California that the foregoing is true and correct.

Dated: _August 15, 1992_   _Samuel D. Server_____
                                        Samuel D. Server

D. Making a Motion for Relief From Stay in Bankruptcy Court

If you ask the bankruptcy court to lift the automatic stay, there is a good chance that your motion will be granted. Tenants usually do not file a response or even show up in court to contest motions for relief from the automatic stay.

1. Finding the Right Bankruptcy Court

To file a motion in bankruptcy court to have the automatic stay lifted, you must first find out which bankruptcy court the tenant filed in. Look for the court's address and phone number on any bankruptcy paper you receive from the court, the tenant or his bankruptcy lawyer. If you can't find the information on the papers, look for the district and branch names on the bankruptcy papers and use the chart below.

Once you have the phone number of the bankruptcy court, call the court clerk and ask to be sent a copy of the local court rules, together with a "Relief from Stay Cover Sheet." Once you have the rules, read the section entitled "Motion Practice," "Notice" or something similar. It will tell you how the court wants motions to be filed. It's very important to follow all local court rules scrupulously; if you don't, your papers could get thrown out.

Call the clerk back and ask to "calendar" (set a date for) a court hearing on a motion for relief from the automatic stay. The clerk should give you a court date over the phone. Be sure it is enough days ahead so you have time to prepare the papers and give the tenant the number of days' written notice of your motion required by your local rules (usually ten days). Also ask the clerk for the time and location of the hearing.

2. Preparing the Papers

Before your court date, you must prepare these documents:

- Relief from Stay Cover Sheet
- Notice of Motion for Relief from Automatic Stay and Proof of Service

---

Federal Bankruptcy Courts in California

CENTRAL DISTRICT	EASTERN DISTRICT	SOUTHERN DISTRICT	NORTHERN DISTRICT
Federal Building 312 N. Spring St. Los Angeles, CA 90012 213-894-4696	8308 U.S. Courthouse 650 Capitol Mall Sacramento, CA 95814 916-551-2662	5-N-26 U.S. Courthouse 940 Front Street San Diego, CA 92189 619-557-5620	P.O. Box 7341 235 Pine Street San Francisco, CA 94120 415-705-3200
506 Federal Building 34 Civic Center Plaza Santa Ana, CA 92701 714-836-2993	5301 U.S. Courthouse 1130 O St., Fresno, CA 93721 209-487-5217		P.O. Box 2070 1300 Clay St. Oakland, CA 94604 510-273-7212
222 E. Carrillo St. Room 101 Santa Barbara, CA 93101 805-897-3880	P.O. Box 5276 Modesto, CA 95352 209-521-5160		280 South First St. Room 3035 San Jose, CA 95113 408-291-7286
699 N. Arrowhead Ave. Room 105 San Bernardino, CA 92401 714-383-5873			99 South E. St. Santa Rosa, CA 95404 707-525-8520

- Motion for Relief from Automatic Stay
- Declaration in Support of Motion for Relief from Automatic Stay
- Order Granting Relief from Automatic Stay.

Samples are shown below for all these forms except the Relief from Stay Cover Sheet, a preprinted form which you should get from your local court clerk. You will need to use pleading paper (the 8-1/2" x 11" paper with the numbers down the left side) for all forms. Make copies of the blank sheet in the Appendix.

Have the following papers in front of you when you get ready to start preparing your own documents; they contain much of the information you need:

- the tenant's bankruptcy papers that were sent to you;
- the papers you filed in municipal court for the eviction; and
- any papers the tenant filed in municipal court to oppose the eviction.

Fill out the top of the forms accurately. Be sure the caption on the top of all the papers accurately states the bankruptcy district, the case name as indicated on the tenant's bankruptcy papers, the bankruptcy case number and the type of bankruptcy (Chapter 7 or 13) the tenant is filing, as well as the court date, time, place of hearing and other information the bankruptcy court clerk has given to you. The clerk will fill in the item "R.S. No." when you file each form.

Tell the truth. The facts you state in the Motion for Relief from Automatic Stay and the Declaration in Support of Motion for Relief from Automatic Stay must be true. Remember that you are signing these documents under penalty of perjury and that it is a federal crime to lie.

You may properly state that you believe the tenant is using bankruptcy merely to avoid eviction, based simply on the timing of the bankruptcy filing while your eviction lawsuit is pending—unless you know that the tenant is honestly filing to discharge many other debts. In the Motion and Declaration, state that the tenant has filed a "skeleton petition" (the bare minimum of forms in

bankruptcy court without a detailed list of assets and debts, which must be filed later) only if that is true. (You can find this out from the bankruptcy court or the tenant's bankruptcy attorney.) The same is true with respect to a bankruptcy petition that lists only a few creditors, including you. Don't state this as fact in your Motion unless you have confirmed it with the bankruptcy court.

3. Filing the Papers

File the original documents, including a Proof of Service by Mail (see Section 4, below) with the bankruptcy court. Be sure to attach relevant eviction documents to the Declaration in Support of Motion for Relief from Automatic Stay, including copies of the complaint you filed in the eviction lawsuit, the tenant's answer, if any and any judgment. Label each attachment (on the bottom of the form) as "Exhibit A," "Exhibit B" and so on.

You can mail the documents to the bankruptcy court, but you are better off taking them in person in case you have mistakes you need to correct. In fact, if you live a great distance from the bankruptcy court, you may want to take along extra copies of pleading paper and a portable typewriter so you can fix the papers on the spot. Also, take your checkbook. You must pay a $60 filing fee, and if you have to retype any papers, the clerk will charge you 75 cents or more a page to make copies.

When making copies of your motion papers, be sure to make a set for yourself, the tenant and anyone else who must receive copies (see Section 4, below) and an extra few copies for the court clerk.

4. Mailing the Motion Papers and Preparing a Proof of Service

Someone over age 18 who isn't a party to the eviction case must mail copies of your motion papers to tenants who have filed bankruptcy, their bankruptcy attorney, if any, the "trustee" (a person appointed by the bankruptcy court to oversee the bankruptcy) and all the creditors listed on the debtor's bankruptcy papers. The trustee's and creditors' names and addresses should be listed on the tenant's bankruptcy papers; you can also get this information from the court clerk.

The person who mails the motion papers must complete and sign a Proof of Service by Mail, which you will attach to the original Notice of Motion for Relief from Automatic Stay you file with the court.

Prepare your forms carefully. Your documents should look something like the samples shown below. However, it is crucial that you adapt the documents according to your own particular circumstances, based on the facts you know to be true.

If You Want To Hire an Attorney

If you don't want to represent yourself in filing a motion for relief from the automatic stay, you need to hire an attorney. But be careful—not just any attorney will do. You will want to hire an attorney with experience representing creditors in bankruptcy. If you know other landlords who have used bankruptcy attorneys, call for a referral. Otherwise, look in the Yellow Pages under attorneys, subheading Bankruptcy.

Call one and ask if she handles motions for relief from automatic stays for landlords. If she says yes, explain that a tenant filed bankruptcy to delay your eviction and that you'd like to hire the lawyer to file a motion for relief from the automatic stay. Ask her what the fee is, assuming one court appearance. Anything much above $750 is excessive. If the attorney bills by the hour, ask for an estimate of how many hours the job should take—and get it in writing before you agree.

---

5. Preparing for the Hearing

If the debtor files and sends you an opposition paper, be sure to study it before the hearing. Go through your records and jot down some notes in response to each argument the debtor raises. Get statements from appraisers stating that the tenant's rent is not below market rate to show that the lease is not a valuable asset. Make copies of your monthly mortgage payment bills to show that you are suffering a hardship because the tenant is delaying eviction with bankruptcy.

6. The Hearing

On the day of the hearing, arrive at the bankruptcy courtroom about a half hour early. If there are several courtrooms, and you don't know where your motion will be heard, check the calendar that is usually posted outside each courtroom. Typically, bankruptcy courts hear many cases, and many different types of motions, on a given day and time. If a calendar is not posted, or if you can't find your case on the list, check with the court clerk.

Once you find the correct courtroom, pay attention to the cases that are called before yours—even if the motions are not similar to yours—to get a feel for how the judge conducts hearings.

When your case is called, walk up to the podium, state your name and say that you are appearing "in pro per." If the tenants and their attorney show up, they should identify themselves, too. Since you are the party making the motion, the judge may ask you questions or ask you to speak first. Very briefly summarize the points you made in your papers and be sure you can back up your assertions. For example, you may want to say:

- The bankruptcy was filed only after you filed the unlawful detainer lawsuit in municipal court or just before the eviction was to take place.
- The tenancy is from month to month.
- The tenancy is not a valuable asset of the bankruptcy estate because the rent you're charging is not significantly less than the fair-market rental.

S A M P L E

1	LENNY D. LANDLORD
	12345 Angeleno St.
2	Los Angeles, CA 90010
	Tel: (213) 555-1234
3	
	Creditor and Moving Party in Pro Per
4	

1
2
3
4
5
6
7

8   UNITED STATES BANKRUPTCY COURT

9
          CENTRAL DISTRICT OF CALIFORNIA
10

11   In re:)   Case No. 292-12345-ABCDE
)
12   TERRENCE D. TENANT,   )   CHAPTER 7
     TILLIE D. TENANT   )
13   )   R.S. No. _____
)
14   Debtors.   )   Hearing Date: 9/15/92
     _____)   Time: 10:00 AM
15

16   NOTICE OF MOTION FOR RELIEF FROM AUTOMATIC STAY

17   TO TERRENCE D. TENANT AND TILLIE D. TENANT, DEBTORS,
18   AND TO THEIR ATTORNEY OF RECORD:

19   PLEASE TAKE NOTICE that on September 15, 1992 at 10:00 AM, in

20   the above-entitled Court, at 312 North Spring Street, Los Angeles,

21   California, Creditor LENNY D. LANDLORD will move for relief from

22   the automatic stay herein, with regard to obtaining a judgment in

23   state court that includes possession of the real property at 6789

24   Angel Boulevard, Apartment 10, Los Angeles, California. The

25   grounds for the motion are set forth in the accompanying motion

26   and declaration.

27   You, and the trustee in this case, are advised that no

28   written response is required to oppose this motion, and that no

oral testimony will normally be permitted in opposition to the motion. You and/or your attorney, or other party including the trustee, however, must appear to oppose the motion or the relief requested may be granted. Applicable law is 11 U.S.C. § 362, Bankruptcy Rules 4001 and 9014 and *In re Smith* (C.D. Cal 1989) 105 B.R. 50.

DATED: August 30, 1992

Lenny D. Landlord
_____

Lenny D. Landlord
Creditor in Pro Per

```
 1   LENNY D. LANDLORD
     12345 Angeleno St.
 2   Los Angeles, CA 90010
     Tel: (213) 555-6789
 3
     Creditor and Moving Party in Pro Per
 4

 5

 6

 7

 8                 UNITED STATES BANKRUPTCY COURT

 9               CENTRAL DISTRICT OF CALIFORNIA

10
     In re:                          )  Case No. 292-12345-ABCDE
11                                    )
     TERRANCE D. TENANT               )  CHAPTER 7
12   TILLIE D. TENANT                 )
                                      )  R.S. No. _____
13        Debtors.                    )
                                      )  Hearing Date: 9/15/92
14   _____)  Time: 10:00 AM

15

16          MOTION FOR RELIEF FROM AUTOMATIC STAY

17        Creditor LENNY D. LANDLORD moves this Court for an Order

18   granting relief from the automatic stay, on the following grounds:

19        On September 1, 1992, Debtors filed a petition under Chapter

20   7 of the U.S. Bankruptcy Code.

21        Debtors occupy the real property at 6789 Angel Boulevard,

22   Apartment 10, Los Angeles, California, pursuant to a tenancy from

23   month to month. Debtors failed to pay the rent of $900 for the

24   period of August 1, 1992 to August 31, 1992, and have paid no rent

25   for any period subsequent. As a result, on August 5, 1992,

26   Creditor served Debtors with a three-day notice to pay rent or

27   quit, to which Debtors failed to respond. Creditor filed an

28   unlawful detainer action entitled Landlord v. Tenant, Case No.
```

1   A-12345-B in the Municipal Court of California for the County of

2   Los Angeles, on August 9, 1992. Creditor obtained against Debtors

3   a judgment for possession of the premises on August 15, 1992.

4   Creditor is informed and believes that Debtors filed the

5   petition in bankruptcy solely to avoid execution of any judgment

6   for possession of real property in the state court proceeding,

7   and without intending to seek the fresh start provided under

8   Title 11 of the U.S. Code. In addition, as evidence of bad faith

9   in their bankruptcy filing, Debtors filed only a "skeleton

10 petition" and listed this Creditor as the only substantial

11 creditor in the case. Creditor attaches his declaration under

12 penalty of perjury, which includes true copies of all litigation

13 documents in the state court unlawful detainer proceeding.

14 Dated: __August 15, 1992__   *Lenny D. Landlord*

15   Creditor in Pro Per

16

17

18

19

20

21

22

23

24

25

26

27

28

1 LENNY D. LANDLORD
   12345 Angeleno St.
2 Los Angeles, CA 90010
   Tel: (213) 555-6789
3
   Creditor and Moving Party in Pro Per
4

5

6

7

8   UNITED STATES BANKRUPTCY COURT

9   CENTRAL DISTRICT OF CALIFORNIA

10
   In re:) Case No. 292-12345-ABCDE
11   )
   TERRANCE D. TENANT   ) CHAPTER 7
12 TILLIE D. TENANT   )
) R.S. No. _____
13   Debtors.   )
) Hearing Date: 9/15/92
14 _____) Time: 10:00 AM

15

16 DECLARATION IN SUPPORT OF MOTION FOR RELIEF FROM AUTOMATIC STAY

17   I, LENNY D. LANDLORD, declare:

18   I am over the age of 18 years. I am the moving party in the

19 above-entitled action. If called as a witness, I could testify

20 competently to the following:

21   On August 9, 1992, I caused to be filed in the Municipal Court

22 of the State of California, for the County of Los Angeles, Los

23 Angeles Judicial District, a verified complaint in unlawful

24 detainer, a copy of which is attached hereto as Exhibit "A." The

25 case number is A-12345-B. All the allegations stated therein are

26 true to my knowledge.

27   I obtained a judgment for possession of the real property at

28 6789 Angel Boulevard, Apartment 10, Los Angeles, California, in the

1   state-court action against Debtors, on August 15, 1992.

2   As is indicated in the unlawful detainer complaint, the

3   tenancy is a residential month-to-month tenancy. I am the owner of

4   the premises. In my opinion, the rent that Debtors agreed to pay

5   as alleged in the unlawful detainer complaint is the reasonable

6   rental value of the premises.

7   Debtors remain in possession of the premises. I will suffer

8   irreparable harm if the automatic stay is not vacated as to

9   enforcement of any judgment for possession of the real property,

10 because each day I incur additional costs as the result of

11 Debtors' nonpayment of rent and their failure to vacate the

12 premises, in that I must make mortgage payments on the property

13 while I am unable to rent it to prospective tenants, other than

14 Debtors, who would pay rent that I could use to defray the

15 mortgage.

16   I am informed and believe that the tenancy is not a sellable

17 asset of the bankruptcy estate, so that continued possession of

18 the real property by Debtors is not necessary to freeze their

19 assets for sale to benefit their creditors or to effect any

20 reorganization by Debtors.

21   I declare under penalty of perjury under the laws of the

22 United States that the foregoing is true and correct.

23

24 Dated: August 15, 1992   *Lenny D. Landlord*
                                      Creditor in Pro Per

25

26

27

28

S A M P L E

1	LENNY D. LANDLORD
	12345 Angeleno St.
2	Los Angeles, CA 90010
	Tel: (213) 555-6789
3	
	Creditor and Moving Party in Pro Per
4	
5	
6	
7	
8	UNITED STATES BANKRUPTCY COURT
9	CENTRAL DISTRICT OF CALIFORNIA
10	
	In re:) Case No. 292-12345-ABCDE
11	)
	TERRANCE D. TENANT) CHAPTER 7
12	TILLIE D. TENANT)
	) R.S. No. _____
13	Debtors.)
	) Hearing Date: 9/15/92
14	_____) Time: 10:00 AM
15	
16	ORDER GRANTING RELIEF FROM AUTOMATIC STAY
17	The motion of Creditor LENNY D. LANDLORD for relief from the
18	automatic stay under 11 U.S.C. § 362 came on for hearing in the
19	above-entitled Court on September 15, 1992 at 10:00 AM; the
20	Creditor appearing in pro per. The Court having taken the matter
21	under submission following argument,
22	IT IS HEREBY ORDERED that Creditor LENNY D. LANDLORD have
23	relief from the automatic stay provided by Debtors' filing of the
24	petition in this case, in that Creditor may proceed with the
25	prosecution of the state court unlawful detainer action of Landlord
26	v. Tenant, et al., Case No. A-12345-B in the Municipal Court of
27	California for the County of Los Angeles, Los Angeles Judicial
28	District, and that Creditor may execute on any judgment for

possession or restitution of the premises at 6789 Angel Boulevard,
Apartment 10, Los Angeles, California, notwithstanding the
pendency of the within-entitled action.

DATED: _____, 19___

_____
UNITED STATES BANKRUPTCY JUDGE

SAMPLE

1	PROOF OF SERVICE BY MAIL
2	My address is _____123 Main Street_____,
3	_____Los Angeles_____, California.
4	On ____August 15____, 19_92_, I served the within:
5	Notice of Motion for Relief from Automatic Stay, Motion for
6	Relief from Automatic Stay, Declaration in Support of Motion for
7	Relief from Automatic Stay, and Proposed Order Granting Relief
8	from Automatic Stay
9	by depositing true copies thereof, enclosed in separate, sealed
10	envelopes, with the postage thereon fully prepared, in the United
11	States Postal Service mail in ____Los Angeles____ County,
12	addressed as follows:
13	Terrence D. Tenant Tillie D. Tenant
14	6789 Angel Boulevard, Apt. 10 Los Angeles, CA 90010
15	(Debtors)
16	Thomas T. Trustee
17	12345 Business Blvd. Los Angeles, CA 90010
18	(Trustee)
19	Lana L. Lawyer 246 Litigation Lane
20	Los Angeles, CA 90010
	(Debtors' Attorney)
21	
22	I am, and was at the time herein-mentioned mailing took
23	place, a resident of or employed in the County where the mailing
24	occurred, over the age of eighteen years old and not a party to
25	the within cause.
26	I declare under penalty of perjury under the laws of the
27	State of California that the foregoing is true and correct.
28	Dated: ____August 15, 1992____ *Samuel D. Server* Samuel D. Server

- The tenant filed only a "skeleton petition," without detailed schedules of assets and liabilities.

- The tenant listed only a few creditors, including you.

Whether or not the tenant shows up (many don't), the hearing will probably be very brief. The judge may ask you some questions, but hearings are not like trials. There are no formal rules of evidence—the facts supporting your motion should have been included in your declaration.

The judge will probably decide on the spot whether or not to grant the motion. If he does, ask him to use the proposed Order Granting Relief from Automatic Stay. If he won't sign this Order, ask him if he wants you to prepare one with different language, or whether he will have his own order typed up and, if so, when that will be ready.

Once the judge signs the order, give a copy of it to the municipal court clerk or the sheriff or marshal performing the eviction. They might require a certified copy of the order. If so, you will have to pay the bankruptcy court clerk's office a small fee for a certified copy. You're now ready to proceed with your eviction. ■

Appendix

Rent Control Chart
Forms

---

*Be sure that the back of the forms you submit to the court
are printed upside-down, as they are on the Appendix forms.

Rent Control Chart

Reading Your Rent Control Ordinance

The following chart contains most of the information about how your rent control ordinance affects evictions, but we recommend that you check the ordinance itself and the chart in *Volume 1*, Chapter 4 (which goes into more detail), and always make sure that it hasn't changed since this was printed. In case you are (understandably) intimidated at the prospect of deciphering your city's ordinance, here are a few hints about reading and understanding rent control ordinances.

Almost all rent control ordinances begin with a statement of purpose, followed by definitions of terms used in the ordinance. If such terms as "rental unit" and "landlord" aren't defined specifically enough to tell you who and what is covered by the ordinance, another section dealing with applicability of the ordinance usually follows. After that the ordinance usually sets out the structure and rules of the rent board and will say whether or not landlords must register their properties with the board.

Your ordinance probably then has a section entitled something like "Annual Increases" or "General Rent Ceiling." If the city allows increases when the unit becomes vacant, this will be stated under this category or in a "Vacancy Decontrol" section.

Following the rent sections should be a section on "Individual Adjustments" or "Hardship Adjustments." This section tells you how to get an increase over and above any general across the board increase. Finally, any requirement that you show "just cause" for eviction should be found under a section entitled "Just (or Good) Cause for Eviction." It will contain a list of the permissible reasons for eviction, along with any extra requirements for eviction notices, and prohibit evictions for any other reason.

To see if you've complied with your city's rent control ordinance before you begin an eviction, check the ordinance for:

- **Registration requirements.** If you're required to register your unit with the rent board but didn't, your tenant may be able to win an eviction lawsuit.

- **Rent increase restrictions.** Read the individual adjustment section to see if the landlord must apply to the rent board for increases over a certain amount. If so, make sure any rent increases were properly applied for and legal. This is especially important if you're planning to evict for nonpayment of rent, because you must list the rent that's legally due on the three-day notice.

- **Special notice requirements.** Check both the general and individual rent adjustment sections, as well as any regulations adopted by the rent board, for special notice requirements for rent-increase notices. Again, if you're evicting for nonpayment of rent, you want to be sure that all previous increases were given with a valid notice.

- **Just cause requirements.** This is crucial; you can evict only for one of the permissible reasons and you must comply with any additional notice requirements. If you want to evict tenants so you can demolish the building or simply go out of business, you may do so under the Ellis Act (Govt. Code §§ 7060-7060.7), even if this reason isn't listed in the ordinance. However, you definitely should have a lawyer handle the eviction.

If you're evicting to move a relative or manager into the unit or to remodel, demolish, or convert the unit, any just cause requirement will have numerous technical notice and compensation requirements. You should consult a lawyer.

BERKELEY

Name of Ordinance	Rent Stabilization and Eviction for Good Cause Ordinance, Ordinance 5261-N.S.	**Just Cause**	Required. (§ 13.a.) This requirement applies even if the property is exempt from other rent control requirements because it qualifies as new construction (§ 5) or government-owned/operated housing. Specific good cause to evict must be stated in both the notice and in any unlawful detainer complaint. (Regulation § 1310.)
Adoption Date	6/3/80. Last amended 11/90, by initiative.		
Exceptions	Units constructed after 6/3/80, owner-occupied single-family residences and duplexes. (§ 5.)		
Administration	Rent Stabilization Board 2100 Milvia Street Berkeley, CA 94704 (510) 644-6128	**Other Features**	The landlord's complaint must allege compliance with both the implied warranty of habitability and the rent control ordinance, except for evictions for remodeling or demolition. (§ 1311.) If the remodeling, demolition, or the moving in of the landlord or a relative on which the eviction was based doesn't occur within two months of the tenant's leaving, the tenant can sue the landlord to regain possession of property and recover actual damages (treble damages or $750 if reason willfully false). (§ 15.)
Registration	Required or landlords cannot raise rent. (The provision that a tenant can withhold rents if the landlord fails to register was ruled unconstitutional in *Floystrup v. Berkeley Rent Stablization Board* (1990) 219 Cal. App. 3d 1309. Stiff penalties for noncooperation. (§§ 8, 11.f.4, 11.g.)		
Vacancy Decontrol	None. Ordinance § 6.q allows for decontrol only if the rental unit vacancy rate exceeds 5% and both Board and City Council agree; under current and foreseeable housing situations, this is a virtual impossibility.		

Reasons Allowed for Just Cause Evictions

Nonpayment of rent.

Breach of lease provision.

Willful causing or allowing of substantial damage to premises and refusal to both pay the reasonable cost of repair and cease causing damage, following written notice.

Tenant refuses to agree to rental agreement or lease on expiration of prior one, where new proposed agreement contains no new or unlawful terms.

Additional Local Notice Requirements and Limitations

Ordinary Three-Day Notice To Pay Rent or Quit is used. (See Chapter 2.)

Three-Day Notice To Perform Covenant or Quit (Chapter 4) is used. Provision must be "reasonable and legal and.... been accepted by the tenant or made part of the rental agreement." If the provision was added after tenant moved in, landlord can evict for breach only if tenant was told in writing that she did not have to accept the new term. Tenant must be given "written notice to cease," which precludes an Unconditional Three-Day Notice To Quit even if the breach is considered uncorrectible.

Even though damage is involved, an Unconditional Three-Day Notice To Quit (Chapter 4) is not allowed. Only a three-day notice that gives the tenant the option of ceasing to cause damage and pay for repair is allowed.

This applies only if a lease or rental agreement expires of its own terms. No notice is required (see Chapter 5). However, tenant must have refused to sign a new one containing the same provisions; an improvised notice giving the tenant several days to sign the new agreement or leave is a good idea, even though not required by ordinance or state law.

Tenant continued to be so disorderly as to disturb other tenants, following written notice to cease or is otherwise subject to eviction under CCP § 1161(4), for committing a nuisance, very seriously damaging the property or subletting contrary to the lease or rental agreement.

Although a warning notice should precede three-day notice based on disturbing neighbors, the three-day notice, according to CCP §1161(4) may be an unconditional Three-Day Notice To Quit.

Tenant, after written notice to cease, continues to refuse landlord access to the property as required by Civ. Code § 1954.

If provision is in lease, use three-day notice giving tenant option of letting you in or moving. If not, and tenancy is month to month, use 30-day notice specifying reason, following written demand for access.

Landlord wants to make substantial repairs to bring property into compliance with health codes, and repairs not possible while tenant remains.

Under state law, eviction for this reason is allowed only if rental agreement is month to month, not for a fixed term. Landlord must first obtain all permits required for the remodeling, must provide alternative housing for the tenant (at the same rent) if he owns other vacant units in city, and must give evicted tenant right of first refusal to rerent after remodeling is finished. (Tenant given alternate temporary housing may be evicted from it if he refuses to move into old unit after work is completed. § 13.a.11.)

Landlord wants to demolish property.

Landlord must first obtain city "removal permit." (Although ordinance requires "good faith" to demolish, a euphemism for not doing it because of rent control, the state Ellis Act severely limits cities from refusing demolition permits on this basis.)

Landlord wants to move self, spouse, parent or child into property, and no comparable vacant unit exists in the property.

30-day notice terminating month-to-month tenancy for this reason must specify name and relationship of person moving in. (Regulation 1380.) (Month to month tenancies only.)

Tenant, after written notice to cease, continues to conduct illegal activity on the premises.

Although a warning notice should precede a three-day notice based on illegal activity, the three-day notice, according to C.C.P. § 1161(4), may be an unconditional Three-Day Notice To Quit.

Landlord wants to move in herself, lived there previously and lease or rental agreement specifically allows for this.

Termination procedure must be in accordance with lease provision. 30 days' written notice is required to terminate month-to-month tenancy unless agreement provides for lesser period as short as 7 days.

Landlord wants to go out of rental business under state Ellis Act.

The requirement that the landlord must give the tenant six months' notice and pay $4,500 in relocation fees to tenants of each unit was ruled illegal, as pre-empted by the State Ellis Act, in *Channing Properties v. City of Berkeley* (1992) 11 Cal. App. 4th 88, 14 Cal. Rptr. 2d 32.

BEVERLY HILLS

Name of Ordinance	Rent Stabilization Ordinance (Beverly Hills Municipal Code, Chapter 5), Ordinance No. 79-0-1731.
Adoption Date	4/27/79. Last amended 12/9/91.
Exceptions	Units constructed after 10/20/78, units that rented for more than $600 on 5/31/78, single-family residences, rented condominium units. (§ 4-5.102.)
Administration	Rent Adjustments Board 455 N. Rexford Beverly Hills, CA 90210 (310) 285-1031.
Registration	Not required.
Vacancy Decontrol	Landlord may charge any rent after a tenant vacates voluntarily, but not when tenancy is terminated by landlord. Once the property is re-rented (when the termination is voluntary), it is subject to rent control based on the higher rent. (§ 4-5-310.)
Just Cause	Required for units other than those that rented for more than $600 on 5/31/78; for these units, a month-to-month tenancy may be terminated only on 60 days' notice, however.
Other Features	Though not required by the ordinance, termination notice should state specific reason for termination; this indicates compliance with ordinance, as alleged (item 16) in your unlawful detainer complaint. Landlord is required to pay tenant substantial relocation fee if evicting to move in self or relative, or to substantially remodel, demolish or convert to condominiums. Tenant may sue landlord who uses moving-in of self or relative as a "pretext" for eviction, for three times the rent that would have been due for the period the tenant was out of possession.

Reasons Allowed for Just Cause Evictions

Nonpayment of rent.

Breach of lease provision, following written notice to correct problem.

Commission of a legal nuisance (disturbing other residents) or damaging the property.

Tenant is using the property for illegal purpose. This specifically includes overcrowding as defined in ordinance based on number of bedrooms and square footage.

Tenant refuses, after written demand by landlord, to agree to new rental agreement or lease on expiration of prior one, where proposed agreement contains no new or unlawful terms.

Tenant has refused the landlord reasonable access to the property as required by Civil Code § 1954.

Fixed-term lease has expired, and person occupying property is subtenant not approved by landlord.

Additional Local Notice Requirements and Limitations

Ordinary Three-Day Notice To Pay Rent or Quit is used. (See Chapter 2.)

Three-Day Notice To Cure Covenant or Quit (Chapter 4) is used. The tenant must be given "written notice to cease," which precludes an unconditional Three-Day Notice To Quit even if the breach is uncorrectible.

Unconditional Three-Day Notice To Quit (Chapter 4) may be used.

Unconditional Three-Day Notice To Quit (Chapter 4) may be used.

This applies when a lease or rental agreement expires of its own terms. The ordinance requires the landlord to have made a written request for renewal or extension at least 30 days before the old one expired.

If access provision is in lease, use three-day notice giving tenant option of letting you in or moving. If not, and tenancy is month to month, use 30-day notice specifying reason, following written demand for access to property.

Eviction is allowed on this basis only if person living there is not original tenant or approved subtenant. If lease has not expired and contains no-subletting clause, use Three-Day Notice To Quit to evict for breach of lease. (See Chapter 4.)

Landlord wants to move self, parent or child into property, and no comparable vacant unit exists in the property. In multiple-unit dwelling, landlord can evict only the most recently-moved-in tenant for this reason.

Landlord must give tenant 90-day notice which states the name, relationship and address of person to be moved in, and a copy of the notice must be sent to the City Clerk. Landlord must also pay tenant(s) a "relocation fee" of up to $2,500, depending on the length of tenancy and the size of unit. The fee must be paid when the tenant leaves, or tenant can sue landlord for three times the fee plus attorney's fees. (§ 11-7.05.) Landlord does not have to pay fee if tenant fails to leave at end of 90-day period or pays to relocate tenant to comparable housing elsewhere. (§§ 11-6.01-11-6.07.)

Employment of resident manager has been terminated and the property is needed for occupancy by the new manager.

This type of eviction is not covered in this book because the question of what notice is required is extremely complicated, depending in part on the nature of the management agreement. You should seek legal advice.

Landlord wants to demolish property or convert to condominiums, or otherwise remove property from rental market.

Landlord must first obtain removal permit from city. For substantial remodeling, tenant gets right of first refusal when work done. Landlord must give tenant one year's notice. Landlord must also pay tenant(s) a "relocation fee" of up to $2,500, depending on the length of tenancy and the size of unit. The fee must be paid when the tenant leaves, or tenant can sue landlord for three times the fee plus attorney's fees. (§ 11-7.05.) Landlord does not have to pay fee if tenant fails to leave at end of 90-day period or pays to relocate tenant to comparable housing elsewhere. (§§ 11-6.01-11-6.07.) Notice, if not accompanied by fee, must inform tenant of its amount and that it is payable when the tenant vacates. The notice cannot be given until city approval of the project is obtained, and a copy of the notice must be sent to the City Clerk.

Landlord wants to substantially remodel property.

Landlord must first obtain removal permit from city. For substantial remodeling, tenant gets right of first refusal when work done. Landlord must give tenant one year's notice. Landlord must also pay tenant(s) a "relocation fee" of up to $2,500, depending on the length of tenancy and the size of unit. The fee must be paid when the tenant leaves, or tenant can sue landlord for three times the fee plus attorney's fees. (§ 11-7.05.) Landlord does not have to pay fee if tenant fails to leave at end of 90-day period or pays to relocate tenant to comparable housing elsewhere. (§§ 11-6.01-11-6.07.) Notice, if not accompanied by fee, must inform tenant of its amount and that it is payable when the tenant vacates. The notice cannot be given until city approval of the project is obtained, and a copy of the notice must be sent to the City Clerk. Landlord must petition Board for permission and in some cases must provide replacement housing during remodeling.

CAMPBELL

Note	This ordinance is not truly a rent control ordinance. Compliance with rent board decisions appears to be voluntary only.	**Administration**	Campbell Rent Mediation Program 1245 S. Winchester Blvd., Suite 20 San Jose, CA 95128 (408) 243-8565.
Name of Ordinance	Campbell Rental Increase Dispute Resolution Ordinance (Campbell Municipal Code, Chapter 6.09).	**Registration**	Not required.
		Vacancy Decontrol	Because there is no "real" rent control, there's no decontrol provision.
Adoption Date	1983.		
Exceptions	Single-family residences, duplexes and triplexes. (§ 6.09.030(l).)	**Just Cause**	Not required.

COTATI

Name of Ordinance	"Rent Stabilization" (Cotati Municipal Code, Chapter 19.19), Ordinance No. 300.	**Registration**	Required.
Adoption Date	9/23/80. Last amended 3/10/87.	**Vacancy Decontrol**	None. (Ordinance § 19.12.030.P allows Board to decontrol only a category of housing whose rental unit vacancy rate exceeds 5%; this is highly unlikely.)
Exception	Units constructed after 9/23/80 (Board has authority to remove exemption), owner-occupied single-family residences, duplexes, and triplexes. (§ 19.12.020.D.)	**Just Cause**	Required. Landlord must state cause with specificity in the complaint, as well as in the termination notice. (§ 19.12.080.)
Administration	Rent Appeals Board 201 W. Sierra Cotati, CA 94931 (707) 792-4600		

Reasons Allowed for Just Cause Evictions

Nonpayment of rent.

Breach of lease provision, following written notice to cease.

Willful causing or allowing of substantial damage to premises, or commission of nuisance that interferes with comfort, safety or enjoyment of the property, following written notice to cease.

Tenant has been using the property illegally.

Tenant refuses to agree to rental agreement or lease on expiration of prior one, where new proposed agreement contains no new or unlawful terms.

Tenant has refused the landlord access to the property, as required by Civil Code § 1954.

Fixed-term lease has expired, and person occupying property is subtenant not approved by landlord.

Landlord wants to move self, parent, child, brother, sister or spouse of foregoing into property.

Landlord wants to demolish property, or otherwise remove property from rental market.

Landlord shares kitchen or bathroom facilities with tenant.

Additional Local Notice Requirements and Limitations

Ordinary Three-Day Notice To Pay Rent or Quit is used. (See Chapter 2.)

Three-Day Notice To Perform Covenant or Quit (Chapter 4) is used. The ordinance precludes use of an Unconditional Three-Day Notice To Quit, even if the breach is uncorrectible.

Conditional Three-Day notice giving tenant the option of correcting the problem (Chapter 4) must be used.

Three-Day Notice To Quit is used. (See Chapter 4.)

This applies only when a lease or rental agreement expires of its own terms. No notice is required (see Chapter 5). However, an improvised notice giving the tenant several days to sign the new agreement or leave is a good idea.

If provision is in lease, use three-day notice giving tenant option of letting you in or moving. If not, and tenancy is month to month, use 30-day notice specifying reason.

Eviction on this basis is allowed only if person living there is not original tenant or approved subtenant. If lease has not expired and contains no-subletting clause, use Three-Day Notice To Quit to evict for breach of lease. (See Chapter 4.)

Under state law, eviction for this reason is allowed only if rental agreement is month to month. Use 30-day notice.

Under state law, eviction for this reason is allowed only if rental agreement is month to month. Use 30-day notice. (Although ordinance requires "good faith" to demolish, a euphemism for not doing it because of rent control, the state Ellis Act severely limits cities from refusing demolition permits on this basis.)

Under state law, eviction for this reason is allowed only if rental agreement is month to month. Use 30-day notice. (Since owner-occupied single-family homes are exempt from all aspects of the ordinance, this section is unlikely to be of much use.)

EAST PALO ALTO

Name of Ordinance	Rent Stabilization and Eviction for Good Cause Ordinance, Ordinance No. 076.
Adoption Date	11/23/83. Last amended 4/88.
Exception	Units constructed after 11/23/83, units owned by landlords owning four or fewer units in city, property rehabilitated in accordance with federal Internal Revenue Code § 174(k). (§ 5.)
Administration	Rent Stabilization Board 2415 University Ave. East Palo Alto, CA 94303 (415) 853-3100.
Registration	Required.
Vacancy Decontrol	None.
Just Cause	Required (§ 13.A). This aspect of the ordinance applies even to new construction, which is otherwise exempt. Specific just cause to evict must be stated in both the notice and in any unlawful detainer complaint. (§ 13.B.)

Other Features

Landlord's complaint must allege compliance with both the implied warranty of habitability and the rent control ordinance, except for evictions for remodeling or demolition (§ 13.C). If remodeling, demolition, or moving self or a relative, on which eviction was based, doesn't occur within two months of the tenant's leaving, tenant can sue landlord to regain possession of property and recover actual damages (treble damages or $500 if reason willfully false). (§ 15.B.)

East Palo Alto's ordinance does not specifically allow eviction for illegal use of the premises, such as dealing drugs. Still, if the lease has a clause prohibiting illegal use of the premises, you can evict for breach of lease provision (see below). If there's no such lease provision, see an attorney about whether C.C.P. § 1161(4)s allowance of an eviction for illegal activity may "pre-empt" the local ordinance.

Reasons Allowed for Just Cause Evictions

Nonpayment of rent.

Breach of lease provision, following written notice to cease.

Willful causing or allowing of substantial damage to premises and refusal to both pay the reasonable cost of repair and cease causing damage, following written notice.

Tenant refuses to agree to rental agreement or lease on expiration of prior one, where new proposed agreement contains no new or unlawful terms.

Tenant continues to be so disorderly as to disturb other tenants, following written notice to cease.

Tenant, after written notice to cease, continues to refuse the landlord access to the property as required by Civil Code § 1954.

Additional Local Notice Requirements and Limitations

Ordinary Three-Day Notice To Pay Rent or Quit is used. (See Chapter 2.)

Three-Day Notice To Cure Covenant or Quit (Chapter 4) is used. Provision must be reasonable and legal and been accepted by the tenant or made part of the rental agreement. If the provision was added after the tenant first moved in, the landlord can evict for breach only if the tenant was told in writing that she didn't have to accept the new term. Ordinance forbids use of an unconditional notice.

Even though damage is involved an ordinary unconditional Three-Day Notice To Quit (Chapter 4) is not allowed. Only a three-day notice that gives the tenant the option of ceasing to cause damage and pay for the costs of repair, as demanded by the landlord, is allowed.

This applies only when a lease or rental agreement expires of its own terms. No notice is required (see Chapter 5). However, an improvised notice giving the tenant several days to sign the new agreement or leave is a good idea.

Even if the tenant is committing a legal nuisance for which state law would allow use of a Three-Day Notice To Quit, ordinance requires that three-day notice be in conditional "cease or quit" form. (Ch. 4).

If provision is in lease, use three-day notice giving tenant option of letting you in or moving. If not, and tenancy is month to month, use 30-day notice specifying reason, following written demand for access to property.

Landlord wants to make substantial repairs to bring property into compliance with health codes, and repairs not possible while tenant remains.

Under state law, eviction for this reason is allowed only if rental agreement is month to month. 30-day notice giving specific reason must be used. Landlord must first obtain all permits required for the remodeling, must provide alternative housing for the tenant if he has other vacant units in city and must give evicted tenant right of first refusal to rerent after remodeling is finished. (Tenant given alternate housing may be evicted from it if he refuses to move into old unit after work is completed. § 13.A.10.)

Landlord wants to demolish property.

Under state law, eviction for this reason is allowed only if rental agreement is month to month. 30-day notice giving specific reason must be used. Landlord must first obtain all permits required for the remodeling, must provide alternative housing for the tenant if he has other vacant units in city and must give evicted tenant right of first refusal to re-rent after remodeling is finished. (Tenant given alternate housing may be evicted from it if he refuses to move into old unit after work is completed. § 13.A.10.) (Although ordinance requires "good faith" to demolish, a euphemism for not doing it because of rent control, the state Ellis Act severely limit cities refusing demolition permits on this basis).

Landlord wants to move self, spouse, parent, grandparent, child or grandchild into property.

Under state law, eviction for this reason is allowed only if rental agreement is month to month. 30-day notice giving specific reason must be used. Also, 30-day notice terminating month-to-month tenancy for this reason should specify name and relationship of person moving in.

HAYWARD

Name of Ordinance "Residential Rent Stabilization," Ordinance No. 83-023 C.S.

Adoption Date 9/13/83. Last amended 3/16/93.

Exceptions Units first occupied after 7/1/79, units owned by landlord owning four or fewer rental units in the city. (§ 2(l).)

Administration Rent Review Office
25151 Clawiter Rd.
Hayward, CA 94545
(510)293-5540.

Registration Not required.

Vacancy Decontrol Rent controls are permanently removed from each unit following a voluntary vacancy (without any legal action by or notices from the landlord, even for cause), the expenditure of at least $200 or more on improvements by the landlord afterward, and city certification of compliance with city Housing Code.(§ 8.)

Just Cause Required. (§ 19(a).) This aspect of the ordinance applies even to voluntarily-vacated property no longer subject to rent control. Specific good cause to evict must be stated in both the notice and in any unlawful detainer complaint. (§ 19(b).)

Special Features Tenant may defend any eviction lawsuit on the basis of the landlord's failure to provide tenant with any of the information required under the ordinance. (§ 8(f).)

Reasons Allowed for Just Cause Evictions

Nonpayment of rent.

Breach of lease provision following written notice to cease.

Willful causing or allowing of substantial damage to premises *and* refusal to both pay the reasonable cost of repair and cease causing damage, following written notice.

Tenant refuses to agree to rental agreement or lease on expiration of prior one, where new proposed agreement contains no new or unlawful terms.

Tenant continues to be so disorderly as to disturb other tenants, following written notice to cease.

Tenant, after written notice to cease, continues to refuse the landlord access to the property as required by Civil Code § 1954.

Additional Local Notice Requirements and Limitations

Ordinary Three-Day Notice To Pay Rent or Quit is used. (See Chapter 2.)

Three-Day Notice To Cure Covenant or Quit (Chapter 4) is used. Provision must be reasonable and legal and been accepted by the tenant or made part of the rental agreement. If the provision was added after the tenant first moved in, the landlord can evict for breach only if the tenant was told in writing that she didn't have to accept the new term. Notice must give the tenant the option of correcting the problem.

Even though damage is involved an ordinary unconditional Three-Day Notice To Quit (Chapter 4) is not allowed. Only a three-day notice that gives the tenant the option of ceasing to cause damage and pay for the costs of repair, as demanded by the landlord, is allowed.

This applies only when a lease or rental agreement expires of its own terms. No notice is required (see Chapter 5). However, an improvised notice giving the tenant several days to sign the new agreement or leave is a good idea.

Even if the tenant is committing a legal nuisance for which state law would allow use of a Three-Day Notice To Quit, ordinance requires that three-day notice be in conditional "cease or quit" form.

If provision is in lease, use three-day notice giving tenant option of letting you in or moving. If not, and tenancy is month to month, use 30-day notice specifying reason, following written demand for access to property.

Landlord wants to make substantial repairs to bring property into compliance with health codes, and repairs not possible while tenant remains.

Under state law, eviction for this reason is allowed only if rental agreement is month to month. 30-day notice (see Chapter 3) giving specific reason must be used. Landlord must first obtain all permits required for the remodeling, and must give tenant notice (see Chapter 3) giving him first chance to rerent after remodeling is finished. (No requirement for alternative housing.)

Landlord wants to demolish property.

Under state law, eviction for this reason is allowed only if rental agreement is month to month. 30-day notice (see Chapter 3) giving specific reason must be used. Landlord must first obtain all necessary permits. (Although ordinance requires "good faith" to demolish, a euphemism for not doing it because of rent control, the state Ellis Act severely limits cities from refusing demolition permits on this basis.)

Landlord wants to move self, spouse, parent, child, stepchild, brother or sister into property, and no comparable vacant unit exists in the property.

Under state law, eviction for this reason is allowed only if rental agreement is month to month. 30-day notice (see Chapter 3) giving specific reason must be used. Landlord must first obtain all permits required for the remodeling, and must give tenant notice (see Chapter 3) giving him first chance to rerent after remodeling is finished. (No requirement for alternative housing.) 30-day notice terminating month-to-month tenancy for this reason should specify name and relationship of person moving in.

Landlord wants to move herself, and lease or rental agreement specifically allows this.

Termination procedure must be in accordance with lease provision. 30 days' written notice is required to terminate month-to-month tenancy unless agreement provides for lesser period as short as 7 days.

Tenant is using the property illegally.

Three-Day Notice To Quit is used. (See Chapter 4.)

Tenant continues, after written notice to cease, to violate reasonable and legal regulations applicable to all tenants generally, if tenant accepted regulations in writing in the lease or rental agreement, or otherwise.

If tenancy is not month-to-month and violation is very serious, use Three-Day Notice To Perform Covenant or Quit. (See Chapter 4.) If tenancy is month-to-month, use 30-day notice preceded by written warning.

Lawful termination of apartment manager's employment, where he or she was compensated with use of apartment.

This type of eviction is not covered in this book because the question of what notice is required is extremely complicated, depending in part on the nature of the management agreement. You should seek legal advice.

LOS ANGELES

Name of Ordinance	Rent Stabilization Ordinance (Los Angeles Municipal Code, Chapter XV).
Adoption Date	4/21/79. Last amended 2/19/91.
Exceptions	Units constructed (or substantially renovated with at least $10,000 in improvements) after 10/1/78, "luxury" units (defined as 0, 1, 2, 3 or 4+ bedroom units renting for at least $302, $420, $588, $756 or $823, respectively, as of 5/31/78), single-family residences, except where three or more houses are located on the same lot. (§ 151.02.G. M.)
Administration	Rent Adjustment Commission 215 West 6th St.,Room 800 Los Angeles, CA 90014 (213) 485-4727 For questions regarding ordinance, call (213) 624-7368.
Registration	Required.
Vacancy Decontrol	Landlord may charge any rent after a tenant either vacates voluntarily or is evicted for nonpayment of rent, breach of a rental agreement provision, or to substantially remodel. (Controls remain if landlord evicts for any other reason, fails to remodel after evicting for that purpose, or terminates or fails to renew a subsidized-housing lease with the city housing authority.) However, once the property is rerented, it is subject to rent control based on the higher rent. (§ 151.06.C.)

Just Cause — Required. (§ 151.09.) Every termination notice must state "the reasons for the termination with specific facts to permit a determination of the date, place, witnesses and circumstances concerning the reason." (§ 151.09.C.1.) Tenant may not defend unlawful detainer action on the basis of lack of good cause or failure of the notice to state the reason if tenant has disobeyed a pretrial court order requiring him or her to deposit rent into court; see C.C.P. § 1170.5 and *Green v. Superior Court* (1974) 10 Cal.3d 616. (§ 151.09.E.)

Other Features — Tenant may defend on the basis that the landlord failed to register the property in accordance with the ordinance. (§ 151.09.F.)

Reasons Allowed for Just Cause Evictions

Nonpayment of rent.

Breach of lease provision, following written notice to cease. (Landlord may not evict based on breach of no-pets clause added by notice of change of terms of tenancy, where no such clause existed at the outset of the tenancy. § 151.09.D.)

Commission of a legal nuisance (disturbing other residents) or damaging the property.

Tenant is using the property for illegal purpose.

Tenant refuses to agree to rental agreement or lease on expiration of prior one, where new proposed agreement contains no new or unlawful terms.

Additional Local Notice Requirements and Limitations

Ordinary Three-Day Notice To Pay Rent or Quit is used. (See Chapter 2.)

Three-Day Notice To Cure Covenant or Quit (Chapter 4) is used. The ordinance requires that the tenant be given "written notice to cease," which precludes an unconditional Three-Day Notice To Quit, even if the breach can be considered uncorrectible.

Unconditional Three-Day Notice To Quit (Chapter 4) may be used.

Unconditional Three-Day Notice To Quit (Chapter 4) may be used.

This applies only when a lease or rental agreement expires of its own terms. No notice is required. (See Chapter 5.) However, an improvised notice giving the tenant several days to sign the new agreement or leave is a good idea, even though not required by ordinance or state law.

Tenant, after written notice to cease, continues to refuse the landlord access to the property as required by Civil Code § 1954.

If provision is in lease, use three-day notice giving tenant option of letting you in or moving. If not, and tenancy is month to month, use 30-day notice specifying reason, following previous written demand for access to property.

Fixed-term lease has expired, and person occupying property is subtenant not approved by landlord.

Eviction on this basis is allowed only if person living there is not original tenant or approved subtenant. No notice is required (see Chapter 5). If lease has not expired and contains no-subletting clause, use Three-Day Notice To Quit to evict for breach of lease. (See Chapter 4.)

Landlord wants to move self, spouse, parent, child or legally-required resident manager into property. Landlord must pay relocation fee of $2,000-$2,500 to tenants except where moving legally-required manager into property.

Only month-to-month tenant can be evicted on this ground. Landlord must serve tenant with copy of a form, the original of which must first be filed with the Community Development Department, that specifies the name and relationship of the person to be moving in. (§ 151.09.C.2.)

Landlord wants to demolish the unit or substantially renovate it at a cost of at least $10,000 and the renovation will take at least 25 days.

Only month-to-month tenant can be evicted on this ground. Use 30-day notice specifying this reason. Landlord must serve tenant with copy of a filed Community Development Department form describing the renovation work or demolition. (§ 151.09.G.)

Landlord seeks to permanently remove the unit from the rental housing market.

Only month-to-month tenant can be evicted on this ground. Use 30-day notice specifying this reason.

LOS GATOS

Name of Ordinance	Los Gatos Rental Dispute Mediation and Arbitration Ordinance (Los Gatos Town Code, Chapter 24).
Adoption Date	10/27/80. Last amended 12/2/92. (Later amendments apply to mobile home parks only.)
Exception	Property on lots with two or fewer units; single-family residences; rented condominium units. (§ 24.20.015.)
Administration	Los Gatos Rent Mediation Program 1245 S. Winchester Blvd., Suite 200 San Jose, CA 95128 (408) 243-8565.
Registration	Not required. (However, a "regulatory fee" to pay for program is added to annual business license fee, when business license is required.)
Vacancy Decontrol	Landlord may charge any rent after a tenant vacates voluntarily or is evicted following Three-Day Notice for Nonpayment of Rent or other breach of the rental agreement. However, once the new rent for a vacated unit is established by the landlord and the property is re-rented, it is subject to rent control based on the higher rent. (§ 24.70.015(1).)
Just Cause	Not required.
Other Features	Tenant faced with termination notice may invoke mediation/arbitration hearing procedure on eviction issue and stay landlord's eviction suit; if tenant wins mediation/arbitration hearing, eviction will be barred. (§§ 24.40.010-24.50.020.)

OAKLAND

Name of Ordinance	"Ordinance Establishing a Residential Rent Arbitration Board ...", Ordinance No. 9980 C.M.S.
Adoption Date	10/7/80. Last amended 9/23/86.
Exceptions	Units constructed after 1/18/84, buildings "substantially rehabilitated" at cost of 50% of that of new construction, as determined by Chief Building Inspector. (§ 2.i).
Administration	Residential Rent Arbitration Board 300 Lakeside Drive, 15th Floor Oakland, CA 94612 (510) 238-3721 (to leave message) or call Sentinel Fair Housing (510) 836-2687
Registration	Not required.
Vacancy Decontrol	Landlord may charge any rent after a tenant vacates voluntarily. Modified controls remain if tenant vacates involuntarily ("where the landlord initiated the termination of tenancy"). However, once the new rent for a vacated unit is established by the landlord and the property is re-rented, it is subject to rent control based on the higher rent. (§ 5.b.) Controls may be permanently removed if landlord spends at least 50% of new-construction cost to "substantially rehabilitate" property.
Just Cause	Not required.
Other Features	Landlord evicting to "rehabilitate" the property (presumably to obtain permanent exemption from controls) must obtain building permit before eviction.

PALM SPRINGS

Name of Ordinance	"Rent Control" (Palm Springs Municipal Code, Title 4),
Adoption Date	9/1/79. Last amended, by initiative, 4/90.
Exceptions	Units constructed after 4/1/79; owner-occupied single-family residences, duplexes, triplexes, and 4-plexes; units where rent was $450 or more as of 9/1/79. (§§ 4.02.010, 4.02.030.)
Administration	Rent Review Commission 3200 E. Tahquitz Canyon Palm Springs, CA 92262 (619) 778-8465.
Registration	Required. (§ 4.02.080.)
Vacancy Decontrol	None.
Just Cause	Not required, but in an unlawful detainer action where retaliation is at issue, ordinance places burden of proof on landlord to prove nonretaliation (§ 4.02.100(b)). Because this is best done by showing a legitimate non-retaliatory reason for eviction, ordinance may still impose a de facto just-cause eviction requirement. Ordinance specifically allows tenant to defend eviction lawsuit on basis of retaliation for refusal to agree in writing to rent increase above annual adjustment amount. (§ 4.02.060(b).)

SAN FRANCISCO

Name of Ordinance   Residential Rent Stabilization and Arbitration Ordinance (San Francisco Administrative Code, Chapter 37).

Adoption Date   6/79. Last amended 12/8/92.

Exceptions   Units constructed after 6/79; buildings over 50 years old and "substantially rehabilitated" since 6/79; owner-occupied single-family residences, duplexes, triplexes, and 4-plexes. (§ 37.2(p).)

Administration   Residential Rent Stabilization and Arbitration Board
25 Van Ness Avenue, Suite 320
San Francisco, CA 94102
(415) 554-9550 and (415) 554-9551

Registration   Not required.

Vacancy Decontrol   Landlord may charge any rent after a tenant either vacates voluntarily or is evicted for good cause. However, once the new rent for a vacated unit is established by the landlord and the property is re-rented, it is subject to rent control based on the higher rent. (§ 37.3(a).)

Just Cause   Required. Every termination notice must state "the grounds under which possession is sought" and must advise the tenant that advice regarding the notice is available from the Board. (§ 37.9.)

Other Features   Tenant or Board may sue landlord, following either unsuccessful eviction attempt or successful eviction based on falsified reason, for treble damages and attorney's fees. (§ 37.9(e).) Landlord must file copy of tenancy termination notice (except Three-Day Notice To Pay Rent or Quit) with rent board within 10 days after it is served on the tenant. (37.9(c).)

Reasons Allowed for Just Cause Evictions

Nonpayment of rent.

Tenant "habitually pays the rent late or gives checks which are frequently returned ... ."

Breach of lease provision, following written notice to cease.

Commission of a legal nuisance (disturbing other residents) or damaging the property.

Tenant is using the property for illegal purpose.

Tenant refuses, after written demand by landlord, to agree to new rental agreement or lease on expiration of prior one, where new proposed agreement contains no new or unlawful terms.

Tenant, after written notice to cease, continues to refuse the landlord access to the property as required by Civil Code § 1954.

Fixed-term lease has expired, and person occupying property is subtenant not approved by landlord.

Additional Local Notice Requirements and Limitations

Ordinary Three-Day Notice To Pay Rent or Quit is used. (See Chapter 2.)

This can only be used if tenancy is month to month, by using 30-day notice.

Three-Day Notice To Perform Covenant or Quit (Chapter 4) is used. Tenant must be given "written notice to cease," which precludes an unconditional Three-Day Notice To Quit, even if the breach is uncorrectible.

Unconditional Three-Day Notice To Quit (Chapter 4) may be used.

Unconditional Three-Day Notice To Quit (Chapter 4) may be used.

This applies only when a lease or rental agreement expires of its own terms. No notice is required. (See Chapter 5.) However, a written notice giving the tenant at least three days to sign the new agreement or leave should be served on the tenant with the proposed new lease or rental agreement.

If provision is in lease, use Three-Day notice giving tenant option of letting you in or moving. (See Chapter 4.) If not, and tenancy is month to month, use 30-day notice specifying reason, following written demand for access to property. (See Chapter 3.)

No notice is required. (See Chapter 5.) Ordinance allows eviction on this basis only if person living there is not original tenant or approved subtenant. (If lease has not expired and contains no-subletting clause, use Three-Day Notice To Quit to evict for breach of lease. See Chapter 4.)

Landlord owning at least 25% interest wants to move self, parent, grandparent, child, grandchild, brother, sister or spouse of any of the foregoing into the property.

Eviction for this reason is allowed only if rental agreement is month to month. (See Chapter 3.) Also, ownership must have been previously registered with Board.

Landlord wants to sell unit following condominium-conversion approval pursuant to separate city ordinance.

Eviction for this reason is allowed only if rental agreement is month to month. (See Chapter 3.) Also, ownership must have been previously registered with Board. Landlord must get all necessary approvals first. New tenants must stay there for a year.

Landlord wants to demolish the unit.

Eviction for this reason is allowed only if rental agreement is month to month. (See Chapter 3.) Also, ownership must have been previously registered with Board. Landlord must obtain all necessary permits first. (Although ordinance requires "good faith" to demolish, a euphemism for not doing it because of rent control, the state Ellis Act severely limit cities from refusing demolition permits on this basis.)

Landlord wants to rehabilitate the property or add capital improvements.

Eviction for this reason is allowed only if rental agreement is month to month. (See Chapter 3.) Also, ownership must have been previously registered with Board. Can't evict if rehab financed by city with "RAP" loans. If improvements are not "substantial rehabilitation" of building 50 or more years old, landlord must give tenant right of first refusal to reoccupy property when work is completed.

Landlord wants to permanently remove property from the rental housing market.

Eviction for this reason is allowed only if rental agreement is month to month. (See Chapter 3.) Also, ownership must have been previously registered with Board. Although the ordinance requires that the landlord must pay relocation compensation of $1,500-$3,000, the Court of Appeal ruled in a case involving Berkeley's ordinance that this requirement was illegal, as pre-empted by the State Ellis Act. (See *Channing Properties v. City of Berkeley* (1992) 11 Cal. App. 4th 88, 14 Cal. Rptr. 2d 32.)

SAN JOSE

Name of Ordinance	San Jose Rental Dispute Mediation and Arbitration Ordinance (San Jose Municipal Code, Title 17, Chapter 17.23).	**Registration**	Not required.
Adoption Date	7/7/79. Last amended 7/19/91.	**Vacancy Decontrol**	Landlord may charge any rent after a tenant vacates voluntarily or is evicted following Three-Day Notice To Pay Rent or Quit other breach of the rental agreement. However, once the new rent for a vacated unit is established by the landlord and the property is re-rented, it is subject to rent control based on the higher rent. (§ 17.23.190.)
Exceptions	Units constructed after 9/7/79, single-family residences, duplexes, townhouses and condominium units. (§ 17.23.150.)		
Administration	Advisory Commission on Rents 4 N. Second Street, Suite 600 San Jose, CA 95113 (408) 277-5431	**Just Cause**	Not required. Notice requirements and unlawful detainer procedures are governed solely by state law.

SANTA MONICA

Name of Ordinance	Rent Control Charter Amendment (City Charter Article XVIII).	**Administration**	Rent Control Board 1685 Main Street, Room 202 Santa Monica, CA 90401 (310) 458-8751
Adoption Date	4/10/79. Last amended 9/13/91.	**Registration**	Required. (C.A. §§ 1803(q), 1805(h).)
Exceptions	Units constructed after 4/10/79; owner-occupied single-family residences, duplexes and triplexes; single-family dwellings not rented on 7/1/84. (Charter Amendment (C.A.) §§ 1801(c), 1815, Regulation (Reg.) §§ 2000 and following, 12000 and following.)) However, rental units other than single-family dwellings not rented on 7/1/84 must be registered and the exemption applied for.	**Vacancy Decontrol**	None. (C.A. § 1803(r) allows Board to decontrol any category of property only if the rental unit vacancy rate exceeds 5%; this is a virtual impossibility.)
		Just Cause	Required. Specific good cause to evict must be stated in the termination notice. (Reg. § 9001.)
		Other Features	Landlord's complaint must allege compliance with rent control ordinance. (C.A. § 1806.)

Reasons Allowed for Just Cause Evictions

Nonpayment of rent.

Breach of lease provision.

Willful causing or allowing of substantial damage to premises, or commission of nuisance that interferes with comfort, safety or enjoyment of the property, following written notice.

Tenant is convicted of using the property for illegal purpose.

Tenant refuses to agree to rental agreement or lease on expiration of prior one, where new proposed agreement contains no new or unlawful terms.

Tenant, after written notice to cease, continues to refuse the landlord access to the property as required by Civil Code § 1954.

Additional Local Notice Requirements and Limitations

Ordinary Three-Day Notice To Pay Rent or Quit is used. (See Chapter 2.)

Three-Day Notice To Perform Covenant or Quit (Chapter 4) is used. Ordinance requires that the tenant have "failed to cure such violation," which precludes an unconditional Three-Day Notice To Quit, even if the breach is uncorrectible.

No requirement for alternative three-day notice giving tenant the option of correcting the problem. Three-Day Notice To Quit may be used. (See Chapter 4.)

Three-Day Notice To Quit (Chapter 4) may be used, but only if tenant is actually convicted. This appears to mean that drug dealers can't be evicted unless first convicted. This provision may violate state law, which does not require a conviction. See C.C.P. § 1161(4). If you wish to evict for illegal use without a conviction, try it based on a violation of a lease provision which forbids illegal use of the premises. Otherwise, see a lawyer about making the argument that this part of the ordinance is preempted by state law.

This applies only when a lease or rental agreement expires of its own terms. No notice is required. (See Chapter 5.) However, an improvised notice giving the tenant several days to sign the new agreement or leave is a good idea.

If provision is in lease, use three-day notice giving tenant option of letting you in or moving. If not, and tenancy is month to month, use 30-day notice specifying reason, following written demand for access to property.

Fixed-term lease has expired, and person occupying property is subtenant not approved by landlord.

No notice is required. (See Chapter 5.) Eviction on this basis is allowed only if person living there is not original tenant or approved subtenant. (If lease has not expired and contains no-subletting clause, use Three-Day Notice To Quit to evict for breach of lease. See Chapter 4.)

Landlord wants to move self, parent, child, brother, sister or spouse of foregoing into property.

Eviction for this reason is allowed only if rental agreement is month to month. Landlord must include on the termination notice the name of the current tenant, the rent charged, and the name, relationship and address of person to be moving in. The notice must be filed with the Board within three days of service on the tenant. (Reg. § 9002(e).) The landlord must also offer any comparable vacant unit in the same building to the tenant and must allow the tenant to move back into the property if the relative does not occupy it within 30 days after the tenant moves out.

Landlord wants to demolish property, convert to condominiums or otherwise remove property from rental market. (City's very strict ordinance has been modified by the state Ellis Act, which severely limits cities from refusing removal permits. See *Javidzad v. City of Santa Monica* (1988) Cal. App. 3d 524, 251 Cal. Rptr. 350.)

Eviction for this reason allowed only if tenancy is month-to-month. Although the ordinance requires a landlord to pay a relocation fee of up to $4,000, the Court of Appeal ruled in a case involving Berkeley's ordinance that this requirement was illegal, as pre-empted by the State Ellis Act. (See *Channing Properties v. City of Berkeley* (1992) 11 Cal. App. 4th 88, 14 Cal. Rptr. 2d 32). That ruling appears to apply only in cases where the landlord just wants to remove the property from the housing market.

THOUSAND OAKS

Name of Ordinance	Rent Stabilization Ordinance, Ordinance No. 755-NS.	**Registration**	Required. (§ XIV.)
Adoption Date	7/1/80. Last amended 3/24/87.	**Vacancy Decontrol**	Property that becomes vacant after 5/1/81 due to tenant voluntarily leaving or being evicted for nonpayment of rent is no longer subject to any provision of the ordinance. (§ VI.)
Exceptions	Units constructed after 6/30/80; "luxury" units (defined as 0, 1, 2, 3 or 4+-bedroom units renting for at least $400, $500, $600, $750, or $900, respectively, as of 6/30/80); single-family residences, duplexes, triplexes, and 4-plexes, except where five or more units are located on the same lot. (§ III.L.)	**Just Cause**	Required.(§ VIII.) Termination notice must state specific reason for termination.
Administration	City Offices 2150 W. Hillcrest Drive Thousand Oaks, CA (805) 497-8611, ext. 657		

Reasons Allowed for Just Cause Evictions

Nonpayment of rent.

Breach of lease provision, following written notice to correct.

Tenant continues to damage property or disturb other tenants, following written notice to cease.

Tenant is using the property for illegal purpose.

Tenant refuses, after written demand by landlord, to agree to new rental agreement or lease on expiration of prior one, where new proposed agreement contains no new or unlawful terms.

Tenant has refused the landlord access to the property as required by Civil Code § 1954.

Fixed-term lease has expired, and person occupying property is subtenant not approved by landlord.

Landlord wants to substantially remodel, convert to condominiums, or demolish property.

Landlord seeks to permanently remove the unit from the rental housing market.

Additional Local Notice Requirements and Limitations

Ordinary Three-Day Notice To Pay Rent or Quit is used. (See Chapter 2.)

Three-Day Notice To Cure Covenant or Quit (Chapter 4) is used, Ordinance requires that the tenant be given "written notice to cease," which precludes an unconditional Three-Day Notice To Quit, even if the breach is uncorrectible.

Even if the tenant is causing nuisance or damage for which state law would allow use of a Three-Day Notice To Quit, ordinance requires that Three-Day notice be in alternative "cease or quit" form.

Ordinance allows use of unconditional Three-Day Notice To Quit.

This applies only when a lease or rental agreement expires of its own terms. No notice is required. (See Chapter 5.) However, written notice giving the tenant at least three days to sign the new agreement or leave should be served on the tenant with the proposed new lease or rental agreement.

If provision is in lease, use Three-day notice giving tenant option of letting you in or moving. If not, and tenancy is month to month, use 30-day notice specifying reason.

No notice is required. (See Chapter 5.) Eviction on this basis is allowed only if person living there is not original tenant or approved subtenant. (If lease has not expired and contains no-subletting clause, use Three-Day Notice To Quit to evict for breach of lease. See Chapter 4.)

Allowed under state law only if fixed-term tenancy has expired, or month-to-month tenancy is terminated by 30-day notice.

Allowed under state law only if fixed-term tenancy has expired, or month-to-month tenancy is terminated by 30-day notice. (Although ordinance requires "good faith" to demolish, a euphemism for not doing it because of rent control, the state Ellis Act severely limit cities from refusing demolition permits on this basis.)

WEST HOLLYWOOD

Name of Ordinance Rent Stabilization Ordinance (West Hollywood Municipal Code, Article IV, Chapter 4).

Adoption Date 6/27/85. Last amended 10/21/92.

Exceptions Units constructed after 7/1/79 ("just-cause" eviction requirements do apply, however). However, many exemptions must be applied for in registration document (see below). (§ 6406.)

Administration Rent Stabilization Commission
8704 Santa Monica Blvd.
West Hollywood, CA 90069
(310) 854-7450

Registration Required. (§ 6407.)

Vacancy Decontrol When tenant of property other than a single-family dwelling voluntarily vacates or is evicted for cause, landlord may increase rent 10%; however, no more than one such increase is permitted within any 24-month period. When tenant of single-family dwelling voluntarily vacates or is evicted for cause (other than for occupancy by owner or relative), landlord can raise rent to any level; however, once the single-family dwelling is re-rented, it is subject to rent control at the new rent. In either case, landlord must file "vacancy increase certificate" with city and show he has repainted and cleaned carpets within previous six months; certificate must be filed within 30 days after tenant vacates, or landlord cannot raise rent under this provision. (§ 6410.)

Just Cause Required. (§ 6413.) This aspect of the ordinance applies even to new construction, which is otherwise exempt from ordinance. Termination notice must state "with particularity the specific grounds" and recite the specific paragraph of ordinance, § 6413.A, under which eviction sought.

Other Features Copy of any unlawful detainer summons and complaint must be filed with Rent Stabilization Commission. (§ 6413.E,F.) Numerous procedural hurdles apply when evicting to move self or relative into property, and substantial relocation fee must be paid to tenant. (§ 6413.A.12.a-k.)

Reasons Allowed for Just Cause Evictions

Nonpayment of rent.

Failure to cure a lease or rental agreement violation within "a reasonable time" after receipt of written notice to cure it.

The tenant's spouse, child, "domestic partner," parent, grandparent, brother or sister can be evicted if the tenant has left, unless that person lived in the unit for at least a year and the tenant died or became incapacitated.

Commission of a legal nuisance (disturbing other residents) or damaging the property.

Tenant is using the property for illegal purpose.

Additional Local Notice Requirements and Limitations

Ordinary Three-Day Notice To Pay Rent or Quit is used. (See Chapter 2.)

Three-Day Notice To Perform Covenant or Quit (Chapter 4) is used. Tenant must be given "a reasonable time" to correct the violation, which precludes an unconditional Three-Day Notice To Quit. Also, the tenant must have been "provided with a written statement of the respective covenants and obligations of both the landlord and tenant" before the violation. Having given the tenant a copy of the written lease or rental agreement should comply with this requirement. This ground is specifically not applicable if the violation is having another person living on the property in violation of the agreement if the person is a "spouse, domestic partner, child, parent, grandparent, brother or sister" of the tenant. (Tenant, however, is required to notify landlord in writing of this fact and state the person's name and relationship, when that person moves in.)

State law allows eviction for this reason by three-day notice only if the tenant's having moved the other person in was a violation of the lease or rental agreement. 30-day notice can be used if tenancy is month to month.

Unconditional Three-Day Notice To Quit (Chapter 4) may be used.

Unconditional Three-Day Notice To Quit (Chapter 4) may be used.

Tenant refuses, after written demand by landlord, to agree to new rental agreement or lease on expiration of prior one, if new proposed agreement contains no new or unlawful terms.

This applies only when a lease or rental agreement expires of its own terms. No notice is required under state law. (See Chapter 5.) However, tenant must have refused to sign a new one containing the same provisions as the old one; a written notice giving the tenant at least three days to sign the new agreement or leave should be served on the tenant with the proposed new lease or rental agreement.

Tenant continues to refuse the landlord access to the property as required by Civil Code § 1954.

If provision is in lease, use three-day notice giving tenant option of letting you in or moving. If not, and tenancy is month to month, use 30-day notice specifying reason.

Person occupying property is subtenant (other than persons mentioned in 2 and 3 above) not approved by landlord. (No requirement, as in other cities, for lease to have expired.)

30-day notice may be used if tenancy is month to month. Otherwise, Three-Day Notice To Quit (see Chapter 4) may be used if lease or rental agreement contains provision against subletting.

Employment of resident manager, who began tenancy as such (not tenant who was "promoted" from regular tenant to manager) and who lived in manager's unit, has been terminated.

This type of eviction is not covered in this book because the question of what is required is extremely complicated, depending in part on the nature of the management agreement. You should seek legal advice.

Employment of resident manager, who was a regular tenant before "promotion" to manager, has been terminated for cause.

Landlord must give tenant 60-day notice, give copy of notice to city, and pay tenant a relocation fee. There are other restrictions as well. This type of eviction can be extremely complicated; see a lawyer.

Landlord wants to move in, after returning from extended absence, and tenancy was under lease for specific fixed term.

No notice is required under state law when fixed-term lease expires, and ordinance doesn't seem to require notice either. However, written letter stating intent not to renew, or clear statement in lease, is advisable.

Landlord wants to move self, parent, grandparent, child, brother or sister into property, and no comparable vacant unit exists in the property.

Tenant must be given 90-day notice that states the name, relationship, and address of person to be moved in, and a copy of the notice must be sent to the Rent Commission. Landlord must also pay tenant(s) of 15 months or more a "relocation fee" between $1,500 and $2,500 ($3,000 for senior citizen or handicapped person), depending on size of unit. Tenant is liable for repayment of the fee if he has not moved at the end of the 90-day period. Person moved in must live in property for at least one year, or bad faith is presumed and tenant may more easily sue landlord for wrongful eviction. Not allowed if tenant is certified by physician as terminally ill.

Landlord wants to make substantial repairs to bring property into compliance with health codes, and repairs not possible while tenant remains.

Under state law, eviction for this reason is allowed only if rental agreement is month to month. Landlord must first obtain all permits required for the remodeling. 30-day notice (see Chapter 3) giving specific reason must be used.

Landlord has taken title to single-family residence or condominium unit by foreclosure.

Tenant must be given 90-day notice that states the name, relationship, and address of person to be moved in, and a copy of the notice must be sent to the Rent Commission. Landlord must also pay tenant(s) of 15 months or more a "relocation fee" between $1,500 and $2,500 ($3,000 for senior citizen or handicapped person), depending on size of unit. Tenant is liable for repayment of the fee if he has not moved at the end of the 90-day period. Person moved in must live in property for at least one year, or bad faith is presumed and tenant may more easily sue landlord for wrongful eviction. Not allowed if tenant is certified by physician as terminally ill. (Vacancy decontrol provisions are not applicable if property is rerented following eviction.)

WESTLAKE VILLAGE

This small city (population 10,000) has a rent control ordinance that applies to apartment complexes of five units or more (as well as to mobilehome parks, whose specialized laws are not covered in this book). However, the city never had more than one apartment complex of this size, and that one was converted to condominiums. Since there is therefore now no property (other than mobilehome parks) to which the ordinance applies, we don't explain the ordinance here.

THREE-DAY NOTICE TO PAY RENT OR QUIT

To: _____ ,
            (name)

Tenant(s) in possession of the premises at

_____ ,
            (street address)

City of _____ , County of _____ , California.

Please take notice that the rent on these premises occupied by you, in the amount of $ _____ , for the

period from _____ to _____ ,

is now due and payable.

YOU ARE HEREBY REQUIRED to pay this amount within THREE (3) days from the date of service on

you of this notice or to vacate and surrender possession of the premises. In the event you fail to do so, legal

proceedings will be instituted against you to recover possession of the premises, declare the forfeiture of

the rental agreement or lease under which you occupy the premises, and recover rents, damages and costs

of suit.

Date: _____   _____
                                                          Owner/Manager

....

PROOF OF SERVICE

I, the undersigned, being at least 18 years of age, served this notice, of which this is a true copy, on _____ ,
one of the occupants listed above as follows:

☐   On _____ , 19____, I delivered the notice to the occupant personally.

☐   On _____ , 19____, I delivered the notice to a person of suitable age and discretion at the occupant's
      residence/business after having attempted personal service at the occupant's residence, and business if known. On
      _____ , 19____, I mailed a second copy to the occupant at his or her residence.

☐   On _____ , 19____, I posted the notice in a conspicuous place on the property, after having attempted
      personal service at the occupant's residence, and business, if known, and after having been unable to find there a person of suitable
      age and discretion. On _____ , 19____, I mailed a second copy to the occupant at the property.

I declare under penalty of perjury under the laws of the State of California that the foregoing is true and correct.

Dated: _____ , 19____   _____
                                                                            Signature

THREE-DAY NOTICE TO PERFORM COVENANT OR QUIT

To: _____ ,

(name)

Tenant(s) in possession of the premises at

_____ ,

(street address)

City of _____ , County of _____ , California.

YOU ARE HEREBY NOTIFIED that you are in violation of the lease or rental agreement under which you occupy these premises because you have violated the covenant to:

_____

_____

_____

_____

_____

in the following manner:

_____

_____

_____

_____

_____

YOU ARE HEREBY REQUIRED within THREE (3) DAYS from the date of service on you of this notice to remedy the violation and perform the covenant or to vacate and surrender possession of the premises.

If you fail to do so, legal proceedings will be instituted against you to recover possession of the premises, declare the forfeiture of the rental agreement or lease under which you occupy the premises, and recover damages and court costs.

Date: _____   _____

Owner/Manager

....

PROOF OF SERVICE

I, the undersigned, being at least 18 years of age, served this notice, of which this is a true copy, on _____ , one of the occupants listed above as follows:

☐ On _____ , 19____ , I delivered the notice to the occupant personally.

☐ On _____ , 19____ , I delivered the notice to a person of suitable age and discretion at the occupant's residence/business after having attempted personal service at the occupant's residence, and business if known. On _____ , 19____ , I mailed a second copy to the occupant at his or her residence.

☐ On _____ , 19____ , I posted the notice in a conspicuous place on the property, after having attempted personal service at the occupant's residence, and business, if known, and after having been unable to find there a person of suitable age and discretion. On _____ , 19____ , I mailed a second copy to the occupant at the property.

I declare under penalty of perjury under the laws of the State of California that the foregoing is true and correct.

Dated: _____ , 19____   _____

Signature

THREE-DAY NOTICE TO QUIT
(IMPROPER SUBLETTING, NUISANCE, WASTE OR ILLEGAL USE)

To: _____ ,
(name)

Tenant(s) in possession of the premises at

_____ ,
(street address)

City of _____ , County of _____ , California.

YOU ARE HEREBY NOTIFIED that you are required within THREE (3) DAYS from the date of service on you of this notice to vacate and surrender possession of the premises because you have committed the following nuisance, waste, unlawful use or unlawful subletting:

_____

_____

_____

_____

_____

_____

_____

_____

As a result of your having committed the foregoing act(s), the lease or rental agreement under which you occupy these premises is terminated. If you fail to vacate and surrender possession of the premises within three days, legal proceedings will be instituted against you to recover possession of the premises, damages and court costs.

Date: _____   _____
                                                                Owner/Manager

....

PROOF OF SERVICE

I, the undersigned, being at least 18 years of age, served this notice, of which this is a true copy, on _____ , one of the occupants listed above as follows:

☐ On _____ , 19____ , I delivered the notice to the occupant personally.

☐ On _____ , 19____ , I delivered the notice to a person of suitable age and discretion at the occupant's residence/business after having attempted personal service at the occupant's residence, and business if known. On _____ , 19____ , I mailed a second copy to the occupant at his or her residence.

☐ On _____ , 19____ , I posted the notice in a conspicuous place on the property, after having attempted personal service at the occupant's residence, and business, if known, and after having been unable to find there a person of suitable age and discretion. On _____ , 19____ , I mailed a second copy to the occupant at the property.

I declare under penalty of perjury under the laws of the State of California that the foregoing is true and correct.

Dated: _____ , 19____   _____
                                                                Signature

SUMMONS
(CITACION JUDICIAL)

UNLAWFUL DETAINER—EVICTION
(PROCESO DE DESAHUCIO—EVICCION)

NOTICE TO DEFENDANT: *(Aviso a acusado)*

YOU ARE BEING SUED BY PLAINTIFF:
(A Ud. le está demandando)

You have *5 DAYS* after this summons is served on you to file a typewritten response at this court. (To calculate the five days, count Saturday and Sunday, but do not count other court holidays.)	*Después de que le entreguen esta citación judicial usted tiene un plazo de 5 DIAS para presentar una respuesta escrita a máquina en esta corte. (Para calcular los cinco días, cuente el sábado y el domingo, pero no cuente ningún otro día feriado observado por la corte).*
A letter or phone call will not protect you. Your typewritten response must be in proper legal form if you want the court to hear your case.	*Una carta o una llamada telefónica no le ofrecerá protección; su respuesta escrita a máquina tiene que cumplir con las formalidades legales apropiadas si usted quiere que la corte escuche su caso.*
If you do not file your response on time, you may lose the case, you may be evicted, and your wages, money and property may be taken without further warning from the court.	*Si usted no presenta su respuesta a tiempo, puede perder el caso, le pueden obligar a desalojar su casa, y le pueden quitar su salario, su dinero y otras cosas de su propiedad sin aviso adicional por parte de la corte.*
There are other legal requirements. You may want to call an attorney right away. If you do not know an attorney, you may call an attorney referral service or a legal aid office *(listed in the phone book).*	*Existen otros requisitos legales. Puede que usted quiera llamar a un abogado inmediatamente. Si no conoce a un abogado, puede llamar a un servicio de referencia de abogados o a una oficina de ayuda legal (vea el directorio telefónico).*

The name and address of the court is: *(El nombre y dirección de la corte es)*

CASE NUMBER: *(Número del caso)*

The name, address, and telephone number of plaintiff's attorney, or plaintiff without an attorney, is:
(El nombre, la dirección y el número de teléfono del abogado del demandante, o del demandante que no tiene abogado, es)

DATE: _____
(Fecha)

Clerk, by _____, Deputy
(Actuario)   *(Delegado)*

[SEAL]

NOTICE TO THE PERSON SERVED: You are served

1. ☐ as an individual defendant.
2. ☐ as the person sued under the fictitious name of *(specify)*:
3. ☐ on behalf of *(specify)*:

    under: ☐ CCP 416.10 (corporation)   ☐ CCP 416.60 (minor)
              ☐ CCP 416.20 (defunct corporation)   ☐ CCP 416.70 (conservatee)
              ☐ CCP 416.40 (association or partnership)   ☐ CCP 416.90 (individual)
              ☐ other:

4. ☐ by personal delivery on *(date)*:
       (See reverse for Proof of Service)

Form Adopted by Rule 982
Judicial Council of California
982(a)(11) [Rev. January 1, 1990]

SUMMONS — UNLAWFUL DETAINER

Code Civ. Proc., §§ 412.20, 1197

PROOF OF SERVICE

1. At the time of service I was at least 18 years of age and not a party to this action, and **I served copies** of the (specify documents):

2. a. Party served (specify name of party as shown on the documents served):

   b. Person served: ☐ party in item 2a ☐ other (specify name and title or relationship to the party named in item 2a):

   c. Address:

3. I served the party named in item 2
   a. ☐ **by personally delivering** the copies (1) on (date):   (2) at (time):
   b. ☐ **by leaving** the copies with or in the presence of (name and title or relationship to person indicated in item 2b):

      (1) ☐ **(business)** a person at least 18 years of age apparently in charge at the office or usual place of business of the person served. I informed him or her of the general nature of the papers.
      (2) ☐ **(home)** a competent member of the household (at least 18 years of age) at the dwelling house or usual place of abode of the person served. I informed him or her of the general nature of the papers.
      (3) on (date):   (4) at (time):
      (5) ☐ A **declaration of diligence** is attached. (Substituted service on natural person, minor, conservatee, or candidate.)
   c. ☐ **by mailing** the copies to the person served, addressed as shown in item 2c, by first-class mail, postage prepaid,
      (1) on (date):   (2) from (city):
      (3) ☐ with two copies of the Notice and Acknowledgment of Receipt and a postage-paid return envelope addressed to me.
      (4) ☐ to an address outside California with return receipt requested.   ◄ (Attach completed form.) ►
   d. ☐ **by causing** copies to be mailed. A declaration of mailing is attached.
   e. ☐ **other** (specify other manner of service and authorizing code section):

4. The "Notice to the Person Served" (on the summons) was completed as follows:
   a. ☐ as an individual defendant.
   b. ☐ as the person sued under the fictitious name of (specify):
   c. ☐ on behalf of (specify):
      under: ☐ CCP 416.10 (corporation)   ☐ CCP 416.60 (minor)   ☐ other:
             ☐ CCP 416.20 (defunct corporation)   ☐ CCP 416.70 (conservatee)
             ☐ CCP 416.40 (association or partnership) ☐ CCP 416.90 (individual)

5. **Person serving** (name, address, and telephone No.):

   a. **Fee** for service: $
   b. ☐ Not a registered California process server.
   c. ☐ Exempt from registration under B&P § 22350(b).
   d. ☐ Registered California process server.
      (1) ☐ Employee or independent contractor.
      (2) Registration No.:
      (3) County:

6. ☐ **I declare** under penalty of perjury under the laws of the State of California that the foregoing is true and correct.

7. ☐ **I am a California sheriff, marshal, or constable and** I certify that the foregoing is true and correct.

Date:

▶ _____

(SIGNATURE)

NOTICE
Iraq-Kuwait Crisis
Dependents of Military Reservists

You may be entitled to have the judge stay (postpone) the eviction procedures **IF** the occupants of the rented property are dependents of a member of the United States Military Reserve on active duty because of the Iraq-Kuwait crisis.

Dependents include the military reservist's

- spouse
- dependent children
- any other dependent.

If you qualify for a stay, you must notify the court

1. in your typewritten response to the Summons
   —or—
2. in a separate typewritten request for a stay.

AVISO
La crisis de Iraq-Kuwait
Dependientes de reservistas militares

Es posible que usted tenga derecho a que el juez prorrogue (posponga) el proceso de desahucio para obligarle a desalojar una propiedad alquilada, **SI** los ocupantes de dicha propiedad son dependientes de un miembro de la Reserva Militar de los Estados Unidos (United States Military Reserve) en servicio activo debido a la crisis Iraq-Kuwait.

Los dependientes incluyen los parientes del reservista indicados a continuación:

- su cónyuge
- sus hijos dependientes
- cualquier otro dependiente.

Si usted es elegible para obtener la prórroga o posposición mencionada, deberá notificar a la corte

1. en su respuesta a la Citación Judicial, escrita a máquina
   —o—
2. en una solicitud separada de prórroga, escrita a máquina.

(NOTE: Attach this notice form to the Summons—Unlawful Detainer)

**SUMMONS — UNLAWFUL DETAINER
ATTACHMENT**

Code of Civil Procedure, § 1167.6
Mil. & Vet. Code, §§ 399.5, 800 et seq.
Stats. 1991, ch. 49 (Sen. Bill No. 1)

NOTICE: EVERYONE WHO LIVES IN THIS RENTAL UNIT MAY BE EVICTED BY COURT ORDER. READ THIS FORM IF YOU LIVE HERE AND IF YOUR NAME IS NOT ON THE ATTACHED SUMMONS AND COMPLAINT.

1. If you live here and you do not complete and submit this form within 10 days of the date of service shown on this form, you will be evicted without further hearing by the court along with the persons named in the Summons and Complaint.
2. If you file this form, your claim will be determined in the eviction action against the persons named in the Complaint.
3. If you do not file this form, you will be evicted without further hearing.

CLAIMANT OR CLAIMANT'S ATTORNEY *(Name and Address)*:

TELEPHONE NO.:

FOR COURT USE ONLY

ATTORNEY FOR *(Name)*:

NAME OF COURT:

STREET ADDRESS:

MAILING ADDRESS:

CITY AND ZIP CODE:

BRANCH NAME:

PLAINTIFF:

DEFENDANT:

PREJUDGMENT CLAIM OF RIGHT TO POSSESSION

CASE NUMBER:

Complete this form only if ALL of these statements are true:
1. You are NOT named in the accompanying Summons and Complaint.
2. You occupied the premises on or before the date the unlawful detainer (eviction) Complaint was filed.
3. You still occupy the premises.

(To be completed by the process server)
DATE OF SERVICE:

(Date that this form is served or delivered, and posted, and mailed by the officer or process server)

I DECLARE THE FOLLOWING UNDER PENALTY OF PERJURY:

1. My name is *(specify)*:

2. I reside at *(street address, unit No., city and ZIP code)*:

3. The address of "the premises" subject to this claim is *(address)*:

4. On *(insert date)*: [   ], the landlord or the landlord's authorized agent filed a complaint to recover possession of the premises. *(This date is the court filing date on the accompanying Summons and Complaint.)*

5. I occupied the premises on the date the complaint was filed *(the date in item 4)*. I have continued to occupy the premises ever since.

6. I was at least 18 years of age on the date the complaint was filed *(the date in item 4)*.

7. I claim a right to possession of the premises because I occupied the premises on the date the complaint was filed *(the date in item 4)*.

8. I was not named in the Summons and Complaint.

9. I understand that if I make this claim of right to possession, I will be added as a defendant to the unlawful detainer (eviction) action.

10. *(Filing fee)* I understand that I must go to the court and pay a filing fee of $ or file with the court the form "Application for Waiver of Court Fees and Costs." I understand that if I don't pay the filing fee or file with the court the form for waiver of court fees within 10 days from the date of service on this form (excluding court holidays), I will not be entitled to make a claim of right to possession.

(Continued on reverse)

CP10.5 [New January 1, 1991]

PREJUDGMENT CLAIM OF RIGHT TO POSSESSION

Code of Civil Procedure, §§ 415.46, 715.010, 715.020, 1174.25

PLAINTIFF (Name):	CASE NUMBER:
DEFENDANT (Name):	

NOTICE: If you fail to file this claim, you will be evicted without further hearing.

11. *(Response required within five days after you file this form)* I understand that I will have *five days* (excluding court holidays) to file a response to the Summons and Complaint after I file this Prejudgment Claim of Right to Possession form.

12. **Rental agreement.** I have *(check all that apply to you)*:

  a. ☐ an oral rental agreement with the landlord.
  b. ☐ a written rental agreement with the landlord.
  c. ☐ an oral rental agreement with a person other than the landlord.
  d. ☐ a written rental agreement with a person other than the landlord.
  e. ☐ other (explain):

I declare under penalty of perjury under the laws of the State of California that the foregoing is true and correct.

WARNING: Perjury is a felony punishable by imprisonment in the state prison.

Date:

▶

....
(TYPE OR PRINT NAME)   (SIGNATURE OF CLAIMANT)

NOTICE: If you file this claim of right to possession, the unlawful detainer (eviction) action against you will be determined at trial. At trial, you may be found liable for rent, costs, and, in some cases, treble damages.

—NOTICE TO OCCUPANTS—

YOU MUST ACT AT ONCE if all the following are true:

1. You are NOT named in the accompanying Summons and Complaint.
2. You occupied the premises on or before the date the unlawful detainer (eviction) complaint was filed. *(The date is the court filing date on the accompanying Summons and Complaint.)*
3. You still occupy the premises.

(Where to file this form) You can complete and SUBMIT THIS CLAIM FORM WITHIN 10 DAYS from the date of service (on the reverse of this form) at the court where the unlawful detainer (eviction) complaint was filed.

(What will happen if you do not file this form) If you do not complete and submit this form (and pay a filing fee or file the form for proceeding in forma pauperis if you cannot pay the fee), YOU WILL BE EVICTED.

After this form is properly filed, you will be added as a defendant in the unlawful detainer (eviction) action and your right to occupy the premises will be decided by the court. If you do not file this claim, you will be evicted without a hearing.

1

2

3

4

5

6

7

8

9

10

11

12

13

14

15

16

17

18

19

20

21

22

23

24

25

26

27

28

ATTORNEY OR PARTY WITHOUT ATTORNEY (Name and Address):   TELEPHONE NO.:   FOR COURT USE ONLY

ATTORNEY FOR (Name):

Insert name of court and name of judicial district and branch court, if any:

PLAINTIFF:

DEFENDANT:

| REQUEST FOR (Application) | ☐ ENTRY OF DEFAULT   ☐ CLERK'S JUDGMENT
☐ COURT JUDGMENT | CASE NUMBER: |

1. TO THE CLERK: On the complaint or cross-complaint filed
   a. On (date):
   b. By (name):
   c. ☐ Enter default of defendant (names):

   d. ☐ I request a court judgment under CCP 585(b), (c), 989, etc. (Testimony required. Apply to the clerk for a hearing date, unless the court will enter a judgment on an affidavit under CCP 585(d).)
   e. ☐ Enter clerk's judgment
      (1) ☐ For restitution of the premises only and issue a writ of execution on the judgment. CCP 1174(c) does not apply. (CCP 1169) ☐ Include in the judgment all tenants, subtenants, named claimants, and other occupants of the premises. The Prejudgment Claim of Right to Possession was served in compliance with CCP 415.46.
      (2) ☐ Under CCP 585(a). (Complete the declaration under CCP 585.5 on the reverse (item 3).)
      (3) ☐ For default previously entered on (date):

2. **Judgment to be entered**

		Amount	Credits Acknowledged	Balance
a.	Demand of complaint . . . . $		$	$
b.	Statement of damages (CCP 425.11) (superior court only)*			
	(1) Special . . . . $		$	$
	(2) General . . . . $		$	$
c.	Interest . . . . $		$	$
d.	Costs (see reverse) . . . . $		$	$
e.	Attorney fees . . . . $		$	$
f.	**TOTALS** . . . . $		$	$

   g. **Daily damages** were demanded in complaint at the rate of: $ per day beginning (date):

Date:

▶

. . . .
           (TYPE OR PRINT NAME)   (SIGNATURE OF PLAINTIFF OR ATTORNEY FOR PLAINTIFF)

* Personal injury or wrongful death actions only.

FOR COURT USE ONLY	(1) ☐ Default entered as requested on (date): (2) ☐ Default NOT entered as requested (state reason):

                                             By: _____

(Continued on reverse)

REQUEST FOR ENTRY OF DEFAULT
(Application to Enter Default)

Code of Civil Procedure, §§ 585-587, 1169

*See note on reverse.

REQUEST FOR ENTRY OF DEFAULT
(Application to Enter Default)

SHORT TITLE:

CASE NUMBER:

---

3. ☐ **DECLARATION UNDER CCP 585.5** *(Required for clerk's judgment under CCP 585(a))*   This action

    a. ☐ is   ☐ is not   on a contract or installment sale for goods or services subject to CC 1801, etc. (Unruh Act).

    b. ☐ is   ☐ is not   on a conditional sales contract subject to CC 2981, etc. (Rees-Levering Motor Vehicle Sales and Finance Act).

    c. ☐ is   ☐ is not   on an obligation for goods, services, loans, or extensions of credit subject to CCP 395(b).

4. ☐ **DECLARATION OF MAILING (CCP 587)**   A copy of this Request for Entry of Default was

    a. ☐ **not mailed** to the following defendants whose addresses are **unknown** to plaintiff or plaintiff's attorney *(names)*:

    b. ☐ **mailed** first-class, postage prepaid, in a sealed envelope addressed to each defendant's attorney of record or, if none, to each defendant's last known address as follows:

        (1)   Mailed on *(date)*:   (2)   To *(specify names and addresses shown on the envelopes)*:

I declare under penalty of perjury under the laws of the State of California that the foregoing items 3 and 4 are true and correct.

Date:

....   ▶   ....
(TYPE OR PRINT NAME)   (SIGNATURE OF DECLARANT)

---

5. ☐ **MEMORANDUM OF COSTS** *(Required if judgment requested)*   Costs and **Disbursements** are as follows (CCP 1033.5):

    a. Clerk's filing fees .... $

    b. Process server's fees .... $

    c. Other *(specify)*: .... $

    d. .... $

    e. **TOTAL** .... $

    f. ☐ Costs and disbursements are waived.

I am the attorney, agent, or party who claims these costs. To the best of my knowledge and belief this memorandum of costs is correct and these costs were necessarily incurred in this case.

I declare under penalty of perjury under the laws of the State of California that the foregoing is true and correct.

Date:

....   ▶   ....
(TYPE OR PRINT NAME)   (SIGNATURE OF DECLARANT)

---

6. ☐ **DECLARATION OF NONMILITARY STATUS** *(Required for a judgment)*   No defendant named in item 1c of the application is in the military service so as to be entitled to the benefits of the Soldiers' and Sailors' Civil Relief Act of 1940 (50 U.S.C. Appen. § 501 et seq.).

I declare under penalty of perjury under the laws of the State of California that the foregoing is true and correct.

Date:

....   ▶   ....
(TYPE OR PRINT NAME)   (SIGNATURE OF DECLARANT)

NOTE: Continued use of form 982(a)(6) (Rev. July 1, 1988) is authorized until June 30, 1992, *except* in unlawful detainer proceedings.

ATTORNEY OR PARTY WITHOUT ATTORNEY *(Name and Address)*:	TELEPHONE NO.:	*FOR COURT USE ONLY*

ATTORNEY FOR *(Name)*:

Insert name of court and name of judicial district and branch court, if any:

PLAINTIFF:

DEFENDANT:

REQUEST FOR (Application)	☐ **ENTRY OF DEFAULT** ☐ **COURT JUDGMENT**	☐ **CLERK'S JUDGMENT**	CASE NUMBER:

1. TO THE CLERK: On the complaint or cross-complaint filed
   a. On *(date)*:
   b. By *(name)*:
   c. ☐ Enter default of defendant *(names)*:

   d. ☐ I request a court judgment under CCP 585(b), (c), 989, etc. *(Testimony required. Apply to the clerk for a hearing date, unless the court will enter a judgment on an affidavit under CCP 585(d).)*
   e. ☐ Enter clerk's judgment
      (1) ☐ For restitution of the premises only and issue a writ of execution on the judgment. CCP 1174(c) does not apply. (CCP 1169) ☐ Include in the judgment all tenants, subtenants, named claimants, and other occupants of the premises. The Prejudgment Claim of Right to Possession was served in compliance with CCP 415.46.
      (2) ☐ Under CCP 585(a). *(Complete the declaration under CCP 585.5 on the reverse (item 3).)*
      (3) ☐ For default previously entered on *(date)*:

2. Judgment to be entered

	Amount	Credits Acknowledged	Balance
a. Demand of complaint	$	$	$
b. Statement of damages (CCP 425.11) *(superior court only)**			
(1) Special...............	$	$	$
(2) General	$	$	$
c. Interest	$	$	$
d. Costs *(see reverse)*	$	$	$
e. Attorney fees	$	$	$
f. **TOTALS**	$	$	$

   g. **Daily damages** were demanded in complaint at the rate of: $ per day beginning *(date)*:

Date:

▶

....
(TYPE OR PRINT NAME)   (SIGNATURE OF PLAINTIFF OR ATTORNEY FOR PLAINTIFF)

* *Personal injury or wrongful death actions only.*

FOR COURT USE ONLY	(1) ☐ Default entered as requested on *(date)*: (2) ☐ Default NOT entered as requested *(state reason)*:

By: _____

(Continued on reverse)

Form Adopted by the
Judicial Council of California
982(a)(6) [Rev. September 30, 1991*]

REQUEST FOR ENTRY OF DEFAULT
(Application to Enter Default)

Code of Civil Procedure, §§ 585-587, 1169

*See note on reverse.

SHORT TITLE:	CASE NUMBER:

3. ☐ **DECLARATION UNDER CCP 585.5** *(Required for clerk's judgment under CCP 585(a))* This action

   a. ☐ is ☐ is not   on a contract or installment sale for goods or services subject to CC 1801, etc. (Unruh Act).

   b. ☐ is ☐ is not   on a conditional sales contract subject to CC 2981, etc. (Rees-Levering Motor Vehicle Sales and Finance Act).

   c. ☐ is ☐ is not   on an obligation for goods, services, loans, or extensions of credit subject to CCP 395(b).

4. **DECLARATION OF MAILING (CCP 587)** A copy of this Request for Entry of Default was

   a. ☐ **not mailed** to the following defendants whose addresses are **unknown** to plaintiff or plaintiff's attorney *(names)*:

   b. ☐ **mailed** first-class, postage prepaid, in a sealed envelope addressed to each defendant's attorney of record or, if none, to each defendant's last known address as follows:

      (1) Mailed on *(date)*:   (2) To *(specify names and addresses shown on the envelopes)*:

I declare under penalty of perjury under the laws of the State of California that the foregoing items 3 and 4 are true and correct.

Date:

. . . .   ▶   . . . .

           (TYPE OR PRINT NAME)   (SIGNATURE OF DECLARANT)

5. **MEMORANDUM OF COSTS** *(Required if judgment requested)* **Costs and Disbursements** are as follows (CCP 1033.5):

   a. Clerk's filing fees . . . . $

   b. Process server's fees . . . . $

   c. Other *(specify)*: . . . . $

   d. . . . . $

   e. **TOTAL** . . . . $ _____

   f. ☐ Costs and disbursements are waived.

I am the attorney, agent, or party who claims these costs. To the best of my knowledge and belief this memorandum of costs is correct and these costs were necessarily incurred in this case.

I declare under penalty of perjury under the laws of the State of California that the foregoing is true and correct.

Date:

. . . .   ▶   . . . .

           (TYPE OR PRINT NAME)   (SIGNATURE OF DECLARANT)

6. ☐ **DECLARATION OF NONMILITARY STATUS** *(Required for a judgment)* No defendant named in item 1c of the application is in the military service so as to be entitled to the benefits of the Soldiers' and Sailors' Civil Relief Act of 1940 (50 U.S.C. Appen. § 501 et seq.).

I declare under penalty of perjury under the laws of the State of California that the foregoing is true and correct.

Date:

. . . .   ▶   . . . .

           (TYPE OR PRINT NAME)   (SIGNATURE OF DECLARANT)

NOTE: Continued use of form 982(a)(6) (Rev. July 1, 1988) is authorized until June 30, 1992, *except* in unlawful detainer proceedings.

ATTORNEY OR PARTY WITHOUT ATTORNEY *(Name and Address)*	TELEPHONE NO:	FOR COURT USE ONLY

ATTORNEY FOR *(Name)*

Insert name of court and name of judicial district and branch court, if any:

PLAINTIFF:

DEFENDANT:

CLERK'S JUDGMENT FOR RESTITUTION OF PREMISES—UNLAWFUL DETAINER	CASE NUMBER:

In this action, the defendant(s) hereinafter named, having been regularly served with summons and copy of complaint, having failed to appear and answer the complaint within the time allowed by law, and the default of said defendant(s) having been entered, upon application of plaintiff(s) pursuant to C.C.P. Section 1169, the Clerk entered the following judgment:

Judgment is hereby entered that plaintiff(s) _____

have and recover from defendant(s) _____

the restitution and possession of the premises situated in the County of _____,

State of California, described as follows:

_____

_____

This judgment

☐ does (if Prejudgment Claim of Right to Possession served per C.C.P. Section 415.46)

☐ does not

include all tenants, subtenants, named claimants, and other occupants of the premises.

Judgment entered on _____ _____, Clerk

Judgment Book _____ Page_____ By _____, Deputy Clerk

NP   **CLERK'S JUDGMENT FOR RESTITUTION OF PREMISES**   Code of Civil Procedure, § 1169
                          —UNLAWFUL DETAINER

MUNICIPAL COURT OF CALIFORNIA, COUNTY OF SANTA CLARA

NAME OF MUNICIPAL OR JUSTICE COURT DISTRICT AND ADDRESS **MUNICIPAL COURT SANTA CLARA COUNTY JUDICIAL DISTRICT** **SANTA CLARA FACILITY** 1095 Homestead Road, Santa Clara, California 95050	**FOR COURT USE ONLY**
TITLE OF CASE *(ABBREVIATED)* Plaintiff: Defendant(s):	
NAME, ADDRESS, AND TELEPHONE NUMBER OF SENDER	
	CASE NUMBER

**UNLAWFUL DETAINER
DEFAULT JUDGMENT
BY CLERK
FOR POSSESSION OF REAL
PROPERTY, ONLY**

The defendant(s) _____
having been regularly served with summons and copy of complaint, having failed to appear and answer said complaint within the time allowed by law, and the default of said defendant(s) having been duly entered; upon application of plaintiff to the Clerk for JUDGMENT.

It is adjudged the plaintiff(s) _____
have and recover from defendant(s) _____
the restitution and possession of those certain premises situated in the County of Santa Clara, State of California, and more particularly described as follows:

This judgment ☐ does ☐ does not include all tenants, subtenants, named claimants, and other occupants of the premises.

I hereby certify this to be a true copy of the Judgment in the above action entered on _____
_____

Judgment entered on _____ _____ , Clerk

Judgment Book _____ Page _____ By _____ , Deputy Clerk

UNLAWFUL DETAINER DEFAULT JUDGMENT BY CLERK
(For Possession of Real Property, Only)

Post Record Catalog #607A

| JUDGMENT
DEFAULT BY
CLERK
UNLAWFUL DETAINER | **IN THE MUNICIPAL COURT OF**
.... **JUDICIAL DISTRICT**
COUNTY OF LOS ANGELES, STATE OF CALIFORNIA

.... | **Case Number** |

.... v. ....

Plaintiff(s)   **Defendant(s)**

The defendant(s) _____

_____

_____ having been served with a copy of the summons and complaint and having failed to answer complaint of plaintiff(s) within the time allowed by law and default of said defendant(s) having been entered, upon application of plaintiff(s) the clerk entered the following judgment:

Plaintiff(s) _____

_____

_____

_____

recover from defendant(s) _____

_____

the restitution and possession of those premises situated in the County of Los Angeles, State of California, and more particularly described as: _____

_____

_____

_____

_____

This judgment ☐ does ☐ does not include all tenants, subtenants, named claimants, and other occupants of the premises.

_____

Deputy Clerk

I certify the foregoing Judgment was entered in the Judgment Book on

.... ,Copy filed.
CLERK OF THE ABOVE NAMED COURT

By ....
                      Deputy

JUDGMENT — DEFAULT BY CLERK

UNLAWFUL DETAINER

76J752CI-24(5) (New - 1/83) PS 2-83   1169ccp

ATTORNEY OR PARTY WITHOUT ATTORNEY *(Name and Address)*:   TELEPHONE NO.:   FOR RECORDER'S USE ONLY

[ ] Recording requested by and return to:

[ ] **ATTORNEY FOR**   [ ] **JUDGMENT CREDITOR**   [ ] **ASSIGNEE OF RECORD**

NAME OF COURT:

STREET ADDRESS:

MAILING ADDRESS:

CITY AND ZIP CODE:

BRANCH NAME:

PLAINTIFF:

DEFENDANT:

WRIT OF
[ ] **EXECUTION (Money Judgment)**
[ ] **POSSESSION OF** [ ] **Personal Property**
                  [ ] **Real Property**
[ ] **SALE**

CASE NUMBER:

FOR COURT USE ONLY

1. **To the Sheriff or any Marshal or Constable of the County of:**

   You are directed to enforce the judgment described below with daily interest and your costs as provided by law.

2. **To any registered process server:** You are authorized to serve this writ only in accord with CCP 699.080 or CCP 715.040.

3. *(Name)*:

   is the [ ] judgment creditor [ ] assignee of record

   whose address is shown on this form above the court's name.

4. **Judgment debtor** *(name and last known address)*:

   [ ] additional judgment debtors on reverse

5. **Judgment entered** on *(date)*:

6. [ ] **Judgment renewed** on *(dates)*:

7. **Notice of sale** under this writ

   a. [ ] has not been requested.

   b. [ ] has been requested *(see reverse)*.

8. [ ] Joint debtor information on reverse.

9. [ ] See reverse for information on real or personal property to be delivered under a writ of possession or sold under a writ of **sale.**

10. [ ] This writ is issued on a sister-state judgment.

11. Total judgment . . . . $

12. Costs after judgment (per filed order or memo CCP 685.090) . $

13. Subtotal *(add 11 and 12)* . . . . . $ _____

14. Credits . . . . $

15. Subtotal *(subtract 14 from 13)* . $ _____

16. Interest after judgment (per filed affidavit CCP 685.050) . . . . . . $

17. Fee for issuance of writ . . . . . . $

18. **Total** *(add 15, 16, and 17)* . . . . $ _____

19. Levying officer: Add daily interest from date of writ *(at the legal rate on 15)* of . . . . $

20. [ ] The amounts called for in items 11–19 are different for each debtor. These amounts are stated for each debtor on Attachment 20.

[SEAL]

Issued on *(date)*:

Clerk, by _____ , Deputy

— **NOTICE TO PERSON SERVED: SEE REVERSE FOR IMPORTANT INFORMATION** —

(Continued on reverse)

Form Approved by the
Judicial Council of California
EJ-130 [Rev. September 30, 1991*]

WRIT OF EXECUTION

Code of Civil Procedure, §§ 699.520, 712.010, 715.010

*See note on reverse.

SHORT TITLE:	CASE NUMBER:

Items continued from the first page:

4. ☐ **Additional judgment debtor** (name and last known address):

7. ☐ **Notice of sale has been requested by** (name and address):

8. ☐ **Joint debtor** was declared bound by the judgment (CCP 989–994)
    a. on (date):
    b. name and address of joint debtor:

    a. on (date):
    b. name and address of joint debtor:

    c. ☐ additional costs against certain joint debtors (itemize):

9. ☐ (Writ of Possession or Writ of Sale) **Judgment** was entered for the following:
    a. ☐ Possession of real property: The complaint was filed on (date):
      (Check (1) or (2)):
      (1) ☐ The Prejudgment Claim of Right to Possession was served in compliance with CCP 415.46.
        The judgment includes all tenants, subtenants, named claimants, and other occupants of the premises.
      (2) ☐ The Prejudgment Claim of Right to Possession was NOT served in compliance with CCP 415.46.
        (a) $ was the daily rental value on the date the complaint was filed.
        (b) The court will hear objections to enforcement of the judgment under CCP 1174.3 on the following
        dates (specify):
    b. ☐ Possession of personal property
      ☐ If delivery cannot be had, then for the value (itemize in 9e) specified in the judgment or supplemental order.
    c. ☐ Sale of personal property
    d. ☐ Sale of real property
    e. Description of property:

— NOTICE TO PERSON SERVED —

WRIT OF EXECUTION OR SALE. Your rights and duties are indicated on the accompanying Notice of Levy.

WRIT OF POSSESSION OF PERSONAL PROPERTY. If the levying officer is not able to take custody of the property, the levying officer will make a demand upon you for the property. If custody is not obtained following demand, the judgment may be enforced as a money judgment for the value of the property specified in the judgment or in a supplemental order.

WRIT OF POSSESSION OF REAL PROPERTY. If the premises are not vacated within five days after the date of service on the occupant or, if service is by posting, within five days after service on you, the levying officer will remove the occupants from the real property and place the judgment creditor in possession of the property. Personal property remaining on the premises will be sold or otherwise disposed of in accordance with CCP 1174 unless you or the owner of the property pays the judgment creditor the reasonable cost of storage and takes possession of the personal property not later than 15 days after the time the judgment creditor takes possession of the premises.

► A Claim of Right to Possession accompanies this writ (unless the Summons was served in compliance with CCP 415.46).

* NOTE: Continued use of form EJ-130 (Rev. Jan. 1, 1989) is authorized until June 30, 1992, except if used as a Writ of Possession of Real Property.

MUNICIPAL COURT OF CALIFORNIA, LOS ANGELES COUNTY _____JUDICIAL DISTRICT	COURT USE ONLY

ADDRESS:

PLAINTIFF:

DEFENDANT:

APPLICATION FOR ISSUANCE OF WRIT OF: ☐ POSSESSION ☐ SALE ☐ OTHER _____	CASE NUMBER

I, the undersigned, say: I am _____Attorney for the

Judgment Creditor in the above-entitled action and that the following judgment was:

(check if applicable)

☐ entered on _____.

☐ renewed on _____.

In favor of the Judgment Creditor as follows (name and address):

against the Judgment Debtor(s) as follows (name and address):

for the amount of: $_____Principal

$_____Accured Costs

$_____Attorney Fees

$_____Interest

$_____TOTAL

and the possession of the premises located at:_____

_____

The daily rental value of the property as of the date the complaint was filed is:

$_____.

It is prayed that a writ as checked above be issued to the County of Los Angeles.

The writ will be directed to _____.
(Law Enforcement Agency and Location)

I declare under the penalty of perjury under the laws of the State of California

that the foregoing is true and correct.

Executed on_____ at _____, California.

_____
Signature

APPLICATION FOR WRIT OF POSS/SALE   712.010 CCP

Name:
Address:

Phone:
Plaintiff in Pro Per

MUNICIPAL COURT OF CALIFORNIA, COUNTY OF _____

_____ JUDICIAL DISTRICT

Plaintiff,	) Case No. _____
	)
v.	) DECLARATION IN SUPPORT
	) OF DEFAULT JUDGMENT
	) FOR RENT, DAMAGES, AND
	) COSTS
	)
Defendant(s).	) (C.C.P. SECS. 585(a), 1169)

I, the undersigned, declare:

1. I am the plaintiff in the above-entitled action and the

owner of the premises at _____,

City of _____, County of _____, California.

2. On _____, 19___, defendant(s) rented the

premises from me pursuant to a written/oral **[cross out one]** agreement

under which the monthly rent was $_____ payable in advance on

the _____ day of each month.

3. The terms of the tenancy **[check one]**:

( ) were not changed; or

( ) were changed, effective _____, 19__, in that

monthly rent was validly and lawfully increased to $_____ by

1   ( ) agreement of the parties and subsequent payment of such rent;

2   or

3   ( ) **[month-to-month tenancy only]** service on defendant(s) of a written

4   notice of at least 30 days, setting forth the increase in rent.

5   4. The reasonable rental value of the premises per day, i.e.,

6   the current monthly rent divided by 30, is $_____.

7   5. Pursuant to the agreement, defendant(s) went into

8   possession of the premises.

9   6. On _____, 19___, defendant(s) were in

10   default in the payment of rent in the amount of $_____, and I

11   caused defendant(s) to be served with a written notice demanding

12   that defendant(s) pay that amount or surrender possession of the

13   premises within three days after service of the notice.

14   7. Defendant(s) failed to pay the rent or surrender

15   possession of the premises within three days after service of the

16   notice, whereupon I commenced this action, complying with any

17   local rent control or eviction protection ordinance applicable,

18   and caused summons and complaint to be served on each defendant.

19   Defendant(s) have failed to answer or otherwise respond to the

20   complaint within the time allowed by law.

21   8. Defendant(s) surrendered possession of the premises on

22   _____, 19__, after entry of a clerk's judgment

23   for possession and issuance of a writ of execution thereon.

24   9. The rent was due for the rental period of

25   _____, 19__ through _____, 19__. After this

26   latter date, and until defendant(s) vacated the premises, I

27   sustained damages at the daily reasonable rental value of $_____,

28   for total damages of $_____.

1   10. I have incurred filing, service, and writ fees in the

2   total amount of $_____ in this action.

3   11. If sworn as a witness, I could testify competently to

4   the facts stated herein.

5   I declare under penalty of perjury under the laws of the

6   State of California that the foregoing is true and correct.

7   DATED:_____, 19___

8   _____

9   Plaintiff in Pro Per

10

11

12

13

14

15

16

17

18

19

20

21

22

23

24

25

26

27

28

```
 1   Name:
     Address:
 2
     Phone:
 3   Plaintiff in Pro Per

 4

 5

 6

 7

 8        MUNICIPAL COURT OF CALIFORNIA, COUNTY OF

 9                               COUNTY JUDICIAL DISTRICT

10                                    )  Case No.
11                                    )
          Plaintiff,                  )  DECLARATION IN SUPPORT
12   v.                               )  OF DEFAULT JUDGMENT
                                      )  FOR DAMAGES AND COSTS
13                                    )
                                      )
14        Defendant(s).               )  (C.C.P. SECS. 585(a), 1169)
     _____)

15

16        I, the undersigned, declare:

17        1. I am the plaintiff in the above-entitled action and the

18   owner of the premises at _____, City

19   of _____, County of _____, California.

20        2. On _____, 19__, defendant(s) rented the pre-

21   mises from me pursuant to a written/oral [cross out one] agreement for a

22   month-to-month tenancy at a monthly rent of $_____.

23        3. The terms of the tenancy [check one]:

24        ( ) were not changed; or

25        ( ) were changed, effective _____, 19___,

26   in that the monthly rent was validly and lawfully increased to

27   $_____ by ( ) agreement of the parties and subsequent

28   payment of such rent; or
```

( ) **[month-to-month tenancy only]** service on defendant(s) of a written notice of at least 30 days, setting forth the increase in rent.

4. The reasonable rental value of the premises per day, i.e., the current monthly rent divided by 30, is $_____.

5. Pursuant to the agreement, defendant(s) went into possession of the premises.

6. On _____, 19___, I served defendant with a written 30-day termination notice.

7. Defendant was still in possession of the property 31 days later on _____, 19_____, and stayed until _____, 19___ when the sheriff evicted him/her/them pursuant to a clerk's judgment for possession and issuance of a writ of execution.

8. I sustained damages at the daily reasonable rental value of $_____ for 21 days between _____, and _____, for a total of $_____.

9. I have incurred filing, service, and writ fees in the total amount of $_____ in this action.

10. If sworn as a witness, I could testify competently to the facts stated herein.

I declare under penalty of perjury under the laws of the State of California that the foregoing is true and correct.

DATED:_____, 19___

_____
Plaintiff in Pro Per

IN THE MUNICIPAL COURT OF

.... JUDICIAL DISTRICT

COUNTY OF LOS ANGELES, STATE OF CALIFORNIA

CASE NUMBER

....

.... vs ....

Plaintiff(s)   Defendant(s)

In Division .... , Honorable .... , Judge Presiding.

Court convened on .... ; and the following proceedings were had:

Plaintiff(s) not appearing ....

the defendant(s) ....

having been served with summons and copy of complaint, having failed to answer complaint of plaintiff(s) within the time allowed by law and default of said defendant(s) having been entered, plaintiff(s) applied to the court for judgment.

☐ Affidavit or declaration of .... under 585.5 C.C.P. having been filed.

☐ Witness(es) sworn for plaintiff(s): ....

    Exhibit(s) received in evidence for plaintiff(s): ....

    The court, after having considered the evidence,

        ☐ found the amount of rent due the plaintiff(s) to be $......................... , and assessed the damages for the unlawful detainer at $ .... and determined that said sums should not be trebled, ordered the following judgment: It is adjudged that on the complaint,

plaintiff(s)   ....

                    .... recover from

defendant(s)   ....

                    ....

☐ the restitution and possession of those premises situated in the County of Los Angeles, State of California, and more particularly described as: ....

....

and the sum of $ .... , and $ .... attorney fees, with costs as provided by law in the sum of $...................... , and that the lease or agreement under which the aforesaid property is held be, and the same is hereby declared forfeited.

☐ the possession of the following described personal property, to wit: ....

....

or its value, which is fixed at $ .... in case possession of said personal property cannot be had ; and in either event the sum of $........................... damages $ .... attorney fees, and $......................... interest with costs as provided by law in the sum of $ .... ,

☐ the sum of $ .... , $ .... , attorney fees,

and $ .... interest with costs as provided by law in the sum of $ ....

The foregoing minutes are correct and the judgment conforms to the decision of the court.

.... Deputy Clerk

I certify the foregoing Judgment was entered in the Judgment Book on

.... , Copy filed.

CLERK OF THE ABOVE NAMED COURT

By ....

Deputy

MINUTES AND DEFAULT JUDGMENT

C.C.P.585, 585.5, 664, 668, 1033½, 1161-1174

MUNICIPAL COURT OF CALIFORNIA, COUNTY OF SANTA CLARA

NAME OF MUNICIPAL OF JUSTIC COURT DISTRICT AND ADDRESS	FOR COURT USE ONLY
TITLE OF CASE *(ABBREVIATED)*	
NAME, ADDRESS, AND TELEPHONE NUMBER OF SENDER	CASE NUMBER

**UNLAWFUL DETAINER
DEFAULT JUDGMENT**

The defendant(s) ....
having been regularly served with summons and copy of complaint, having failed to appear and answer said complaint within the time allowed by law, and the default of said defendant(s) having been duly entered, and after having heard the testimony and considered the evidence, or pursuant to affidavit on file herein, the Court ordered the following JUDGMENT:

It is ordered and adjuged the plaintiff(s)...
have and recover from defendant(s)..
the restitution and possession of those certain premises situated in the County of Santa Clara, State of California, and more particularly described as follows:

and the sum of $...................... rent, and $...................... damages for unlawful detainer, making a total amount of $............................, plus $.........0......... attorney fees, with costs as provided by law in the sum of $..................... and that said lease or agreement under which the aforesaid property is held be, and it is hereby declared forfeited.

.... days stay of execution.

Dated:..................................

....
Judge of the Municipal Court

I hereby certify this to be a true copy of the Judgment in the above action rendered on ....
....

Judgment entered on ....

Minute Book.......................... Page...........................

...., Clerk

By................................., Deputy Clerk

UNLAWFUL DETAINER DEFAULT JUDGMENT   CCP 585, 664, 668, 1033½, 1174

NAME AND ADDRESS OF ATTORNEY:	TELEPHONE NO.:	For Court use only:

MUNICIPAL COURT OF CALIFORNIA, COUNTY OF SAN DIEGO

PLAINTIFF: (ABBREVIATED)

DEFENDANT: (ABBREVIATED)

JUDGMENT BY DEFAULT BY COURT—UNLAWFUL DETAINER	CASE NUMBER

In this action the Defendant (s), ...
having been regularly served with summons and copy of complaint, having failed to appear and answer the complaint of Plaintiff (s) within the time allowed by law, and the default of said Defendant (s) having been duly entered, upon application of Plaintiff (s) to the Court, and

☐ after having heard the testimony and considered the evidence,

☐ a declaration under CCP 585 (4), in lieu of testimony, having been considered, the Court ordered the following judgment:

That Plaintiff (s) do have and recover from Defendant (s) ....

....

the restitution and possession of those certain premises situated, lying and being in the City and County of San Diego, State of California, and is described as follows,

....

....

And that the lease or agreement under which said property is held be, and the same is hereby forfeited.

It is further ordered that plaintiff (s) recover from said Defendant (s) the sum of:

Damages $.................................

Attorney fees $.................................

Interest $.................................

Costs $.................................

Total $.................................

Done in open Court this date:.................................

_____
Judge of Said Court

CLERK OF COURT

By _____, Deputy

SDMC 14 (Rev. 5-75)   **JUDGMENT BY DEFAULT BY COURT—UNLAWFUL DETAINER**   CCP 585

```
 1   Name:
     Address:
 2
     Phone:
 3   Plaintiff in Pro Per

 4

 5

 6

 7

 8        MUNICIPAL COURT OF CALIFORNIA, COUNTY OF _____

 9        _____ JUDICIAL DISTRICT

10
     _____  )  Case No. _____
11                                      )
            Plaintiff,                  )  STIPULATION FOR JUDGMENT
12   v.                                 )
                                        )
13   _____   )
                                        )
14   _____   )
                                        )
15          Defendant(s).               )
     _____   )
16

17        Plaintiff _____ and

18   defendant(s) _____

19   hereby agree to settle the above-entitled unlawful detainer action

20   for possession of the real property at _____

21   _____, City of _____

22   County of _____, California, hereinafter

23   described as the "premises," on the following terms and conditions:

24        1. Defendant(s) agree to vacate the premises on or before

25   _____, 19___. Plaintiff shall therefore have a

26   judgment for possession of those premises. The judgment may issue

27   immediately, but execution on the judgment is to be stayed until

28   _____, 19___.
```

2. Defendants shall pay to plaintiff the sum of $_____,

as full payment of the rent for the following period:

_____, 19___ through _____, 19___.

This sum shall be paid as follows: **[check one]**

( ) Immediately, on signing this stipulation;

( ) On or before _____, 19___; should defen-

dants fail to pay this sum as promised, plaintiff shall be en-

titled, on ex parte application to the Court, to a judgment or

amended judgment for that sum and for immediate possession of the

premises, with no stay of execution thereon.

3. The tenant's security deposit of $_____ shall be

handled as follows: **[check one]**

( ) Treated according to law;

( ) Applied as follows: _____

_____.

In addition, plaintiff and defendants agree to waive all

claims or demands that each may have against the other for any

transaction directly or indirectly arising from their landlord/

tenant relationship, and further agree that this stipulation not

be construed as reflecting on the merits of the dispute.

DATED:_____, 19___ DATED:_____, 19 __

_____   _____
Plaintiff in Pro Per   Defendant/Attorney
                                     for Defendant

```
1   Name:
    Address:
2
    Phone:
3   Plaintiff in Pro Per

4

5

6

7

8        MUNICIPAL COURT OF CALIFORNIA, COUNTY OF _____

9        _____ JUDICIAL DISTRICT

10
    _____  )  Case No. _____
11                                       )
            Plaintiff,                   )  JUDGMENT PURSUANT
12   v.                                  )  TO STIPULATION
                                         )
13   _____  )
                                         )
14   _____  )
                                         )
15          Defendant(s).                )
    _____   )
16

17        Pursuant to stipulation by and between plaintiff and

18   defendant(s),

19        IT IS HEREBY ORDERED AND ADJUDGED AS FOLLOWS:

20   Plaintiff _____ shall have judgment against

21   defendant(s) _____

22   for restitution and possession of the real property at

23   _____,

24   City of _____, County of

25   _____, California.

26        ( )  [check, if applicable] Execution thereon shall be stayed until

27   _____, 19____.

28
```

        ( ) [check, if applicable] Plaintiff shall also have judgment against

defendants in the sum of $_____.

DATED:_____, 19___   _____
                                          JUDGE OF THE MUNICIPAL COURT

```
 1   Name:
     Address:
 2
 3   Phone:
     Plaintiff in Pro Per
 4

 5

 6

 7

 8        MUNICIPAL COURT OF CALIFORNIA, COUNTY OF _____

 9        _____ JUDICIAL DISTRICT

10

11   _____ )   Case No. _____
                                        )
12          Plaintiff,                  )   NOTICE OF MOTION FOR
     v.                                 )   SUMMARY JUDGMENT;
13                                      )   PLAINTIFF'S DECLARATION;
     _____  )   POINTS AND AUTHORITIES
14                                      )   (C.C.P. 437C, 1170.7)
            Defendant(s).               )
15   _____  )   Hearing Date:
                                        )   Time:
16                                          Courtroom:

17

18   TO DEFENDANTS _____

19        AND THEIR ATTORNEY OF RECORD:

20        PLEASE TAKE NOTICE that on _____, 19___

21   at _____ __.M in the above-entitled Court, at

22   _____,

23   City of _____, California, the above-named

24   plaintiff will move the Court for an Order granting summary

25   judgment for possession of the subject premises herein, rent,

26   damages, and costs in the above-entitled action.

27        This motion is made on the ground that defendants' defense has

28   no merit and there exists no triable issue of fact as to
```

1 plaintiff's cause of action, plaintiff having established that

2 defendants are guilty of unlawfully detaining the subject premises

3 following nonpayment of the rent due, service of a 3-day notice to

4 pay rent or quit, and failure to pay the rent or vacate the

5 premises within the time given in the said notice.

6   This motion is based on this notice, the declaration of

7 plaintiff attached hereto, the points and authorities attached

8 hereto, the pleadings, records, and files herein, and on such

9 argument as may be presented at the hearing on the motion.

10 DATED: _____, 19___

11

12   _____
                                       Plaintiff in Pro Per

13   DECLARATION OF PLAINTIFF

14   I, the undersigned, declare:

15   1. I am the plaintiff in the within action and the owner of

16 the subject premises located at _____

17 _____, City of _____,

18 County of _____, California.

19   2. On _____, 19___, defendant(s) rented the premises

20 from me pursuant to a written/oral agreement. The monthly rent was

21 $_____ payable in advance on the day of each month, the

22 reasonable rental value of the premises per day being $_____.

23   3. Pursuant to the agreement, defendant(s) went into

24 possession of the premises.

25   4. On _____, 19___, defendant(s) were in default

26 in the payment of rent in the amount of $_____, and I served

27 defendant(s) _____

28 _____

with a written notice demanding that defendant(s) pay that amount or surrender possession of the premises within three days of service of the said notice. A true copy of that notice is attached to the complaint herein as Exhibit "B" thereto.

5. Prior to my service of the said three-day notice, defendant(s) had not notified me of any substantial defect in the premises relating to the tenantability or habitability thereof.

6. Defendant(s) failed to pay the said rent or surrender possession of the said premises within three days of service of the said notice, whereupon I commenced the instant action, complying with all applicable rent control and/or eviction protection ordinances. Defendant(s) still remain in possession of the premises.

7. This rent was due for the rental period of _____, 19_____ through _____, 19_____. After this latter date and to the present, I sustained damages at the daily reasonable rental value indicated above in paragraph 2, for total damages in the amount of $_____, and total rent and damages in the amount of $_____.

8. I have incurred service and filing fees in the total amount of $_____ in the within action.

9. If sworn as a witness, I could testify competently to the facts stated herein.

I declare under penalty of perjury under the laws of the State of California that the foregoing is true and correct.

DATED: _____, 19_____   _____
                                      Plaintiff in Pro Per

POINTS AND AUTHORITIES

I. PLAINTIFF'S MOTION FOR SUMMARY JUDGMENT IS PROPERLY BEFORE THE COURT.

In an unlawful detainer action a motion for summary judgment may be made on five days' notice. C.C.P. Sec. 1170.7. The time limits imposed by subdivision (a) of section 437c, as well as the requirement in subdivision (b) of a separate statement of material facts not in dispute, are not applicable to summary judgment motions in unlawful detainer actions. C.C.P. Sec.437c(n). In all other respects, the motion is required to be granted on the same terms and conditions as a summary judgment motion under C.C.P. Sec. 437c, and such a motion must be decided solely on the affidavits or declarations filed. Ibid., subd. (c).

II. PLAINTIFF HAS ESTABLISHED THE PRIMA FACIE ELEMENTS OF AN UNLAWFUL DETAINER ACTION FOR NONPAYMENT OF RENT.

Under section 1162(2) of the Code of Civil Procedure, a tenant or subtenant is guilty of unlawful detainer.

> When he continues in possession . . . after default
> in the payment of rent . . . and three days' notice,
> in writing requiring its payment, stating the amount
> which is due, or possession of the property, shall
> have been served on him . . . .

Elements other than default in rent, service of the notice, the expiration of three days without payment, and the continuance in possession include the existence of a landlord-tenant relationship (Fredricksen v. McCosker (1956) 143 Cal. App. 2d 114) and proper contents of the notice (Wilson v. Sadleir (1915) 26 Cal. App. 357, 359 (incorporation of proper notice is sufficient)). Plaintiff's declaration establishes all these elements, so that plaintiff is entitled to summary judgment.

III. DEFENDANT(S) CANNOT PREVAIL UNDER A DEFENSE OF BREACH OF THE IMPLIED WARRANTY OF HABITABILITY.

Under the rule of Green v. Superior Court (1974) 10 Cal. 3d 616, the California Supreme Court held that in an unlawful detainer action founded on nonpayment of rent, the tenant could assert as a defense that the landlord breached an implied warranty to keep the premises habitable. The Court cited with approval the case of Hinson v. Delis (1972) 26 Cal. App. 3d 62 in this regard. In Hinson, the tenant sued the landlord in a regular civil action for breach of this implied warranty. After the trial court ruled in favor of the landlord, the Court of Appeal reversed, holding that there existed such a warranty in the law, as to which, "The tenant must also give notice of alleged defects to the landlord and allow a reasonable time for repairs to be made." Hinson at p. 70. When the Green court held that the warranty of habitability established by the Hinson court could be asserted by the tenant as a defense to an unlawful detainer action, as well as a basis for suit by the tenant, it did not modify or remove this requirement of notice by the tenant to the landlord of the alleged defects by which the tenant seeks to withhold rent. Therefore, the notice requirement also applies where the defense is asserted by the tenant in an unlawful detainer action.

Plaintiff's declaration establishes that defendant(s) failed to give plaintiff notice of the alleged defects in the premises. Unless a triable issue of fact exists in this regard, defendant(s) cannot assert this defense, as a matter of law.

DATED: _____, 19_____

_____
Plaintiff in Pro Per

PROOF OF SERVICE

I the undersigned, declare:

I am over the age of 18 years and not a party to the within action.

On _____, 19____, I served the within Notice of Motion for Summary Judgment, Declaration of Plaintiff, and Points and Authorities on defendant(s) by delivering true copies thereof to each such defendant, or other person not less than 18 years of age, at defendants' residence address of

_____,

City of _____, California, between _____.M. and _____.M.

I declare under penalty of perjury under the laws of the State of California that the foregoing is true and correct.

DATED: _____, 19__ _____

Name:

```
 1   Name:
     Address:
 2
     Phone:
 3   Plaintiff in Pro Per

 4

 5

 6

 7

 8        MUNICIPAL COURT OF CALIFORNIA, COUNTY OF _____

 9        _____ JUDICIAL DISTRICT

10
     _____     )   Case No. _____
11                                       )
              Plaintiff,                 )   PROPOSED ORDER
12   v.                                  )   GRANTING MOTION FOR
                                         )   SUMMARY JUDGMENT
13   _____      )
                                         )
14        Defendant(s).                  )
     _____      )
15

16
          Plaintiff's motion for summary judgment came on for hearing in
17
     Department _____ of the above-entitled Court on
18
     _____, 19___ , said plaintiff appearing in pro per
19
     and defendant(s)        appearing by
20
     The matter having been argued and submitted,
21
          IT IS HEREBY ORDERED that plaintiff's motion for summary
22
     judgment for restitution of the premises the subject of this
23
     action, rent and damages in the sum of $_____, and costs
24
     of suit be, and the same is, granted.
25
     DATED: _____, 19___
26
                                         _____
27                                       JUDGE OF THE MUNICIPAL COURT

28
```

```
 1   Name:
     Address:
 2
     Phone:
 3   Plaintiff in Pro Per

 4

 5

 6

 7

 8        MUNICIPAL COURT OF CALIFORNIA, COUNTY OF _____

 9        _____ JUDICIAL DISTRICT

10
     _____   )   Case No. _____
11                                        )
             Plaintiff,                   )   JUDGMENT
12   v.                                   )
                                          )
13   _____    )
                                          )
14           Defendant(s).                )
                                          )
15   _____    )

16        The motion of plaintiff for summary judgment having been

17   granted,

18        IT IS HEREBY ORDERED AND ADJUDGED that plaintiff have and

19   recover from defendant(s) _____

20   _____

21   possession and restitution of the real property located at

22   _____, City of _____,

23   County of _____, California, rent and damages

24   in the sum of $_____, plus costs of suit in the sum of

25   $_____ for the total sum of $_____.

26   DATED: _____, 19___

27                                     _____
                                       JUDGE OF THE MUNICIPAL COURT
28
```

Name:
Address:

Phone:
Plaintiff in Pro Per

MUNICIPAL COURT OF CALIFORNIA, COUNTY OF _____

_____ JUDICIAL DISTRICT

_____)   Case No. _____
)
        Plaintiff,   )   JUDGMENT AFTER TRIAL
v.   )
)
_____)
)
        Defendant(s).   )
_____)

        The above-entitled cause came on for trial on

_____, 19___ in courtroom No.____ of the

above-entitled Court, the Hon. _____

presiding, plaintiff appearing in pro per and defendant(s)

_____

        ( ) not appearing

        ( ) appearing in pro per

        ( ) appearing by attorney(s): _____.

        Jury trial having been waived, and the Court having heard the

testimony and considered the evidence,

        IT IS HEREBY ORDERED AND ADJUDGED that the above-entitled

plaintiff have and recover from the said defendant(s) possession of

the real property described as _____

_____, City of _____,

County of_____, California, rent and damages

in the sum of $_____, and costs in the sum of $_____.

DATED: _____, 19___

_____

JUDGE OF THE MUNICIPAL COURT

ATTORNEY OR PARTY WITHOUT ATTORNEY *(Name and Address)*:

TELEPHONE NO.:

ATTORNEY FOR *(Name)*:

NAME OF COURT:
STREET ADDRESS:
MAILING ADDRESS:
CITY AND ZIP CODE:
BRANCH NAME:

PLAINTIFF:

DEFENDANT:

CASE NUMBER:

APPLICATION AND ORDER FOR APPEARANCE AND EXAMINATION

[ ] **ENFORCEMENT OF JUDGMENT**   [ ] **ATTACHMENT (Third Person)**
[ ] **Judgment Debtor**   [ ] **Third Person**

ORDER TO APPEAR FOR EXAMINATION

1. TO *(name)*:
2. YOU ARE ORDERED TO APPEAR personally before this court, or before a referee appointed by the court, to
   a. [ ] furnish information to aid in enforcement of a money judgment against you.
   b. [ ] answer concerning property of the judgment debtor in your possession or control or concerning a debt you owe the judgment debtor.
   c. [ ] answer concerning property of the defendant in your possession or control or concerning a debt you owe the defendant that is subject to attachment.

Date: Time: Dept. or Div.:   Rm.:
Address of court [ ] shown above [ ] is:

3. This order may be served by a sheriff, marshal, constable, registered process server, **or the following specially appointed person** *(name)*:

Date: _____

(SIGNATURE OF JUDGE OR REFEREE)

This order must be served not less than 10 days before the date set for the examination.

IMPORTANT NOTICES ON REVERSE

APPLICATION FOR ORDER TO APPEAR FOR EXAMINATION

1. [ ] Judgment creditor   [ ] Assignee of record   [ ] Plaintiff who has a right to attach order
   applies for an order requiring *(name)*:   to appear and furnish information
   to aid in enforcement of the money judgment or to answer concerning property or debt.
2. The person to be examined is
   [ ] the judgment debtor
   [ ] a third person (1) who has possession or control of property belonging to the judgment debtor or the defendant or (2) who owes the judgment debtor or the defendant more than $250. An affidavit supporting this application under CCP §491.110 or §708.120 is attached.
3. The person to be examined resides or has a place of business in this county or within 150 miles of the place of examination.
4. [ ] This court is **not** the court in which the money judgment is entered or *(attachment only)* the court that issued the writ of attachment. An affidavit supporting an application under CCP §491.150 or §708.160 is attached.
5. [ ] The judgment debtor has been examined within the past 120 days. An affidavit showing good cause for another examination is attached.

I declare under penalty of perjury under the laws of the State of California that the foregoing is true and correct.
Date:

· ▶ _____
(TYPE OR PRINT NAME)   *(SIGNATURE OF DECLARANT)*

Form Approved by the
Judicial Council of California
AT-138, EJ-125 [New July 1, 1984]

**APPLICATION AND ORDER
FOR APPEARANCE AND EXAMINATION**
(Attachment—Enforcement of Judgment)

CCP 491.110, 708.110, 708.120
Post Record Catalog # AT-138

APPEARANCE OF JUDGMENT DEBTOR (ENFORCEMENT OF JUDGMENT)

NOTICE TO JUDGMENT DEBTOR If you fail to appear at the time and place specified in this order, you may be subject to arrest and punishment for contempt of court, and the court may make an order requiring you to pay the reasonable attorney fees incurred by the judgment creditor in this proceeding.

APPEARANCE OF A THIRD PERSON (ENFORCEMENT OF JUDGMENT)

(1) NOTICE TO PERSON SERVED If you fail to appear at the time and place specified in this order, you may be subject to arrest and punishment for contempt of court, and the court may make an order requiring you to pay the reasonable attorney fees incurred by the judgment creditor in this proceeding.

(2) NOTICE TO JUDGMENT DEBTOR The person in whose favor the judgment was entered in this action claims that the person to be examined pursuant to this order has possession or control of property which is yours or owes you a debt. This property or debt is as follows *(Describe the property or debt using typewritten capital letters)*:

If you claim that all or any portion of this property or debt is exempt from enforcement of the money judgment, you must file your exemption claim in writing with the court and have a copy personally served on the judgment creditor not later than three days before the date set for the examination. You must appear at the time and place set for the examination to establish your claim of exemption or your exemption may be waived.

APPEARANCE OF A THIRD PERSON (ATTACHMENT)

NOTICE TO PERSON SERVED If you fail to appear at the time and place specified in this order, you may be subject to arrest and punishment for contempt of court, and the court may make an order requiring you to pay the reasonable attorney fees incurred by the plaintiff in this proceeding.

APPEARANCE OF A CORPORATION, PARTNERSHIP, ASSOCIATION, TRUST, OR OTHER ORGANIZATION

It is your duty to designate one or more of the following to appear and be examined: officers, directors, managing agents, or other persons who are familiar with your property and debts.

QUESTIONNAIRE FOR JUDGMENT-DEBTOR EXAMINATION

Date of Examination: _____, 19 _____

PART 1. BASIC IDENTIFYING FACTS

Your full name: _____

Any other names (including married/maiden names) used by you:

_____

Are you married?:_____   If so, give your spouse's full name: _____

If married, what other name(s) has your spouse used? _____

Your current residence (not P.O. box) address:

_____

_____

Your telephone numbers: home:_____   work:_____

Do you have any children? _____   If so, give their names and ages, and state whether they live with you:

_____

_____

_____

PART 2.A. EMPLOYMENT OF DEBTOR:

Are you employed?_____   Your employer's name and address:

_____

_____

How long have you worked for this employer? _____

What is your job classification? _____

Rate of pay? $_____ gross per month $ _____ per hour.

Hours per week you work for this employer: _____

What are your job duties? _____

Do you receive any kind of incentive payments or bonuses from your employer? _____

If so, state the conditions under which you get them, and when you get them:

_____

_____

_____

_____

PART 2.B. EMPLOYMENT OF SPOUSE

Is your spouse employed? _____   Employer's name and address:

_____

_____

How long has s/he worked for this employer? _____

What is his/her job classification? _____

Rate of pay? $_____ gross per month $_____ per hour.

Hours per week s/he works for this employer: _____

What are his/her job duties? _____

Does s/he receive any kind of incentive payments or bonuses from the employer? _____

If so, state the conditions under which s/he gets them, and when s/he gets them: _____

_____

_____

PART 2.C. OTHER EMPLOYMENT OF DEBTOR OR SPOUSE

Your employer's name and address:

_____

_____

_____

How long have you worked for this employer? _____

What is your job classification? _____

Rate of pay? $ gross per month; $ per hour. _____

Hours per week you work for this employer: _____

What are your job duties? _____

Do you receive any kind of incentive payments or bonuses from your employer? _____

If so, state the conditions under which you get them, and when you get them: _____

_____

_____

PART 2.D. SELF-EMPLOYMENT OF DEBTOR OR SPOUSE

If you or your spouse is engaged in any type of full or part-time self employment, give the name and type of business, and its location: _____

_____

_____

How long in this business?_____

Did you or your spouse start up or purchase it? _____

If started up, when? _____

If purchased, state the purchase price, date of purchase, and full names and addresses of sellers: _____.

_____

_____

_____

_____

Do you or your spouse have an accountant for this business?

Accountant's name and address:

_____

_____

Who prepares your business and personal income tax returns?

_____

_____

PART 3. CASH, SAVINGS OR CHECKING ACCOUNTS, SAFE-DEPOSIT BOXES

How much cash do you have on your person right now? _____

Do you or your spouse have a checking account? _____

If so, give bank, S&L, or credit union name and branch: _____

_____

Do you have a checkbook with you now? _____

If yes, give the account number(s): _____

Who is authorized to sign checks on the account? _____

_____

What is the current approximate balance? $_____

When did you make your last deposit? _____

Amount of last deposit: $_____

How often do you make deposits? _____

How often does your spouse make deposits? _____

When did you write your last check on that account? _____

How much was the check for? $_____

Do you or your spouse have a savings account? _____

If so, give bank, S&L, or credit union name and branch: _____

_____

State the account number(s): _____

Who is authorized to withdraw funds? _____

_____

What is the current approximate balance? $ _____

When did you make your last deposit? _____

Amount of last deposit? $_____

When did you last make a withdrawal? _____

Do you have access to any business account for which you are an authorized signer? _____

Give the bank or S&L name, branch, and business name and address: _____

_____

_____

Do you or your spouse have a safe deposit box? _____

Who has access to the box? _____

What property is kept in it? _____

_____

_____

_____

_____

_____

Give the box location and number: _____

_____

PART 4. MOTOR VEHICLES

What motor vehicles do you and your spouse drive?

Vehicle 1: Make:_____ Model: _____ Year: _____

License Plate Number: _____ State: _____

Registered Owner(s): _____

_____

Where garaged? _____

Est. Value: $_____   Is it fully paid for?_____

If not paid for, state amount owed: $_____

Name and address of lender/lienholder/legal owner:

_____

_____

Vehicle 2: Make:_____ Model: _____ Year: _____

License Plate Number: _____ State: _____

Registered Owner(s): _____

_____

Where garaged? _____

Est. Value: $_____   Is it fully paid for? _____

If not paid for, state amount owed: $_____

Name and address of lender/lienholder/legal owner:

_____

_____

Do you or your spouse own any recreational vehicles, such as carnpers, trailers, boats,dirt-bikes, etc?_____

If yes, give the following information:

Type of vehicle:_____ Make: _____ Year: _____

License/Registration Number: _____ State: _____

Registered Owner(s): _____

_____

Where kept?_____

Est. Value: $_____   Is it fully paid for? _____

If not paid for, state amount owed: $_____

Name and address of lender/lienholder/legal owner:

_____

_____

PART 5. CURRENT RESIDENCE

Do you live in an apartment, single-family house, mobilehome, condominium unit, or townhouse? _____

Do you rent or own your home? _____

PART 5.A. IF DEBTOR RENTS

How much rent do you pay? $_____   When paid? _____

How do you pay; check, cash, or money order? _____

Do you rent out any rooms? If so, state rents received and names of persons paying:

_____

_____

State landlord's name, address, and phone: _____

_____

_____

_____

How long have you rented at this address? _____

PART 5.B. IF DEBTOR AND/OR SPOUSE OWN HOME

Who is listed as owner(s) on the deed to the property?

_____

When was the home purchased? _____

What was the purchase price? $_____

How much was the down payment? $_____

How much are the monthly payments? $_____

To what bank, S&L, or mortgage company are the monthly payments made?

_____

Who makes the actual payments? _____

How are the payments made; cash, check, or money order? _____

How much is still owed on the loan? $_____

How much do you think the property could sell for today? $_____

Is there a second deed of trust or second mortgage against the property? _____

For what amount? $_____

How much are the monthly payments? $_____

Who are these payments paid to? _____

Are there any other liens against the property? _____

If so, state the amounts, the names of the lienholders, and how the liens occurred:

_____

_____

_____

Do you rent out any of the rooms in the residence? _____

If so, state rents received and names of persons paying: _____

_____

_____

_____

PART 6. REAL PROPERTY OTHER THAN HOME

Do you or spouse own any real estate anywhere (other than any already discussed in 5.B above)? _____

If yes, what kind of property is it? (vacant land? commercial property, etc): _____

_____

Is there a structure of any type on the land? _____

If yes, what kind? _____

Who is listed as owner(s) on the deed to the property? _____

When was the property purchased? _____

What was the purchase price? $_____

How much was the down payment? $_____

How much are the monthly payments? $_____

To what bank, S&L, or mortgage company are the monthly payments made? _____

_____

_____

Who makes the actual payments? _____

How are the payments made; cash, check, or money order?_____

How much is still owed on the loan? $ _____

How much do you think the property could sell for today? $_____

Is there a second deed of trust or second mortgage against the property? _____

For what amount? $_____

How much are the monthly payments? $_____

Who are these payments paid to? _____

Are there any other liens against the property? _____

If yes, state the amounts, the names of lienholders, and how the liens occurred: _____

_____

_____

_____

Do you receive any rents from the property? _____

If so, state rents received and names of persons paying: _____

_____

_____

_____

PART 7. OTHER PROPERTY

Do you or your spouse own any stocks, bonds, or corporate securities of any kind? _____

If yes, state corporation name and address, type of holding, name(s) of owner(s), and value of holding(s):

_____

_____

_____

_____

Do you or your spouse own any deeds of trust or mortgages on any real property or personal property? _____

If yes, state nature of property, location, nature of payments to you, and location of property:

_____

_____

_____

Are there any unsatisfied judgments in favor of you or your spouse? _____

If yes, state plaintiffs and defendants, amount of judgment, court, county, and judicial district:

_____

_____

_____

Do you or your spouse own any rings, watches, diamonds, other jewelry or antiques of any kind worth $100 or more? _____

If yes, list property and value: _____

_____

_____

Do you or your spouse own any other personal property not already discussed, that is worth over $100? _____

If yes, list property and value: _____

_____

_____

_____

In the past year have you or your spouse received any payments of money other than already discussed? _____

If yes, state amounts, dates received, reason money was received, and what happened to the money:

_____

_____

_____

Are you the beneficiary in any will? _____

If yes, state name and address of author of will, relationship of that individual to you, and type and value of property to be received: _____

_____

_____

_____

PART 8. BUSINESS RELATIONS AND EMPLOYMENT HISTORY

Are you or your spouse an officer, director, or stockholder of any corporation? _____

If yes, state corporation's name and address, nature of business, your or spouse's position, and the nature and value of any shares of stock owned: _____

_____

_____

_____

For the past five years, list names and addresses of all businesses conducted by you and employment had by you, giving your position, duration of employment, and rate or amount of pay:

_____

_____

_____

_____

_____

_____

_____

_____

_____

_____

_____

_____

_____

_____

_____

_____

ATTORNEY OR PARTY WITHOUT ATTORNEY *(Name and Address)*:	TELEPHONE NO.:	LEVYING OFFICER *(Name and Address)*:

ATTORNEY FOR *(Name)*:

NAME OF COURT, JUDICIAL DISTRICT OR BRANCH COURT, IF ANY:

PLAINTIFF:

DEFENDANT:

APPLICATION FOR EARNINGS WITHHOLDING ORDER (Wage Garnishment)	LEVYING OFFICER FILE NO.:	COURT CASE NO.:

TO THE SHERIFF OR ANY MARSHAL OR CONSTABLE OF THE COUNTY OF
OR ANY REGISTERED PROCESS SERVER

1. The judgment creditor *(name)*:

requests issuance of an Earnings Withholding Order directing the employer to withhold the earnings of the judgment debtor (employee).

Name and address of employer   Name and address of employee

Social Security Number *(if known)*:

2. The amounts withheld are to be paid to
   a. ☐ The attorney (or party without an attorney) named at the top of this page.
   b. ☐ Other *(name, address, and telephone)*:

3. a. Judgment was entered on *(date)*:
   b. Collect the amount directed by the Writ of Execution unless a lesser amount is specified here:
      $

4. ☐ The Writ of Execution was issued to collect delinquent amounts payable for the **support** of a child, former spouse, or **spouse** of the employee.

5. ☐ Special instructions *(specify)*:

6. *(Check a or b)*
   a. ☐ I have not previously obtained an order directing this employer to withhold the earnings of this employee.
      —OR—
   b. ☐ I have previously obtained such an order, but that order *(check one)*:
      ☐ expired at least 10 days ago.
      ☐ was terminated by a court order, but I am entitled to apply for another Earnings Withholding Order under the provisions of Code of Civil Procedure section 706.105(h).
      ☐ was ineffective.

▶

. . . . *(TYPE OR PRINT NAME)*   *(SIGNATURE OF ATTORNEY OR PARTY WITHOUT ATTORNEY)*

I declare under penalty of perjury under the laws of the State of California that the foregoing is true and correct.

Date:

▶

. . . . *(TYPE OR PRINT NAME)*   *(SIGNATURE OF DECLARANT)*

Form Adopted by the
Judicial Council of California
982.5(1) [Rev. January 1, 1985]

APPLICATION FOR EARNINGS WITHHOLDING ORDER
(Wage Garnishment)

CCP 706.121
Post Record Catalog #982.5(1)

ATTORNEY OR PARTY WITHOUT ATTORNEY *(Name and Address)*:

TELEPHONE NO.:

ATTORNEY FOR *(Name)*:

NAME OF COURT:

STREET ADDRESS:

MAILING ADDRESS:

CITY AND ZIP CODE:

BRANCH NAME:

PLAINTIFF:

DEFENDANT:

CASE NUMBER:

ACKNOWLEDGMENT OF SATISFACTION OF JUDGMENT

[ ] FULL [ ] PARTIAL [ ] MATURED INSTALLMENT

FOR COURT USE ONLY

1. Satisfaction of the judgment is acknowledged as follows *(see footnote* before completing)*:

    a. [ ] Full satisfaction

        (1) [ ] Judgment is satisfied in full.

        (2) [ ] The judgment creditor has accepted payment or performance other than that specified in the judgment in full satisfaction of the judgment.

    b. [ ] Partial satisfaction

        The amount received in partial satisfaction of the judgment is

        $

    c. [ ] Matured installment

        All matured installments under the installment judgment have been satisfied as of *(date)*:

2. Full name and address of judgment creditor:

3. Full name and address of assignee of record, if any:

4. Full name and address of judgment debtor being fully or partially released:

5. a. Judgment entered on *(date)*:

        [ ] (1) in judgment book volume no.:   (2) page no.:

    b. [ ] Renewal entered on *(date)*:

        [ ] (1) in judgment book volume no.:   (2) page no.:

6. [ ] An [ ] abstract of judgment [ ] certified copy of the judgment has been recorded as follows *(complete all information for each county where recorded)*:

COUNTY	DATE OF RECORDING	BOOK NUMBER	PAGE NUMBER

7. [ ] A notice of judgment lien has been filed in the office of the Secretary of State as file number *(specify)*:

NOTICE TO JUDGMENT DEBTOR: If this is an acknowledgment of full satisfaction of judgment, it will have to be recorded in each county shown in item 6 above, if any, in order to release the judgment lien, and will have to be filed in the office of the Secretary of State to terminate any judgment lien on personal property.

▶

Date:

_____
(SIGNATURE OF JUDGMENT CREDITOR OR ASSIGNEE OF CREDITOR OR ATTORNEY)

*The names of the judgment creditor and judgment debtor must be stated as shown in any Abstract of Judgment which was recorded and is being released by this satisfaction. **A separate notary acknowledgment must be attached for each signature.**

Form Approved by the
Judicial Council of California
EJ-100 [Rev. July 1, 1983](Cor. 7/84)

ACKNOWLEDGMENT OF SATISFACTION OF JUDGMENT

CCP 724.060, 724.120, 724.250

Post Record Catalog # EJ-100

PROOF OF SERVICE BY MAIL

My address is _____,

_____, California.

On _____, 19_____, I served the within:

_____

_____

_____

_____

by depositing true copies thereof, enclosed in separate, sealed envelopes, with the postage thereon fully prepared, in the United States Postal Service mail in Los Angeles County, addressed as follows:

_____

_____

_____

_____

_____

_____

_____

_____

_____

_____

_____

_____

_____

I am, and was at the time herein-mentioned mailing took place, a resident of or employed in the County where the mailing occurred, over the age of eighteen years old and not a party to the within cause.

I declare under penalty of perjury under the laws of the State of California that the foregoing is true and correct.

Dated: _____   _____

150 B.R. 50
United States Bankruptcy Court,
C.D. California.
Aug. 30, 1989.

I

INTRODUCTION

Mike Marquand, dba San Marcos Apartments, ("Movant") filed and served a motion (the "Motion") pursuant to 11 U.S.C. § 362(d) for relief from the automatic stay provided by 11 U.S.C. § 362(a) (the "Stay"). In the Motion, Movant seeks an order relieving him of the Stay so he may enforce a "Judgment for Unlawful Detainer" (the "Judgment") obtained by Movant in the Municipal Court of the State of California, County of Los Angeles (the "State Court"). Movant obtained the Judgment in the State Court to regain possession of residential real property commonly known as 15238 Orange Avenue, No. 111, Paramount, California (the "Apartment"), from Sanya Smith ("Debtor"), the debtor in this Chapter 7 bankruptcy case.

The Motion is not unique or rare; I have heard over one hundred such motions in each month since April 1988 when I assumed the bench. With few and insignificant variations, these hundreds of motions involve facts identical to those I find below.

II

FACTS

On June 30, 1988, Debtor entered into an Apartment Rental Agreement (the "Rental Agreement") with Movant. Under the terms of the Rental Agreement, Debtor agreed to pay Movant $695.00 per month beginning on July 1, 1988. On or about June 1, 1989, Debtor failed to pay the agreed upon monthly rent to Movant. Thereafter, on June 10, 1989, Movant, served a Notice to Pay Rent or Surrender Possession of Premises pursuant to Cal. Code of Civ.Proc. § 1161. Debtor did not pay the overdue rent. Movant then filed a complaint for unlawful detainer in the State Court (the "Complaint") on June 30, 1989. Debtor did not appear or otherwise respond to the Complaint.

On July 17, 1989, the Judgment was awarded to Movant. Before Movant could

enforce the Judgement to regain possession of the Apartment, Debtor filed her Voluntary Petition Under Chapter 7 of the United States Bankruptcy Code in the United States Bankruptcy Court, Central District of California on July 28, 1989. Movant was the only creditor listed on Debtor's Bankruptcy Schedules.

On August 1, 1989 Movant filed the Motion. On August 3, 1989 Movant served notice of the Motion and the Motion on Debtor by United States Mail. The Motion was heard on August 30, 1989. Debtor did not appear at the hearing or file any type of opposition to the Motion.

III

THE PROLIFERATION OF "UNLAWFUL DETAINER" CASE FILINGS

More than 39,000 Chapter 7 bankruptcy cases are filed in the Central District of California annually.[1] A significant portion of these cases are apparently filed solely for the purpose of staying a residential landlord from dispossessing a debtor/tenant from a rented apartment or house. There is no exact count of these "unlawful detainer" cases pending in this district, but over the past several months, eighty percent of the motions for relief from Stay filed in Chapter 7 cases that I have heard involve residential unlawful detainer actions.

That these cases are filed solely for the purpose of staying enforcement of unlawful detainer judgments can be inferred from several facts: the commencement of the case by the filing of a "bare bones" petition without any schedules or statement of affairs ever being filed; the listing of no, few, or false creditors, if schedules are indeed filed; the failure of the debtor to appear at the mandatory section 341(a) meeting of creditors; and the refusal of debtors in these cases to comply with the requirements of the Bankruptcy Code, the Bankruptcy Rules, or this court's Local Rules and thereby failing to obtain a discharge.

The debtor/tenant almost never appears at the hearing on the landlord/movant's motion for relief from the Stay. When a debtor/tenant does appear, I always inquire as

---

1. *See* "The Federal Judicial Workload Statistics," Dec. 1988 edition, Administrative Office of the United States Courts, Statistical Analysis and Reports Division.

to the purpose of the bankruptcy case filing. Invariably the debtor tells me that he or she filed in order to stay his or her eviction from residential real property.

IV

THE ROLE OF THE "BANKRUPTCY MILLS"

A principal, and perhaps the primary, reason for the proliferation of these unlawful detainer bankruptcy cases is the advice given to these debtor/tenants by some lawyers and many paralegals who are in business to advise low-income and legally unsophisticated individuals regarding the filing of bankruptcy cases.

Some of these lawyers and paralegals provide valuable services for reasonable compensation to those who are in financial distress and who seek the "fresh start" a Chapter 7 or Chapter 13 discharge provides. Unfortunately there are many others who mislead debtor/tenants into believing that filing a bankruptcy case will stay unlawful detainer evictions for an extended period of time and that no detrimental consequences will occur. These "bankruptcy mills" often take several hundreds of dollars in fees from debtor/tenants who cannot afford to pay rent in the first place.

Often these debtor/tenants are not advised that the filing of a bankruptcy case will have a deleterious effect on their credit records. In fact, many debtor/tenants who have appeared in my court have told me that these "bankruptcy mills" do not even disclose to these debtor/tenants that they were filing bankruptcy—rather, they are led to believe they are obtaining some appropriate form of legal relief in our legal system, which is all too often complex and intimidating to the lay-person.

Of course, not all of these debtor/tenants are innocent victims. Many have learned to manipulate the bankruptcy court system on their own, without the help of

2. *See Local Bankruptcy Practice Manual for the Central District of California,* (Professional Education Systems, Inc., 1989) pp. 366–367.

any of the "bankruptcy mills." These *pro se* debtor/tenants will often file not one, but two or more bankruptcies in order to delay improperly the enforcement of an unlawful detainer judgment. Landlords who have sought relief from the Stay before me have testified that some of these manipulative debtor/tenants have boasted that they can use (or misuse) the bankruptcy court system to delay the landlord's efforts to evict them for several months while paying no rent.

V

THE EFFECT ON BANKRUPTCY COURTS

As discussed in section III above, the bankruptcy courts in the Central District of California are flooded with Chapter 7 and Chapter 13 cases filed solely for the purpose of delaying unlawful detainer evictions. Inevitably and swiftly following the filing of these cases is the filing of motions for relief of the Stay by landlords who are temporarily thwarted by this abuse of the bankruptcy court system. Nearly every bankruptcy judge in the Central District of California allows residential landlords to seek relief from the Stay in these unlawful detainer bankruptcy cases on shortened notice.[2] Thus, contrary to the false representations made by the "bankruptcy mills," the debtor/tenants generally obtain only a brief respite from the consummation of the unlawful detainer evictions, after having paid hundreds of dollars to these mills.

The United States Trustee for the Central District of California has joined forces with the United States Attorney in an attempt to put these "bankruptcy mills" out of business.[3] These laudable efforts have met with little success. This is due to the ease with which operators of these bankruptcy mills can shuck one business identity, assume another, change location, and continue to defraud an unending supply of

3. *See* Los Angeles Times, "Petition Mills Dupe Many Into False Bankruptcies," May 8, 1989, Sec. 1, pp. 1, 23-24.

debtor/tenants and abuse the protection afforded by the Stay.

The Bankruptcy Court for the Central District of California is the busiest bankruptcy court in the nation, with over 50,000 bankruptcy case filings a year.[4] The mountain of paper work that accompanies the thousands of abusive "unlawful detainer" case filings places an unnecessary burden on our already overworked and undercompensated clerk's office. Of course this mountain of paperwork flows from our Clerk's Office to the chambers of our judges when landlords file their relief from Stay motions. Because of the increased workload caused by these blatantly abusive unlawful detainer case filings, our court has had to establish special procedures dismissing these cases as quickly as possible so that the court's dockets and the clerk's files will not become more choked with paperwork than they already are.

These relief from Stay motions are rarely contested and are never lost, as long as the moving party provides adequate notice of the motion and competent evidence to establish a *prima facie* case. Thus, bankruptcy courts in our district hear dozens of these Stay motions weekly, none of which involves any justiciable controversies of fact or law.

VI

THE SCOPE OF THE STAY

A. *Property of the Estate*

Section 362(a) provides in pertinent part:
[A] petition filed under Section 301, 302, or 303 of this title ...

operates as a stay, applicable to all entities of ...

(1) The commencement or continuation, including the issuance or employment of process, of a judicial, administrative, or other action or proceeding against the debtor that was or could have been commenced before the commencement of the case under this title, or to recover a claim against the debtor that arose before the commencement of the case under this title;

(2) *The enforcement*, against the debtor or *against property of the estate, of a judgment* obtained before the commencement of a case under this title;

(3) *any act to obtain possession of property of the estate*, or property from the estate, or to exercise control over property of the estate.... (Emphasis added.)

The term "property of the estate," as used in section 362(a), is defined in section 541(a)(1) to include:

[A]ll legal or equitable interests of the debtor in property as of the commencement of the case.

A bankruptcy court must look to state law to determine what "legal or equitable interests" the debtor had at the commencement of the case. *See Butner v. United States*, 440 U.S. 48, 99 S.Ct. 914, 59 L.Ed.2d 136 (1979); *In re Farmers Markets, Inc.*, 792 F.2d 1400 (9th Cir.1986); and *In re Schewe*, 94 B.R. 938 (Bankr.W.D. Mich.1989).

The United States Court of Appeals for the Ninth Circuit has interpreted California law as to whether a tenant retains any property interest once a lease has been terminated. In the case of *In re Windmill Farms, Inc.*, 841 F.2d 1467 (1988), the Ninth Circuit held that a lease of real property is terminated under California law when the lessor affirms his election to terminate the lease as expressed in a notice to pay rent or quit which the lessor has previously served upon the lessee. *Id.* at 1469–71. This affirmation of the termination of the lease by the lessor is usually accomplished by the filing of a complaint for unlawful detainer. Thus, if the lessor properly notifies the lessee of the lessor's intention to terminate the lease, the unpaid rent is not paid within the appropriate period of notice, and the lessor affirms his intention to terminate the lease by, at least, filing a complaint for unlawful de-

4. *See* "The Federal Judicial Workload Statistics," Dec. 1988 edition, Administrative Office of the United States Courts, Statistical Analysis and Reports Division.

tainer, the lease is terminated and the lessee retains no property interest with regards to the leased real property, except, perhaps, for one—the right to obtain relief from forfeiture of the lease under California Code of Civil Procedure § 1179.[5]

In this case, Debtor failed to pay her rent, Movant gave appropriate notice to Debtor of his intention to terminate Debtor's tenancy if she did not pay her overdue rent, Debtor failed to pay her overdue rent, and Movant affirmed his intention to terminate the tenancy by filing a Complaint. Further, Movant obtained the Judgment which declared his termination of Debtor's tenancy of the Apartment. Therefore it follows from the analysis presented in *Windmill Farms* that the bankruptcy estate of Debtor has absolutely no property interest in the Rental Agreement, or the tenancy it created, which was terminated prior to the commencement of this bankruptcy case. Debtor's retention of physical possession of the Apartment is not a property interest recognized by law.[6]

It is arguable that Debtor's bankruptcy estate does retain a property interest in the right to seek relief from forfeiture under Cal.Code of Civ.Proc. § 1179. No Chapter 7 debtor or trustee has ever sought to exercise this right in any of the residential unlawful detainer cases that I have heard. This is due to the fact that such tenancies have absolutely no value to the bankruptcy estate and its creditors and that these unlawful detainer bankruptcy cases rarely, if ever, have any assets that would enable the bankruptcy trustee to fulfill the condition in Cal.Code Civ.Proc. § 1179 for relief from forfeiture—"full payment of rent due." That relief from forfeiture rights have no meaning in residential unlawful detainer cases is recognized in our Local Bankruptcy Rule 112(1)(a) which provides that the Chapter 7 trustee in such cases neither need be named as a responding party in, nor served with, motions for relief from Stay to enforce unlawful detainer judgments against residential real property.[7]

Based upon the foregoing authorities, I conclude that neither Debtor nor the bankruptcy estate herein has any legal or equitable property interest in the Debtor's Rental Agreement or the Apartment due to the termination of Debtor's tenancy prior to the commencement of this bankruptcy case. Therefore, the Stay does not enjoin the Movant from taking any action to regain possession of the Apartment. As a result, it is not necessary for the Movant to obtain relief from the Stay in order to regain possession of the Apartment.[8]

B. *The Debtor*

It appears from the language of section 362(a)(2), quoted in section VI

---

5. In *re Windmill Farms, supra* at 1469, the Ninth Circuit held that if a trustee was able to obtain relief from forfeiture of the lease pursuant to California Code of Civil Procedure, § 1179, then the lease would be "resurrected" and the bankruptcy estate would regain its property interest in the lease and the subject real property.

6. Many courts have held that actual, physical possession of premises subject to a month-to-month tenancy or lease does not constitute a legal or equitable interest in property within the meaning of section 541. *In re Kennedy*, 39 B.R. 995, 997 (C.D.Cal.1984); *In re Youngs*, 7 B.R. 69, 71 (Bankr.D.Mass.1980); *In re Depoy*, 29 B.R. 466, 470 (Bankr.N.D.Ind.1983).

7. Even if a trustee or debtor wished to obtain relief from forfeiture for a terminated residential lease, nothing in this opinion precludes either party from seeking such relief in the appropriate forum.

8. In some ways, the above analysis is analogous to the Bankruptcy Code's treatment of property that technically is property of the estate but which is of inconsequential value or benefit to the estate. Section 542(a) provides as follows:

An entity, other than a custodian, in possession, custody, or control, during the case, of properties that the trustee may use, sell, or lease under Section 363 of this title, or that the debtor may exempt under section 542 of this title, shall deliver to the trustee, and account for, such property or the value of such property, *unless such property is of inconsequential value or benefit to the estate.* (Emphasis added.)

If an entity has possession of property of the estate that is of inconsequential value or benefit to the estate, section 542 excuses that entity from turning it over to the trustee. Similarly, if a landlord seeks possession of residential real property that is no longer property of the estate, it does not follow that the Stay should enjoin the landlord from doing so.

above, that the Stay enjoins Movant from enforcing an unlawful detainer judgment against *Debtor*, even though the Stay does not prohibit Movant from regaining possession of the Apartment. I believe, however, that the only practical construction of 362(a)(1), (2) and (3) would be that these subsections operate to enjoin an entity from continuing an action or enforcing a judgment against a debtor that would either interfere with the administration of the bankruptcy estate or violate the discharge of debt which gives debtors a "fresh start," a goal sought by debtors who file bankruptcy in good faith.[9] For example, if a landlord, or any other creditor, attempted to enforce a judgment for money damages against the Debtor or the bankruptcy estate, 11 U.S.C. § 362(a)(2) would clearly enjoin such conduct.

As discussed above, those individuals who file bankruptcy cases to stay unlawful detainers usually do not seek a "fresh start" discharge of debt. They are only seeking to delay improperly the landlord from obtaining possession of his property. This delay provides no benefit to the bankruptcy estate or creditors of the estate.

The purpose of the Stay is to give the bankruptcy estate and its fiduciary, either the trustee or the debtor-in-possession, an opportunity to gather together the assets of the estate, determine their value, and liquidate or reorganize them. This goal of the Stay is not achieved by applying it to a landlord's attempt to regain possession of residential real property wrongfully being held by a debtor/tenant.

Instead, if the Stay is allowed to enjoin a landlord from completing a residential eviction, a completely different end is achieved—that of allowing unscrupulous manipulators, the "bankruptcy mills," to prey upon the desperate and ignorant tenants who come to them for help and are defrauded out of money which could better be used to pay rent to their current landlords or to obtain new living quarters.

Another consequence of holding that the Stay applies to residential unlawful detainer evictions is that the cost of doing business as a residential landlord rises with the additional expense of hiring lawyers not only to pursue an eviction in the state court but also to obtain relief from the Stay in Bankruptcy Court. This added cost necessarily increases the rent that must be paid by low-income tenants in the Los Angeles area, which is one of the most expensive urban rental markets in the country.[10] The ever increasing rents for low-income housing, of course, only makes it harder for tenants to pay their rent and therefore leads to more abusive bankruptcy filings.[11] Thus, this vicious cycle repeats and repeats.

Based upon the foregoing, I conclude that the Stay does not enjoin a landlord from regaining possession of residential premises from a wrongfully holding-over bankruptcy debtor/tenant, as long as the landlord seeks only to repossess the property and not to enforce any other portion of his unlawful detainer judgment against the debtor and the bankruptcy estate, such as collecting money damages.

VII

CONCLUSION

This opinion may be viewed by some as judicial legislation. I observe that this abuse of the bankruptcy court system has been communicated to Congress.[12] Congress has failed to address the problem, perhaps because landlords of residential real property do not have as loud a lobby-

9. H.R.Rep. No. 95-595, 95th Cong. 1st Sess. 340–342 (1977), U.S.Code Cong. & Admin.News 1978 pp. 5787, 6296–6299 *reprinted in* King, Klee, and Levin, *Collier on Bankruptcy* (15th Ed.1988) Appendix 2.

10. *See* recent study done by Roulac Real Estate Consulting Group; Deloitte, Haskins & Sells and Institute of Real Estate Management, August 1989.

11. *See* Los Angeles Times, "Crowded Courtrooms Serve as Battleground for L.A.'s Eviction Wars," June 11, 1989, Part II, p. 1.

12. Letter of The Honorable Alan M. Ahart dated March 17, 1989, a copy of which is on file with this court.

ing voice as commercial landlords who have been able to effect large and significant revisions in the Bankruptcy Code in order to protect their interests. *See*, 11 U.S.C. § 365(b)(3) and § 365(c)(3) as amended by the Bankruptcy Amendments and Federal Judgeship Act of 1984.

I further observe that this opinion will have absolutely no effect on this problem unless residential landlords, and the attorneys who represent them, call it to the attention of the state courts that issue unlawful detainer judgments and convince those state courts to order the proper state law enforcement officials to evict debtor/tenants without first requiring residential landlords to obtain relief from the Stay. If this chain of events results, there is a chance that this wide-spread and daily abuse of the Bankruptcy Court system and the shameless defrauding of thousands of tenant victims will cease.

Based upon my conclusion that the Stay does not enjoin Movant from enforcing the Judgment, no order granting relief from stay is required.

Nevertheless, in the interests of justice, and to allow Movant to enforce the Judgment with no further delay, I hereby authorize Movant, to the extent that such authority is required, to enforce the Judgment to regain possession of the Apartment from Debtor.

Index

RECYCLE YOUR OUT-OF-DATE BOOKS
AND GET 25% OFF YOUR NEXT PURCHASE

OUT-OF-DATE = DANGEROUS

Using an old edition can be dangerous if information in it is wrong. Unfortunately, laws and legal procedures change often. Generally speaking, any book more than two years old is of questionable value. Books more than four or five years old are a menace.

To help you keep up-to-date, we extend this offer:

If you cut out and deliver to us the title portion of the cover of any old Nolo book, we'll give you a 25% discount off the retail price of any new Nolo book. For example, if you have a copy of Tenants' Rights, 4th edition and want to trade it for the latest *California Marriage and Divorce Law*, send us the *Tenants' Rights* cover and a check for the current price of *California Marriage and Divorce Law*, less a 25% discount.

Information on current prices and editions is listed in the back of this book and in the catalog in the Nolo News (see offer at the back of this book).

This offer is to individuals only.

ESTATE PLANNING & PROBATE

Plan Your Estate With a Living Trust
Attorney Denis Clifford
National 2nd Edition
This book covers every significant aspect of estate planning and gives detailed, specific instructions for preparing a living trust, a document that lets your family avoid expensive and lengthy probate court proceedings after your death. *Plan Your Estate* includes all the tear-out forms and step-by-step instructions to let you prepare an estate plan designed for your special needs.
$19.95/NEST

Nolo's Simple Will Book
Attorney Denis Clifford
National 2nd Edition
It's easy to write a legally valid will using this book. The instructions and forms enable people to draft a will for all needs, including naming a personal guardian for minor children, leaving property to minor children or young adults and updating a will when necessary. Good in all states except Louisiana.
$17.95/SWIL

The Conservatorship Book
Lisa Goldoftas & Attorney Carolyn Farren
California 1st Edition
When someone becomes incapacitated due to illness or age, a conservator may need to take charge of their medical and financial affairs. *The Conservatorship Book* comes with complete instructions and all the forms necessary to file conservatorship documents, appear in court, be appointed conservator and end a conservatorship.
$24.95/CNSV

How to Probate an Estate
Julia Nissley
California 7th Edition
If you find yourself responsible for winding up the legal and financial affairs of a deceased family member or friend, you can often save costly attorneys' fees by handling the probate process yourself. This book also explains the simple procedures you can use to transfer assets that don't require probate, including property held in joint tenancy or living trusts or as community property.
$34.95/PAE

Who Will Handle Your Finances If You Can't?
Attorneys Denis Clifford and Mary Randolph
National 1st Edition
Contains all the forms and instructions necessary to create a durable power of attorney for finances. Creating this document means that you, not courts and lawyers, decide who will handle your financial affairs if illness or old age makes it impossible for you to handle them yourself. It also saves your family from going through painful conservatorship proceedings later.
$19.95/FINA

law form kits

Nolo's Law Form Kit: Wills
Attorney Denis Clifford and Lisa Goldoftas
National 1st Edition
Provides you with a legally valid will, quickly and easily. You can create a will that distributes your property according to your wishes, select beneficiaries, choose a guardian for your children, set up a children's trust and appoint an executor.
$14.95/KWL

software

WillMaker
Nolo Press
Version 4.0
This easy-to-use software program lets you prepare and update a legal will—safely, privately and without the expense of a lawyer. Leading you step-by-step in a question-and-answer format, *WillMaker* builds a will around your answers, taking into account your state of residence. *WillMaker* comes with a 200-page legal manual which provides the legal background necessary to make sound choices. Good in all states except Louisiana.
IBM PC (3-1/2 & 5-1/4 disks included)
$69.95/WI4
MACINTOSH $69.95/WM4

Nolo's Personal RecordKeeper
(formerly For the Record)
Carol Pladsen & Attorney Ralph Warner
Version 3.0
Nolo's Personal RecordKeeper lets you record the location of personal, financial and legal information in over 200 categories and subcategories. It also allows you to create lists of insured property, compute net worth, consolidate emergency information into one place and export to *Quicken*® home inventory and net worth reports. Includes a 320-page manual filled with practical and legal advice.
IBM PC (3-1/2 & 5-1/4 disks included)
$49.95/FRI3
MACINTOSH $49.95/FRM3

Nolo's Living Trust
Attorney Mary Randolph
Version 1.0
A will is an indispensable part of any estate plan, but many people need a living trust as well. By putting certain assets into a trust, you save your heirs the headache, time and expense of probate. *Nolo's Living Trust* lets you set up an individual or shared marital trust, make your trust document legal, transfer your property to the trust, and change or revoke the trust at any time. The manual guides you through the process step-by-step, and legal help screens and an on-line glossary explain key legal terms and concepts. Good in all states except Louisiana.
MACINTOSH $79.95/LTM1

GOING TO COURT

Everybody's Guide to Municipal Court
Judge Roderic Duncan
California 1st Edition
Explains how to prepare and defend the most common types of contract and personal injury law suits in California Municipal Court. Written by a California judge, the book provides step-by-step instructions for preparing and filing all necessary forms, gathering evidence and appearing in court.
$29.95/MUNI

Everybody's Guide to Small Claims Court
Attorney Ralph Warner
National 5th Edition
California 10th Edition
These books will help you decide if you should sue in Small Claims Court, show you how to file and serve papers, tell you what to bring to court and how to collect a judgment.
National $15.95/NSCC
California $15.95/ CSCC

How to Win Your Personal Injury Claim
Attorney Joseph Matthews
National 1st Edition
Armed with the right information anyone can handle a personal injury claim. This step-by-step guide will show you how to avoid insurance company run-arounds, evaluate what your claim is worth, obtain a full and fair settlement and save for yourself what you would pay a lawyer.
$24.95/PICL

Fight Your Ticket
Attorney David Brown
California 5th Edition
Shows you how to fight an unfair traffic ticket—when you're stopped, at arraignment, at trial and on appeal.
$17.95/FYT

Collect Your Court Judgment
Gini Graham Scott, Attorney Stephen Elias & Lisa Goldoftas
California 2nd Edition
Contains step-by-step instructions and all the forms you need to collect a court judgment from the debtor's bank accounts, wages, business receipts, real estate or other assets.
$19.95/JUDG

How to Change Your Name
Attorneys David Loeb & David Brown
California 5th Edition
Explains how to change your name legally and provides all the necessary court forms with detailed instructions on how to fill them out.
$19.95/NAME

The Criminal Records Book
Attorney Warren Siegel
California 3rd Edition
Shows you step-by-step how to seal criminal records, dismiss convictions, destroy marijuana records and reduce felony convictions.
$19.95/CRIM

Legal Breakdown: 40 Ways to Fix Our Legal System
Nolo Press Editors and Staff
National 1st Edition
Presents 40 common-sense proposals to make our legal system fairer, faster, cheaper and more accessible. It advocates abolishing probate, taking divorce out of court, treating jurors better and a host of other fundamental changes.
$8.95/LEG

The Legal Guide for Starting & Running a Small Business
Attorney Fred S. Steingold
National 1st Edition
An essential resource for every small business owner, whether you are just starting out or are already established.
Find out how to form a sole proprietorship, partnership or corporation, negotiate a favorable lease, hire and fire employees, write contracts and resolve disputes.
$19.95 / RUNS

Sexual Harassment on the Job
Attorneys William Petrocelli & Barbara Kate Repa
National 1st Edition
Describes what harassment is, what the laws are that make it illegal and how to put a stop to it. Invaluable both for employees experiencing harassment and for employers interested in creating a policy against sexual harassment and a procedure for handling complaints.
$14.95/HARS

Your Rights in the Workplace
Dan Lacey
National 1st Edition
Here is the first comprehensive guide to workplace rights —from hiring to firing. Learn the legal rules about wages and overtime, maternity and parental leave, unemployment and disability insurance, worker's compensation, job safety, discrimination and illegal firings and layoffs.
$15.95/YRW

How to Write a Business Plan
Mike McKeever
National 4th Edition
If you're thinking of starting a business or raising money to expand an existing one, this book will show you how to write the business plan and loan package necessary to finance your business and make it work.
$19.95/SBS

Marketing Without Advertising
Michael Phillips & Salli Rasberry
National 1st Edition
Outlines practical steps for building and expanding a small business without spending a lot of money on advertising.
$14.00/MWAD

The Partnership Book
Attorneys Denis Clifford & Ralph Warner
National 4th Edition
Shows you step-by-step how to write a solid partnership agreement that meets your needs. It covers initial contributions to the business, wages, profit-sharing, buyouts, death or retirement of a partner and disputes.
$24.95/PART

How to Form A Nonprofit Corporation
Attorney Anthony Mancuso
National 1st Edition
Explains the legal formalities involved and provides detailed information on the differences in the law among all 50 states. It also contains forms for the Articles, Bylaws and Minutes you need, along with complete instructions for obtaining federal 501 (c) (3) tax exemptions and qualifying for public charity status.
$24.95/NNP

The California Nonprofit Corporation Handbook
Attorney Anthony Mancuso
California 6th Edition
Shows you step-by-step how to form and operate a nonprofit corporation in California. It includes the latest corporate and tax law changes, and the forms for the Articles, Bylaws and Minutes.
$29.95/NON

How to Form Your Own Corporation
Attorney Anthony Mancuso
California 7th Edition
New York 2nd Edition
Texas 4th Edition
Florida 3rd Edition
These books contain the forms, instructions and tax information you need to incorporate a small business yourself and save hundreds of dollars in lawyers' fees.
California $29.95/CCOR
New York $24.95/NYCO
Texas $29.95/TCOR
Florida $29.95/FLCO

The California Professional Corporation Handbook
Attorney Anthony Mancuso
California 4th Edition
Health care professionals, lawyers, accountants and members of certain other professions must fulfill special requirements when forming a corporation in California. This book contains up-to-date tax information plus all the forms and instructions necessary to form a California professional corporation.
$34.95/PROF

The Independent Paralegal's Handbook
Attorney Ralph Warner
National 2nd Edition
Provides legal and business guidelines for those who want to take routine legal work out of the law office and offer it for a reasonable fee in an independent business.
$19.95/ PARA

Getting Started as an Independent Paralegal
(Two Audio Tapes)
Attorney Ralph Warner
National 2nd Edition
If you are interested in going into business as an Independent Paralegal—helping consumers prepare their own legal paperwork in uncontested proceedings such as bankruptcy, divorce, small business incorporation, landlord-tenant actions and probate—you'll want these tapes. Approximately two hours in length, the tapes will tell you everything you need to know about what legal tasks to handle, how much to charge and how to run a profitable business.
$44.95/GSIP

Nolo's Partnership Maker
Attorney Anthony Mancuso &
Mickael Radke
Version 1.0
Nolo's Partnership Maker prepares a legal partnership agreement for doing business in any state. You can select and assemble the standard partnership clauses provided or create your own customized agreement. And the agreement can be updated at any time. Includes on-line legal help screens, glossary and tutorial, and a manual that takes you through the process step-by-step.
IBM PC (3-1/2 & 5-1/4 disks included)
$129.95/PAGI1

California Incorporator
Attorney Anthony Mancuso
Version 1.0 (good only in CA)
Answer the questions on the screen and this software program will print out the 35-40 pages of documents you need to make your California corporation legal. Comes with a 200-page manual which explains the incorporation process.
IBM PC (3-1/2 & 5-1/4 disks included)
$129.00/INCI

The California Nonprofit Corporation Handbook
(computer edition)
Attorney Anthony Mancuso
Version 1.0
This book/software package shows you step-by-step how to form and operate a nonprofit corporation in California. Included on disk are the forms for the Articles, Bylaws and Minutes.
IBM PC 5-1/4 $69.95/ NPI
IBM PC 3-1/2 $69.95/ NP3I
MACINTOSH $69.95/ NPM

How to Form Your Own New York Corporation & How to Form Your Own Texas Corporation
(computer editions)
Attorney Anthony Mancuso
These book/software packages contain the instructions and tax information and forms you need to incorporate a small business and save hundreds of dollars in lawyers' fees. All organizational forms are on disk. Both come with a 250-page manual.
New York 1st Edition
IBM PC 5-1/4 $69.95/ NYCI
IBM PC 3-1/2 $69.95/ NYC3I
MACINTOSH $69.95/ NYCM

Texas 1st Edition
IBM PC 5-1/4 $69.95/ TCI
IBM PC 3-1/2 $69.95/ TC3I
MACINTOSH $69.95/ TCM

Neighbor Law: Fences, Trees, Boundaries & Noise
Attorney Cora Jordan
National 1st Edition
Answers common questions about the subjects that most often trigger disputes between neighbors: fences, trees, boundaries and noise. It explains how to find the law and resolve disputes without a nasty lawsuit.
$14.95/NEI

Dog Law
Attorney Mary Randolph
National 1st Edition
A practical guide to the laws that affect dog owners and their neighbors. You'll find answers to common questions on such topics as biting, barking, veterinarians and more.
$12.95/DOG

Stand Up to the IRS
Attorney Fred Daily
National 1st Edition
Gives detailed stategies on surviving an audit with the minimum amount of damage, appealing an audit decision, going to Tax Court and dealing with IRS collectors. It also discusses filing tax returns when you haven't done so in a while, tax crimes, concerns of small business people and getting help from the IRS ombudsman.
$19.95 / SIRS

Money Troubles: Legal Strategies to Cope With Your Debts
Attorney Robin Leonard
National 1st Edition
Are you behind on your credit card bills or loan payments? If you are, then *Money Troubles* is exactly what you need. It covers everything from knowing what your rights are, and asserting them, to helping you evaluate your individual situation. This practical, straightforward book is for anyone who needs help understanding and dealing with the complex and often scary topic of debts.
$16.95/MT

How to File for Bankruptcy
Attorneys Stephen Elias, Albin Renauer &
Robin Leonard
National 4th Edition
Trying to decide whether or not filing for bankruptcy makes sense? *How to File for Bankruptcy* contains an overview of the process and all the forms plus step-by-step instructions on the procedures to follow.
$25.95/HFB

Simple Contracts for Personal Use
Attorney Stephen Elias & Marcia Stewart
National 2nd Edition
Contains clearly written legal form contracts to buy and sell property, borrow and lend money, store and lend personal property, release others from personal liability, or pay a contractor to do home repairs. Includes agreements to arrange childcare and other household help.
$16.95/CONT

The Copyright Handbook

Attorney Stephen Fishman
National 1st Edition

Provides forms and step-by-step instructions for protecting all types of written expression under U.S. and international copyright law. It contains detailed reference chapters on copyright infringement, fair use, works for hire and transfers of copyright ownership.
$24.95/COHA

LANDLORDS & TENANTS

The Landlord's Law Book, Vol. 1: Rights & Responsibilities

Attorneys David Brown & Ralph Warner
California 3rd Edition

This book contains information on deposits, leases and rental agreements, inspections (tenants' privacy rights), habitability (rent withholding), ending a tenancy, liability and rent control.
$29.95/LBRT

The Landlord's Law Book, Vol. 2: Evictions

Attorney David Brown
California 4th Edition

Updated for 1993, this book will show you step-by-step how to go to court and evict a tenant. Contains all the tear-out forms and necessary instructions.
$32.95/LBEV

Tenants' Rights

Attorneys Myron Moskovitz & Ralph Warner
California 11th Edition

Explains how to handle your relationship with your landlord and understand your legal rights when you find yourself in disagreement. A special section on rent control cities is included.
$15.95/CTEN

HOMEOWNERS

How to Buy a House in California

Attorney Ralph Warner, Ira Serkes & George Devine
California 2nd Edition

This book shows you how to find a house, work with a real estate agent, make an offer and negotiate intelligently. Includes information on all types of mortgages as well as private financing options.
$19.95/BHCA

For Sale By Owner

George Devine
California 2nd Edition

Provides essential information about pricing your house, marketing it, writing a contract and going through escrow.
$24.95/FSBO

Homestead Your House

Attorneys Ralph Warner, Charles Sherman & Toni Ihara
California 8th Edition

Shows you how to file a Declaration of Homestead and includes complete instructions and tear-out forms.
$9.95/HOME

The Deeds Book

Attorney Mary Randolph
California 2nd Edition

If you own real estate, you'll need to sign a new deed when you transfer the property or put it in trust as part of your estate planning. This book shows you how to find the right kind of deed, complete the tear-out forms and record them in the county recorder's public records.
$15.95/DEED

OLDER AMERICANS

Elder Care: Choosing & Financing Long-Term Care

Attorney Joseph Matthews
National 1st Edition

This book will guide you in choosing and paying for long-term care, alerting you to practical concerns and explaining laws that may affect your decisions.
$16.95/ELD

Social Security, Medicare & Pensions

Attorney Joseph Matthews with Dorothy Matthews Berman
National 5th Edition

This book contains invaluable guidance through the current maze of rights and benefits for those 55 and over, including Medicare, Medicaid and Social Security retirement and disability benefits and age discrimination protections.
$15.95/SOA

REFERENCE

Legal Research: How to Find and Understand the Law

Attorneys Stephen Elias & Susan Levinkind
National 3rd Edition

A valuable tool on its own or as a companion to just about every other Nolo book. Gives easy-to-use, step-by-step instructions on how to find legal information.
$19.95/LRES

Family Law Dictionary

Attorneys Robin Leonard & Stephen Elias
National 2nd Edition

Finally, a legal dictionary that's written in plain English, not "legalese"! *The Family Law Dictionary* is designed to help the nonlawyer who has a question or problem involving family law—marriage, divorce, adoption or living together.
$13.95/FLD

Legal Research Made Easy: A Roadmap Through the Law Library Maze

2-1/2 hr. videotape and 40-page manual
Nolo Press/Legal Star Communications
National 1st Edition

University of California law professor Bob Berring explains how to use all the basic legal research tools in your local law library with an easy-to-follow six-step research plan and a sense of humor.
$89.95/LRME

CONSUMER/REFERENCE

Nolo's Pocket Guide to California Law

Attorney Lisa Guerin and Nolo Press Editors
California 1st Edition

The only plain English guide to the laws that affect you everyday. Get quick clear answers to questions about child support, custody, consumer rights, employee rights, government benefits, divorce, bankruptcy, adoption, wills and much more.
$10.95/CLAW

Barbara Kaufman's Consumer Action Guide

Barbara Kaufman
California 1st Edition

This practical handbook is filled with information on hundreds of consumer topics. Barbara Kaufman, the Bay Area's award-winning consumer reporter and producer of KCBS Radio's *Call for Action*, gives consumers access to their legal rights, providing addresses and phone numbers of where to complain when things go wrong, and providing resources if more help is necessary.
$14.95/CAG

N O L O   P R E S S   /   9 5 0   P A R K E R   S T R E E T   /   B E R K E L E Y   C A   9 4 7 1 0

O R D E R   F O R M

Name

Address (UPS to street address, Priority Mail to P.O. boxes)

Catalog Code	Quantity	Item	Unit price	Total

Subtotal		
Sales tax (California residents only)		
Shipping & handling		
2nd day UPS		
TOTAL		
PRICES SUBJECT TO CHANGE		

SALES TAX
California residents add your local tax

SHIPPING & HANDLING
$4.00   1 item
$5.00   2-3 items
+$.50   each additional item
Allow 2-3 weeks for delivery

IN A HURRY?
UPS 2nd day delivery is available:
Add $5.00 (contiguous states) or
$8.00 (Alaska & Hawaii) to your regular shipping and handling charges

FOR FASTER SERVICE, USE YOUR CREDIT CARD AND OUR TOLL-FREE NUMBERS:
Monday-Friday, 7 a.m. to 5 p.m. Pacific Time
Order line	1 (800) 992-6656
General Information	1 (510) 549-1976
Fax us your order	1 (800) 645-0895

METHOD OF PAYMENT
☐ Check enclosed
☐ VISA   ☐ Mastercard   ☐ Discover Card   ☐ American Express

Account #   Expiration Date

Signature Authorizing

Phone   LBEV 4

[Nolo books are]..."written in plain language, free of legal mumbo jumbo, and spiced with witty personal observations."

—ASSOCIATED PRESS

"Well-produced and slickly written, the [Nolo] books are designed to take the mystery out of seemingly involved procedures, carefully avoiding legalese and leading the reader step-by-step through such everyday legal problems as filling out forms, making up contracts, and even how to behave in court."

—SAN FRANCISCO EXAMINER

"...Nolo publications...guide people simply through the how, when, where and why of law."

—WASHINGTON POST

"Increasingly, people who are not lawyers are performing tasks usually regarded as legal work... And consumers, using books like Nolo's, do routine legal work themselves."

—NEW YORK TIMES

"...All of [Nolo's] books are easy-to-understand, are updated regularly, provide pull-out forms...and are often quite moving in their sense of compassion for the struggles of the lay reader."

—SAN FRANCISCO CHRONICLE

NO POSTAGE
NECESSARY
IF MAILED
IN THE
UNITED STATES

BUSINESS REPLY MAIL
FIRST-CLASS MAIL PERMIT NO 3283 BERKELEY CA

POSTAGE WILL BE PAID BY ADDRESSEE

**NOLO PRESS
950 Parker Street
Berkeley CA 94710-9867**